UNITED STATES POLICY TOWARDS LIBERIA 1822 TO 2003: UNINTENDED CONSEQUENCES?

To Janet —
with every good wish!

Chester

4/04

UNITED STATES POLICY TOWARDS LIBERIA 1822 TO 2003: UNINTENDED CONSEQUENCES?

LESTER S. HYMAN

AFRICANA HOMESTEAD LEGACY PUBLISHERS
CHERRY HILL, NEW JERSEY

Africana Homestead Legacy Publishers
PO Box 2957
Cherry Hill, New Jersey 08034-0265
e-mail: publisher@ahlpub.com.
Toll free order line, 24 hours, 7 days a week: 1-800-247-6553.

Library of Congress Cataloging-in-Publication

Hyman, Lester S.
　　United States policy towards Liberia, 1822 to 2003 : unintended
　　consequences / Lester S. Hyman.
　　　　p. cm.
　　Includes bibliographical references and index.
　　ISBN 0-9653308-8-5 (alk. paper)
　　1. United States--Foreign relations--Liberia. 2. Liberia--Foreign relations--
　　United States.
　　I. Title.

E183.8.L5H96 2003
327.7306662--dc21

　　　　　　　　　　　　　　　　　　　　　　　　　　　　　2003051926

Cover design by Brian Lancaster, Omega Group III, Philadelphia, PA.
Cover image co-designed by Brian Lancaster and Carolyn C. Williams, Africana
Homestead Legacy Publishers.
Lester Hyman's photograph by Peter Cutts Photography, Washington, D.C.

There is only one child in the world, And the child's name is All Children.
That child speaks our name.
Carl Sandburg

I dedicate this book to the children of Liberia.
May they be given the basic tools necessary to survive and to learn;
to reach their potential; to live in dignity, peace and freedom;
And to achieve their dreams.

CONTENTS

CONTENTS [CONTINUED]

ACKNOWLEDGMENTS

There are so many people who graciously assisted me over the past two years as I researched and wrote this book that I would like to acknowledge a few of them who have been especially helpful. Let me stress, however, that the viewpoints taken, the conclusions reached, and the proposals made are entirely my own, for which I bear full responsibility.

First and foremost I thank Rachel Diggs, former Liberian Ambassador to the United States, and Joe Diggs, her husband, for their constant support and encouragement throughout the project, and particularly for their kindness in reviewing the manuscript for errors of fact or omission. Rachel also consented to a formal interview relative to her diplomatic position.

Next my appreciation goes to the following people who sat for formal interviews for the book: Herman "Hank" Cohen, Gerald Cooper, George Dalley, President Charles Taylor, Alhaji Kromah, Jim Woolsey, and Bob Yerks. There also were a number of confidential interviews with key officials of the United Nations, the U.S. Congress, the U.S. Department of State, the U.S. Agency for International Development (USAID), the World Bank, the International Monetary Fund (IMF), and Liberian leaders, both in the government and in the opposition.

Profound thanks to Jim Gray of the Friends of Liberia who every day e-mailed to colleagues, without editorial comment, every significant article about Liberia that appeared in the world press, as well as articles from each of the many newspapers published in Liberia. It is a treasure chest of material and essential reading for anyone interested in Liberia. The Liberia Project at the University of Indiana, Bloomington, Indiana has now assumed his work. My thanks to Rob Wishart of the Los Angeles Times for keeping me abreast of the news from Liberia. Living in Washington, I also used the archives of the Washington Post to analyze coverage of many of the incidents described in the book.

Kudos to my long-time secretary Linda Jedlicka for transcribing the oftentimes lengthy, and sometimes raucous interviews, mentioned above and for dealing with me and all of my Liberian friends over the years with patience, good humor and charm—and more recently to Linda Steele who also has helped with the transcriptions. Grateful thanks to the many Liberians of all ages and positions who have kept in touch with me by phone, letter and in person over the past twelve years and instilled in me a tremendous sense of respect and awe for their ability to survive through the most difficult of times while maintaining an optimistic outlook toward the future. A thank you to Hans Johnson who gave me thoughtful stylistic suggestions—and to my long-time law partner Ken Schaner for reviewing the manuscript, giving me constant encouragement, and listening patiently to my frustrations as the Liberian story took more twists and turns than a box of pretzels just as we were getting ready to go to press.

I especially want to thank the wonderful team at Africana Homestead Legacy Publishers: the Publisher and Managing Editor, Carolyn C. Williams, who has been extremely supportive and has handled the project with sensitivity, intelligence and outstanding professionalism; the project editor, E. Lama Wonkeryor, PhD,. who brought a scholarly approach to the work, insisting upon verification and sourcing for every fact stated and every point made; and the graphic designer Brian Lancaster who captured so well the intertwined relationship between Liberia and the United States in his book jacket design.

Finally, grateful thanks to the members of my family—David Hyman, Andrew Hyman,

Elizabeth Hyman and Peter Willard—who patiently tolerated my oftentimes obsessive passion for fairness and justice for the people of Liberia which somehow I managed to bring up <u>ad nauseum</u> in every telephone conversation and dinnertime discussion. Now we can talk about other things as well!

PROLOGUE

Liberia! Most Americans who have heard of the country think: rogue state; authoritarian leadership; failed nation; civil war; a government of thugs and barbarians; a people dedicated to ethnic warfare; diamond smugglers; repression of human rights and freedom of speech.

One cannot be surprised that people hold these views about Liberia because that is precisely what the mainstream press writes, what many members of Congress believe, and what government officials in the United States of America and Great Britain speak. The drumbeat of condemnation continues unabated.

Such a damaging description of Liberia is misleading. By nature, Liberians are a peace-loving people and many of the woes of this tiny West African country were abetted by a short-sighted and badly skewed U.S. foreign policy.

In recent years, U.S. policymakers privately have taken the position that the historic relationship between the United States and Liberia is today irrelevant, and there is no current interest in Liberia.[1] This, despite the fact that, through times of peace and war, Liberia was a staunch ally, and its territory and natural resources were instrumental in achieving Allied victories during the World Wars and Cold War. Students of Liberian history learn that: Liberia was a charter member of the League of Nations (in 1919), and one of the founding members of the United Nations; that, at the behest of the U.S., it cast the deciding vote creating the State of Israel; that, during World War II, the Cold War, and the Gulf War, the U.S. Central Intelligence Agency's (CIA) Africa headquarters were in Liberia; that the Voice of America's station for all of Africa was in Liberia; that Liberian ships were reflagged to the use of the United States; that the Omega Navigational Station in Liberia allowed the U.S. to track ships in the Atlantic; that in 1942 for World War II, Liberia turned over its primary airfield, Roberts International Airport (named after President Joseph Jenkins Roberts), to the United States for use as a major transit point for thousands of American soldiers and for allied operations in North Africa and southern Europe; and that similar help was extended to the U.S. during the Gulf War. Despite this record of consistent cooperation with the United States, there is little evidence that the U.S. has reciprocated in its support of Liberia.

By perusing this volume, the reader will understand the complexity and failures of U.S.–Liberian relations. The examination of U.S. foreign policy also reveals that it has been counter-productive to the cause of peace and stability not only in Liberia, but in the West Africa region.

What impelled me to undertake this project after 12 years of intensive experience with Liberia? I am a lawyer, a participant for many years in peace resolution efforts around the world, and, most particularly, someone who has been professionally involved with Liberian matters. In my travels throughout the country I became well acquainted with most of the "players" on both sides of the tragic drama that has unfolded between Liberia and its supposed patron nation, the United States of America.

As time progressed, I increasingly became frustrated over the disparity between the perception of Liberia and the reality. Almost everything that I read in the U.S. media about the country differed from documented facts and my personal experiences. My concern for the common people of Liberia, many of whom I have come to know well, also grew. I was particularly moved by the many letters I received during the years of civil war from young people in Liberia who bewailed the fact that they had been deprived of years of education. "How can I ever become a lawyer like you when I can't get an education because the schools are closed?" wrote one. Their futures are cloudy and without promise. It may be too late for many of them. But for the next generation of Liberian youngsters the opportunity to help them achieve their promise, advance themselves, and lead fruitful and challenging lives still exists.

After witnessing the consequences of a flawed U.S. policy—the suffering it has wreaked upon the three million citizens of Liberia—I could not in good conscience remain silent. I believe I owed it to them to tell what I know of the Liberian story. In short, my concern for the people led me to write about how Liberia descended to its present state of collapse, with fighting, feuding, and suffering, and how, with the help of the United States and the international community, it can construct a better future.

Mind you, the Liberian government has made egregious mistakes. But, although of quite a different nature and magnitude, the U.S. has made serious errors in judgment in its bilateral relationship. Since 1989 the problems of Liberia have been extraordinarily complex. For example, the sanction policy that the United States and Britain have championed at the United Nations, along with a virtual international embargo on aid, was overly simplistic. Equally important it penalized the wrong parties: the innocent men, women, and children of Liberia who love the United States and do not understand why this great nation abandoned them in their time of need.

Many of my friends and family ask: why have you stuck it out so long in advocating the cause of a "rogue" state? Because I was taught that it is entirely appropriate for a lawyer to represent an unpopular and controversial cause—not to excuse unacceptable behavior, but to try to alter that behavior in constructive ways. That is what I have tried to do. As an honest broker between the U.S. and Liberia, I have tried to affect the policy of both nations toward one another and ameliorate the excesses that have taken place. As you will see, I believe that the United States has been woefully deficient in its relationship with Liberia and insensitive to the needs of the Liberian people. I hold strong views on what I believe United States policy should be as we look toward elections in Liberia in 2004 or 2005. I am determined to do all I can to bring about a change in that policy and hope that this book may affect that policy.

Starting at the beginning, my involvement with Liberia began in 1991. A British businessman came to the Bush White House and asked for a recommendation of a Washington law firm that might help him solve a problem. He was unable to do business effectively in Liberia because, at the time, it had two competing <u>de facto</u> governments, the National Patriotic Reconstruction Government (NPRAG), led by Charles Ghankay Taylor, and the Interim Government of National Unity (IGNU) led by Amos Claudius Sawyer. The White House aide recommended one of my law partners, H.P. Goldfield, who, in turn, asked me to join him in meeting with the client because of my history of involvement in peace resolution efforts (especially in Haiti after the departure of "Baby Doc" Duvalier). We were asked if we could help resolve the differences between the two competing governments. Soon thereafter (March 6, 1991) my law partner and I traveled to Senegal to meet Charles Taylor who was then engaged in meetings with the Senegalese President Abdou Diouf.

We spoke with Mr. Taylor frankly for many hours. He struck me as a complex and fascinating individual, a man of supreme confidence, with an impressive grasp of world events. He expressed his desire to restore his country to peace and prosperity after so many years of suffering under the leadership of Samuel Doe. For hours we peppered Taylor with the toughest possible questions, and he answered them all apparently without evasion. For example, we asked whether it was true that he sought financial aid and armaments from Libya, an arch-enemy of the United States. He readily admitted that he took help wherever he could get it, including Libya—that he would prefer the help came from the United States, but thus far it had not materialized—and that "while my heart is with God, I will accept help from the Devil if that is the only way to help my people."

Shortly after our meeting, we accepted the assignment of trying to bring about a rapprochement between Taylor and Sawyer. We worked with both sides to convince them to invite former President Jimmy Carter to come into the country as a mediator. Carter only serves in such a role if both parties to a dispute request his assistance. Taylor and Sawyer did agree, and President Carter accepted the assignment. That is how it all began. The businessman client was delighted with our work and concluded the representation.

Within a short time, Charles Taylor said he was impressed with our work and asked whether our law firm would represent the National Patriotic Reconstruction Government (NPRAG), explaining its point of view to the opinion-makers in Washington and, in turn, conveying American attitudes toward Liberia. We agreed to do so. We ceased our representation during the civil war in Liberia. After Taylor was inaugurated as Liberia's president in 1997, in an election that President Carter and the international community certified as free and fair, he called me again and asked that our law firm represent the Republic of Liberia in the United States. I was quite surprised by his request since, during the civil war, I had written a very tough letter to him, expressing my disgust at how the various factional leaders were squabbling among themselves while the people suffered. When I made that point during our phone conversation, he replied: "That's why I want your help—because you're one of the few people I know who tell me candidly what you think." We then agreed to represent the country and served in that capacity until 1999. At no time did we ever represent Charles Taylor personally. Thereafter, while maintaining my deep interest and concern for Liberia, I no longer served as U.S. counsel but merely acted as a private citizen who cares deeply for the people of Liberia. From 1999 until March 7, 2003, I had no contact with him of any kind (letter, telephone, or in person).

United States policy toward Liberia consistently has shaped its history. In view of the general contours of this volume, one should reflect on these questions: What impels U.S. policy? Has it been helpful or hurtful to Liberia?

From 1847 to 1980—a period of 133 years—Liberia was relatively at peace. What changed? How did U.S. policy towards Charles Taylor affect the citizens of Liberia? What caused seven years of horrible civil strife? What factors affected the 1997 national democratic election? Why did the succeeding years result in the lack of a U.S. commitment to intervene and support the people of Liberia?

NOTES

[1] Throughout this book, the phrase, "the State Department," refers to a very small cadre of people who make U.S. policy toward Liberia. I have the highest regard and admiration for our Secretary of State Colin Powell and the other 99% of dedicated public servants who work in the U.S. Department of State, and toil, oftentimes, at their own peril in the hot-spots of the world in order to promote American values of freedom and democracy.

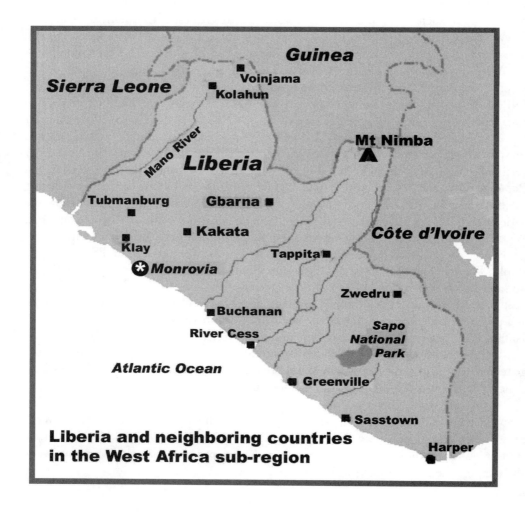

Liberia and neighboring countries in the West Africa sub-region

CHAPTER 1
INTRODUCTION

" Let us not look back in anger;
Nor forward in fear,
But around us...in awareness."
James Thurber

Why should you devote the time and effort to read a book about a small West African nation? Because this work raises issues about U.S. foreign policy that apply not only to Liberia, but to American foreign policy toward developing countries throughout the world.

This book addresses three issues relevant to U.S. foreign policy themes:

1. *Making common cause with one evil-doer in order to defeat a greater evil-doer*. In implementing its foreign policy to protect national security, the United States has allied itself with heads of state (and other parties) who horrifically violate the human and civil rights of their country's citizenry, precisely because of U.S. willingness to overlook such actions. During the Cold War, the focus of the U.S. on the defeat of Communism was compromised by it making common cause with Samuel Doe of Liberia, one of the most vicious dictators in the history of Africa. This U.S. policy contributed to the conditions that led to the effort to depose Doe, an act that culminated in a brutal, 7-year civil war, and the catastrophic suffering of Liberia's citizens. The wartime destruction of Liberia's infrastructure, and death and displacement of its people, which persist to this very day, prompt one to consider these questions: 1.) Was the trade-off worth it? 2). Did Liberia's strategic importance in U.S. policy that was designed to win the Cold War supersede the welfare of its three million citizens?

2. *The timely treatment of post-conflict nations*. Following the end of Liberia's civil war, the citizens elected a permanent government in free and fair national elections. In the promotion of democracy and nation building, there was an immediate need for the U.S. and other world powers to help stimulate the country's economy and rebuild its infrastructure, with relatively small expenditures. However, the U.S. and others failed to act at the opportune moment. Conditions further declined and Liberia's destabilization soon impacted much of the West Africa region, by the spread of conflict to Sierra Leone and Côte d'Ivoire. As a result, the involved parties (primarily the U.S., France, Britain, and the United Nations) have spent billions of dollars trying to restore peace.

3. *Focusing on a country's leader instead of its people*. In conjunction with points one and two described above, the U.S. has often developed its foreign policy relative to the leader of a country, rather than the citizenry. From the start of Charles Taylor's military effort to depose Samuel Doe, the U.S. worked to prevent him from assuming the presidency of Liberia. This U.S. policy prolonged the civil war unnecessarily. After Taylor's election as Liberia's president in 1997, the United States implemented a policy that undermined

his administration, by denying all but minimal humanitarian aid, and imposing sanctions for his role in fostering regional conflict. While containing Charles Taylor, the U.S. policy fostered both the rise of rebel groups who sought to depose him militarily, and the worsening of the humanitarian crisis to catastrophic proportions as a result of the renewed warfare.

Liberia, then, is a *case study* of these vital themes of American foreign policy. How the United States resolves the situation in Liberia will indicate how well it will deal with the rest of the world, especially developing nations, in the years to come. U.S. relations with Liberia, even if formulated with the best of intentions, have had unintended consequences—the unnecessary suffering of the very people whom it purports to help.

A BRIEF HISTORY OF LIBERIA

It is essential to know something of Liberia's past history in order to understand the special relationship that exists between the United States and Liberia. It evolved from the founding of this West African country.

In 1816, a distinguished group of United States citizens established the American Colonization Society (ACS). Its goal was to found a colony in West Africa, later called Liberia (for "liberty"…the land of the free), for freed blacks. In his 2002 study, Edward Lama Wonkeryor wrote that the stated goals of the ACS were:

> • To rescue the free colored people of the United States from their political and social disadvantages.
>
> • To place them in a country where they may enjoy the benefits of free government, with all the blessings which it brings in its train.
>
> • To spread civilization, sound morals, and true religion throughout the continent of Africa.
>
> • To arrest and destroy the slave trade.
>
> • To afford slave owners, who wished, or were willing, to liberate their slaves, an asylum for their reception. (Vermont Colonization Society, 1858)

> In December 1816 the Reverend Robert Finley, a Presbyterian clergyman from Basking Ridge, New Jersey, organized the American Society for Colonizing Free People of Color (commonly called the American Colonization Society). The goals of the society appealed to many northern and Southern whites who held a variety of objections to slavery; Finley was able to enlist the help of such prominent men as John Randolph, Daniel Webster, Andrew Jackson, Henry Clay, and Judge Bushrod Washington, nephew of George Washington. (Williams, 1984).

> As previously stated, the ACS was formed in 1816, and it became active in many states. The states with ACS chapters included Alabama, Connecticut, Indiana, Kentucky, Maine, Maryland, New Hampshire, New Jersey, New York, North Carolina, Ohio, Pennsylvania, Tennessee, Vermont, and Virginia. Many distinguished policymakers, including President James Monroe, actively cooperated with the ACS. The aim of the ACS was to expediently and

practically address the perceived problems of freed African Americans in the United States by establishing a colony either on the American continent or in Africa. Equally important, when Abraham Lincoln became president of the United States, he endorsed many positions of the ACS, especially the ones that dealt with relocating African Americans to Africa, the Caribbean, and Latin America. Since black Americans were in minority and could not co-exist peacefully and equally with whites (dominant majority) in America, ACS supporters felt that ACS, by establishing a colony to accommodate blacks, could lead blacks to achieve freedom and self-determination as a political, ideological, and Christian entity.[1]

Despite its stated goals, however, among the ACS were members who wanted to rid the United States of the emancipated slaves for fear that their continued presence would have an incendiary effect, prompting those who were still enslaved to seek their freedom particularly through uprisings or other violent resistance. Henry Clay said he was determined to "rid our country of a useless and pernicious, if not dangerous portion of its population." The liberal wing of the colonization movement, however, believed that a successful colony in Africa would prove that Africans were capable of self-improvement and deserving of freedom. As with nearly all that happened over the years between the United States and Liberia, there was altruism combined with self-interest and that dichotomy continues to this day.[2]

The members of the ACS also were aware of the earlier effort of Paul Cuffee (also Cuffe), a wealthy African-American Quaker to help American blacks emigrate to Africa. For this reason, the Reverend Samuel J. Mills, a "professional fundraiser for many sectarian benevolent societies, and the advance man for the newly formed American Society for Colonizing the Free People of Color in the United States..." corresponded with and

> solicited Cuffe's opinion, not only on African colonization, but also on many facets of black-white relations in America. Cuffe's considered replies made a deep impression on Mills. No doubt Cuffe's judgments weighed heavily as well with other promoters of the American Colonization Society.[3]

Born near Bedford, Massachusetts, Cuffee was notably one of the first in the 19th century black colonization movement to call for emigration to Africa. After founding in 1811 the Friendly Society of Sierra Leone, Cuffee, a shipbuilder and shipowner, financed and captained a voyage that took 38 settlers there in 1815. His plans for future expeditions ended with his death in 1817. "Cuffe's death terminated the first phase of the black nationalist movement in the United States."[4] The ACS also sent its first settlers to Sierra Leone; after the settlement failed, its survivors were sent to Liberia.[5]

The U.S. Congress appropriated an initial $100,000 to the ACS to buy the land in what became Liberia, build houses and forts, acquire farm tools, pay teachers, and help the settlers care for, and defend themselves. The first settlers arrived on the shores of Liberia in a U.S. Navy ship supported by grants from the U.S. Treasury. In 1822 the king of the Bassa country agreed to sell land at Cape Mesurado to the new settlers. The price: 6 muskets, 1 box of beads, 2 hogshead of tobacco, 1 cask of gunpowder, 6 iron bars, 10 iron pots, 1 dozen knives, forks and spoons, 6 pieces of blue baft, 4 hats, 3 coats, 3 pair of shoes, 1 box of pipes, 1 keg of nails, 20 mirrors, 3 handkerchiefs, 3 pieces of calico, 3 canes, 4 umbrellas, 1 box of soap, and 1 barrel of rum. Total value: $300.00. The contracting parties pledged themselves to live in peace and friendship forever.[6]

Between 1821 and 1843 the American Colonization Society resettled a little more than 4,000 African Americans in West Africa. Initially called Christopolis, the capital of Liberia was named Monrovia in honor of the sitting U.S. President James Monroe. There were other American contributions to Liberia's founding: its constitution was written at Harvard Law School; the Capitol building was a replica of the U.S. Capitol; its main port was named for U.S. President James Buchanan. Incidentally, Francis Scott Key, the author of the Star-Bangled Banner, was one of the founding members of the ACS. Liberia's flag bears a single star, hence the "Lone Star" country, and eleven stripes, representing the 11 signers of the Declaration of Independence, and the red, white and blue of the American flag.[7,8]

Most of the leaders of Liberia from that period to this day were educated in the United States. At first, few African Americans in the United States were convinced of the viability of the new nation of Liberia. However, after the Fugitive Slave Act was passed in 1850 (easing the process whereby a white person who claimed ownership of a black person in American could sue for possession of that person, but denying black people the right to testify in their own defense), more blacks reconsidered their position toward emigration to Africa. Between 1822 and 1867, the ACS resettled about 23,000 blacks, of which approximately 12,000 were freed slaves, in Liberia.[9] Initially structured as a group of independent colonies, Liberia became first a commonwealth (1838) then a republic (1847), formed by mergers and acquisitions of land from the indigenous populations.

As indicated above, Liberia was not the first experiment in resettling blacks who had been enslaved in North America and Europe, in Africa. Nearly 3,000 American slaves, known as the Black Loyalists, escaped to British lines during the Revolutionary War and were resettled in Nova Scotia in 1783.[10] Because of the harsh climate, lack of promised land grants, and anger at their treatment by the government and hostile populace, they sent a representative, Thomas Peters, to England to petition the British government for the land they had been promised.[11] While there, members of the Sierra Leone Company persuaded Peters to recruit Black Loyalists to settle in Sierra Leone, which the company had founded as a place to settle destitute blacks from London and freed slaves. Slightly less than one-third of the Black Loyalist population left Nova Scotia for Sierra Leone in 1792, and founded Freetown, which became the capital city.[12] A majority of 543 Jamaica Maroons, who had successfully fought the British for years until they were finally expelled and sent to Nova Scotia in 1796, resettled in Sierra Leone in 1800.[13]

In his book, *Founding Brothers: The Revolutionary Generation,* Joseph Ellis provided insights into the attempts to relocate freed slaves abroad. He described the 1790 petitions to the U.S. House of Representatives of two Quaker delegations which sought to abolish the slave trade. This effort brought about a spirited open debate on the subject of slavery which, until then, had been a forbidden issue for public discussion. Ellis cited Congressman James Jackson who made the case for the South to retain slavery and summarized his argument as follows:

> Those advocating emancipation…need to confront the intractable dilemma posed by the sheer size of an African population that, once freed, must be removed to some other location…(W)here could the freed blacks be sent? Those advocating an African solution might profitably study the recent English efforts to establish a black colony in Sierra Leone, where most of the freed blacks died or were enslaved by the local African tribes.[14]

One can imagine Congressman Jackson's surprise at the eventual growth and development of Sierra Leone despite his dire warnings.

In March of 1790 a prominent Virginian by the name of Fernando Fairfax drafted a "Plan for Liberating Negroes within the United States" which envisioned "that the bulk of the freed slaves would be transported elsewhere, the Fairfax plan favoring an American colony in Africa on the British model of Sierra Leone." Ellis concluded that two issues prevented any effort at that time to emancipate the slaves, the first being compensation of the slave owners which would cost the new government an exorbitant amount of money, and second, the problem of where the newly freed slaves would go. He wrote:

> Two unpalatable but undeniable historical facts must be faced: First, that no emancipation plan without this feature (relocation) stood the slightest chance of success; and second, that no model of a genuinely biracial society existed anywhere in the world at that time, nor had any existed in recorded history...The subsequent failure of the American Colonization Society and the combination of logistical and economic difficulties in the colony of Liberia exposed the impracticality of any mass migration back to Africa...[15]

Whenever there were serious suggestions to free the slaves and keep them here in the United States, the Southern states that depended upon slavery for their economic prosperity threatened to leave the Union (as they would do years later, leading to the Civil War), a tragedy which the newly formed country could not afford as it struggled to establish itself.

From the time of their arrival, the Americo-Liberians, who brought American values and culture, clashed with the indigenous peoples of Liberia, who had their ancient tribal culture and ethnic differences. The motto of the early governments, "The Love of Liberty Brought Us Here" was biased, presenting only the settlers' viewpoint; after all, the indigenous people already *were* there. Tensions between the two groups continued for many years, leading to short periods of armed conflict. To the outside world, Liberia was America's colony in Africa. But in truth Liberia was the first independent black republic in the period of colonial history of that continent. Besides Ethiopia, an independent republic that was never colonized, it took another 100 years before the other African nations achieved their freedom from their colonial masters. Great Britain (Sierra Leone) and France (Senegal, Côte d'Ivoire, and Guinea), among others, still exert hegemony over their former colonies.

One of the accusations against the new settlers that has reverberated throughout history until the present was that the emancipated slaves emulated their former white masters in terms of their treatment of the indigenous tribes. Among historians, there are differing views on this point. Some maintain Americo-Liberians saw themselves as entitled to appropriate native lands by force. Others write that settlers believed in "civilizing" the indigenous people, intermarrying with them, and bringing them into the body politic of Liberian republican government. As discussed in successive chapters, this same issue was raised when Sergeant Samuel K. Doe (an indigenous Liberian) overthrew President William R. Tolbert, Jr. (an Americo-Liberian) in a bloody coup d'etat on April 12, 1980.

The memoirs of a number of early settlers gave conflicting accounts of life in the Republic. For example, the Reverend Daniel H. Peterson wrote in 1854 of his visit to Liberia the previous year,

> During the morning we went ashore at the port, and were received with much joy, and in a very friendly manner, by all the people...I must say that I never saw a more attractive place...I had never before seen freedom and liberty existing among our people, until I saw it in Monrovia, Liberia...There is nothing to be compared with this on the face of the earth for the colored nation, nor ever has been since the days of Noah.[16]

Yet William Nesbit, who wrote an account in 1855, said of his four month stay in Liberia:

> Monrovia, which is eligibly situated on high land on Cape Montserrado, contains about eighteen hundred of population, colonist, and native, and presents an ancient and dilapidated appearance...the climate has a blighting effect...As there are no horses, cattle, or beasts of burden of any kind, all the labor has to be performed by the naked natives..the face of the country is one magnificent swamp...All are traders...thus they get their living, entirely neglecting agriculture and everything else that would tend to develop the resources of the country...I am not able to imagine any more abject state of misery...The unhealthfulness of the climate is proverbial...I would a thousand times rather be a slave in the United States than in Liberia.[17]

In 1857, Reverend Samuel Williams, in response to Nesbit's view, described his four years in Liberia.

> Monrovia has about fifteen hundred inhabitants, and is a beautifully located place, on a high elevation...The productions of Liberia are very numerous...They can raise cassava, sweet potatoes and yams...and buy rice from the natives...It is now more for the want of fences than any other cause that they have not horses, asses and oxen...The morals of Liberia are as good, perhaps, as those of any other country...They have the orange, lemon, lime soursop. Guava, pawpaw, mango, plum, and pine apple...the fresh meats are nearly the same as we get in our own market, with the exception of goat meat. They have beef, pork, mutton and venison of a very good quality.[18]

Reverend Williams bewailed the indolence of many of the colonists ("all love to have a servant wait on them"). Reverend Williams's account, appearing to be the most credible, wrote:

> Liberia, like all other countries is not a paradise...Nor is it on the other hand a purgatory; but like all other lands, it has its sweets and its bitters, its sorrows and its pleasures, its life and its death.[19]

Agents of the ACS served as governors of Liberia for 25 years following its establishment. On July 26, 1847, Liberia declared its independence, the first independent black republic in the colonial history of Africa. The Republic of Liberia was unique in that it became the only part of the continent that was governed by blacks. A U.S. born governor Joseph Jenkins Roberts was its first president. It should be noted that 16 of the 19 men who served as Liberia's president were educated in schools and colleges in the United States. Liberia's Declaration of Independence includes this passsage:

The Western coast of Africa was the place selected by American benevolence and philanthropy for our future home...In coming to these shores of Africa, we indulged the pleasing hope that we should be permitted to exercise and improve those faculties which impart to man his dignity— to nourish in our hearts the flame of honorable ambition, to cherish and indulge those aspirations which a beneficent creator hath implanted in every human heart; and to evince to all who, despite ridicule, and oppress our own race that we possess with them a common nature, are with them susceptible of equal refinement, and capable of equal advancement in all that adorns and dignifies man.[20]

Although a number of European countries recognized Liberia shortly after it declared independence, the United States waited another 15 years until President Abraham Lincoln finally extended recognition in 1862. According to political scientist J. Gus Liebenow, "the Civil War had removed the principal objectors to the presence of a Black envoy in Washington, D.C."[21] This was the first example, in a lengthy series, of a begrudging United States' policy towards the country it founded.

As the Honorable Rachel Gbenyon Diggs, former Liberian Ambassador to the United States stated:

Far from rejecting the institutions, values, dress and speech of a society that had rejected them, the settlers painstakingly attempted to reproduce a similar culture in their own home.[22]

The Liberian Constitution, for example, provides for a President, a Senate and House, and a Supreme Court. All along Liberia's coast one passes little settlements that bear such familiar names as Virginia, New Georgia, Louisiana, Hartford, Greenville, and Lexington. Until the mid–1990s the American dollar was the official currency.

THE AFRICAN EXPERIENCE

As the new nation of Liberia put down its roots in the African soil and began a slow but continuous development as a peaceful nation, it is important to be aware of what was happening throughout the rest of Africa...events that soon made Liberia unique as the only independent black country on the continent. Before Liberia was established, and until the 1880s, most of the continent of Africa was still ruled by Africans and barely explored. Yet, by 1902, 5 European powers and 1 extraordinary individual had grabbed almost the entire continent, giving themselves 30 new colonies, 10 million square miles of new territory, and 110 million new subjects.

Students remember learning in school about Stanley and Livingstone (and those immortal words: "Dr. Livingstone, I presume"). David Livingstone was the world's best-known explorer, as well as a dedicated missionary and philanthropist. Henry Morton Stanley was a young reporter for the New York Herald who "found" Livingstone in the heart of Africa and reported the explorer's exploits to an entranced American readership. Thomas Pakenham recounted Livingstone's experiences in his seminal work, *The Scramble for Africa*:

For among the giant lakes and waterfalls (that Livingstone had discovered), the teeming populations where geographers had supposed all was desert, in that Arcadia he had found the heart of darkness, a new outburst of the slave trade. He called it 'the open sore of the world' and believed he could find the means to heal it by making an 'open path' from civilization.[23]

Livingstone exposed the horrors of the slave trade then still in progress. His call for Africa to be redeemed by the three Cs—commerce, Christianity, and civilization—was aimed at the conscience of the civilized world. He was looking for the source of the Nile River which he thought would bring commerce and civilization to the interior of Africa. Instead he discovered the previously unknown source of the Congo River. As Pakenham wrote: "Four times the size of the Nile…the Congo would serve, far better than the Nile, as the open path to bring commerce and Christianity into the heart of Africa."[24]

Livingstone died in Africa in 1873. His last words were: "All I can add in my solitude, is, may heaven's rich blessing come down on every one, American, English, or Turk, who will help heal this open sore of the earth."[25]

Then in 1876 King Leopold of Belgium announced to the world that he was embarking upon a crusade to end the slave trade. The King said he was prepared to spend his own money for this humanitarian cause. As stated earlier, so much of what happened in Africa was ambiguous—King Leopold's intentions were no exception. In the guise of humanitarianism, Leopold's true intent was to colonize the Congo and gain for Belgium the extraordinary riches, especially gold, that was in abundant supply there. In public, King Leopold said: "To open to civilization the only part of our globe where it has yet to penetrate, to pierce the darkness which envelops whole populations, is, I dare say, a crusade worthy of this century of progress."[26] A few months later the very same King Leopold wrote to his ambassador in London: "I do not want to miss a good chance of getting us a slice of this magnificent African cake."[27]

Once other European powers realized Leopold's actual intent, they moved quickly to take their own slices of the pie. Coming at a time when most European countries were experiencing a great depression, their hope was that Black Africa would prove to be an Eldorado, a huge new market and tropical treasure house. Soon colonial fever swept Europe, and overseas empire was identified with national prestige. Thus began the scramble for Africa that ended up with most of the continent coming under oppressive colonial rule. Under an 1890 Anglo-French agreement, Britain got The Gambia, Sierra Leone, the Gold Coast, and Nigeria while the French acquired Morocco, Algeria, Tunisia, Senegal, Guinea, Gabon, the Niger and French Congo. Only Liberia stood alone as a self-governed and independent nation-state. Other countries went to Germany, Portugal, Italy, and Spain.[28]

Almost from the beginning of its existence, Liberia was threatened by these colonial powers. In particular the British, who had recognized Liberian sovereignty in 1848, and the French, who had given recognition in 1852, sought to take pieces of Liberian territory and annex them to their neighboring colonies. President Grover Cleveland, in an 1886 message to Congress, spoke of the "moral right and duty of the United States" to help Liberia since "it must not be forgotten that this distant community is an offshoot of our own system." When there was a need for action, however, these bold words proved meaningless. While the U.S. sent one of its warships to the area whenever Liberian land was threatened, Cleveland and succeeding administrations refused Monrovia's plea for military assistance to defend their soil. Because of the U.S. failure to act, the British forced concessions of Liberian territory to Sierra Leone in 1883 and 1903. Similarly, the French forced Liberia to cede part of its territory to Côte d'Ivoire (the Ivory Coast) in 1892 with the signing of a treaty. These events resulted in tension along the borders of the three countries with consequences that resonate to this day.[29]

AMERICO-LIBERIANS VERSUS INDIGENOUS LIBERIANS

While the rest of Africa looked to Europe as its ruler, the Liberian settlers felt very special ties to America. As Ambassador Gbenyon Diggs wrote:

> Because of these special ties, ...one of Liberia's formidable national challenges was its social and political imbalance. The founders had conceived an African state where settlers and aboriginal tribes could co-exist peacefully. Yet in the face of clashes in cultural differences and disparities in customary and statutory laws, the People of the Republic remained disunited and divided by fear and distrust. It was almost a century later that a concerted effort was made to remove many of the odious distinctions through a Unification Program.[30]

This disparity between the Americo-Liberians (sometimes called "Congos") and the indigenous peoples (often called "country" or "tribal" people) still was apparent during the administration of President William V. S. Tubman (1944–1971).[31] The distinguished American actor Ossie Davis was stationed as a GI in Liberia from 1942 to 1945. In his book (co-authored with his wife Ruby Dee), *With Ossie and Ruby—In This Life Together,* he described his experiences with the Americo-Liberians:

> The Americo-Liberians were descendants of the repatriated slaves, and though they spoke with a lilt that sounded like West Indian calypso, they looked so much like us, it was amazing. They were now the ruling class. They had nice homes and were wealthy but their servants, drawn mostly from the other indigenous tribes, were by and large poor and could not vote. The Americo-Liberians behaved toward them as any other ruling class, obviously forgetting what it had meant to be slave. That bothered me a great deal. I felt proud to be there among my people, in a double sense of the word, but I also felt ashamed.
>
> The Americo-Liberians, black though they were, tended to live like Europeans or Americans, and that surprised me. They had new cars; they regularly sent their children off to Europe or America to college, and they fraternized with their peers at Firestone. They seldom mixed with the natives, with whom I had already bonded, who were authentic Africans and much more fun. I was not only uneasy with the class conflict I felt was brewing in Liberia, I was disturbed by it. But most of the soldiers on the post were not. They, too, quite easily took to treating all the natives, not as brothers and comrades, but like servants, in much the same way folks treated black folks down in Georgia.
>
> This arrogance disturbed me, too, and I began to entertain a horrible suspicion. For most of my life, I had believed that black folks were in many ways morally superior to white folks, especially in our dealings with each other. I was profoundly disappointed that the Americo-Liberians, the children of slaves themselves, would come to Africa and behave as if they themselves were the slaveholders now.[32]

This friction between the two groups was extremely important later—in 1980—when Samuel Doe, allegedly representing the indigenous people of Liberia, perpetrated a coup d'etat that overthrew the Americo-Liberian President William R. Tolbert, Jr. Many observers believe, however, that the Americo-Liberian versus Indigenous Liberian problem was a convenient excuse for a bloody coup that was much more complicated and based upon other imperatives.

CONCLUSION

The earliest policy of the United States towards Liberia, from its founding to the late 19th century, created serious problems for the developing nation. By delaying its recognition of the independent Republic for a period of 15 years, due to the racism of the day, the U.S. weakened Liberia's position as a sovereign nation. In particular, U.S. failure to assist Liberia in preventing parts of its border territory from annexation by the colonial powers of Great Britain and France was an egregious error that led to still unresolved tensions with Sierra Leone and Côte d'Ivoire.

NOTES

[1] Edward Lama Wonkeryor, "America's African Colonization Movement: Implications for New Jersey and Liberia," *Liberian Studies Journal* Vol. XXVII, Number 1, 2002, pp. 28–29.

[2] Wilson Jeremiah Moses (ed.), *Liberian Dreams: Back-to-Africa Narratives from the 1850s*, Pennsylvania State University Press, 1998, p. xvii.

[3] Sheldon H. Harris, *Paul Cuffe: Black America and the African Return*, New York, Simon and Shuster, 1972, pp. 74, 251–253.

[4] Ibid., pp. 15, 27, 29, 39–71. Cuffe Slocum, Paul Cuffe's father, was brought from the west coast of Africa to Buzzards Bay, Massachusetts in 1728 at age 10 or 11.

[5] Sir Charles Lucas, *The Partition & Colonization of Africa*, Oxford: Clarendon Press, reprint New York: H. Fertig, 1922[1972].

[6] Moses, pp. xxi, xxiii.

[7] Ibid., p. xvi.

[8] In 1999 I gave a speech on the subject of the Rule of Law to about 1,500 Liberians gathered in Monrovia for a National Reconciliation Conference. Behind me on the podium hung the Liberian flag. At the conclusion of my address I said: "My hope is that one day *your* star spangled banner will hang over *your* home of the brave and land of the free." After I concluded, an old chief from the country approached me and said: "Mr. Hyman, that was a very good speech, but you made a big mistake." "What was that?" I inquired. With a sly smile he said: "Don't you know that you can't 'spangle' a single star?" I never condescended to a Liberian again.

[9] J. Gus Liebenow, *Liberia: The Quest for Democracy*. Bloomington, Indiana: Indiana University Press, 1987, p. 19; Rachel Gbenyon Diggs, Presentation to Vanderbilt University, October 25, 2001, p. 2.

[10] Graham Russell Hodges, ed. *The Black Loyalist Directory: African Americans in Exile after the American Revolution*. (New York, 1996). In 1775 Lord Dunmore, Royal Governor of Virginia, issued a proclamation for slaves and indentured persons to receive freedom in exchange for fighting for the British, and 2,000 persons joined the British side. Other proclamations followed, including the Philipsburg proclamation when they realized they were losing the war, issued by Sir Henry Clinton, the British

Commander-in-chief at New York. It stated that any Negro who deserted the rebel (American) cause would receive full protection, freedom, and land. After the Americans won the war and the Treaty of Paris was signed in 1783, British forces and their supporters went to New York to wait for evacuation. Although General George Washington, on behalf of the Americans who wanted to regain their "property," demanded that the British return all slaves who had joined them before November 30, 1782, Sir Guy Carleton, who was the new British Commander-in-chief, refused. Instead they made an agreement for the British to pay money to the Americans. A joint British-American Commission identified the Blacks who had joined the British before the surrender, issued them "certificates of freedom," inspected all Blacks on ships in New York harbor awaiting departure (a total of 114 ships between April and November, 1783), and recorded the names and status of more than 3,000 persons in a document called the *Book of Negroes*. This included those who escaped, the slaves and indentured servants of White Loyalists, and Blacks who had bought their freedom. Before and after that period, there were an unknown number of ships with Blacks loyal to the British that also left New York and other ports. The estimates were as high as 5,000 black people who resettled in Nova Scotia, New Brunswick, the West Indies, Quebec, England, Germany, and Belgium. Of that number, 3,500 went to Nova Scotia.
[11] White resentment of the Black Loyalist farmers and skilled tradesmen, who were willing to work for lower wages, was evident in the Nova Scotian settlements. On July 1784, the racial tensions between whites and blacks erupted into a race riot by white soldiers against blacks in the community of Shelburne, causing the Black Loyalists to flee to Birchtown.
[12] James W. St. G. Walker, *The Black Loyalists—The Search for a Promised Land in Nova Scotia and Sierra Leone 1783–1870,* 1992. On January 15, 1792, fifteen ships with 1196 Black Loyalists, including the prominent leaders David George, Boston King, and Moses Wilkinson, left Halifax for Sierra Leone.
[13] The bellicose behavior of the Jamaica Maroons, who disliked the climate and agrarian life, led the Nova Scotian government to arrange for their resettlement to Sierra Leone in 1799. The Sierra Leone Company initially objected to this plan for two reasons: many of the Black Loyalist settlers had rebelled against the company one year after arrival and the Company did not want a second hostile group; most Maroons were not Christians, in opposition to the religious goals of the colony. Upon their arrival in 1800 and at the behest of the Sierra Leone Company, the Maroons repressed the revolt of Black Loyalists.
[14] Joseph J. Ellis, *Founding Brothers: The Revolutionary Generation,* Alfred A. Knopf, 2000.
[15] Ibid.
[16] Moses, p. 47.
[17] Ibid., p. 89.
[18] Ibid., p. 134.
[19] Ibid., p. 144.
[20] Gbenyon Diggs, *The Role of America in the Liberian Experience,* speech, p. 1, no date.
[21] Liebenow, p. 17.
[22] Gbenyon Diggs, Vanderbilt University speech, p. 3.
[23] Thomas Pakenham, *The Scramble for Africa,* Jonathan Ball Publishers, 1991, p. 1.
[24] Ibid., p. 7.
[25] Ibid., Introduction.

[26] Ibid, p. 21.

[27] Ibid., p. 22.

[28] Ibid., p. 360.

[29] Reed Kramer, "Liberia: A Casualty of the Cold War's End," *CSIS Africa Notes.* July, 1995, p. 3.

[30] Diggs, Vanderbilt University speech, p. 3.

[31] The term "Congo" was a name given to the Africans who were rescued from slave ships that were intercepted by the British to halt the slave trade. Many of these individuals settled in Liberia, rather than return to their native countries.

[32] Ossie Davis and Ruby Dee, *With Ossie and Ruby—In this Life Together*, William Morrow, November 1998, pp. 126–132.

CHAPTER 2
LIBERIA IN THE TWENTIETH CENTURY

During the first 100 years of its existence, Liberia had great difficulty raising sufficient money to operate the American-style administration that it emulated. The country's lack of infrastructure made it difficult to collect taxes on commerce. Beginning in 1870 a long series of foreign loans from European countries and the United States put Liberia into serious debt. At the start of this period, a high interest bank loan from Great Britain to the government led to a political uproar, followed by the removal from office in 1871 of Edward J. Roye, Liberia's fifth president.

With the start of the 20th century and through the first quarter, Liberia's financial situation remained dire, as it continued to struggle through its economic crisis. In 1912, the U.S., Great Britain, and Germany loaned the country $1.7 million. However, when Liberia failed to meet its obligation it lost its financial sovereignty. In 1914 President Daniel E. Howard requested a $5 million loan from the U.S.; the Woodrow Wilson administration rejected the request because of Liberia's poor credit rating. Pervasive corruption in the administration of Charles D. B. King was the cause of its failure to obtain a loan from the U.S. in 1922, during the administration of Warren G. Harding.

Americo-Liberians ruled Liberia from 1847 until the coup of 1980, through the dominant True Whig Party. (See Appendix B for list of Liberia's Presidents.) Characteristically these administrations were totalitarian, corrupt, and brutal towards all of Liberia's other ethnic groups.

In this chapter, the author emphasizes the presidencies of two Americo-Liberians, William V. S. Tubman and William R. Tolbert Jr., for several reasons. Tubman oversaw major developments (industrial, domestic, political, and social integration) and increased international recognition of Liberia, through his Open Door Policy. In this way, he successfully fostered diplomacy and trade with the U.S., and other western industrialized countries. In addition, Tubman, who headed a totalitarian administration, had the longest tenure as president, 27 years, from 1944 to 1971. Tolbert was confronted with bipolar military rivalry and competition for spheres of influence that existed between the United States and the United Soviet Socialist Republic (Soviet Union) during the height of the Cold War. Since he advocated domestic and international policies of neutrality that contradicted the interests of the U.S. in Liberia and in continental Africa, the United States saw him as dangerous. In addition, Tolbert attempted a quick integration of the Liberian bureaucracy with indigenous Liberians, which led to his rejection by most Americo-Liberians. On the other hand, the indigenous Liberians wanted higher representation in the government than he offered. For example, they sought positions such as vice president, speaker of the house, ambassador, cabinet minister, director of public corporations, among others. Because Tolbert did not yield to their demands or reform the government, they also rejected him. These conditions led to his overthrow and were the precursors to the civil war.

Overall, the factors that shaped U.S relations towards Liberia in the 20th century were the economic interests of both countries, the government of Liberia's corruption and human rights abuses, the fight against Fascism in World War II, and U.S. intelligence operations during the Cold War to defeat Communism. U.S. policies both helped and hindered Liberia's development as a successful country. Improved relations, especially during

World War II, led to a long period of prosperity in Liberia. However, U.S. policies also fostered the conditions that led to Liberia's political instability, and its devastating decline during the civil war in the last decade.

THE FIRESTONE DEAL

Against the background of Liberia's economic distress came the Firestone deal. In 1926 Liberian President Charles D. B. King negotiated a contract with the Firestone Rubber and Tire Company of Akron, Ohio. At the time, British companies, which controlled 80% of the world's rubber production, had driven up the price of rubber, especially since 70% of the world's rubber supply was consumed by the United States due to its expanding automobile industry. Harvey Firestone signed a 99 year lease on one million acres of land in Liberia at a price of *six cents an acre*. It was the world's largest rubber plantation. Workers at the time received wages of 24 cents a day. Firestone agreed to invest $20 million in the Liberian rubber industry. As security for the deal, Firestone loaned Liberia five million dollars but the country's custom receipts were used as collateral against the debt, and an American was placed in charge of the customs revenue to ensure collection of levies and liquidation of the loans. In other words, Liberia was in receivership. To this day, Firestone (now owned by the Japanese) exports all the raw material out of Liberia. The country has no manufacturing facility; Liberians cannot make their own tires, raincoats, condoms, or even rubber bands.[1]

Using the Firestone deal as the prime example, many have argued that there has been growth in Liberia but not development. The contrary view is that the Firestone investment has provided approximately 20,000 jobs for Liberian laborers. As S. Augustu P. Horton wrote in his book, *Liberia's Underdevelopment—In Spite of the Struggle*: "Harvey Firestone set the stage for Liberia's economic growth; he also laid the foundation for external forces to influence and manipulate Liberia's economy."[2] The Firestone arrangement became a model for future concessions to foreign investors; in this way the government obtained the funds necessary to run the country.

LEAGUE OF NATIONS INQUIRY

The relationship between Liberia and the United States was severely strained in the late 1920s and through the 1930s. Joseph Saye Guannu contends that one of the darkest periods in Liberian history was between 1929 and 1934. In 1929 The United States charged Monrovia with practicing slavery and forced labor of indigenous Liberians. The consequent inquiry conducted by a commission of the League of Nations almost culminated in the loss of Liberia's national sovereignty and political independence. President Charles Dunbar B. King, his vice-president Allan N. Yancy, and other government officials resigned from office. At the conclusion of the investigation, the Commission of Inquiry recommended a series of socioeconomic reforms, which Liberia accepted in principle.[3]

According to Guannu, Edwin James Barclay, who was Secretary of State and later President of Liberia, stated:

> Liberia and Liberians in the past few years have had to pass through the crucible of both responsible and irresponsible criticism. The severest self-analysis will not leave us unconvinced that some of the criticism was just. This experience will have been without benefit if it has not developed in us the courage to face realities.[4]

Guannu wrote that the resignation of President Charles D. King, Vice-President Allen Yancy and others prevented their impeachment. He also made the point that state authorities had maltreated indigenous Liberians "in the process of recruitment of laborers for public works and the private farms of government officials in Liberia and for Spanish plantations at Fernando Po."[5] A radio message transmitted to Secretary of State Edwin Barclay, dated 5 October 1927, from Post Master General Reginald Sherman at Sinoe stated, according to the League Report:

> Ross wired yesterday asking for boys to be shipped steamer which request please deny. I am informed that boys are decoyed from Hinterland under the promise of bringing rice for sale which is taken from them and forced aboard just as in slave days.[6]

In his urgent response, Secretary Barclay noted in part:

> Thinking Ross acting bona fide I granted him permit for shipment of 300 labourers. Those were supposed to be men voluntarily engaging for services. Your message reveals iniquity. Am canceling permit. You will instruct Grisby in my name and in the name of Government to have man who was involuntarily held released immediately. This is peremptory.[7]

Appearing before the League Commission of inquiry at Kakata in May 1930, a witness testified, as phrased by Guannu:

> Every work they gave us to do, the whip is our pay. In our country, we are there as slaves...We are not going up again because they flog us. Our own rice they put on our backs and call it government loads. We are country people. We do not own our own work. We work to give them chop.[8]

Equally important, another witness in Harper City, Maryland County, told the League Commission of Inquiry that:

...these men who go on the roads, are used on private farms. Out of the 12 boys sent from this section, 6 of them went on the road. The other six on the private farm of Vice President Yancy.[9]

After becoming president, Edwin J. Barclay failed to implement the measures prescribed by the League of Nations. In response the United States, under the administration of President Franklin Delano Roosevelt (FDR), suspended recognition of Barclay's administration. Lester Aglar Walton, who served as United States Envoy Extraordinary and Minister Plenipotentiary to Liberia from 1935 to 1946, assisted the Republic in improving its relations with the U.S. Walton was a prominent African-American who had a prestigious career in journalism before and after his diplomatic tenure.[10] He was one of the persons who facilitated Liberia receiving important resources during World War II which fostered its first major growth in development. These included the construction of the Free Port of Monrovia, discussed in further detail in the next section, and the agreement with Pan American Airways that established Roberts International Airport (Roberts Field). However during his tenure, Walton reported ongoing corruption in Liberia to the U.S. Department of State, having observed Liberian officials who had "...the reputation for acquiring a big bank account on a small salary." He also wrote of further human right violations by Americo-Liberians against indigenous Liberians to Harry McBride, who was a Liberianist and an assistant to U.S. Secretary of State Cordell Hull. McBride had helped Liberia regain U.S. recognition and was the U.S. financial advisor to the republic under the Loan Agreement. In his communication Walton told Harry McBride:

> Forced labor, vicious exploitation of the natives by Frontier Force, unjust and excessive fines are some of the contributory factors to occasion resentment and dissatisfaction, impelling many natives to reluctantly settle in Sierra Leone.[11]

Due to Liberia's strategic importance in World War II, the U.S. ultimately disregarded these factors in its policy decisions to restore recognition to the republic and use its resources for the Allied effort against Germany and its Axis allies.

WORLD WAR II AND POST-WAR ERA

FRANKLIN DELANO ROOSEVELT VISITS LIBERIA

U.S.–Liberian cooperation and positive relations were enhanced by a visit to Liberia by President Franklin D. Roosevelt on his return to the U.S. from the Casablanca conference in 1943. In so doing, he was the first President of the United States ever to visit that country, although it was an unofficial visit (President Jimmy Carter was the first U.S. president who paid an official visit to Liberia in 1978).[12] One source says that FDR's plane stopped in Liberia merely for refueling.[13] According to Dr. Raymond Teichman, head of research at the FDR Library in Hyde Park, New York, on January 27, 1943, Roosevelt flew from Bathurst Airport in The Gambia to Robertsfield in Liberia, landing at 12:15pm and remaining there until 3:30 p.m. He attended a luncheon given in his honor by then President Edwin J. Barclay of Liberia, and later reviewed the troops.

In the memoirs of U.S. Secretary of State Cordell Hull, he revealed that FDR's visit was of paramount importance because Liberia was to play a key role in the strategic plan that the U.S. had developed to fight Germany and its Axis. Cordell Hull wrote:

> North Africa was not the only portion of the Dark Continent that engaged our diplomatic efforts in 1942. One of our most fruitful achievements was in Liberia, on the west bulge of Africa, across the South Atlantic from Brazil. At this time fortunately our relations were of the best with the little country which a hundred years before had been founded by American freed slaves with the assistance of our Government. As I entered office in 1933, no formal diplomatic ties existed between the United States and Liberia. The United States, as well as Great Britain, had severed such relations in 1930 as a result of various abuses of power by Liberian officials.
>
> In 1935 I had sent to Liberia my assistant, Harry McBride, who already had a first-hand knowledge of that country, and his conferences with President Edwin Barclay resulted in the resumption of diplomatic relations and the beginning of a new era of friendship. We signed a treaty of friendship, commerce, and navigation with Liberia in 1938, and a consular convention, an air navigation agreement and a treaty of conciliation in the following months. In 1939 Pan American Airways signed a contract with the Liberian Government for the operation of transatlantic service to Liberia.
>
> Shortly after Pearl Harbor I again sent McBride to Liberia to induce that Government to coordinate its defenses with ours. It consented to the use by

the United States Army Air Forces of the Pan American airports in Liberia, and Liberia became a vital link in the air route across the South Atlantic to the Near and the Far East. We formalized this arrangement on March 31, 1942, by signing an agreement providing for the defense of Liberia by the United States and giving us the right to establish defense areas in Liberia and to build military installations there. Three weeks before, at the Department's suggestion, President Roosevelt had opened Lend-Lease to Liberia. With Japan's occupation of the rubber producing areas in the Far East, Liberia became of greatly increased importance to us as one of the few remaining available sources of natural rubber.

Throughout the remainder of the war the United States contributed materially to developing Liberia by constructing a port, enlarging the airports, building roads, and providing the Liberian Government with technical assistants. Liberia declared war on the Axis, expelled Axis citizens, and signed the United Nations Declaration. Visits were exchanged between President Roosevelt and President Barclay and President-elect Tubman. We worked out a long-range policy toward Liberia designed to lift the standard of living of this traditional godchild of the United States and to strengthen our economic and political ties.[14]

State Department archives contain a note from the U.S. Chargé d'Affaires in Liberia, Frederick P. Hibbard, written to the U.S. Secretary of State on January 28, the day after Roosevelt's visit. He wrote, in part:

It is regretted that the visit was of such short duration, so much being crowded into it, that it was impossible for me to explain in greater detail the problems of our relations with Liberia, nor did I have an opportunity to hear the conversation with President Barclay. The occasion has been hailed as a most historic one by all Liberians who are enthusiastic over the honor thus paid their country by the President of their oldest friend. While maintaining his customary reserve, it was easy to detect in President Barclay's face a thrill at being able to meet on equal terms the President of the United States and to have him in Liberia...[15]

During his visit to Liberia, FDR extended an invitation to President Barclay to visit him in the United States, which Barclay accepted. At a dinner at Blair House on May 29, 1943, Barclay met with the Assistant Chief of the Division of Near Eastern Affairs in the U.S. Department of State, Mr. Villard, who wrote:

President Barclay said bluntly at the outset that while he appreciated the courteous treatment given to him since his arrival in the United States, he was keenly disappointed at the lack of opportunity to discuss the problems of Liberia with responsible officials of the American Government. He observed that he was a very busy man; that he would not have left Liberia if he had known that his visit to Washington was to be devoted to social functions or that he was scheduled to leave without a chance to take up in the proper quarters various matters which he considered vital to the future of Liberia.[16]

President Barclay had referred to FDR's discussion at lunch in Liberia about the possibility of the United States building a port in Liberia. The U.S. wanted the port in Liberia, as Mr. Villard's communique reported, "as a means of implementing the President's declaration that Dakar would never again become a threat to the Western hemisphere."

FDR, who had such a dislike and mistrust of General Charles DeGaulle, did not want to depend on the cooperation of the French to have a port in West Africa that could be used by the U.S. in the furtherance of the war. Roosevelt waited until the next morning to express the desire to see a port developed in Liberia—a port which would be dependable for the U.S. The President indicated that a port near Monrovia would be ideal and he "made it clear that he would not entertain any port project which would benefit primarily the Firestone Plantations…" Villard explains that,

> President Barclay said that while he appreciated all that Firestone had done for his country, he regarded Firestone as an American interest which had to be curbed. He said that the Firestone organization considered itself to be of paramount importance in Liberia as if the country should be run for its benefit alone. He was obviously suspicious of any extension of Firestone's influence, including the sponsoring by Firestone of new American enterprises or a port development connected with the rubber plantations.[17]

On June 2, 1943, President Barclay complained to Harry Hopkins, the Special Assistant to President Roosevelt, that supplies of money and materials had been promised Liberia in consideration of certain substantial grants which the Liberian government had made towards the war effort, namely, the establishment of American air bases in Liberian territory, and the granting to the United States of military bases therein, but not yet delivered. In a memorandum President Barclay (who was speaking both for himself and his chosen successor William Tubman) described those products of Liberia that he wished to develop for the world market: palm oil, palm kernels, copra, kola nuts, coffee, cocoa, and pissava fibre, as well as mineral deposits (gold, diamonds and iron ore) and went on to say:

> In placing the resources and territorial facilities of the Republic at the disposal of the Government of the United States so readily and fully to serve its war objectives, Liberia had expected that comparable consideration would be given to her basic requirements for economic development. Certain understandings and commitments were, of course, arrived at the time the Liberian Government took the above steps, but it cannot be said that they have materialized.[18]

Meanwhile FDR indicated to the U.S. Assistant Secretary of State Adolph Berle that he wanted a port built in Liberia that could be used by the U.S. Navy, primarily for submarines. On June 17, 1943 Barclay reiterated that the only condition he attached to the development of a port in his country was that it should be economically beneficial to Liberia. The total cost of the port construction (including surveys) was $8,665,000 with the funds coming from the Lend-Lease Administration. On September 14, 1943 Roosevelt wrote to his Secretary of State that, in the negotiations with Liberians, "provision should be made for protection of United States military, air and naval interests in the port with particular reference to our future operational rights there."[19]

Finally, the U.S. insisted that it have operational control of the port, which was to be run by a Port Authority made up of five members—three from the United States and two from Liberia. The U.S. considered this a fair arrangement since it was paying for the entire cost of construction. At the same time, they stated that Liberians should be involved in preparation for Libera's assumption of its control.

Although President Barclay did not receive the economic assistance he sought from the U.S., the deal nevertheless benefitted Liberia since it had a port built at no expense, a facility which today is one of the two main ports in the country. In addition, the Lend-

Lease funds which paid for the construction of the seaport in Monrovia made accessible the country's huge iron ore deposits just as the worldwide demand for steel was growing. Republic Steel took a major stake in the venture, prompting construction of a rail line and roadway and providing new openings to Liberia's interior. For the next phase of the country's history, iron ore paid the way to relative prosperity.

LIBERIAN SHIP REGISTRY

Developments in U.S. foreign policy advanced by President Franklin Delano Roosevelt towards Great Britain and the war in Europe in the early 1940s culminated in the peacetime creation of the Liberian Ship Registry. It was founded and operated under the administration of a U.S. corporation, Liberian Services (later International Trust Company of Liberia and International Registries, Inc. (IRI)), in December 1948. During 2000, the Liberia International Ship and Corporate Registry (LISCR), a corporation based in Vienna, Virginia assumed operations of the registry from IRI. The registry enhanced Liberia's international standing as a maritime nation and has provided as much as 25% of the nation's gross revenue.[20]

In the years immediately preceding its entry into World War II, the United States government wished to assist Great Britain in that country's effort to deter the Nazi invasion of Europe that had resulted in German occupation of several countries. The American electorate, however, opposed entanglements in any foreign wars. With isolationism rampant, the U.S. Congress had passed The Neutrality Act on May 1, 1937.[21] Several of its key resolutions prohibited President Roosevelt from using American ships to transport arms and other goods that could help Great Britain stave off the powerful Nazi military machine. In response to this restriction, the Department of Defense recommended that the U.S. reflag merchant ships under the flag of Panama.[22] Since the vessels technically would not be American ships, there would be no violation of the Neutrality Act in using those ships to send help to Britain. In the Neutrality Act of 1939, the amendment passed by Congress allowed the munition sales to the French and British. Congress repealed additional provisions in 1941 and passed the Lend-Lease Act of March 11, 1941, to allow the U.S. to provide military aid to foreign nations. The act authorized the president to transfer arms or any other defense materials for which Congress appropriated money to "the government of any country whose defense the President deems vital to the defense of the United States." But even with these legislative changes, the practice of reflagging merchant vessels continued.

After the conclusion of the war, Edward Stettinius, who had served in FDR's wartime administration as director in the Office of Production Management (1940–1942), Lend-Lease Administrator (1942–1943), Undersecretary of State (1943–1944) and Secretary of State (December 1944–June 1945), considered that Liberia was an ideal country to have a ship registry. He had resigned from his position in the Truman administration as the first U.S. ambassador to the United Nations (1945–1946).[23] In 1948, Stettinius and his partners founded the peacetime company Liberian Services to run the registry from the United States. The group profited from their venture. After his death in 1949, ownership of Liberian Services and its affiliates passed to the International Bank of Washington, D.C., and development of the registry was then headed by General George Olmsted.[24] The Liberian Ship Registry rapidly evolved as one of the best, safest, most security conscious, and most environmentally sensitive ship registries in the world.

Starting in the early 1950s and into the 1960s, European maritime nations and international maritime unions attacked the emergence of "Flags of Convenience" or Free

Flags, as they called the ships under the flags of Liberia, Panama, Honduras, and later Costa Rica.[25] The United States joined with Liberia and the other nations to defend and secure their full rights in the International Maritime Organization, and other maritime associations. In 1958, because Liberia, the third largest maritime nation by registered tonnage at the time, and Panama (the eighth largest) were not elected to positions on the Maritime Safety Committee of the Inter-governmental Maritime Consultative Organisation (IMCO), Liberia drafted a resolution that was approved that IMCO should request an "Advisory Opinion from the International Court of Justice at the Hague" regarding the issues raised by their European adversaries.[26] During the 15 years of opposition, the U.S., which fully supported and assisted Liberia in this matter, maintained that

> Since the transportation of these bulk commodities is vital to our national economy and defence needs, the Liberian, Panamanian, and Honduran flags are essential to our national interests.[27]

PRESIDENT WILLIAM VACANARAT SHADRACH TUBMAN

Edwin J. Barclays's successor, William V. S. Tubman, became President of Liberia in 1944. In an effort to advance Liberia's economic growth, he developed what he called the Open Door policy, welcoming foreign investors on very favorable terms. Tubman's Open Door policy was also designed to promote the development of the country's largely undeveloped interior based on joint ventures between the government and foreign investors. In the three decades of his Presidency (seven terms from 1944 to 1971), Tubman built a one-party state (through the vehicle of the True Whig Party) which he ruled with an iron hand. His was government by personality cult. As his crowning achievement and in the name of nation-building, he abolished separate jurisdictions for the coast and the hinterland, and in their places established a united republic with nine counties. Unity was a grand accomplishment, but it also made it easier for Tubman to retain a powerful hold on the nation—and on the patronage involved. In order to give their children an opportunity at government jobs and patronage, country people began to form alliances with the elite.

In implementation of his foreign policy, President Tubman formed alliances with other nations in Africa and established relationships with many European countries. By the time of the Cold War, he had carefully cultivated his relationship with the United States. In fact the United States set up a mission to train the Liberian military (something it would refuse to do in the late 1990s) and brought Liberian military officers to U.S. institutions for further training. However in his domestic policy, Tubman suppressed all efforts to organize opposition political parties.

In 1959 Liberia entered into a mutual defense pact with the United States. Over the next decade, the U.S. government built two sophisticated communications facilities to handle diplomatic and intelligence traffic to and from Africa, to monitor radio and other broadcasts in the region, and to relay a powerful Voice of America signal throughout the continent. In 1976, the U.S. Coast Guard erected an Omega navigational station—one of eight around the world—to guide and monitor shipping traffic in the eastern Atlantic and up and down Africa's west coast. These instances of U.S. assistance to Liberia are proof of the long and close historic relationship between the two countries—a relationship that the United States, immediately after the Cold War, dismissed as non-existent. The assistance varied since the United States, between 1946 and 1961 provided Liberia with $41 million in assistance. Between 1962 and 1980, economic and military aid totaled $278 million.[28]

PRESIDENT WILLIAM RICHARD TOLBERT JR.

In 1971 upon Tubman's death, William R. Tolbert, Jr. became president. He was immediately faced with demands from students (including many country people), who had been well educated, to provide them with suitable jobs in the government. He also faced a rising, militant African nationalism espoused by such groups as Movement for Justice in Africa (MOJA) in which Amos Sawyer (later to become president of an interim government in 1990) was one of the leaders.[29] In response to this criticism, Tolbert moved away from a 100% pro-American line in foreign affairs and, in so doing, earned the antipathy of the U.S. CIA, which had its headquarters for the African continent in Monrovia, and the U.S. Pentagon.

To complicate matters, Tolbert raised the price of rice—the universal staple of the Liberian people—in order to discourage costly imports, and encourage domestic production of rice. This led to the April 14, 1979 rice riots in Monrovia which further weakened his government. Historian Stephen Ellis wrote,

> So pervasive was the sense of impending change that one man intent on making a political career, a leader of the Liberian student movement in the United States, headed back to Liberia to be at the heart of the thing. His name was Charles Taylor.[30]

As part of his tilt to the left in foreign policy, Tolbert refused to allow the United States bunkering facilities at Robertsfield Airport for a U.S. Rapid Deployment Force. At this point, the U.S. began to withdraw its support of Tolbert and look for a likely successor. Although there is no definitive evidence, many Liberians who were active in government at that time believed that the U.S. had chosen Major Jarbo to succeed Tolbert.[31] But while Jarbo was mounting his effort to unseat Tolbert (via a bloodless coup), he was superseded by another group that included Samuel Kanyon Doe. The U.S. wanted to precipitate Tolbert's ouster, but failed to anticipate conditions after Tolbert was gone. This unhappy pattern was repeated in U.S.–Liberian relations—the theory of unintended consequences.

In 1980 the leaders of MOJA formed alliances with some lower-ranking soldiers of the Liberian Army. Because the soldiers were led to believe that the government was about to execute some political prisoners on the anniversary of the 1979 rice riots, they decided to pre-empt that action. Seventeen inebriated non-commissioned soldiers of the Armed Forces of Liberia (AFL), led by Thomas Gunkama Quiwonkpa and Thomas Weh Syen launched a coup on the night of April 12, 1980.[32] They called themselves the People's Redemption Council (PRC). Some of the party went to look for President Tolbert at his home. At the same time, however, Master Sergeant Samuel Kanyon Doe, Colonel Harrison Dennue, and other members of their group entered the Executive Mansion, found Tolbert there, and murdered him. A former Voice of America reporter wrote: "Samuel Doe cut the liver and heart out of President Tolbert and ritually mutilated them, leaving teeth marks in the flesh." Thus ended 133 years of relative peace in Liberia, by the man whom the United States would support for many years, to the detriment of the Liberian populace.[33]

MILITARY COUP D'ETAT

SAMUEL KANYON DOE AND THE PEOPLE'S REDEMPTION COUNCIL

Samuel Kanyon Doe, a 28 year old illiterate, became the leader of the coup. The first act of his tenure as head of state was to arrest 13 high-ranking members of the Tolbert government who then were marched naked through the streets of Monrovia and summarily

executed on the beach, as a shocked international community looked on…in silence.[34]
Why did the United States Embassy in Monrovia stand by while these people were
assassinated? Why didn't the international human rights community broadcast to the world
Doe's blatant violations of every principle of international law? Major Jarbo tried to flee
the country but was hunted down and killed by the Doe junta.[35] In an incident that was to
have geopolitical consequences in the future, one of the people sought out by the junta
was Adolphus Benedict Tolbert, the son of President Tolbert.[36] He sought refuge in the French
Embassy in Monrovia. Adolphus's wife Desiree was the god-daughter of the late President Felix
Houphouet-Boigny of the Côte d'Ivoire (Ivory Coast), a legendary and revered leader of West
Africa. Desiree appealed to Houphouet-Boigny who, in turn, contacted Samuel Doe and asked
that he spare Adolphus Tolbert's life. Despite Doe's professed commitment to honor Houphouet-
Boigny's wishes, and in violation of international law, Tolbert was abducted from the French
Embassy in Monrovia in June of 1980 and murdered. Forever after, Houphouet-Boigny vowed
to avenge the death of Adolphus and became the implacable enemy of Samuel Doe.

The conventional wisdom was that, after so many years of America-Liberian
governance, the indigenous people finally rose up and took over the government for
themselves. But one can fairly conclude that the U.S., by withdrawing its support from
President Tolbert, encouraged those elements that wanted to overthrow Tolbert. Apparently,
however, U.S. intelligence did not realize that the Quiwonkpa-Doe faction was ready to
move—and that the Major Jarbo faction was not. As the result, Liberia ended up with
Samuel Doe as its head of state (later president), with dire consequences for the future. In
this instance, then, short-sighted U.S. policy toward Liberia exemplified the theory of
unintended consequences. The problem with the policy was the failure to look ahead. The
U.S. withdrew its support of Tolbert without considering the possibility that an unknown,
brutal faction—Doe's faction—could emerge. Then, faced with a vicious Doe government
that slaughtered people at will, the U.S. vigorously supported that government for reasons
that will be subsequently discussed. The initial error of judgment (pulling the rug from
under Tolbert) thus was compounded (by placing the rug under the corrupt Samuel Doe).

Initially, Samuel Doe was head of the civilian government and General Thomas Gunkama
Quiwonkpa was leader of the army. Doe was from the Krahn ethnic group and Quiwonkpa
was from the Mano ethnic group. At his very first press conference, Doe was asked what
his program was for Liberia—he had not the slightest idea.[37] Both Doe and Quiwonkpa,
still allies, placed members of their ethnic groups, families, and close associates in high
government posts. One of the people selected by Thomas Quiwonkpa was Charles Taylor,
a graduate of Bentley College in Boston, Massachusetts who was married to a close relative
of Quiwonkpa. Taylor was born in 1948 near Monrovia, the third of 15 children in an
America-Liberian and indigenous family of modest means. At the suggestion of Quiwonkpa
when he was still in favor with Doe, Taylor became Director General of the Liberian
General Services Administration which (as in the U.S.) was the government procurement
office. He served from June of 1980 until August of 1983. Many MOJA members also
joined the Doe government in high offices. Many of these people concluded that, although
they were appalled that a young man of Doe's inexperience was their President, it was their
duty, as patriotic Liberians, to try and administer the country in a responsible way.

In 1981 Doe, in order to secure his personal control of the government, ordered the
execution of his compatriots, such as Thomas Weh Syen, vice-chairman of the ruling
military People's Redemption Council. Despite this, after Ronald Reagan took office in
1981, the U.S. dramatically increased its support for Liberia. In 1982, President Reagan

invited Doe to Washington (where, to the embarrassment of all, Reagan publicly referred to the Liberian President as "Chairman Moe") and urged Doe to end all political executions. As former Assistant U.S. Secretary of State for Africa, Herman "Hank" Cohen, writes in his book, *Intervening in Africa*,

> Doe readily agreed, since most Liberians who might be a threat were now dead or living in exile...Within five years, the Doe regime went from the embodiment of indigenous majority rule to an oppressive government dominated by Liberia's most backward ethnic group, the Krahn. The other tribal people now regretted the ouster of the Americo-Liberians in 1980.[38]

Yet the U.S., in President Reagan's favorite phrase, decided to "stay the course" with Samuel Doe. Support for Liberia, and Samuel Doe in particular, under the Reagan administration skyrocketed. Aid levels rose from about $20 million in 1979 to $75 million and then $95 million, for a total of between $402 and $500 million between 1981 and 1985, more than the country received during the entire previous century.

In 1983 under U.S. pressure, Doe announced that he was considering becoming an elected civilian president under a constitution. Since his role was confined to heading the army which had brought Doe to power, Quiwonkpa would lose influence. A short time later and based on allegations that Quiwonkpa was conspiring against him, Doe announced that he intended to remove him as head of the army and have him serve as secretary-general of the PRC.[39] However, General Quiwonkpa stated that he refused to accept the position unless Chairman Doe did the following: 1) set a definite time-table for the return to civilian democratic rule; 2) determine the identity of Quiwonkpa's accusers who said that he wanted to overthrow the government; and 3) punish those who were guilty with a revolutionary penalty.[40] Doe refused to comply with Quiwonkpa's conditions. Quiwonkpa, too, continued to reject his appoinment as secretary general of the PRC. Afraid that Quiwonkpa, who was the most powerful and incorruptible general, would try to wrest state power from him while he was on a foreign trip, Doe removed the commanding general from the army with the forfeiture of all benefits. He also charged General Quiwonkpa and 12 prominent Liberians with treason—a trumped up charge—for attempting to overthrow his government.[41] Quiwonkpa, who saw Doe's refusal as an effort to emasculate him politically and a threat to his life, went into exile in Sierra Leone. Later he resurfaced in the United States. Quiwonkpa returned to Africa in 1985 and staged an unsuccessful coup against Doe. One of the people accompanying him was Prince Yourmie Johnson, a Gio, the man who assassinated Samuel Doe in 1990.

At about the same time Charles Taylor, of Gola and Americo-Liberian parentage, fled to the United States, fearing for his own life. Taylor was transferred from the GSA to the Ministry of Commerce as deputy minister; he had been accused of financial irregularities at GSA, as well as being suspect because of his close alliance with Quiwonkpa. Many other Liberians serving in the Doe government became disillusioned and disgusted by what they observed. Several people fled the country, fearing for their lives, as Doe embarked upon a new campaign of harassment and torture against his political opponents, both in and out of the military establishment.

THE CHARLES GHANKAY TAYLOR EMBEZZLEMENT CHARGE

Over the years, the view that Charles Taylor is a convicted felon, who broke out of jail in the United States and escaped to West Africa, was accepted as fact. A U.S. Senator called Taylor "a jailbird." Since the incident relates to the Doe era, it is worth examining the facts. As with most issues in Liberian politics, the truth is far more complex than the conventional wisdom.

Once Samuel Doe had overthrown the Tolbert government by force of arms, then embarked upon the brutal assassination of his political opponents, the question of who would run the government was critical. Many of the brightest and most dedicated Liberians felt that the wisest course of action was to join the Doe government and hopefully set it on a respectable path for the good of the citizenry. They were encouraged to do so by the support of the United States government for the Doe government. In the 1980s the United States and the Soviet Union were in the midst of the Cold War, battling for the minds and hearts of the nations of the world. Liberia played a role in U.S. plans since the CIA station for Africa, as well as the Voice of America station, and the Omega Navigational System (for tracking shipping) all were located within Liberia's borders.

One could argue that the U.S. was initially justified in supporting the government in power, despite Doe and the PRC having achieved that power through the bloodiest of coups. But as the weeks and months passed, it became evident that the administration of Samuel Doe was corrupt to its core, and vicious in its methods of silencing opposition. It is thought that most of the $500 million that the United States lavished on Doe in a 10-year period went into his own pockets. Representative Donald M. Payne of New Jersey, the ranking member of the Subcommittee on Africa of the Committee on International Relations, House of Representatives in the 108th Congress said:

> However, preceding Taylor, you know, Sergeant Doe killed Tolbert and assassinated or executed the cabinet level people and leaders of Liberia right on the beaches, and our country did not have disdain. As a matter of fact, after Sergeant Doe took over in the early 1980s we tripled the U.S. aid to Liberia. Now, to me that makes no sense.[42]

High-ranking State Department officials stated that continued U.S. support of the Doe administration was one of the most unfortunate consequences of the Cold War and a serious mistake.[43] As Thomas Friedman put it in his book, *The Lexus and the Olive Tree*: "Precisely because the superpowers were ready to write blank checks, a lot of Cold War regional conflicts smoldered on much longer than they should have."[44]

Bill Berkeley of the New York Times in his book, *The Graves are Not Yet Full: Race, Tribe and Power in the Heart of Africa,* accused Chester Crocker, U.S. Undersecretary of State for Africa, of legitimizing the tyranny of Samuel Doe, calling his policies "a case study in the ruinous consequences of the cold war at its least-known fringes—what might better be called destructive engagement."[45] No one seriously believed that, if the U.S. abandoned its support of Doe, the Russians would come to Liberia and somehow tip the balance in the Cold War.

In October of 1983, Doe accused Charles Taylor of having embezzled $922,382.70 from the government. Taylor was removed from his position at the GSA and transferred to become Deputy Minister of Commerce, while an investigation into the charges ensued. Taylor, along with a number of other prominent Liberians (including Ellen Johnson-Sirleaf who, in 1997, ran against Taylor for the presidency of Liberia, and is expected to run again in the next election), fled to the United States. On December 19, 1983 in Liberia, a warrant was issued for the arrest of Taylor, for the alleged "Theft of Property."[46] Doe requested the Reagan administration to jail and extradite Taylor back to Liberia for trial. At this time, there were no U.S. charges filed against Charles Taylor. The U.S.

government acceded to Doe's request. On May 24, 1984 Taylor was arrested and confined to the Plymouth County, Massachusetts jail, that had a contract with the U.S. government to house federal prisoners. Bail was denied and Taylor spent the next 15 months in jail. Doe then asked the the Reagan administration to extradite Taylor back to Liberia. The U.S. willingly complied and the United States Attorney for Massachusetts acted in this case "for and in behalf of the government of Liberia"—in other words, the U.S. represented Doe.[47]

The money in question was designated to purchase U.S. spare parts for heavy equipment owned by the Liberian Ministry of Public Works. It was wired to the Citibank account (in New York) of a company called IEE which was the designated parts supplier. Only $100,000 of the total amount of $922,382.70 went to Mr. Taylor. He claimed that this amount represented monies he had collected from various individuals in Liberia and had given to Mr. B.S. Dhillon, President of IEE, for safekeeping with the exception of a small amount which was his own. The remainder of the money ended up in Mr. Dhillon's bank account.[48]

Taylor was represented by former U.S. Attorney General Ramsey Clark, who argued in court that: 1) there was insufficient evidence to warrant extradition; 2) that the evidence established the overwhelming probability that Taylor would be executed if he was extradited to Liberia; 3) that there was no valid extradition treaty between the United States and Liberia (since the treaty was signed in 1938 and no longer was valid because of Doe's military coup in overthrowing the legitimate government of Liberia); and 4) that Taylor's extradition should be denied because it would violate the responsibility of the United States to respect and protect human rights.[49]

The Massachusetts authorities rejected Ramsey Clark's argument on behalf of Taylor, because of "the insistence by the Executive Department of the United States, acting through the Secretary of State, that the Treaty is in full force and effect." The United States Magistrate concluded—

> I find the evidence submitted totally insufficient to support findings of fact
> to brand the Government of Liberia as a lawless military dictatorship with a
> complete disregard of fundamental human rights, international due process
> of law and its own rules

and he stated further that it was the sole responsibility of the Executive Branch to assess the good faith of the requesting government.[50] In another opinion of the court (regarding a *habeas corpus* petition, dated October 31, 1985), U.S. District Court Judge Robert Keeton wrote: "It is well-established that the decision to extradite ultimately is left to the Secretary of State." The court basically referred the issue back to the White House, which had decided to comply with Samuel Doe.

After the ruling, Taylor, prompted by his fear, escaped from the second story cellblock area in which he had been confined at the Plymouth County jail and fled the United States. On September 15, 1985 (15 months after he was jailed), he sawed and removed the bars on a window in the 1910 facility, climbed down knotted sheets to the ground, and escaped in the car of a fellow Liberian exile. Ever since, rumors and speculation were rampant as to who helped Taylor escape, especially since no one else, before or after, had escaped from the Plymouth County facility. Although there were no U.S. charges against Taylor, Massachusetts kept its charges against him for jail-breaking on its books.

A signed affidavit by the Attorney General and Minister of Justice of Liberia during the Doe years stated that Doe was told that if he didn't prosecute Taylor, the public would believe that he and Taylor were co-conspirators in the alleged embezzlement of government funds. At the same time Taylor was informed that his life would be in jeopardy if he returned to Liberia; in the affidavit the attorney-general concluded that "Taylor's real fear for his own personal safety…motivated him to avoid extradition at any cost."

Since the Reagan Administration's foreign policy objective was to maintain good relations with Samuel Doe, it had granted his request to extradite Charles Taylor back to Liberia. This was despite Doe's past actions that indicated he would have surely killed Taylor. Whether the charge of embezzlement brought by the Doe government against Charles Taylor had merit or not, or whether Taylor and Doe conspired together, the United States government did not hesitate to accommodate Samuel Doe's desire to have Taylor sent back to Liberia. This was despite the high probability that the U.S. knew he would be jailed, tortured, and then killed, like many other opponents of Doe.

Taylor's boldness in attacking the record of corruption and killing of the Doe administration was anathema to the U.S. The administration policy disregarded this abysmal record to justify its full support of Doe, whose cooperation it felt was essential in the Cold War effort. It is also conceivable that this was the genesis for the opposition that the U.S. State Department had to Charles Taylor in successive years.

THE FIGHT TO OUST SAMUEL KANYON DOE

THE CAMPAIGN OF GENERAL THOMAS GUNKAMA QUIWONKPA

Samuel Doe was a member of the Krahn tribe. His former ally, Thomas Quiwonkpa was of the Mano tribe, as previously stated. As the ethnic rivalry between the two groups increased, Doe moved to rid himself of his rivals. In November 1985 Quiwonkpa, who had fled the country, reentered Liberia from Sierra Leone with a group of dissidents in an attempt to overthrow the Doe government. His coup failed and Doe's people murdered him, mutilated his corpse and dragged it around the city for all to see. Television footage observed by the Lawyers Committee shows Krahn soldiers (Doe's men) verging on hysteria, kicking and pummeling Quiwonkpa's body beyond recognition. The body then was taken to the Barclay Training Center in downtown Monrovia directly across the street from a large outdoor market filled with shoppers and market women. There, as hundreds looked on, the rebel leader was castrated, dismembered, and consumed. Doe then embarked upon a purge of anyone who had supported Quiwonkpa. It has been estimated that, at that time, between 600 and 1,500 people were killed on the orders of Samuel Doe.

After these incidents, Doe filled all important government posts with members of his Krahn tribe. To replace Gio dominance in Nimba County, Doe appointed Mandingo officials and also selected Alhaji Kromah, a Mandingo, to head the Liberian Broadcasting Service. Mandingos were not considered as "true Liberians" and thus posed no potential threat to Doe as a rival voting group. Most Mandingos are Muslims and traders. They claim to be descended from the great Malinke tribe of Guinea, but others assert that the Mandingo was a forest-dweller who was enslaved by the Malinke. Later the Mandingos allegedly were slave traders themselves.

There is a distinctive prejudice in Liberia against the Mandingo that stems from several issues. As part of their long-standing culture in the treatment of all strangers, indigenous Liberians offered "space," meaning land, commercial property, homes, or rooms within a residence—free of charge—to Mandingos to use for dwelling and trading. In return, many Mandigos used legal and illegal means to claim the property without adequately compensating the owner(s); if payment was made it was not equal to the value of the property. Culturally, Mandingos have considered all non-Muslims as irreligious people. Because of this, they refused to allow their children to marry members of other indigenous ethnic groups. In contrast, Mandingo men, while professing to greater spirituality within the confines of Islamic law than indigenous people, had sexual liaisons with indigenous women. Yet, in the past, Mandigo women who dated indigenous men were severely punished. These social and economic practices by many Mandigos promoted resentment that was the seed of prejudice against their entire group. The U.S. Department of State found that Muslims complained of Christians being given preference in employment and access to facilities, especially in cities. In October 2002, a property dispute erupted in violence and the burning of a mosque;12 suspected perpetrators were arrested.[51]

Long before the world coined the phrase "ethnic cleansing," Doe practiced it to remove all opposition to his government which meant killing people of tribes other than his own Krahn tribe. Blaine Harden wrote: "Before Doe, Liberia was one of the few African countries without serious ethnic hostility."[52] During the Doe regime, ethnic warfare reigned supreme.

NATIONAL ELECTIONS OF 1985

With his opposition under close surveillance by his security forces, Samuel Doe felt sufficiently secure to call for a national election, a move that had been urged upon him by the U.S. government which was anxious that there be a return to civilian rule. Held in October of 1985, a man named Jackson Doe, a former education minister under President Tolbert—no relation to Samuel Doe—contested for the presidency under the banner of the Liberia Action Party against Samuel Doe. Jackson Doe, who was a member of the Gio ethnic group in Nimba County, was highly regarded by the United States and by all accounts won the election. The Lawyers Committee for Human Rights, in its publication *Liberia: A Promise Betrayed* states that—

> the results based on the official tally sheets showed Jackson Doe, the LAP standard bearer, winning the presidential election with more than 60 percent of the vote...President Doe managed to overcome this result by resorting to one of the most brazen electoral frauds in recent African history. His subordinates in the Special Election Commission (SECOM) destroyed thousands of ballots in a bonfire that was discovered outside Monrovia and photographed by the local press.[53]

Samuel Doe ignored the votes of his people and declared that he had won the election with 50.9% of the vote. Astoundingly, the United States continued to support Samuel Doe after his blatant disregard of democratic principles. State Department officials later admitted that the U.S. made another bad mistake in propping up the government of Samuel Doe, instead of recognizing the true winner of the election and a man well qualified to be President, Jackson Doe. But the Cold War was more important than Liberia's future.

David Halberstam wrote in *War in a Time of Peace* about Somalia,

> The importance of Somalia had been for a time, for reasons that had absolutely nothing to do with the quality of life for the people there, greatly inflated by the Cold War, as if the outcome of what were always nothing more than their indigenous tribal struggles would in some way help determine a larger, global struggle and show which of the giant superpowers held the key to the future. Arms poured in from both superpowers, promises of more aid were made. Warlords were described in the media as either tough, no-nonsense military men (our proxies) or left-leaning radicals (their proxies).[54]

This could just as well have been Liberia that he described.

While the U.S. Secretary of State George Schultz praised the Doe government for its "genuine progress" toward democracy, the Washington Post published a different view. Blaine Harden of the Post wrote:

> What the Americans ended up buying was neither stability nor democracy. They paid, instead, for Doe's legitimacy: weapons to coerce loyalty, money to rent it. The skinny backwoods sergeant was more cunning than he looked. Repeatedly, he outfoxed the State Department. He promised to return to his barracks, which he did not. He promised free and fair elections, which he rigged. He promised financial discipline, which he faked. For his every promise, the US government rewarded him with aid. For his every betrayal, the US government accepted another promise.[55]

Once again, U.S. Cold War imperatives overruled the concern for human rights. In restrospect former Secretary of State Schultz expressed one of the difficulties he engendered by the U.S. policy towards Samuel Doe. In his memoir titled, *Turmoil and Triumph,* Mr. Schultz discussed his unsuccessful attempts to convince the House Intelligence Committee to permit U.S. intervention in Suriname in 1982, in opposition to an army sergeant who had led a group of soldiers in the overthrow of the government. The Committee refused permission. Schultz wrote:

> (W)e were asked why we wanted to intervene in Suriname when we were not seeking to intervene in Liberia, where Master Sergeant Samuel Doe was brutally consolidating his powers…The President and I stewed in frustration at our inability to produce effective counteraction.[56]

THE ARMED CAMPAIGN OF CHARLES GHANKAY TAYLOR

It was against this background that Charles Taylor began his campaign to oust Samuel Doe. After his escape from jail on September 15, 1985, Taylor went to Mexico, then to Ghana. From there, he traveled to Burkina Faso where Blaise Compaore had overthrown that country's President, Thomas Sankara, aided by a number of Liberians of the Quiwonkpa faction who had fled that country in fear of retribution by Doe. As a result both Compaore of Burkina Faso and Houphouet-Boigny of Côte d'Ivoire were anti-Doe. At the same time, President Gaddafi of Libya encouraged revolutionary movements which might lead to his dream of a pan-African union, a dream which in 2003 is becoming a reality, although not under Gaddafi's leadership.

One should separate the unsavory record of Gaddafi from the worthwhile goal of African unity, similar to the now fulfilled dream of European unity through the European Union (EU). The difference, of course, is that the U.S. supported the EU, but historically none of the major powers have been enthusiastic about an African union that could endanger their continued ability to exploit that continent's natural resources (gold, diamonds, iron ore, cocoa). The U.S.'s disenchantment with President Tolbert in large part was caused by his promoting pan-Africanism, which, especially during the Cold War, was perceived as a threat to the West.[57]

These three countries (Côte d'Ivoire, Burkina Faso, and Libya) gave Taylor the financial support that was necessary to mount and lead the struggle against Doe. Although there were other Liberian exile groups who had similar plans, none had the financial backing that Taylor had. One of Taylor's closest associates stated privately that Taylor was a wealthy man before he embarked on his crusade against Doe, and because of the assistance of the three nations' presidents Taylor never needed to profit personally from his undertaking— he already had enough money.[58]

In 1988 in the hope of unseating Samuel Doe, Taylor planned to launch his return to his homeland from Sierra Leone, which shares a border with Liberia. He offered money to Sierra Leone's President, Joseph Momoh, to gain his permission to operate out of that country.[59] At the same time he encouraged Taylor, however, Momoh told Doe of Taylor's offer, and extracted a higher sum from Doe. He then turned down Taylor's request. That incident led to Taylor forming an alliance with a rebel group in Sierra Leone known as the Revolutionary United Front (RUF) headed by Foday Sankoh, whose goal it was to overthrow Momoh. Taylor's group took the name of the National Patriotic Front of Liberia (NPFL). After Joseph Momoh's rebuff, Charles Taylor moved his group to Côte d'Ivoire, and prepared to enter Liberia at the point where the two countries shared a common border, in Nimba County, Liberia.

On December 24, 1989 Taylor and 100 fighters crossed the Côte d'Ivoire border into Liberia. He said at the time that he was going to get "that boy Doe off the backs of the Liberian people." Taylor's people moved quickly across Liberia, well received by people who despised President Samuel Kanyon Doe. As he proceeded toward the capital of Monrovia, his military victory seemed imminent.

In April of 1990, a political development altered the balance of power in Taylor's struggle to remove Doe; Nigeria's President Ibrahim Babangida decided to help his beleaguered ally, Samuel Doe, by sending plane loads of arms and ammunition to help halt the NPFL advance.[60] The Nigerian arms insured that Liberia's war did not end in April of 1990. Details of this Nigerian intervention were documented in *Through the Liberian Storm,* a book written by Dr. Joseph Njoh. A Nigerian born doctor, Njoh was head of the Department of Internal Medicine at the John F. Kennedy Hospital in Monrovia, Liberia during this period. He tells of his visit to the Nigerian Embassy in Liberia on May 17, 1990, where he met with an old friend who was a high-ranking officer at the embassy. Here, in the words of Dr. Njoh, is what he discovered:

> We had grown to like and trust each other very much. I believed that if anyone could enlighten me as to the extent of Nigeria's involvement in the Liberian conflict, it would be he...After the initial courtesies were exchanged, I quickly closed the door and went straight to the point. I asked him questions to which I sought answers. I was reasonably certain that he knew the answers and that if he did not answer them, it would be because he did not want to. Certainly he was high enough at the embassy to know the goings on.

> The first question was: 'Is it true that the Nigerian government is helping Doe by sending arms to him?' He nodded and grunted to say it was true. Then he added: 'I went myself to Roberts Airport (near Monrovia) to receive one of the planes when it arrived from one of the airports in the northern part of Nigeria. It was a private aeroplane, an OKADA airline plane, loaded with arms and ammunition. Some of the arms were unloaded from the plane in my presence and reloaded into military trucks of the AFL (Doe's army).'

> 'Do you mean that the Nigerian government sent arms and ammunition to Doe to fight this war,' asked Dr. Njoh. His friend nodded and smiled.[61]

After his discussion, Dr. Njoh went to the office of the Nigerian ambassador for confirmation, but the ambassador denied the entire story. *The New African* magazine which revealed Dr. Njoh's story in its September 1997 edition, wryly remarked: "As they say in Britain, an ambassador is an official sent abroad to lie for Her Majesty."

The magazine article continued,

At the rate the rebels were advancing, most Liberians believed the NPFL would take Monrovia in a matter of weeks. The war would be over and normalcy would return. Therefore Nigeria's arms shipments at that crucial time was a lifeline which ordinary Liberians thought Doe did not deserve. Soon anti-Nigerian feelings were all over.[62]

Taylor's NPFL was welcomed by those Liberians who wished to be rid of the government of Samuel Doe. Liberia had lived in relative peace for all 133 years of its existence until the blood bath perpetrated by Doe and his contemporaries in 1980. By July 2, 1990 the NPFL was five miles from the center of Monrovia. The United States, publicly, though not privately, continued to support Samuel Doe and his Armed Forces of Liberia (AFL). Herman "Hank" Cohen, former U.S. Assistant Secretary of State for African Affairs, wrote:

> Reports of AFL human rights violations against civilians provoked our first public reaction. The NPFL rebels were killing members of Doe's Krahn tribe but behaved well toward other ethnic groups. Doe in turn sent in his Krahn troops, who specialized in pillaging, extortion and killing.[63]

An ethnic war was in full force. As the NPFL was about to enter Monrovia, 2,000 U.S. marines arrived in warships off the coast of Monrovia on June 4 and 5 in order to safely evacuate American personnel from Liberia. While in the country, they did nothing to help the Liberians. Hank Cohen stated:

> We deployed a large marine amphibious force near Liberia to evacuate U.S. citizens, an operation accomplished with great efficiency...A modest intervention at that point to end the fighting in Monrovia could have avoided the prolonged conflict.[64]

At the same time, the AFL (on July 29 and 30) attacked St. Peter's Lutheran Church in Monrovia where 2,000 refugees, mostly Gio and Mano, had sought shelter. Doe's AFL troops opened fire and 600 people were massacred. One of the people killed in that massacre was Mr. Nelson Taylor, the father of Charles Taylor.

When one hears of the massacre of 600 people, often the number is noted but the human terms of such incidents may not be considered. An eyewitness description by the one of the doctors at the hospital revealed the consequences:

> As the bodies were brought in [to the Catholic hospital near the site of the massacre], in a seemingly endless stream, even the hardened men and women on the hospital staff lost their composure. Tears flowed freely down their cheeks as they toiled to ease the pain, to stop the oozing of blood and to bind the wounds.

> Particularly painful was the sight of children who were mercilessly butchered. I will never forget a baby who had a deep gash in her buttocks and sucked intermittently at her mother's partly amputated left breast. The mother appeared unconscious, her right nipple had a sore. The pattern of the cuts showed that the machetes were wielded in a random fashion. For most part of that fateful day, the air around the hospital was thick with the smell of raw meat.[65]

Still the U.S. observed, but did nothing. Liberians could not understand why the United States allowed this carnage to take place without intervening to help end the conflict. All factions would have deferred to a U.S. intervention, but the administration declined to help. During that year, more than 700,000 refugees fled from Liberia. Especially in the case of Liberia, because of its long historical association with the United States, and because of the near reverence in which Liberians hold Americans, the slightest indication from the United States as to dissatisfaction with the excesses of the Doe government almost surely would have led to its overthrow. Conversely, the failure of the U.S. to condemn the Doe government led many to believe that the U.S. supported its continuance. Further analysis supports that Liberians would have been correct in that assumption.

Journalist Reed Kramer writes in a paper published by the Center for Strategic and International Studies (July 1995):

> As fighting escalated in early 1990, the George W. Bush administration faced a serious conundrum. Western Europe and most of Africa looked to the United States to take the lead in seeking a peaceful resolution to the Liberian crisis, since the country's history bears an unmistakable 'made in America' stamp. But senior administration officials, determined to limit U.S. involvement in what was viewed as a 'brush fire', rejected the notion of inherent American interest or responsibility.[66]

In May of 1990 the U.S. finally tried to convince Doe to go quietly into exile and allow all the political factions, including that of Charles Taylor, to negotiate a democratic transition by holding an election as soon as possible. Efforts to stimulate discussions between Doe and the NPFL continued. At first Liberia was the mission of the U.S. Department of State's Coordinating Committee headed by Herman Cohen. Things progressed fairly well until responsibility for Liberia was taken from the Coordinating Committee and given to the Deputies Committee headed by Deputy National Security Advisor Robert Gates, a career CIA official brought in by President Bush. Cohen wrote that, to his distress, Gates "refused to recognize any special U.S. responsibility for Liberia's crisis on the basis of historical ties" and took the view that "we were not responsible for solving the Liberian problem, no matter what the Africans or anyone else expected." In other words, the U.S. decided to wash its hands of Liberia.

Assistant Secretary Cohen had proposed a constitutionally viable scheme to both sides in which Doe would resign in favor of his vice president, who then would appoint Charles Taylor in his stead as vice president, and himself resign. Thus, as the result of Doe's abdication, Taylor would become president of Liberia and organize an election to be held in October of 1991. This was a reasonable and sound plan, but Doe still refused to leave quietly. Cohen planned to go to Liberia to persuade and escort Doe into exile. But on June 5, 1990, the U.S. National Security Council reported that the president of the United States had decided that the U.S. would not take charge of the Liberian problem and that Cohen should not go to Liberia. Cohen wrote:

> My not going to Monrovia to pressure Doe was less of a disappointment than the admonition not to take charge of the problem. What I wanted was to use the considerable influence of the United States to push frightened Liberians into a 'win-win' solution that might spare the country further agony. If the United States refused to take risks to do that, who else would? I was personally outraged, particularly by the absence of any real dialogue between those with the knowledge and those with the ultimate power of decision.[67]

If Cohen had prevailed, there undoubtedly would have been a peaceful diplomatic solution to the Liberian problem. But once Taylor learned that Cohen had been silenced by his superiors, he realized that he would have to prevail by military means.

Taylor and the NPFL seemed on the verge of total victory. The NPFL had cut off Monrovia except by sea and the road northwest to Sierra Leone. Hank Cohen wrote: "…I acknowledged to Charles Taylor that victory was in his grasp and suggested that it would be better for everyone if a battle for Monrovia could be avoided." Cohen recommended that Taylor leave the road to Sierra Leone open so the Krahns would have an escape route. At this point, the recollections of the U.S. and Liberia diverge. Cohen said that Taylor went ahead and attacked Monrovia on July 2, and was repelled by the ferocious fighting of the Krahns. Furthermore, the road to Sierra Leone was blocked by the sudden appearance of Prince Johnson's Independent National Patriotic Front of Liberia (INPFL) forces, who also opposed Taylor. On the other hand, Taylor stated that he acceded to Cohen's request *not* to attack Monrovia and that it was the biggest mistake he ever made; if he had entered Monrovia, he could have quickly prevailed, the war would have ended, and he would have become president of all Liberia.[68]

In an interview on July 30, 1992 with African journalist Baffour Ankomah, Taylor related his account of the NPFL not entering Monrovia:

> The US officially asked us not to take Monrovia. We had been in constant contact with the Americans from the very early days of the uprising. Not only did we consult with them as we went along, but we did assist in the evacuation of American citizens in Monrovia. Direct link was established with them step by step…The Americans told me directly that once Roberts Airport fell, the US government would put pressure on Samuel Doe to leave Monrovia. If you remember, they did ask Doe to leave. This was agreed upon before Roberts Airport fell to us…The airport fell, nothing happened. We then locked up the city of Monrovia. We were asked by the Americans to open the road to Sierra Leone to permit fleeing Liberians to leave the city. We opened the road. The Americans said to us that the destruction of Monrovia would be too much. That we should not take Monrovia. So we agreed that we would put pressure on Monrovia, we circled Monrovia and did not go into the city proper because we had promised the Americans that we would not destroy Monrovia. So for more than two months, my troops were poised on the campus of the University of Liberia, just a street divided us from the Executive Mansion where Doe was. We could have taken the Mansion any moment but we had a promise to keep. After we circled Monrovia, the U.S. Assistant Secretary of State for African Affairs, Herman Cohen drove into this territory during the fighting…and met us…Cohen asked me not to take Monrovia and to call a ceasefire, Herman Cohen! That is why we did not take Monrovia, that is why we then declared a unilateral ceasefire.[69]

Both Americans and Liberians have agreed that Taylor told Herman Cohen that he would agree to a U.S.–brokered truce. "With the U.S. involved," Taylor said, "we can have peace." The White House, however, was unhappy with Cohen, who was accused of exceeding his authority and called home to explain his actions. Taylor felt tricked. Tom Woewiyu, who was Taylor's defense minister at the time and is now a member of the Liberian Senate, said, "The Americans told us 'It looks like Doe is going to leave–why don't you hold off (entering Monrovia)?'—and we did because we didn't want to see Monrovia and its people destroyed." Reed Kramer wrote this about the situation:

After Taylor realized that Washington had no intention of actively backing the accord he had made with Cohen, he feared he had been the victim of an American and Nigerian scheme to keep him from taking power. The delay probably cost the Front (Taylor's force) the chance to seize control of Monrovia, because the Nigerian-directed West African force was later able to push the rebels out of the capital, the only part of Liberia they never captured.[70]

In a 1993 interview former President Jimmy Carter said: "Unless television images come into American living rooms of little starving babies, the U.S. government just looks the other way and pays very little attention to what's going on in Africa."[71]

Asked whether Taylor's decision not to take Monrovia was a mistake, Taylor, in this same interview said:

> Terrible mistake, terrible mistake, very, very bad mistake...(If) you check all the records, my soldiers never entered Monrovia proper, never! We had promised the Americans and kept the promise...This is when Prince Johnson (who broke away from Taylor's NPFL) used the opportunity and entered (Monrovia with his faction, the INPFL). We believe that he was brought in.[72]

The ruler of Nigeria, General Babangida, who was a supporter of Samuel Doe, had decided that a Taylor victory would destroy the businesses which Nigeria had jointly funded with Doe in Liberia. He convinced Jimmy (ECOWAS), which was meant to be an economic organization of the West African nations, to form a military organization known as the Economic Community of West African States Cease-Fire Monitoring Group (ECOMOG) to intervene in Liberia, and on August 7 ECOWAS so voted.[73] At that point, most of West Africa would have welcomed U.S. intercession to help settle the Liberian problem. But on August 1, Iraq invaded Kuwait. Understandably the attention of the U.S. was shifted to that struggle, which had serious national interest ramifications (including oil) for the U.S. Liberia no longer concerned U.S. policymakers. This gave free rein to ECOMOG's Nigerian-led adventure in Liberia. The ECOMOG force (3,000 troops, 90% of which were Nigerian) landed in Monrovia on August 24, 1990, and Taylor's NPFL had to contend with a new non-Liberian enemy. Looting by the Nigerians was so pervasive that Liberians jokingly referred to the acronym ECOMOG as meaning "Every Car or Moveable Object Gone." Taylor was infuriated by the Nigerian pretense as peacekeepers and actual effort as determined foes of the Taylor regime. Nigeria, with its hegemonic ambitions, thus became the enemy of Charles Taylor.[74]

On August 27, 1990 yet another event transpired that delayed Taylor's victory over Monrovia. A small group of Liberian politicians met at an ECOWAS-sponsored conference in Banjul, Gambia, claiming to represent all the major Liberian political parties—except Taylor's NPFL or Johnson's faction. This handful of people "elected" an academic and political activist named Amos Claudius Sawyer as interim president of the country (the same Sawyer who had trained in Libya and was a leader of the radical MOJA movement), while the rank and file voters of Liberia had no say in the matter. The Sawyer "government," called the Interim Government of National Unity (IGNU), soon was known to the Liberian population as "the Incompetent Government of No Use." Deemed as a puppet of Nigeria, Sawyer's rule was limited to the capital city of Monrovia, under the protection of Nigerian soldiers; Taylor continued to control the remaining 95% of the country.[75]

The appearance of Prince Yourmie Johnson (who had deserted first Samuel Doe and later Charles Taylor) as a putative presidential contender was a serious development. In many quarters Johnson had a reputation both as being an alcoholic and mentally unstable, with a record of murdering people, including his own men, at will.[76] Johnson reasoned that the U.S. was fed up with Doe but unhappy at the prospects of a Taylor government and would support his candidacy. This never came to pass. Sawyer was the preferred candidate of Nigeria, the power behind ECOMOG. IGNU never was officially recognized by the United States which described the Sawyer regime as a "de facto" (rather than a "de jure," legally constituted) government. Yet in a court case the U.S. recognized the interim government as a proper party.[77] The judge in the Federal District Court of New York called upon a U.S. State Department "observer" who was sitting quietly in the courtroom and asked whether the U.S. considered IGNU to be the sole appropriate government of Liberia. The man from State answered in the affirmative, and the judge accordingly overruled counsel's argument that both National Patriotic Reconstruction Government (NPRAG), NPFL's government, and IGNU were legitimate de facto governments. Interestingly, Herman "Hank" Cohen, then the U.S. Assistant Secretary of State for Africa, gave a speech shortly thereafter, in which he stated that there was no "de jure" government of Liberia, and that both IGNU (Sawyer) and NPRAG (Taylor) were "de facto" governments (in fact) of Liberia.[78] Yet in October of 1991 when Amos Sawyer visited the U.S. in order to address the United Nations in his claimed capacity as Liberian head of state, he was received by the Acting U.S. Secretary of State. The higher level executives in the U.S. Department of State considered Amos Sawyer to be the President of Liberia, and denied Taylor all credibility.[79]

Thus, because of the emergence of the Nigeria and ECOMOG coalition, Prince Johnson, and the artificial creation of an Amos Sawyer government, Charles Taylor was unable to take control of Monrovia, which would have made him president of the entire country.

THE ASSASSINATION OF SAMUEL KANYON DOE

On September 9, 1990, the besieged President Samuel Doe left the Executive Mansion where he had bunkered for days and visited the commander of ECOMOG, Lt. General Arnold Quainoo, who was Ghanaian. Primarily Doe complained that the ECOMOG Commander had failed to make a courtesy call upon him as President. Within minutes of Doe entering the ECOMOG headquarters, Prince Johnson and his men suddenly appeared. Curiously they were not required to surrender their weapons before entering the building as was required of Doe's entourage. Doe's guards were surrounded by Johnson's men, who insisted they wanted to make peace but instead opened fire on Doe's bodyguards. In a thirty minute period, 64 of Doe's men were killed and Doe was dragged away by Johnson to his own base.

Over a period of two days, Doe was tortured and mutilated, then killed by Prince Johnson and his men.[80] A recent public television documentary film, *Liberia: America's Stepchild,* showed Johnson using a cell phone to talk directly to the U.S. Embassy as the assassination was about to take place.[81] The torture and murder was recorded on videotape, and has been viewed by various parties. In the horrible confrontation, Doe was stripped naked and his ears sliced off one by one, as Prince Johnson presided over the event with glee. Ever since, there has been much speculation as to why Doe went to the ECOMOG headquarters, how Johnson knew to appear minutes later, and why nothing was done to stop the carnage by U.S. intelligence officers who were in radio communication with all the parties. Why did the United States and the international human rights community, who knew of the two full days of Doe's torture and dismemberment, remain silent? The consensus was that U.S. officials wanted to get rid of Samuel Kanyon Doe, who had become a serious embarrassment to them; at the same time, they deprived Taylor of the "honor" of ridding Liberia of Doe and chose not to stop Johnson when he assassinated President Doe.[82] The taped killing of Doe was essentially irrefutable documentary evidence of Johnson's character. The paper, *Critical Factors in Demobilization, Demilitarization and Reintegration: An Analysis of Ethiopia, Liberia, Mozambique and Zimbabwe*, published by Office of the Secretary of Defense, International Security Affairs, Office of African Affairs, stated that "Prince Yourmie Johnson...was described as mentally unstable (Clayton, 1995), psychopathic and a new species of human kind (Ellis, 1995: 165, 167)."[83] Johnson later was exiled to Nigeria where he was, by his own testimony, "born again." Currently he has asked the Nigerians to let him return to Liberia, insisting that he run a candidacy for the presidency in the next elections.[84]

CONCLUSION

U.S. policy towards Liberia in the early 20th century failed to alleviate the Republic's economic crisis. Until the Firestone deal in 1926, Liberia's economy lacked growth and development, and it had enormous debt that it could not repay. Liberia's human rights violations by the forced labor of indigenous people and the failure of the Edwin J. Barclay administration (1930–1944) to implement measures stipulated by the League of Nations to remedy the abuses caused the FDR administration to suspend recognition of the country in 1933. But its economic and strategic importance led to resumption of relations in 1935. U.S.–Liberia relations improved dramatically during World War II, and, particularly during the administration of President William V.S. Tubman (1944–1971), contributing to Liberia's most successful period of growth and development.

Liberia played a key role in U.S. Africa policy; the CIA station for Africa, the Voice of America station, and the Omega Navigational System (for tracking shipping) were located within its borders. But U.S. policy during the Cold War era also undermined the administration of President William R. Tolbert, and perpetually supported the vicious military dictator, President Samuel K. Doe. As the campaigns to remove Doe led Liberia into civil war, the U.S. State Department policy was remiss. Instead of aiding a peaceful transition to a new government that soon would hold national elections, the U.S. hands-off policy led to anarchy and prolonged civil war. The people of Liberia were the ultimate victims. Reed Kramer wrote,

> What is certain is that failure to stop the fighting during 1990, before the entire country was demolished, erected barriers to a solution that still have not been overcome. The result was to condemn Liberia and much of the region to continuing suffering and to divert scarce international assistance from economic development to sustaining refugees.[85]

Blaine Harden in his article, *Who Killed Liberia? We Did, The Ugly American Policy: Create the Mess, Then Stand Back and Watch the Slaughter*, for the Washington Post stated,

> (T)he State Department...continued to stand by a widely hated, wildly corrupt and laughably incompetent leader...Had the United States acted responsibly, forced Doe out and supervised another election in the mid-1980s, the recent history of Liberia would probably be far different. It is a good bet that there would have been no post-election coup attempt, no tribal killings, no rebel invasion in 1990, no six-year civil war...Our government, though, has not deemed Liberia's chaos to be sufficiently important to warrant serious consideration of any kind of American intervention...The United States was perfectly positioned to head it off. But we washed our hands of responsibility. We watched from a safe distance as Liberia descended into hell.[86]

NOTES

[1] In August of 1991 the author toured the Firestone plantation and wrote a memorandum which said, in part:

> Just beneath the surface is a great deal of resentment toward Firestone. We…heard the following:
>
> • Firestone executives, none of whom are Liberians, live like kings (observers saw, for example, the Firestone Golf Club and the Firestone Yacht Club for top management) while the rank and file Liberian employees do not even have electricity in their company housing units…
>
> • All raw rubber is shipped out of Liberia and processed abroad. There has been no willingness to have Liberians manufacture rubber products indigenously to give value-added jobs and income to that country. Ironically, Liberia, with its huge natural rubber resource, must import ever single rubber-band or tire it uses from abroad!"

[2] S. Augustu P. Horton, *Liberia's Underdevelopment—In Spite of Struggle: A Personal Analysis of the Underlying Reasons for Liberia's Underdevelopment,* Lanham/London: University Press of America, 1994.

[3] Joseph S. Guannu, "The Perennial Problems of Liberian History," *An Occasional Paper*, Vol. II, No. 1, 1989, 1–19.

[4] Ibid., p. 5.

[5] Ibid., p. 5.

[6] League Report as cited in Guannu, p. 5.

[7] Ibid.

[8] Ibid.; The definition of "chop" is food.

[9] League Report as cited in Guannu, p. 5.

[10] Source: "American Liberia Realtions during World War II," at <http://pages.prodigy.net/jkess3/History.html>. by Joseph Tellewoyan. (See Lester Aglar Walton diplomatic dispatches, U.S. State Department Archives.)

[11] Ibid.

[12] J. Gus Liebenow, *Liberia: The Quest for Democracy*. Bloomington: Indiana University Press, 1987.

[13] Reed Kramer, "Liberia: A Casualty of the Cold War's End," *CSIS Africa Notes.* July, 1995,.p. 6.

[14] Cordell Hull, *The Memoirs of Cordell Hull, Volume II,* New York: The Macmillan Company, 1948, pp. 1185–1186.

[15] Foreign Relations of the U.S., Diplomatic Papers, 1943, Volume IV, The Near East and Africa, Washington, D.C.:United States Government Printing Office, 1964, p. 657.

[16] Ibid.

[17] Ibid.

[18] Ibid.

[19] Ibid., p. 686.

[20] Erling D. Naess, *The Great PanLibHon Controversy*, Epping, Gower Press, 1972, p. 1–167.

[21] The Neutrality Act of 1937 amended the Joint Resolution of August 31, 1935.

[22] Naess, ibid.

[23] U.S. Department of State, *Hall of the Secretaries of State: Edward Reilly Stettinius*, Electronic Research Collection, Washington D.C, available at <http://dosfan.lib.uic.edu/ERC/secretaries/estettinius.htm>, updated April 2002.

[24] American National Biography. Vol. 20. New York: Oxford University Press, 1999, 687-689; The Dictionary of American Biography. Supplement 4. New York: Charles Scribner's Sons, 1974, 776-778. International Registries Inc. Company profile. <http://www.register-iri.com/content.cfm?catid=10>.

[25] Naess, ibid.

[26] Ibid., p. 124-128. Rochefort L. Weeks, a former attorney general of Liberia and president of the University of Liberia successfully advanced the republic's maritime shipping rights.

[27] Ibid., p. 135.

[28] Kramer, p. 6.

[29] Stephen Ellis, *The Mask of Anarchy: The Destruction of Liberia and the Religious Dimension of an African Civil War,* London: Hurst & Company, p. 52.

[30] Ibid.

[31] Ibid, p. 53.

[32] Ibid.

[33] SanfordUngar, *Africa: The People and Politics of an Emerging Continent,* Simon and Schuster, 1985, p. 90; Kenneth R. Timmerman, *Shakedown: Exposing the Real Jesse Jackson,* Regnery Publishing, 2002, pp. 297-298. In the early 1800s there were brief periods of fighting between the Americo-Liberian population and various indigenous groups.

[34] Ungar, p. 90.

[35] Ellis, p. 53.

[36] Ibid.; James Youboty, *Liberian Civil War: a graphic account,* Parkside Impressions Enterprises, pp. 59-61.

[37] Nancy Oku Bright, Jean-Phillipe Boucicaut, *Liberia: America's Stepchild: The Untold Story of America's African Progeny,* Grain Coast Production, © 2002, video.

[38] Herman J. Cohen, *Intervening in Africa: Superpowr Peacemaking in a Troubled Continent,* New York: Palgrave, 2000, p. 127.

[39] Ellis, p. 57.

[40] Edward L. Wonkeryor, *Liberia Military Dictatorship: A Fiasco Revolution,* Chicago: Strugglers Community Press, p.84.

[41] Ibid.

[42] Subcommittee on Africa of the Committee on International Relations, House of Representatives, 108th Congress, First Session, *Prospects for Peace in Ivory Coast,* February 12, 2003. Serial No. 108–2. p. 38. Hearing before the Subcommittee, transcript available at <http://wwwa.house.gov/international_relations/108/84945.pdf>.

[43] Personal communication to author.

[44] Thomas L. Friedman, *The Lexus and the Olive Tree: Understanding Globalization,* Knopf Publishing Group, 2000, p. 200.

[45] Bill Berkeley, *The Graves Are Not Yet Full,* New York: The Berkley Publishing Group, 1999.

[46] Criminal Complaint, U.S. District Court of Massachusetts, May 23, 1984.

[47] Ibid., Affidavit accompanying Criminal Complaint.

[48] Ibid., pp. 12, 13, 20.

[49] Memorandum regarding Extradition, U.S. District Court of Massachusetts, pp.2, 3, March 29, 1985.

[50] Ibid., pp. 4, 5. Since investigation of Liberia's human rights record had documented mass killing of civilians and political opponents, that statement was not credible.

[51] Personal communication with Liberian citizens; U.S. Department of State, *Liberia: International Religious Freedom Report*, Bureau of Democracy, Human Rights, and Labor, October 26, 2001, <http://www.state.gov/g/drl/rls/irf/2001/5619.htm>.

[52] Blaine Harden, "Who Killed Liberia? We Did, The Ugly American Policy: Create the Mess, Then Stand Back and Watch the Slaughter," *Washington Post*, May 26, 1996, p. C1.

[53] Bill Berkeley, *Liberia: A Promise Betrayed*, Lawyers Committee for Human Rights, New York, 1986, p. 118.

[54] David Halberstam, *War in a Time of Peace: Bush, Clinton and the Generals,* Scribner, 2001, p. 249.

[55] Harden, ibid.

[56] George Schultz, *Turmoil and Triumph: My Years as Decretary of State*, New York: Charles Scribner's Sons, 1993, p. 296.

[57] Ellis, p. 50.

[58] Author's personal communication with close associate of Charles Taylor.

[59] Ellis, pp. 70, 71.

[60] Baffour Ankomah, "How Nigeria Prolonged Liberia's Agony," *New African*, September 1997, p. 16. Apparently the U.S. government neither acknowledged nor opposed the Nigerian role.

[61] Njoh, Joseph, *Through the Liberian Storm*, London: Minerva Press, 1996.

[62] Ankomah, "How Nigeria Prolonged Liberia's Agony," p. 16.

[63] Cohen, p. 131.

[64] Ibid.

[65] Ankomah, p. 35.

[66] Kramer, p. 1.

[67] Cohen, p. 145.

[68] Ankomah, "Interview by with Charles Taylor on July 30, 1992," *New African*, September 1997, p. 15.

[69] Ibid.

[70] Kramer, p. 10.

[71] Ibid., p. 10.

[72] Ankomah, ibid., p. 15.

[73] Ankomah, "How Nigeria Prolonged Liberia's Agony," p. 35.

[74] Kramer, p. 10; conversation between the author and Charles Taylor. He drove me to Harbel and showed me the bomb crater made by Nigerian air attacks. We then toured the hospital and saw patients who had been further injured by the bombing.

[75] Ellis, p. 14; K. Moses Nagbe, Bulk Challenge, Cape Coast, Ghana, 1996, p. 12.

[76] Ellis, p. 15, 10.

[77] Ibid., p. 14.

[78] Ibid.

[79] Ibid.

[80] Ibid., p. 9, 10.

[81] Bright and Boucicaut, *Liberia: America's Stepchild.*

[82] Ellis, 12.

[83] Office of the Secretary of Defense, International Security Affairs, Office of African Affairs, *Critical Factors in Demobilization, Demilitarization and Reintegration,* 2002, p. 115.

[84] Ellis, 26.

[85] Kramer, 11.

[86] Harden, p. C1.

CHAPTER 3
PROLONGED CIVIL WAR 1990–1996

Historic accounts give the starting date of the Liberian Civil War as December 24, 1989, when Charles G. Taylor and his small force crossed the Côte d'Ivoire border into Liberia in order to oust President Samuel Kanyon Doe. In 1990, despite the military success of Taylor and the National Patriotic Front of Liberia (NPFL) and their establishment of the National Patriotic Reconstruction Government (NPRAG), they did not succeed with their mission. Prince Yourmie Johnson and his break-away group, the Independent National Patriotic Front of Liberia (INPFL) executed Doe.

During the civil war, several other factions entered the fray: the United Liberation Movement of Liberia for Democracy (ULIMO) was formed by a merger of four sub-groups: George E. Seigbe Boley, Sr., leader of the Liberian Peace Council (LPC); General Albert Karpeh, the Liberian United Defense Force; Alhaji G. V. Kromah, the Movement for the Redemption of Liberian Moslems (MRLM); and a small segment of Liberia's army, the Armed Forces of Liberia (AFL). Kromah became leader of the merged ULIMO, and remained the head of the later division known as ULIMO-K. Roosevelt Johnson was head of the ULIMO-J, the other offshoot of ULIMO. Other factions were François Massaquoi, head of the Lofa Defence Force (LDF); Thomas Woewiyu, head of the National Patriotic Front of Liberia-Central Revolutionary Council (NPFL-CRC); Chea Cheapoo, head of the Liberia National Conference (LNC). Amos Claudius Sawyer was elected as president of the Interim Government of National Unity (IGNU). Lieutenant General J. Hezekiah Bowen commanded the Armed Forces of Liberia, which was aligned with IGNU. Although the principal signers of the key peace accords were Charles Taylor (and Enoch Dogolea Vice-President of NPFL/NPRAG), Alhaji Kromah, Amos Sawyer, and J. Hezekiah Bowen, a total of eight factions signed the last peace accord in 1995 that ostensibly ended the civil war.[1]

Besides the factions, intervention by the Economic Community of West African States (ECOWAS) and its peacekeeping unit, the Economic Community of West African States Cease-Fire Monitoring Group (ECOMOG), and the U.S. hands-off policy deterred Taylor in his claim to the Liberian presidency. Because of its size and military power, Nigeria influenced ECOWAS and ECOMOG policy formulation and implementation. All factors prolonged the conflict that devastated Liberia.

STRATEGIC ALLIANCES

In September of 1990, Lt. General Arnold Qainoo, of the Ghanain Army who headed ECOMOG, was summarily replaced by Nigerian Major General Joshua Nimyel Dogonyaro, who immediately organized as much support as possible for the Sawyer government. General Dogonyaro was the person who had announced on Nigerian radio the military coup that brought his friend General Ibrahim Babangida to power in 1985. Dogonyaro moved quickly to secure Monrovia, drove Taylor's forces out of the city (this was known as the first battle for Monrovia), supported the IGNU government of Amos Sawyer, and began an endless round of negotiations with Taylor to find a peaceful solution to the impasse. Nigeria, acting alone and through ECOMOG which it controlled, was determined to stop Charles Taylor from taking Monrovia and the presidency of Liberia. Prevented at the last minute from uniting the country and becoming its president, Taylor withdrew from Monrovia and secured the remaining 95% of Liberia (known as "Greater Liberia") and then set up his own government in the town of Gbarnga. Taylor called his government the National Patriotic Reconstruction Assembly Government (NPRAG), rather than the appellation, the National Patriotic Front of Liberia (NPFL), which referred to his army.[2]

A journalist who visited Gbarnga in 1992 wrote that Charles Taylor's political organization, the National Patriotic Party (NPP) was already up and running.[3] "It had party offices all over, staffed by enthusiastic followers—even in 1992! And this was the man who was supposed to be afraid of elections." Those who traveled with him around the countryside saw the enthusiasm with which the people greeted him.[4] He brought rice to the small villages that dotted the countryside. But the official position of the U.S. Department of State was that the people of Liberia feared Taylor and that their support for him was not genuine.

Charles Taylor set up a system of roadblocks throughout the countryside (usually a string across the road manned by young soldiers); ECOMOG roadblocks, made of huge cement blocks and manned by Nigerian soldiers, were set up in Monrovia.[5] In this manner each side protected itself against incursions by the other. Taylor was able to support his part of the country because rubber, timber, iron ore, and diamonds were in his area, as well as the Port of Buchanan. Local businessmen willingly did business with him.[6] With regard to the port at Buchanan, the State Department contended that there was no activity and it was patrolled day and night by Taylor's armed soldiers. However, observers at the port saw the bustling nature of the operation, with ships (usually from French-speaking countries) arriving and departing regularly, and no evidence of armed soldiers.[7] The support that Taylor garnered from Ivorian and French business people made the U.S. wary of him; they feared that if he won the presidency, he would "tilt" toward the French rather than toward Americans.

As indicated earlier, Taylor wanted to punish President Momoh of Sierra Leone, who had double-crossed him when Taylor wanted to mount his offensive to depose Doe from Sierra Leone. In retaliation he formed an alliance with a Sierra Leonian group known as the Revolutionary United Front (RUF) headed by Foday Sankoh. In 1991 RUF moved against Momoh to reignite the Sierra Leone civil war, which had recently ended. In contrast, the ULIMO, who supported Momoh because he was anti-Taylor, re-entered Liberia from Sierra Leone to oppose Taylor. The growing military prowess of ULIMO served Nigeria's and ECOMOG's anti-Taylor strategy. Furthermore ULIMO entered the diamond fields along the Liberia-Sierra Leone border to support its activities, and took diamonds by force from the miners. They then smuggled the diamonds out of the country and sold or bartered them for weapons.

In September of 1991 the Bush administration attempted to further the peace process in Liberia. Charles Taylor had taken the position that he would not disarm to ECOMOG as long as they were dominated by Nigeria which he considered his arch-enemy. A proposal was made that Senegal would send 1,500 troops (paid for by the United States) to reconfigure ECOMOG. When six Senegalese soldiers were killed in May of 1992, allegedly by NPFL troops, ECOWAS decided that Taylor was returning to his old ways and intended to conquer Liberia by force. ECOMOG then distributed arms to IGNU, ULIMO and the AFL, all opponents of Taylor. To prop up his military force, Taylor obtained arms from outside Liberia and the all-out war resumed and continued through mid-1996.

PEACE ACCORDS

A series of negotiations and peace accords that took place in several countries in Africa and in Geneva, Switzerland, led to short term cease-fires and agreements in an effort to resolve the Liberian conflict.[8] These diplomatic initiatives were undertaken between 1990 and 1995. They included, in part:

- Bamako (Mali) talks and cease fire Agreement, November 1990
- Banjul (The Gambia) talks and Agreement, December 1990
- Yamassoukro (Côte d'Ivoire) talks (I, II, III, and IV), June to October 1991; Yamassoukro IV Accord October 1991, pursued for implementation from 1991 to 1992
- Geneva, Switzerland peace talks, July to August 1993
- Cotonou (Benin) talks and Agreement, July to August 1993
- Akosombo (Ghana) talks and Agreement, September 1994;
- Accra (Ghana) talks, November to December 1994; Agreement on the clarification of the Akosombo Agreement, December 1994
- Abuja (Nigeria) talks and Abuja Agreement to Supplement the Cotonou and Akosombo Agreements as subsequently clarified by the Accra Agreement, August 1995.

From 1991 to 1993 the United Nations made a considerable commitment to implementing Yamassoukro IV to its full extent. They felt this accord, unlike the previous agreements, was complete and would contribute toward the unconditional resolution of the Liberian civil war. For this reason, it is examined below. Following the failure of Yamassoukro IV, other negotiations followed. The Cotonou ceasefire was another critical event that is briefly discussed. Ultimately, the Abuja Accord, also examined below, led to the formation of the transitional government that included leaders of the various Liberian factions. This transitional government was delegated with the responsibility to establish a conducive atmosphere for democratic elections.

YAMASSOUKRO TALKS AND YAMASSOUKRO IV ACCORD

Between June and October 1991, there were four peace conferences held under the sponsorship of ECOWAS, Yamassoukro I, II, III and IV. Some of the meetings were held in the palace of Houphouet-Boigny, the president of Côte d'Ivoire.[9, 10] Although most people think that Abidjan is the capital of Côte d'Ivoire; the capital is Yamassoukro, about one hour's drive north of Abidjan.

Each meeting was attended by high-ranking representatives (often the chief executive) of the member states of ECOWAS. At the Yamassoukro III meeting of September 16 to 17, 1991, officials from Nigeria, Sierra Leone, The Gambia, Ghana, and Guinea attended. Also invited were Charles Taylor of NPRAG and Amos Sawyer of IGNU, representing the two de facto governments of Liberia. Former President Jimmy Carter participated in one conference, accompanied by his assistant Dayle Spencer. At the Yamassoukro IV meeting, October 29 to 30, most West African leaders were present: President Houphouet-Boigny; President Blaise Compaore of Burkina Faso; President Joao Bernardo Vieira of Guinea Bissau; President Amadou Toumani Toure of Mali; President Abdou Diouf of Senegal; Prime Minister Kokou Joseph Koffigoh of Togo; Vice President Agustus Aikhomu of Nigeria; Vice President J.B. Dauda of Sierra Leone; Minister Alhaji Omar Sey of The Gambia; Foreign Minister Obed Asamoah of Ghana; and Attorney General Facine Toure of Guinea.[11]

The U.S. Department of State was exercised about Taylor's willingness to sign the various agreements which called for security, encampment, and disarmament, because Taylor had abrogated previous agreements. Dayle Spencer stated: "The problem in Liberia wasn't so much getting the parties to sign agreements, as it was getting them to honor them once signed." Taylor insisted that since he controlled 95% of the country, he must be the interim president until elections were held. The other nations resisted his demand. Taylor had a legitimate argument. He controlled the entire country except for the capitol which he had failed to capture only because of the urging of the United States that he not enter the city in order to avoid further bloodshed.

Dayle Spencer summarized the situation as follows:

> From my perspective the Liberian issues were complicated not only by the inter-racial conflicts among the Liberians, which spilled over boundary lines into other countries, but by economic concerns (who would ultimately control the resources), and regional power plays as well. The United States was caught in a bind, because although it had natural, historical ties with the Liberians, it didn't want to be seen dictating solutions to Africa at a time when, for once, Africa was trying to mount its own peacekeeping forces to resolve African problems. Then, of course, you had the regional African leaders with their own agendas, trying to shore up their political bases. Maybe it was a case of too many cooks.[12]

However Dayle Spencer's analysis did not recognize Nigeria's determination to prevent Charles Taylor from becoming president of a united Liberia; its actions were not as a peacekeeper, but rather as an active combatant. The Carter solution was a set of agreements for both IGNU and NPRAG to find solutions to the Liberian civil conflict. President Carter personally drafted the confidential set of agreements and hand-delivered them to Amos Sawyer (President, Interim Government of National Unity) and Charles Taylor.

In judgment of the Yamassoukro outcome, some analysts believe that if the ECOWAS nations had accepted the Carter solution, there would not have been a renewed outburst of fighting.[13] But fighting did erupt, which led to Taylor's final assault on Monrovia.[14]

The second battle for Monrovia, known as Operation Octopus, began on October 15, 1992. ECOMOG used aircraft and naval guns to bomb NPFL positions causing tremendous damage and civilian casualties. Historian Stephen Ellis wrote,

> Of the thousands of casualties in Monrovia during Operation Octopus, probably the bulk may be attributed to ECOMOG shelling and the use of napalm and cluster bombs. The NPFL (Taylor's forces) claimed the total number of deaths through ECOMOG bombardment to be over 6,500, occurring mostly in the suburbs of Monrovia in October and November of 1992 and in Buchanan in April 1993.[15]

As previously stated, the ECOMOG peace-keeping force became an overt combatant in an effort to destroy Taylor.[16] ULIMO and Nigeria also actively joined the anti-Taylor battle, undergoing training in Guinea. Taylor withdrew and ECOMOG took over both Monrovia and the Port of Buchanan. From the time of the Yamassoukro IV Accord, and through 1992 and early 1993, the UN and other nations urged that the combatants adhere to the agreement. But the combatants failed to adhere to the UN mandate.

COTONOU CEASEFIRE

On June 6, 1993, 600 displaced people, mostly women and children, were massacred at a camp in the Firestone Plantation in Harbel. The AFL (Doe forces) and NPFL (Taylor forces) each blamed the other. However an inquiry instituted by the Secretary-General of the United Nations and conducted by Amos Wako, the Attorney General of Kenya, concluded that the Harbel massacre had been carried out by the AFL. This event gave credibility to Taylor's pleas for a peaceful settlement. On July 25, 1993, the three main Liberian armed factions (NPFL, ULIMO, and AFL) signed a ceasefire in Cotonou, Benin, and agreed upon a transitional government (in place of IGNU) and a timetable for national elections. At the same time the United Nations established a United Nations Observer Mission (UNAMIL) to monitor the peace process and report to the Secretary-General. By providing for the dissolution of the Sawyer government, and replacing it with a transitional government that included both the NPFL and ULIMO, the NPFL for the first time had a stake in the Liberian government. But the interference of surrogate groups prolonged the war for control of Liberia. Nigeria continued to oppose any peace agreement that would allow Taylor to become President of Liberia and used its military (for example, in supporting the attack on Taylor's Gbarnga headquarters in September of 1994) to undercut Taylor whenever they wished.[17]

The United States government became concerned about the duality of Nigeria's role: on the one hand, it was the leading member of the ECOMOG force which was supposed to act as a peacekeeper in Liberia; and, on the other hand, it supported military efforts to undermine Charles Taylor.[18] The U.S. concluded that Nigeria was fueling the civil war in Liberia. Sources stated that the United States persuaded ECOWAS (the West African organization of which ECOMOG was a member) to accept the services of Pacific Architects and Engineers (PAE), an American private security company with close links to the Pentagon, to take charge of many of ECOMOG's logistics at U.S. expense. In this way the U.S. exerted more influence on the ground, a constructive move on its part.

ABUJA ACCORDS

In 1994, as the civil war continued, Charles Taylor concluded that, if he were to prevail, he would have to make peace and enter into some sort of an accommodation with his arch-enemy Nigeria. This goal was made more realistic by the fact that, in the previous year (1993), General Sani Abacha, who was much less hostile toward Taylor, had replaced President Babangida. Accordingly in August of 1995, Taylor, the seven other Liberian factions, and Abacha reached the 13th agreement of the civil war, in what became known as the Abuja Accords. The agreement provided for a new Council of State, with all of the key warring factions involved, a disarmament process, and national elections

On August 31, 1995 Charles Ghankay (which means "strong in the face of adversity" in the Gola language) Taylor entered Monrovia for the first time since he left Liberia for the United States in 1983. Dressed all in white, he was greeted by an outpouring of the citizens of Monrovia.[19]

Negotiators of the Abuja Accord hoped that, instead of fighting for power, the factions would resolve their differences through political means. But the opposition's envy of Taylor was palpable, especially since he was the only leader acknowledged by the people of Greater Liberia and the only leader who had amassed the funds necessary to pursue a presidential campaign as the result of his control of all business transactions in greater Liberia. On October 31, 1996 an assassination attempt was made on his life in the Executive Mansion.

By hiding in the bathroom, Taylor narrowly escaped death and thereafter realized that he must rely more on ECOMOG for his personal security.

At this point Liberia was run by a collective presidency made up of the six major faction leaders, or, as the press always called them, the warlords. It was an uneasy relationship. Late in 1996 Madeleine Albright, U.S. Ambassador to the United Nations (later Secretary of State), came to Liberia and met with the six leaders. An African journalist named Maxwell Ziamo described the meeting:

> Mrs. Albright addressed the presidency like kids in a kindergarten class. Charles Taylor was the only one who stood up to the unwanted chastisement... Madeleine Albright was evidently not accustomed to such 'challenges' and 'confrontations' from an African. Madame Albright later became Secretary of State when an unfavorable policy toward President Taylor and Liberia ensued and continued throughout her tenure. Charles Taylor was convicted and condemned by the last American administration long before his first day in office.

Other sources gave similar reports.[20] Later whenever Secretary Albright went to Africa, she was asked to include Liberia in her itinerary and to meet with then President Taylor.[21] For whatever reason, she consistently refused, thus giving credence to Ziamo's story of her dislike of Mr. Taylor.[22]

Despite the agreement to rely upon political rather than military means of achieving power, the third battle of Monrovia began on April 6, 1996. ULIMO-J attacked the ECOMOG forces. Some people suggest this was done at Taylor's private urging but no verifiable evidence has proven that point. In response, ECOMOG, joined by ULIMO-K and the NPFL moved to arrest Roosevelt Johnson, the head of ULIMO-J. It became apparent that Taylor had the greatest strength and soon would be the sole victor in the battle for Monrovia. Again, both the United States and ECOMOG were determined that Taylor not be victorious by military means. Nigeria, through its military, armed both ULIMO-K and ULIMO-J. In other words they armed both sides. The Nigerian government, upset at the duplicitous role that its soldiers were playing, sent a new general, Victor Malu, to command the ECOMOG forces. His orders were to stabilize Liberia

---

When the peacekeeper becomes a combatant, one must raise the question whether the current U.S. policy of utilizing regional peacekeeping efforts, such as ECOMOG, is valid. On the one hand, countries in the region, presumably from self-interest, would act in an even-handed manner to restore peace and stability when civil disturbances adversely affect them. Alternately, sometimes regional peacekeepers are headed by nations that have hegemonic desires of their own, and thus are not neutral in enforcing peace, as in the case of Nigeria vis-a-vis Liberia. That latter instance would argue for bringing in truly neutral peacekeeping forces. As career U.S. diplomat Monteagle Stearns wrote in his superb book on American diplomacy, *Talking to Strangers*:

> The problem with regional surrogates is that they usually have regional axes to grind and do not make disinterested peacemakers. States outside the region are more often trusted and have a better chance of producing viable settlements of regional disputes.

Policymakers should pay much more attention to this important issue.

while, at the same time, return to the Abuja Accords which called for a national election. Based on his strength, most Liberians assumed Taylor would become president in a legitimate manner. ECOMOG forces were deployed not only in Monrovia but throughout the country, refugees returned to their homes, and the national election campaign began. On April 21, 1996 a high level U.S. delegation offered $30 million of U.S. assistance as an incentive to the warring parties to resume the transition. As Cohen wrote,

> The lure of America's historical tie to Liberia had proved irresistible to the Clintonites, unlike Bush's people. The impact was dramatic. The transition was resumed, leading to a presidential election in July of 1997 considered cleanly run and basically free and fair. The winner was none other than Charles Taylor, the man we wanted to install as President in 1990.

Analysis of the course of events in the seven-year civil war convinced many participants and observers that United States foreign policy was misguided. It resulted in a long, devastating civil war from which Liberia has yet to recover. Herman Cohen, frustrated by the action of senior officials in the administration who were not experts on Africa, and who reversed the strategy that he had put in place, wrote:

> The May-June 1990 decision that the United States would not play a leading role in peacemaking in Liberia was a big mistake. If we had been allowed to pursue the plan adopted in the interagency process to persuade Doe to go into exile, thus opening the door for Taylor to take power, years of devastating civil war might have been prevented. And without the collateral need for ECOWAS peacekeeping, a francophone-anglophone surrogate war could also have been prevented...Had Taylor been allowed to take power in 1990...the destruction of Liberia would have been avoided, and Taylor might have been more open to constructive external influence."

US CENTRAL INTELLIGENCE AGENCY (CIA)

As discussed earlier, members of the National Security Council with CIA background (such as Robert Gates) undermined all efforts to end fighting in Liberia that would help Charles Taylor become President.

There is reason to believe that the CIA played (and perhaps still plays) an inordinately powerful role in setting U.S. policy toward Liberia. During the Cold War, Libya was considered an enemy of the United States. What no one (other than the CIA) in the U.S. government or the public at large knew at the time, was that the CIA under William Casey in the 1980s undertook a large-scale covert operation to unseat Moamar Gadaffi as the ruler of Libya. It was not until 1987 that Bob Woodward and Don Oberdorfer in the Washington Post, and Seymour Hersh in the New York Times, finally reported the story. The 1986 bombing raid on Libya, they wrote, was directed by the same people who were involved later in the Iran-Contra scandal, namely Oliver North and John Poindexter. Hersh wrote that "the White House and the CIA used internal manipulation and deceit to shield true policy from the professionals in the State Department and the Pentagon."[23]

What had not been revealed before was that the CIA had pinpointed Liberia, where a compliant Samuel Doe did the U.S.'s bidding, as a key operational area, with an easily accessible base for the CIA's heightened clandestine campaign against Libya. The CIA also used Liberia's communication facilities in a covert operation in support of Chad's leader Hissene Habre who had ousted his Libyan-backed rival Goukouni Oueddei. According to Bob Woodward,

CIA Director Casey had selected Samuel Doe as one of 12 heads of state from around the world to receive U.S. support from a special security assistance program. Journalist Reed Kramer writes that "unknown to almost everyone else making decisions about Liberia for the administration, this gave the CIA and the White House a huge stake in keeping the Liberian regime in place." In 1986 the United States, with total cooperation from Samuel Doe, mounted another covert operation in Liberia, this time an airlift to the UNITA (União Nacional para a Independência Total de Angola) faction in Angola which was operated out of Monrovia's Roberts International Airport.[24]

A document was mailed to the author's office that purported to be a CIA Field Intelligence Report—it was written on CIA stationery with the CIA shield and dated September 7, 1996.* The author wrote to the CIA General Counsel in an effort to ascertain whether or not the letter was genuine and was informed that it was not. The CIA expressed no objection, however, to reproducing the letter in full in this book. The author has done so, since, whether genuine or not, he considers that it summarizes the U.S. position towards Liberia at that time:

> Our strategic interest, goals and objectives in the sub-Sahara African region is (sic) still very vital, if not crucial. With the emergence of radical and leftist governments, such as Sudan, Libya, Somalia, Nigeria and Algeria, Liberia remains the most vital source of intelligence gathering whenever we utilize human intelligence resources.
>
> Liberia is still the nerve center of our African operations. It is a country where our operatives are not viewed with suspicion. The entry and exit strategy options for many of our covert operations including Black Ops remain intact.
>
> Despite Liberia's ongoing internecine conflict, Americans have seen a minimal casualty rate. Organized violence against our citizens, personnel, property or installations have been non-existent. More Americans were killed in major U.S. cities last week alone than have been killed in Liberia's seven year conflict.
>
> With its rich and immensely dense African forest, Liberia is a prime source for the training of Special Forces and Navy Seals teams in Black Ops and modern guerilla warfare. We still maintain a large number of Subs within and off the Liberian shores and the scaled down operation at the Omega Navigational Station continues to adequately serve our Atlantic and Mediterranean fleet.
>
> In terms of the May 30, 1997 elections, all transmissions from Capitol Hill and 1600 Penn seem to not favor any of the current candidates in Monrovia. Mr. Taylor is out of the question due to his double dealings with international shady figures, including his ties to Libya's Muammar Gaddafi. Mr. Mathews on the other hand is very inconsistent and unreliable. He is too close to many of the problems in the country. Mr. Tipoteh is a card-carrying Socialist. He is the type who will turn away from the U.S. and align with Socialist nations. Mr. Fahnbulleh is a very divisive figure with a narrow support base. He tends to be a sectionalist. He has close ties to China, Cuba, and other Socialist nations.
>
> Operatives are gathering up to the minute data on each of these individuals and other Presidential aspirants in

In his September 30, 1987 Washington Post article, Bob Woodward wrote:

> The deputy chief of Doe's personal guard, Lt. Col. Moses Flanzamaton, became a CIA agent and later, in 1985, attempted to seize power by leading a machine-gun ambush on Doe's jeep. Doe was not injured, but Flanzamaton was captured, confessed to CIA ties and embroidered his tale to include CIA sponsorship of the assassination. It was white knuckles in Langley for days, where top officials feared that the agency would be accused unfairly of an

Monrovia. In my follow-up report I will submit these findings.

I believe we should infiltrate large Liberian organizations and groups in the U.S. such as the Union of Liberian Association in the Americas to see if they can identify and/or support a candidate here. According to classified reports, the U.S. opposes almost all of the standing politicians in the country. They are generally corruptible and short on vision. Should any one of them become elected, immediate actions will be taken, including threats of a war crimes tribunal, to bring down the government.

As you are aware, $15 billion have been allocated for Liberia's reconstruction. The House and Senate Select Committees on Intelligence and Foreign Affairs, as well as 1600 Penn, have established the conditions on which this money will be released. It clearly stipulates that no portion of this money should be released unless the Head of the new Government is acceptable to Langley.

If, by the end of February 1997, the Station Chief at Mamba Point should indicate that the Liberians have not embraced a candidate who is not connected with widespread corruption and ethnic polarization, and should the political and military climate remain unpredictable, Phase II of "Operation Green Sand" will begin. This Class-3

destabilization campaign will render Liberia primed for complete external control within five years.

Respectfully submitted.

Larry Charters, Senior Intelligence Officer

---

* The document, a chilling predictor of what happened from 1996 onwards, indicates U.S. opposition to Charles Taylor, as well as other presidential aspirants.

The letter from Scott W. Mueller, General Counsel of the Central Intelligence Agency dated 14 May 2003, to Lester S. Hyman, is printed here in full:

I am writing in response to your letter dated 30 April 2003, enclosing a letter dated 7 September 1996 purportedly from the Central Intelligence Agency (CIA), specifically from a 'Larry Charters, Senior Intelligence Officer' to a 'Mr. Steve Wayne, Chief of Mission, West African Bureau... California'. You enquired whether the letter is genuine. My office has consulted with the relevant components of the CIA and determined that the letter is not genuine. As the letter is not genuine, and provided you characterize it accordingly, the Agency has no objection to your reproducing the contents of the letter—without the purported, but fake, CIA seal—in your book.

assassination attempt. But Flanzamaton was executed a week after the coup attempt, and the agency's fears went unrealized.[25]

Two explanations for the CIA's opposition to Charles Taylor are, 1) his attempted ouster of "their boy," Samuel Doe, who had cooperated with every clandestine and covert action that the U.S. ordered, and 2) Libya's financial backing of Taylor and training for some of his men.

When asked whether the CIA should dictate policy, James Woolsey, who was Director of the CIA from 1992 to 1995, replied that,

> the Director of Central Intelligence (DCI) should not be a policy advisor and normally he is not. The CIA Director, however, occasionally has been a policy advisor in the past. (William) Casey famously was. I think it's a bad idea for the DCI to be a policy advisor because people begin to suspect that you may be tilting the intelligence to support what your policy choice is.[26]

That is precisely what happened in the case of Liberia.

There is reason to believe that the CIA today maintains a major presence in Liberia, operating within the confines of the American Embassy. Recently a member of the U.S. Embassy staff told a Liberian diplomat that there was no way that the Americans ever would close down the embassy in Monrovia because "it would cost $50 million to take out all the equipment we have there" and then quickly changed the subject.[27]

CONCLUSION

Remarks given on April 1, 2003 by Howard F. Jeter, Ambassador to Nigeria and former Deputy Assistant Secretary of State for Africa, summarized U.S. perceptions of the impact of the Liberian civil war:

> West Africa's current crisis began in 1989, with the brutal civil war in Liberia. Never before had this region seen such wanton destruction and brutality; never before had the troubles in one country engulfed so many others; never before had a country been taken over by ethnically-based warring factions. That war killed 150,000 Liberians, generated 750,000 refugees and internally displaced 2.4 million Liberians, nearly 70% of the country's population. The civil was in Liberia ended in 1997 with internationally observed national elections. I was there and we all rejoiced...

U.S. policy in the early 1990s, that was directed to stop Charles Taylor from assuming the presidency, prolonged the Liberian civil war for seven years. At the end of the conflict the U.S. fostered democracy, by supporting national elections that were held in 1997. As discussed in Chapter 4, Jeter's optimism did not reflect the long-term position of the U.S on the outcome of the election.

NOTES

[1] Comfort Ero, "ECOWAS and Subregional Peacekeeping in Liberia," *The Journal of Humanitarian Assistance*, 25 September 1995; 3 June 2000. http://www.jha.ac/articles/a005.htm; U.S. Institute of Peace, "Liberia," Peace Agreements Digital Collection, Washington, D.C., <http://www.usip.org/library/pa/liberia/pa_liberia.html>. updated June 19, 2003.

[2] At that time the author represented the National Patriotic Reconstruction Assembly Government (NPRAG).

[3] In Gbarnga on two occasions I met with Taylor and saw that he actually was running a government, with ministers for each area (agriculture, education, etc.).

[4] That view differed from the my personal observations from 1991 to 1996. One teenaged youngster in Gbarnga spoke with the author about his desire to someday become a lawyer. This gave the opportunity to ask him whether he liked Taylor personally. "Do I like him?" he asked incredulously. "No, I love him." There were many more like him.

[5] Personal observation when I visited Monrovia during the civil war. On my second trip to Liberia (1991), I represented the National Patriotic Reconstruction Government (NPRAG); it was unsafe for me to go to Monrovia since it was controlled by Interim Government of National Unity (IGNU) and ECOMOG (made up primarily of Nigerian soldiers). Instead, we drove from Abidjan, Côte d'Ivoire through the back country, and entered Liberia from the east, with our destination being Taylor's headquarters in Gbarnga. I never will forget that ride. It took more than eight hours over rutted, and often washed-out roads. Six of us packed into a small jeep, with a tape of Bob Marley playing at full volume to keep the driver awake. We stopped from time to time to pick up "road kill"—(even a dead possum was loaded into the back of the jeep for someone's future dinner). Days later when I left Liberia, I told Charles Taylor that I wanted to see Monrovia. I had never visited the capital, only up-country. He tried to dissuade me, but I persisted. So he assigned a jeep and driver to me and said I would be taken as far as possible. That turned out to be the outskirts of Monrovia. The driver wished me luck and sped away. After a long wait, I flagged down a taxicab and was taken on a brief tour of the city. I saw countless cement roadblocks manned by, I assumed, Nigerian soldiers with automatic machine guns at the ready. It was quite a contrast to the roadblocks in Taylor-land, which consisted exclusively of a piece of string stretched across the road and guarded by a teenage boy. When I was ready to leave the city, the taxi driver took me to the Spriggs Field Airport on the outskirts. There I was confronted by Nigerian soldiers who carefully checked my passport. Suddenly, I was hustled into a back room and surrounded by more soldiers with drawn pistols. An officer stated that I was in the country illegally. "Why is that?" I asked, panic struck. "Because," he said, "your passport does not show that you ever entered our country." Now I was in a pickle (because we had driven through back roads to Gbarnga). I thought fast. Knowing that President Carter was in Liberia at the time as part of his peace resolution mission, I stretched the truth a bit and said: "I'm here with Jimmy Carter," which literally was true. Suddenly the mood changed dramatically. I was transformed from an illegal trespasser into an honored guest of Liberia. After a $25 contribution to the officer's personal welfare fund, I was taken to the plane to be flown out of Liberia. Thereafter, I felt that I owed my freedom, and perhaps my life, to Jimmy Carter.

[6] I spoke to a number of those businessmen who told me that they dealt directly with Taylor and found him to be fair and thorough in his dealings with them.

[7] I spent time in Buchanan at the port and observed for myself the bustling nature of the operation. In all my trips there, I never saw a soldier or civilian with a rifle.

[8] Scott, Colin, Larry Minear, Thomas G. Weiss, *Humanitarian Action and Security in Liberia, 1989-1994. Occasional Paper # 20.* The Thomas J. Watson Jr. Institute for International Studies, Brown University 1995.

[9] When one approaches the city, the first thing one sees, like an oasis appearing in the desert, is a precise replica of St. Peter's Cathedral in Rome. Although a massive structure, it is done in excellent taste, but looks odd in the midst of a nearly barren area. Dedicated by the Pope, priests from Italy run it (reported to me by guides who gave me a tour). Charles Taylor and I toured the cathedral together. We noticed that, in one of the huge stained glass windows, there was a depiction of the crucifixion of Christ. At the foot of the Cross were Mary and a number of Jesus' followers, one of whom, to our surprise, was a black man with a remarkable resemblance to Houphouet-Boigny himself. At one point, I started to laugh and Taylor asked me what was

so funny. I am Jewish and said: If God were looking for me today, about the last place he'd ever think to look would be in a Catholic Cathedral in the middle of Africa!

[10] My personal observations when attending the Yamassoukro III and IV meetings. A huge hotel in Yamassoukro called the President was where the participants stayed during the meetings. It was usually deserted except for those people who came to do business with Houphouet-Boigny. Nearby is the President's palace. An enormous structure, it is surrounded by a moat filled with alligators (a novel twist to presidential security). A palace literally, it rivals Versailles in its opulence. Outside the meeting hall entranceway stood the Presidential Guard dressed in splendid uniforms with white feathered helmets. To the author, the palace had a dream like quality due to its sumptuous decor. It was like a scene out of "The Student Prince."

[11] Economic Community of West African States, *Final Communique, Committee of Five*, Yamoussoukro, Côte d'Ivoire, September 16-17, 1991.

[12] Dayle Spencer, letter to author, July 13, 2001.

[13] It was fascinating to watch President Carter at work as he tried to resolve differences between competing forces. He would take his laptop computer and go visit with the leader of the first warring party. He would ask precisely what he wished to achieve and what his demands were— and then he would print out the list and hand it to the leader. Then he would do exactly the same thing with the leader of the opposing faction. He then would take the two lists of demands and try to find one item, no matter how minor, on which both parties might agree. Using this as an opening wedge, he would continue to shuttle back and forth between the two parties, narrowing the differences until finally he achieved a broad basis of agreement. It was an impressive balancing act which only someone as respected as Jimmy Carter could accomplish.

President Carter sometime was criticized for the respectful form of address he would use with warring faction leaders. When asked about it, Carter said that he had no qualms about addressing a person with whatever title he wished so long as he could get him to sit down and negotiate with him. With Carter, substance always took precedence over form.

[14] Stephen Ellis, p. 104. I felt then, and continue to believe now that a bloody civil war could have been avoided and hundreds of thousands of lives saved.

[15] Ibid., p. 99.

[16] Ibid, pp. 99, 100.

[17] Ibid., p. 103.

[18] Ibid.

[19] Ibid., 105.

[20] Maxwell Ziamo, "A rejoinder to Jefftey Bartholet's 'An African Strongman,' *Newsweek Magazine*, May 14, 2001, p. 1; author's interview with Charles Taylor, (see Appendix E).

[21] Madeleine Albright letter to President Taylor, October 20, 1999; letter from Susan Rice to author, January 13, 2000.

[22] Ibid. Regretfully, Ms. Albright declined to sit for an interview for this book.

[23] Bob Woodward, "Veil: The Secret Wars of the CIA, 1981-1987, Part 5 of 6," *Washington Post*, September 30, 1987, p. A1.

[24] Ibid.

[25] Ibid.

[26] James Woolsey, interview with the author, March 7, 2002.

[27] Author's personal communication with Liberian diplomat.

[28] Howard Jeter, U.S. Ambassador to Nigeria. Speech delivered at the Shell Muson Center, Lagos, Nigeria, April 1, 2003 as released by the Public Affairs Office of the U.S. Embassy, Nigeria.

CHAPTER 4
THE TAYLOR PRESIDENCY

On Saturday, July 19, 1997, 600,000 of the 700,000 registered voters of Liberia finally cast their ballots to elect a president. The election was overseen by more than 500 members of an international observer team led by former U.S. President Jimmy Carter. The media and the U.S. Department of State long had predicted that Taylor could not win an election. But he did. In an election universally adjudged to be free and fair, Taylor received 75.3% of the vote. His nearest rival, Ellen Johnson-Sirleaf received only about 10% of the vote. The rest of the field of 12 candidates were also-rans. Taylor's party, the National Patriotic Party (NPP) won 49 of the 64 seats in the Liberian House of Representatives and 21 of the 26 seats in the Senate. The landslide was overwhelming.

Those who served with President Carter in a similar effort in Haiti in 1990 (including the author) know the thoroughness with which he covered Liberia to assure that the election was conducted properly. He concluded that this was a free and fair election, noting that more than 80% of the eligible voters cast their ballots. Only weeks before, some officials at the U.S. Department of State were certain that Ellen Johnson-Sirleaf, a World Bank figure who just recently had returned to Liberia from the United States, would be the victor because she could demonstrate international support.[1] However, political analysts know it is difficult for a candidate to build a large constituency when living outside one's country. This was precisely the situation in Haiti when U.S. Department of State was assured that Mark Bazin, a respected World Bank figure living in the U.S., would win the presidency of Haiti over a popular indigenous priest, Father Jean-Bertrand Aristide.[2] They were wrong then—and for the same reason. In August of 1997 Charles Ghankay Taylor was inaugurated as president of Liberia.

The international community, led by the United States (considered by other countries as the "patron" of Liberia), did not cheer the election result. Almost immediately, opponents stated that people voted for Taylor only because they feared him. As proof, they cited a chant that many of the younger people, supporters of Taylor, sang at a huge rally held at a stadium in Monrovia the night before the election: "He killed my Pa; He killed my Ma; I'll vote for him." While American critics of Taylor cited this slogan as proof that the people feared him, Liberians stated the reverse was true. The slogan was the rallying cry of those Liberians who believed that, since Charles Taylor had the strength to replace the evil government of Samuel Doe, the people had equal confidence that he had the strength to lead the country to peace. The analysis of the election by the U.S. Department of State, published in its Liberia Country Report for Democracy, Human Rights, and Labor for 1998 (and repeated in subsequent reports) had these conclusions:

> In July 1997 Taylor won the presidency, and his National Patriotic Party (NPP) won three-quarters of the seats in the Congress, in elections that were administratively free and transparent, but were conducted in an atmosphere of intimidation, as most voters believed that Taylor's forces would resume fighting if Taylor were to lose.[3]

The UN Special Representative of the Secretary-General for Children and Armed Conflict, Olara A. Otunnu, commented on Taylor's election and stated, whether people voted for Taylor out of love, or because they wanted a strong person in the job, or because they feared that further fighting would ensue if Taylor were not elected, the election was conducted in a fair manner. The international community thus should acknowledge that fact and give him a fair chance.[4]

Historian Stephen Ellis wrote,

> Liberia held the fairest election in its history…Three quarters of those who went to the polls voted for Charles Taylor. In some cases people may have reasoned that a vote for Taylor was the best hope for peace…But many may also have voted for Taylor because his very determination made him appear strong…After seven years of ECOMOG presence, the result was exactly the one which the ECOMOG countries had set out to prevent in August, 1990: Charles Taylor was President of Liberia.[5]

The policy of Nigeria, acting through ECOMOG, backfired—the unintended consequence was the election of Charles Taylor.

INAUGURATION

Immediately after Charles Taylor was elected President of Liberia, some members of the press criticized his election. The Washington Post, in an editorial the next day, wrote: "Liberians have chosen a strange way to end—if it is ended—the seven-year civil war that has shredded their 150-year-old West African country. They have overwhelmingly elected president the single person most responsible for Liberia's tragedy." As demonstrated in previous sections, that statement was untrue. The United States and Nigeria bore much of the blame for the events that caused Liberia to endure seven years of civil war.

In response to the Post editorial, the respected New African magazine, in its September,1997 issue, responded:

> Surely the Washington Post must know that Charles Taylor is not the only person 'most responsible for Liberia's tragedy.' Yes, he launched the rebel war on Christmas eve 1989 to oust Samuel Doe's despicable regime, but the role played by America in advising Taylor not to take the capital Monrovia in early 1990, definitely led to the prolongation of the crisis which in turn led to the 'seven-year-tragedy' the Washington Post is complaining about…Taylor's war…would have ended in less than six months if America, Nigeria and other countries had not intervened sadly to prolong the crisis. These countries, therefore, cannot escape blame.[6]

The editorial then said: "The world can help by giving them the chance and facilities for reconstruction rather than trying subtly to stoke the fire by the kind of editorials published by The Washington Post."

On August 2, 1997, Charles Taylor was sworn in as President of the Republic of Liberia and delivered his inaugural address. His optimism was evident as he proclaimed:

> We pledge not only to uphold and defend our laws and norms, but also to ensure that all citizens, irrespective of tribe, religion or status will receive an equal protection before the Law. I wish to assure you that under this administration, there will be no witch-hunting; there will be no recriminations meted out against any citizen or group of citizens by anyone. To my former worthy opponents, we extend the hand of friendship and an invitation to join us in this awesome task of rebuilding the nation and to ensure the future for ourselves and generations yet unborn.[7]

Especially significant was a paragraph that dealt, not just with Liberia, but with Africa as a whole. Taylor said:

> The baton has been bequeathed to a new breed of West African leaders, a new breed of South African leaders, a new breed of East and North Africa leaders who are determined that Africa is no longer willing or prepared to accept being dictated to by outside forces...Africa must determine for herself, on behalf of its people, what its priorities are, based on the wishes and desires of the African people.[8]

The policymakers at the U.S. State Department disapproved of this Kennedyesque proclamation of African independence and self-reliance.

While many nations were represented by their heads of state at the inauguration, the United States sent what many felt was a lower level delegation. It was headed by Congressman Donald Payne of New Jersey, who was Chair of the Congressional Black Caucus. The other members were Congressman John Conyers; Congresswoman Cynthia McKinney; the U.S. Ambassador to Liberia William Milan; the son of President Carter, Chip Carter; and Eve Wilkins of the State Department's Protocol Office. Former President Jimmy Carter also was present but only in his private capacity, not as a representative of the United States. It was not a delegation that signaled a significant U.S. relationship with the new democratically elected government.

It should be noted that each of President Taylor's immediate predecessors was formally received by the then President of the United States. President Edwin J. Barclay by Franklin D. Roosevelt; President William V. S. Tubman by John F. Kennedy; President William R. Tolbert Jr. by Richard Nixon sending First Lady Pat Nixon to his inauguration; and even the infamous Samuel K. Doe by Ronald Reagan. The only gesture President William Clinton made to President Charles Taylor was to telephone him briefly from Air Force One, at the insistence of Reverend Jesse Jackson, as the President flew over Liberia (never to stop there) on his March 1998 African trip.[9]

Not only did President Clinton decline to meet personally with one of the few democratically elected leaders in Africa, but, when, later the same year (in December), Secretary of State Madeleine Albright toured African countries, she refused to meet with the elected Liberian president. Yet eight of the nine leaders whom she met had ascended to power with gun in hand. Secretary Albright's unwillingness to meet with President Taylor on Liberian soil contrasts sharply with the policy of one of her predecessors, Secretary of State James Baker. According to veteran ABC News correspondent John McWethy,

> Baker's strategy was, even though we were a superpower, it was extremely important for him to show up on the other guy's soil. It didn't matter to him how small the other guy's country was, he went to them.[10]

DEMOBILIZATION, DEMILITARIZATION AND REINTEGRATION

As part of the demobilization, demilitarization, and reintegration plan for Liberia and shortly after assuming office, Taylor and his administration oversaw the destruction of thousands of arms. Kofi Annan, Secretary-General of the United Nations, attended the event and praised the Liberian government for its action. The U.S. State Department in its official Liberia Country Report on Human Rights Practices for 1997 stated that more than 20,000 weapons and over 20 million rounds of ammunition were turned in and that "significant disarmament was achieved." In a January 13, 2000 letter, Susan Rice, the

Assistant Secretary of State for Africa, wrote: "President Clinton has also written to President Taylor, welcoming his commitment to the destruction of the arms and ammunition collected at the end of Liberia's civil war, the largest arms destruction in modern Africa."[11]

However, the U.S. Defense Department conceded that the international community was deficient in its support of Liberia at this crucial time, the period just before and after the Liberian election of 1997, when demobilization, demilitarization, and reintegration of its troops took place. In February of 2002, the Office of the Secretary of Defense, International Security Affairs, Office of African Affairs issued a detailed analysis of Liberia's experiences in a paper, titled, *Critical Factors in Demobilization, Demilitarization and Reintegration: An Analysis of Ethiopia, Liberia, Mozambique and Zimbabwe.*

In the Executive Summary, "key implications for future involvement of the US Department of Defense in DDR" (Demobilization, Demilitarization and Reintegration) are listed, one of which confirms a major thesis of this book, to wit: "The United States should become involved early in countries where DDR will eventually need to occur and encourage other countries to do the same..." [12] But as documented in the analysis, this advice was not taken in the case of Liberia.

In the Introduction the report stated the following about Liberia:

> ...(D)isarmament and demobilization of combatants (in the seven year civil war) and repatriation of refugees were to proceed from November through January 1997, and elections were scheduled for May 1998. Due to the short timetable for the implementation of DDR, little more than confiscation of 10,000 weapons occurred before the election. Combatants were not systematically given psychological counseling, training or other vocational opportunities, or even transported and integrated into their home communities. Insufficient resources plagued the process, and planning for long-term demobilization programs did not occur. Liberia's instability continues today.[13]

The international community, not Liberians, forced a quick election before these modalities were achieved. "Planners viewed the election of a permanent government as more important than the demobilization, disarmament and reintegration of the former combatants of the civil war."[14]

Section 3.3 of the report maintained that "DDR requires extended commitment of support by internal and external actors"; and "DDR requires extended funding."[15] The Defense Department further stated that

> (I)n Liberia, plans were outlined for demobilization in the peace accords signed at the end of the conflict. These plans did not take into account a strategic approach to DDR. Instead, they focused on the impending election as the means to restore peace to Liberia, as opposed to the process of DDR. As a result, demobilization was a rushed process. This tight timetable and lack of overt strategy led to a quick-and-dirty approach to demobilization in which ex-combatants finished the process in less than a day. The focus on the elections also meant that the reintegration process was neglected, and few resources made available to carry it out.[16]

The Defense Department also confirmed the commonly held view of the Nigerian-dominated ECOMOG forces and its effect on DDR:

(U)nder the peace accords signed in Liberia, ECOMOG, a regional military group, headed by Nigeria, was tasked with implementing DDR. Unfortunately, ECOMOG did not remain impartial. ECOMOG 'peacekeepers' involved themselves in extensive fighting with many of the factions. Most Liberians saw ECOMOG not as a peacekeeping faction but as a combative group controlled by Nigeria. In addition, underpaid and over-tasked ECOMOG soldiers developed a reputation for looting and other crimes against the Liberian people. These actions severely damaged ECOMOG's integrity as a peacekeeping force. As a result, rather than creating a sense of security, ECOMOG added to the climate of chaos and lawlessness. UNOMIL, a UN-sponsored group in charge of monitoring ECOMOG, was viewed as a weak and ineffective force. This lack of strong central authority with integrity in the eyes of the Liberians was a great hindrance to the successful completion of DDR.[17]

In the section on Demobilization (3.5), the Defense Department revealed that

(t)he well-planned DDR in Liberia, which most likely would have helped sever combatant ties to their command structure, was never fully implemented. The program was ultimately condensed into a quick-and-dirty process compacted into several hours. Additionally, the ex-combatants often were not welcome back in their home villages and so remained together with other ex-military. There were plans also to target assistance toward ex-combatants and groups such as child soldiers. However, donor support was insufficient and the National Disarmament and Demobilization Committee opposed aid packages for ex-combatants—aid that could have served as an incentive for severing those ties. In the end, a majority of the child soldiers walked away from the demobilization areas, ultimately returning to the control of their commanders.[18]

In section 3.7 of the U.S. Defense Department conceded that

Liberia's attempts at DDR are an example of external actors' involvement proving counterproductive to stabilization efforts...Despite external actors' broad and intimate involvement in Liberia's conflict, international interest in and financial assistance to DDR have been lacking.[19]

A candid admission follows: (u)nlike previous DDR plans that have been readily supported and funded by the international community elsewhere, the Liberian program received less than enthusiastic support; donors were strongly disinclined to spend money on it.[20]

Finally, the Defense Department concluded: "In countries where DDR will eventually become a priority, the United States should become involved early and encourage other countries to do the same, as this will develop a sense of commitment needed for effective DDR."[21] And continued its summary as follows: "The United States should support and help promote the process of demilitarization through technical assistance, training, advice and—where possible—support to programs."[22] All of these factors were missing in the case of Liberia, despite repeated Liberian government requests to the United States government for assistance. Taken in conjunction with Assistant Secretary of Defense Vincent Kern's letter (see section *Liberian Army*, p. 64), the report indicated a willingness to assist the republic. But the actions of other sectors of the U.S. government, which rejected overtures from Liberia and the offers of assistance from U.S. Defense, were counter-productive to Liberia's adjustment to peacetime.

REPRISE OF MASSACHUSETTS JUDICIAL CHARGES

After his inauguration, President Charles Taylor was invited to address the United Nations in New York. However the Sheriff of Plymouth County, Massachusetts made it known that if Taylor came to the United States he would arrest him. The Boston Globe, on August 14, 1997, wrote:

> When he makes his first official visit to the United States as President of Liberia in a few weeks, Charles Taylor had better stay away from Boston. Sure, he is Africa's newest democratically elected leader, but the Plymouth County sheriff has been waiting twelve years to arrest him.

The United States legal counsel (in which capacity the author was serving) for the Republic of Liberia, along with the Liberian Ambassador to the United States, Rachel Gbenyon Diggs, negotiated both with the District Attorney of Plymouth County, Massachusetts and the U.S. State Department to expunge the record in Massachusetts so that Charles Taylor, as the legally elected President of his country, could travel within the United States without the Plymouth County Sheriff making an attempt to arrest him.

On September 24, 1997 the U.S. legal counsel wrote to Secretary of State Madeleine Albright about "an impending 'storm cloud' in the form of a bureaucratic snarl that jeopardizes the beginning of the relationship between the U.S. and the new democratically elected Government of the Republic of Liberia for which we are U.S. Counsel." The communication continued:

> In a nutshell, President Charles Taylor planned to come to the U.S. later this week to address the UN General Assembly and engage in other discussions concerning the reconstruction of Liberia. He will not make the trip so long as judicial charges are pending against him in this country...For almost two weeks of intensive effort now, we have sought the assistance of the Department of State in resolving this issue—thus far without success...Only the total removal of the outstanding charges will prevent and guarantee that there will be no potential embarrassment of Charles Taylor as a sovereign head of State...and assure that the total focus of his trip will be the reconstruction of his country. The District Attorney's office in Plymouth County, Massachusetts, has told me repeatedly that they would welcome guidance from the State Department regarding the possibility of their voiding the outstanding charges against Charles Taylor dating back to 1985. After lengthy meetings and conversations with the appropriate legal advisors at State, we were informed that 'there is no <u>legal</u> impediment' to State engaging in a dialogue with the Plymouth County authorities...that it is a <u>political</u> decision. Yet no one at State seems willing to make that political decision...I cannot believe that in the interest of international comity, the United States won't lift a finger to encourage a process that can remove what to the U.S. is a minor irritant, but to our friends in Liberia is a major obstacle to a constructive relationship. I submit that there is no downside for the U.S. to help resolve this troublesome issue and considerable upside for a successful relationship with Liberia.

Although the Massachusetts District Attorney indicated that he would look favorably upon such a request if the U.S. State Department asked him to do so, State still declined. It took the position that the issue was a legal determination that only could be made by the U.S. Department of Justice (DOJ). DOJ then took the position that the issue was a policy decision that only the U.S. State Department could make. The two agencies went back and forth in discussion for quite a while until the Department of State finally seized the issue. But the Department refused to make a request of the Massachusetts D.A., saying that it was entirely his decision. After repeated discussions, the U.S. counsel to Liberia and Liberian ambassador submitted a draft letter for State to sign, which stated that "in the interest of a harmonious relationship between the United States and Liberia, the Department would have no objection and is in support of termination of charges pending in Massachusetts against Mr. Taylor." But the State Department adamantly refused to sign the draft letter, or indicate its support of the proposed Massachusetts action.

Finally on August 25, 1998, after further negotiations, the U.S. Department of State reluctantly issued a letter to the U.S. counsel to Liberia (although pointedly not to the Plymouth County District Attorney), signed by Vicki Huddleston, Deputy Assistant Secretary of State for African Affairs, which eliminated the language about a harmonious relationship and, as well, eliminated the words of support for the contemplated Massachusetts action. The final signed letter merely stated: "I am pleased to inform you that the Department would have no objection to the termination of charges pending in Massachusetts against Mr. Taylor and so advises you." The Massachusetts District Attorney interpreted this language as the U.S. government telling him that he was on his own, that he should make the decision but not at its behest. The District Attorney considered this lukewarm endorsement for several months and finally issued the Commonwealth's Notice of Nolle Prosequi, dropping all Massachusetts charges against Charles Taylor on October 13, 1998.

A footnote to this episode took place on March 26, 2002. Sam Van Kessely, the former President of the Press Union in Liberia, addressed 100 practicing journalists in Liberia. Mr. Kessely's newspaper, the Daily Star, had first reported in the 1980s that Taylor had embezzled one million dollars for his personal use. He admitted that the story was a "blatant lie and deadly propaganda" aimed at driving Mr. Taylor out of Liberia. Kessely stated that members of the newspaper's Board of Directors, some of whom also held high positions in the Doe government, forced the paper to take a partisan approach. He also said that the Doe government had made death threats against the staff unless they reported what they were told by the government. This was another example of the lengths to which the Doe government went to punish (and, if possible, kill) its political opponents.

PLANNED VISIT TO THE UNITED STATES OF AMERICA

In May of 1999, the Liberian Ambassador to the United States, Rachel Gbenyon Diggs was contacted by the President's office and informed that since the Plymouth, Massachusetts problem had been successfully resolved, Mr. Taylor wished to visit the U.S. to personally present his case to the U.S. authorities for assistance to Liberia. At the same time, he wanted to have an opportunity to "introduce" himself to U.S. opinion makers, meet with Liberians residing in the U.S., and, as well, make his case directly to the American public. Generally, most Americans only had knowledge of either Liberia or Charles Taylor presented through the prism of mass media—and it was not favorable. As an example, whenever CNN aired a story about Liberia, it was presented in the form of a voice-over while the picture on the screen showed fierce fighting in the streets. CNN never informed its audience that the pictures were from its archive, taken during Liberia's civil war which had ended—and never reported that there was peace in the country. Many viewers concluded Liberia was still at war. It was this image that President Taylor wanted to correct.

Ambassador Gbenyon Diggs and others produced an itinerary that would achieve the purposes stated above. She succeeded admirably. The following appearances and appointments were confirmed:

- An address before the National Press Club in Washington, D.C.;

- An address before the Council on Foreign Relations in New York;

- An open "town meeting" forum at Howard University in Washington;

- A speech and question-and-answer session at Morehouse College in Atlanta, Georgia;

- A private meeting with former President Jimmy Carter at the Carter Center in Atlanta;

- An Editorial Board meeting at the Washington Post;

- Tea with the Senate International Relations Committee;

- A Trade Fair at the compound of the newly renovated Liberian Embassy Chancery;

- Meetings with the President of the World Bank and Managing Director of the IMF; and

- An appearance at the annual Congressional Black Caucus dinner in Washington.

The only appointment requested by President Taylor that was not granted was a formal meeting with the president of the United States. Presumably because of the negative views of the State Department and the CIA, Liberia was a sensitive subject, and the White House did not want to act in a manner contrary to their advice. However the Liberians were told that, either at the Congressional Black Caucus dinner reception, which President Clinton was to attend, or at the White House where Mr. Taylor could meet with the Vice-President and the President hopefully would drop by Mr. Gore's office to speak briefly with the Liberian president, the two men would have an opportunity to meet. This type of informal get-together is routinely arranged with leaders of nations when the President either does not have the time for a formal meeting or State dinner, or when the White House wants to speak with a foreign leader without necessarily giving him or her the official stamp of approval.

With all the plans in place, Ambassador Gbenyon Diggs awaited the arrival of her President. At the last moment, however, and without any advance warning, a member of President Taylor's staff informed Ambassador Gbenyon Diggs that the trip had been canceled. No explanation was given. Neither President Taylor, nor anyone in his office, wrote or called the people who had agreed to receive him to give an explanation.

The cancellation hurt President Charles Taylor's reputation with those who had planned to receive him. President Carter, for example, previously had scheduled a meeting with the President of Tanzania at the Carter Center at the very time when Mr. Taylor had asked for an appointment. Mr. Carter rearranged his schedule, moving the President of Tanzania to another time slot, in order to convenience Charles Taylor. Yet no word of explanation came from Taylor, understandably angering President Carter.

Immediately after the cancellation call, Ambassador Gbenyon Diggs and others contacted Monrovia, hoping to reverse the decision about the trip—but did not succeed. Various explanations were forthcoming. The first was that Taylor was worried about a possible insurrection at home by his enemies if he left the country and traveled to the United States. Another was that the country could not afford to send a proper delegation to the U.S. (even though it was pointed out that a large delegation would not be appropriate considering the financial difficulties of the new government). It was argued that it would be quite sufficient for Taylor to come with his Foreign Minister and a security guard but that suggestion was rejected. Some Liberians in the United States who were opponents of Taylor suggested that he canceled because he did not want to have fellow Liberians publicly demonstrate against him, but that argument lacked credibility because Taylor, an extremely articulate and persuasive speaker, relished confronting opponents and debating with them.

It was only years later that the real reason came to light. President Taylor felt that, if he came to the United States and was not formally received by the President of the United States (as he was formally received by President Chirac in France on September 28, 1998 and by Nelson Mandela in South Africa in November of 1997), he would lose face at home.

Perhaps if he had known that an informal meeting had been tentatively arranged between him and President Clinton, he would have changed his mind. But it was the formal recognition that he sought. Because of the recommendations of the CIA and State Department, Charles Taylor was snubbed. If instead Taylor had been engaged at the highest level of the United States government, the two leaders would have had an opportunity to discuss what Liberia needed to do in order to obtain U.S. help. Taylor had stated that he loved the United States, and, in the interest of helping his people, he would have done almost anything reasonable that the President of the United States asked of him.[23] But that chance never came.

As much as Taylor made a mistake by not coming to the United States, the United States made a greater mistake by denying Taylor a formal meeting with President Clinton, where persuasion could have been employed effectively. U.S. policy thus ignored the wisdom of 'walk softly and carry a big stick' (a phrase popularized by Theodore Roosevelt who, in turn, borrowed it from an old West African proverb according to Edmund Morris in his Pulitzer Prize-winning biography "The Rise of Theodore Roosevelt") and instead walked all over Liberia while using a big stick to enforce its will.

Robert Oakley, former U.S. Ambassador and former U.S. Deputy Assistant Secretary of State once commented: "Treat a warlord like a statesman and he will behave like a statesman. Treat a warlord like a warlord and he will behave like a warlord." The U.S. State Department adopted the latter course with Mr. Taylor. A good example of the effectiveness of Mr. Oakley's maxim is Ghana. Lieutenant Jerry Rawlings came to power by force of arms. Yet the United States worked with Rawlings and he later was fairly elected to the presidency. He was brought to Washington where he met with President Clinton, became a responsible leader of his country and a reliable ally. When his term ended, Rawlings stood aside and oversaw a fair election to choose his successor.

Analysis shows that his failure to come to the United States early in his presidency was one of the most costly mistakes Charles Taylor made. From President Taylor's point of view, an opportunity to present himself and his case to the American people was lost.

Later the United Nations, at the insistence of the United States, imposed travel sanctions on him and 128 other Liberian and foreign nationals, preventing them from traveling to the U.S. or any other member country of the United Nations. As a result, the American people's knowledge of Liberia and Taylor remained channeled primarily through the U.S. State Department and the media.

US OPPOSITION TO THE TAYLOR ADMINISTRATION

In the months immediately following Charles Taylor's inauguration as president of Liberia, he communicated his unwillingness to be dictated to by outside forces—primarily the United States. This became an important source of dissension between the two countries.

DETERIORATION OF US-LIBERIA RELATIONS

Two questions then arose with respect to U.S.–Liberia relations. How would the United States implement its foreign policy towards Liberia, when its president had stated he would not comply with U.S. efforts to micro-manage his country? Would the U.S. deny aid to Liberia's citizenry given this situation? The U.S. position remained consistent, driven by its position that each time the U.S started to help Liberia, President Taylor took some egregious action that prevented the substantive assistance.[24] At times, Taylor departed from his stated policy of no micro-management. But he consistently asserted that whenever he was about to comply with a U.S.request, the State Department would raise the bar another notch and refuse assistance until the new goal was met. As a result, the relations between the governments of the United States and Liberia continued to deteriorate. A pattern—an effective stalemate—emerged: U.S. offers of aid were linked to conditions with which Taylor and his administration failed to comply, or, if there was compliance, it was customarily deemed suspect or deficient. The failed relationship between the U.S. and Taylor administration, and the U.S. subsequent denial of aid contributed to Liberia's inability to recover from its civil war. As a result of the policies and actions that impaired relations between the two governments, Liberia's populace suffered greatly.

The antipathy shown toward Taylor remained clear and palpable, especially among the die-hard "Cold War warriors." An example indicative of this attitude relates to the following publication. On November 12, 2002, the Washington Post carried a paid advertisement titled, *The people of Liberia extend the hand of friendship and partnership to the people of America.* It included a statement from President Charles Taylor, *We stood by America; we always will stand by America.*

Two days later the Washington Post printed a Letter to the Editor from Gerald S. Rose, who was U.S. Deputy Chief of Mission in Liberia from 1991 to 1996. Printed in full here, he said the following:

> With the full realization that your newspaper is a commercial endeavor, I wonder if it would accept a four-page advertisement extolling the virtues of Saddam Hussein and his government.

> Charles Taylor is the West African equivalent of Hussein. Since 1989, Taylor's NPFL has been responsible for hundreds of thousands of deaths, the dislocation of millions and widespread human rights abuses.

> He has been condemned by the United Nations and his government sanctioned for his direct role in the horrible excesses of the Sierra Leone war. He may not get the publicity Hussein gets, yet he may be just as evil.

Shame on your paper for carrying Taylor's message in its Nov. 12 edition.

Despite his former service in the diplomatic corps, he expressed a clearly hostile viewpoint.

LIBERIAN POLICE AND SECURITY FORCES

Liberia had a great need to train its police and security forces. After the seven-year civil war, many former combatants (who believed they had put Taylor in the position so that a free election could be held) demanded that Taylor place them into jobs in the police and security force. Those who fought so hard for the winning side now looked to the spoils. While ex-combatants sought police and security positions, most did not have the training to uphold the responsibilities of these positions in a peacetime atmosphere. They especially required training to reduce the likelihood of human rights violations.

Taylor sought U.S. assistance to train his people. The vehicle was to be the International Criminal Investigative Training Assistance Program (ICITAP) program of the U.S. Department of Justice. Its mission is to serve as a source of support for U.S. criminal justice and foreign policy goals by assisting foreign governments in developing the capacity to provide professional law enforcement services based on democratic principles and respect for human rights. ICITAP was created by the U.S. Department of Justice in 1986, initially to respond to a request from the Department of State for assistance in training forces in Latin America. Since then, ICITAP's activities have expanded to encompass two principal types of assistance projects: 1) the development of police forces in the context of international peacekeeping operations, and 2) the enhancement of capabilities of existing police forces in emerging democracies. According to the U.S. State Department: "Priority is given to countries in transition to democracy, where unique opportunities exist for major restructuring and refocusing of police and investigative resources toward establishment of a rule of law."

Although Liberia met the ICITAP qualifications, U.S. State and U.S. Justice declined to help Liberia train its police force. The reason for the declination stemmed from the U.S. government issuing a condition with which Liberia refused to comply; the United States insisted that Liberia remove Joe Tate as its police chief. Tate, a relative of Charles Taylor, was known as a hard-nosed, no-nonsense law enforcement official who was doing a good job holding down crime in the country.

President Taylor's position, as stated previously, was that he would not allow the United States to micro-manage his government, as opposed to the Doe regime where whatever Uncle Sam wanted, Uncle Sam got. As David Halberstam wrote: "America sought to be internationalist on the cheap and to remain partially isolationist, sure that it had the right to dictate policy for every other country all over the world."[25]

In an effort to resolve the dispute, the U.S. counsel for the Republic of Liberia met with members of the U.S. State Department and argued that, 1) the U.S. should allow the freely elected Liberian government to choose the people they wished to fulfill key positions, and 2) if they had a valid reason for opposing Tate as police chief, reveal it. The answer given was that Joe Tate has a long record of human rights abuses, and they had the evidence.

Both Rachel Gbenyon Diggs, the Liberian Ambassador to the United States, and the U.S. counsel then met separately with Howard Jeter at the State Department. They told Jeter that if State could demonstrate the allegation was accurate, they would immediately recommend to President Taylor that he relieve Mr. Tate of his position. But Gbenyon Diggs and counsel requested to see the proof. Both said if there was such a record of abuse, and if President Taylor then refused to disassociate himself from Joe Tate, they would resign their positions. After much delay and continual promises that the evidence would be forthcoming, the U.S. State Department did not produce any information regarding Mr. Tate's alleged abysmal human rights record. As the result of the U.S. Department of State's policy, the U.S. missed an important opportunity to help train the police and security forces of Liberia. Without the proof, Taylor did not remove Tate and Liberia did not receive the ICITAP funds.

Along with the issue of the police was security force training. On January 22, 1999 Liberian Ambassador Rachel Gbenyon Diggs was interviewed for the "Diplomatic Dispatches" column in the Washington Post written by Nora Boustany.

> Diggs lamented the fact that the U.S...has yet to send an assessment team to evaluate Liberia's security apparatus and that there has been a delay in implementing a 'security rehabilitation program' that would train security agents and provide judicial and human rights education...(Ambassador Diggs said that) "every day that we lack security training, and every day we have people coming out of a war and taking decisions without observing human rights...is a day lost,' she argued.[26]

The issue of training Liberia's security force arose again in January 2000 when the Liberian Government said it needed about $1 million to properly train its security forces. Star Radio in Liberia (an internationally funded radio station) reported:

> President Charles Taylor said the government doesn't have the amount of money or technical expertise to conduct the training. He said the international community is yet to respond to government's request for training assistance...The President's comments come in the wake of persistent calls for the training of government security training forces...The Movement for the Defense of Human Rights (MODHAR) said ex-fighters made up the bulk of the security forces. MODHAR said lack of training for them was responsible for the continuous human rights abuses. The group believes the restructuring and training of the security forces will ensure respect for the rule of law.[27]

Not only the government, but, as well, the human rights groups, pleaded for international help in providing the training. However, the United States refused to help.

In a speech before the Liberian Senate on February 27, 2002, Tiawon S. Gongloe, counselor-at-law, stated:

> In my view, if the process of recruitment, re-structuring and re-training of our security forces had been allowed to unfold...Liberia would not have been in the state it is today...It is my opinion that the lifting of the arms embargo on Liberia would have immediately followed after the reconstitution of the Liberia security forces as agreed by the parties to the Liberian conflict under the Abuja Accord...ECOWAS and the international community were under moral obligation to protect the government and the people of Liberia until the security forces had been restructured, retrained and re-armed...[28]

An ironic note to the situation was on November 18, 2002, when Thomas White, Deputy Chief of Mission of the U.S. Embassy in Liberia spoke at the University of Liberia. In his speech he said that there was a real need for the training and restructuring of the security apparatus in the country, emphasizing that they needed to provide security, but not act as political overseers in the crucial Liberian national elections to be held in 2003.

Since the U.S. had a great concern about assuring the integrity of the 2003 elections in Liberia, not using the ICITAP program to help Liberia retrain the security forces was a serious policy failure. Whether the decision-maker in this instance was the State Department, the National Security Council, the CIA, or Senator Jesse Helms was irrelevant; the point was that the decision, whoever made it, was wrong. Had the United States assisted Liberia to train the police and security forces, the likelihood was that the excesses that took place at the hands of these forces could have been lessened, or even avoided.[29]

THE DEATH OF SAMUEL DOKIE

The next dispute between the fledgling government and the United States occurred over the death of Samuel Dokie, his wife, and his sister. Mr. Dokie was associated with Charles Taylor in his drive to become president of Liberia but defected in 1994, along with Tom Woewiyu and Lavelli Supuwood, to form his own minor faction, supported by ECOMOG, known as the Central Revolutionary Council. However Dokie served as Deputy Speaker of the Transitional Legislative Assemby (TLA), one of several bodies which guided the country to democratic elections in 1997. After his election in 1997, Taylor made special efforts to bring all the factions that opposed him into the government. Some agreed. Others opted to remain independent. Samuel Dokie was in the latter group.

On November 28 1997, it was alleged that Dokie, his wife Janet, his sister Victoria, and his bodyguard Emmanuel Voker were arrested by security men in Gbarnga (which was the Taylor headquarter city during the civil war) allegedly upon the orders of the director of the Executive Mansion-based special security service chief, Colonel Benjamin Yeaten. The Dokie family was traveling in Sanniquellie in Nimba County to attend to family matters. Days later their bodies were found on the Gbarnga Highway. Following this mysterious incident, the Government of Liberia announced a probe aimed at bringing the criminals to justice.

Initially the State Department blamed the Dokie killing on Joe Tate, the police chief. When it turned out that, at the time of the killings, Tate was attending a funeral in Monrovia at which he was observed by more than a hundred people, the U.S. State Department reluctantly recanted.

Some of the suspects were taken to court where a trial commenced, but they later were released for lack of evidence. Critics alleged that the real perpetrators had gotten away and that the people arrested were selected to "take the fall" for them. Colonel Benjamin Yeaten never was called at the trial, and the government later announced that the suspected murderers had fled to the Ivory Coast. There was judicial process, but clearly it was flawed.

President Taylor gave a public statement on the killing on December 4, 1997:

> For the past 18 hours...I have been groaning in agony, lost for expression, and perplexed about how this tragedy could befall the Liberian nation, especially at this time when we had begun to enjoy the fruits of our successful transition to peace, stability, and reconciliation.

The U.S. State Department increased its focus on the incident.[30] They raised the question of whether Taylor had ordered the killing of Dokie. Many Liberians knew Dokie was extremely unpopular with members of his own ethnic group, Mano, because he had killed leading Nimba county intellectuals, politicians, soldiers and ordinary citizens, both Mano and Gio, on behalf of Taylor's NPFL. While Nimbaians believed he must die for his act, there was no evidence that Nimba civilians killed Dokie.[31] The U.S. denounced Charles Taylor on the belief that suggested Dokie was killed for the following reasons: when Dokie left the NPFL, he unequivocally supported IGNU; and Taylor feared Dokie would expose NPFL's war strategy and its military strength to ECOMOG. The murder of Dokie was another reason that America withheld political and economic support from the Taylor government.[32]

One cannot minimize the death of any individual. However, it should be noted that the United States government initially made no statement when, over a 100 day period in Rwanda in 1994, there was a state-sponsored genocide by the Hutus against the Tutsis when more than 800,000 people were murdered—that was killing at a rate three times faster than the Nazis in World War II.[33] Despite this horrific event, the U.S. provided aid to Rwanda. It also is worth keeping in mind the perceptive comment of David Halberstam in *War in a Time of Peace* when he wrote,

> Rwanda was, in the eyes of many nonwhite critics of Western geopolitics, the quintessential example not just of the indifference of Americans and Europeans to the problems in Africa, but of the double standard used in Washington and other Western capitals to judge the value of African lives compared with Western and Caucasian ones. The West, or at least part of it, they believed, agonized over events in Bosnia, violence inflicted on Europeans by Europeans, but was almost completely unconcerned about violence inflicted on Africans by Africans.[34]

This inconsistent application of policy towards Liberia, as compared to Rwanda (and other countries), was another source of tension between Liberia and the United States.

ARMED FORCES OF LIBERIA

President Taylor also asked the United States to assist in providing professional training for the Armed Forces of Liberia, as the U.S does for so many nations. The Liberian Minister of Defense, Peter D. Chea, wished to reduce the Liberian army to about 5,000 men; the U.S. Defense Department was pleased with his goal. The U.S. counsel to Liberia met on numerous occasions with Vincent Kern, the Deputy Assistant Secretary of Defense for African Affairs, who was very supportive of assistance to Liberia. Yet no decision was forthcoming from the Pentagon. Many months passed, and counsel wrote to Mr. Kern to state that the help was needed immediately. On June 10, 1998, Kern's response arrived:

> Having spoken with Minister of Defense Chea earlier this year, I fully appreciate the concerns that prompted President Taylor's request for U.S. security assistance. We had a very successful exchange and I was impressed by Minister Chea's commitment to benchmarks that, as accomplished, will allow us to begin to establish military programs. These benchmarks include progress in establishing a small, professional, nationally representative army as well as overall progress in human rights performance. As the progress continues, we and the State Department will review ways that DoD can assist the Liberian Army, including those areas where President Taylor has requested our help— training, some limited assistance with infrastructure repair, and a full range of military contacts such as ship visits.
>
> As you know, Liberia is subject to Congressional restrictions which currently limit security assistance. We believe it important for Liberia to take concrete

steps toward these benchmarks to demonstrate that the lifting of these restrictions is warranted. We have allocated funding to restart the IMET training program for 1999, approved several humanitarian assistance projects, and are considering flag officer visits out of EUCOM in recognition of progress Liberia has made to date.

Please convey to President Taylor that we commend Liberia for the significant steps it has taken toward recovery from the horrific civil war and that we look forward to progress on the benchmarks.

At the bottom of the letter, in Mr. Kern's handwriting, the postscript reads, "Sorry about the confusion and delay."

Defense Minister Chea proceeded to achieve the benchmarks referred to above by reducing the size of the Army by 2,628 soldiers, as he had pledged, to 5,000 men. But U.S. Congressional restrictions withholding security assistance to Liberia, which were imposed during the seven years of bloody civil war, were still in place. In that respect, although U.S. Department of State or U.S. Department of Defense were remiss in not urging Congress to lift the restrictions, the U.S. Congress by its failure to do so after Liberia's compliance was at greater fault.

Even the flag officer visits "in recognition of progress Liberia has made to date" failed to materialize. Although symbolic, such visits were extremely important in demonstrating to the people of Liberia, and particularly to those who never accepted the election results and continued to oppose the Taylor government, that the United States would help the people of Liberia.

Mr. Kern was unable to obtain a positive decision from his superiors at the U.S. Department of Defense. When counsel tried repeatedly to meet with Secretary of Defense William Cohen to resolve this problem, he was refused an appointment. Thus, the Pentagon never provided any assistance to Liberia.

In addition, the U.S. State Department, through the U.S. Agency for International Development (USAID) which now is a part of the Department of State, also provides training for armies in other countries. The USAID budgets for FY2003 and FY2004, have under the item "International Military, Education and Training" a list of 40 African countries where the U.S provides military training assistance.[35] Included in the list are nations such as Burkina Faso, Côte d'Ivoire, Guinea, Kenya, Nigeria, Rwanda, and Sierra Leone. One country is conspicuously missing: Liberia.

OVERSEAS PRIVATE INVESTMENT CORPORATION INSURANCE (OPIC)

Once the democratic election was held, a number of United States companies expressed interest in investing in Liberia. For example, TriStar USA of Los Angeles expressed interest in power generation, water supply, and housing projects. The Vice President of the company, Raymond Littleton, held discussions with the Liberian Electricity Corporation (LEC) to identify ways in which his company could help electrify Monrovia and other parts of the country. Another example is Ross Mines which had invested more than $12 million in the development of the Bukon Jedh gold mine in Liberia's Sinoe County. Ross Mines had an application at OPIC for expansion of its production equipment through the purchase of American-made sluices. At the time, Ross's one existing sluice generated 100 jobs for Liberians. With OPIC financing, however, the mines could have bought more sluices and generated five times that number of jobs. The OPIC financing never was forthcoming.

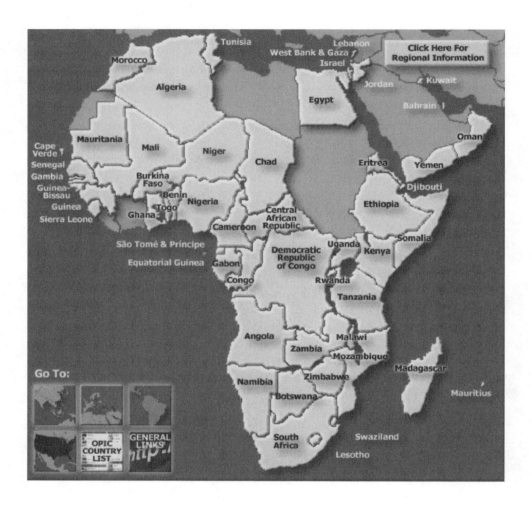

THIS OPIC MAP INDICATES THE COUNTRIES THAT HAVE CERTIFICATION THROUGH THEIR PROGRAM. AS IN THE CASE OF LIBERIA, THOSE COUNTRIES WHICH DO NOT HAVE CERTIFICATION ARE RECESSED, AND THEIR NAMES ARE OMITTED. LIBERIA BORDERS SIERRA LEONE AND GUINEA.
SOURCE: <HTTP://WWW.OPIC.GOV/LINKS/LINKS-AFR.HTM>. REPRINTED WITH PERMISSION FROM THE OFFICE OF THE GENERAL COUNSEL, OPIC.

Former Ambassador Diggs compiled a long list of such companies that wanted to do business in Liberia and help the country rebuild after its devastating civil war.[36]

Essential to such investment, however, is the need for insurance against political risks. There is one organization that addresses such a need. It is the U.S. Overseas Private Investment Corporation, more familiarly known as OPIC. Its mission is

> to mobilize and facilitate the participation of United States private capital and skills in the economic and social development of less developed countries and areas, and countries in transition from nonmarket to market economies, thereby complementing the development assistance objectives of the United States.

OPIC accomplishes its mission by assisting U.S. investors through the following four principal activities designed to promote overseas investment and reduce the associated risks:

- insuring investments overseas against a broad range of political risks;

- financing of businesses overseas through loans and loan guaranties;

- financing private investment funds that provide equity to businesses overseas; and

- advocating the interests of the American business community.

Over its 29 year history, OPIC's political risk insurance and loans have helped U.S. businesses of all sizes to invest and compete in more than 140 developing nations. It supported $138 billion worth of investments that has generated $63.6 billion in U.S. exports and created nearly 250,000 American jobs. OPIC projects also have helped developing countries to generate over $10 billion in host-government revenues and created nearly 668,000 host-country jobs. All of OPIC's guaranty and insurance obligations are backed by the full faith and credit of the United States of America.[37]

In mid-1998 Ambassador Diggs and the U.S. counsel to Liberia approached OPIC in order that Liberia might participate in the program. Their initial meeting with Harvey A. Himberg, then the Director of Investment Policy for OPIC, and Samuel Smoots, Regional Manager for Business Development, went very well. For months thereafter, however, they were shuttled back and forth, like the proverbial "hot potato," between OPIC, the State Department, and the U.S. Trade Representative (USTR), each of which expressed keen interest but insisted that Diggs and counsel see the other.

OPIC's staff told the pair that USTR is the government agency responsible for evaluating the status of the Republic of Liberia. USTR stated that the Government of Liberia had not taken steps to adopt and implement measures that extend internationally recognized worker rights.

After working with the Liberian government, Diggs and the U.S. counsel reported to OPIC that Liberia had passed legislation that placed it in compliance with section 231A of the Foreign Assistance Act, having adopted internationally accepted standards of workers' rights. Labor Unions were active and welcome in Liberia. But USTR informed them that the State Department, in its human rights report, stated that the government "continued violating fundamental human rights and has not taken any substantive measures to prevent such violations." Although Diggs and counsel pointed out both to USTR and to State that the report referred to events *prior* to the democratic election in July of 1997, neither agency heeded their argument.

On April 23, 1998, the U.S. counsel to Liberia wrote to the White House stating that a number of American corporations have expressed interest in making major investments in Liberia (especially with regard to infrastructure projects), but understandably would not go forward without OPIC guarantees. The State Department's human rights report on Liberia (reflecting a seven-year civil war which ended in 1997) was outdated. Under the Taylor government, a human rights commission was established but never implemented (see Chapter 9, Human Rights), the judicial system in practice, a free press and opposition political parties existed. Although there were human rights abuses, it was important to gauge whether the violations of human rights, restrictions on freedom of speech and press, legitimacy of courts systems, etc., had worsened or improved. In the case of Liberia, there was evidence of improvement since the election of 1997, which the State Department's human rights reports acknowledged.

> The Government's human rights record was poor, and there were serious problems in many areas; however, there was some improvement in comparison with 1996...Security forces committed extrajudicial killings; however it was difficult to distinguish in many cases whether some killings were a result of political, criminal, ethnic, or other motives.

This should have allowed the United States to assist Liberia and not penalize its populace. U.S. president William Clinton personally had called President Taylor to encourage him in his efforts, and Mrs. Clinton (in March of 1998) met with Mrs. Taylor and suggested "micro" programs for the women of Liberia. But U.S. policy did not grant Liberia OPIC eligibility, nor allow it to become eligible for OPIC guarantees. If it had, the country would have been assured of the investment of American companies to help provide roads, telecommunications, airports, electricity, schools, etc.

On October 18, 1999, Diggs and counsel asked OPIC to end the shuttling back-and-forth by arranging a meeting with key representatives of OPIC, USTR, and the Department of State in the same room so they could answer once and for all. That meeting never materialized. Since President Clinton had announced a plan to expand OPIC loan guarantees by 650 million dollars to encourage infrastructure development in Africa, Liberia especially wanted to gain eligibility for OPIC assistance. It did not.

Moreover the African Growth and Opportunity Act (AGOA), in Title 11, requested that OPIC initiate two or more equity funds in support of projects in the countries of sub-Sahara Africa. One fund was to be an equity fund with assets of up to $150 million. The primary purpose of that fund was to achieve long-term capital appreciation through equity investments in support of projects in those countries. In addition, one or more funds, with combined assets of $500 million was to be used to support different infrastructure projects in the same countries. Eligibility depended upon the President of the United States determining that the country in question did not engage in gross violations of internationally recognized human rights and had established, or was making continual progress toward establishing, a market-based economy. Despite the fact that Liberia, since August of 1997, met those requirements, OPIC stated it was unlikely that the Republic of Liberia would qualify for any of these funds "at this time."

In checking the OPIC country certification list in Africa, one finds OPIC approved programs in such troubled countries with records of human rights abuses as: Angola, Zimbabwe, Congo, Uganda, Burkina Faso, Algeria, Somalia, Yemen, and Rwanda. Liberia, by contrast, was denied certification. This added to the perception of Liberian officials regarding the inconsistent treatment of their country by the United States government.[38]

THE HUMMER INCIDENT

In January of 1998, just four months after Charles Taylor became President of Liberia, his representatives attempted to purchase a Hummer automobile for his use. Ordinarily the President rides in a conventional automobile, but, during Liberia's five month rainy season, it is impossible for a conventional car to make its way up-country where most of the roads are unpaved. Because of its design, the Hummer is ideal for "flooded, unpaved roads... ." Additionally, for the protection of every head of state, a bullet-proof vehicle is essential. In Liberia the back roads still contain land-mines left over from the seven year civil war. Taylor's security detail was concerned that if the President's car accidentally drove over one of those mines and set it off, he would be injured or killed. Accordingly, Gerald Cooper, Liberia's Ambassador to the IMO (the International Maritime Organization, a United Nations group based in London), authorized a British company, Liberian Purchasing Agent UK, to locate a U.S. local agent (Joe Aikhuele of Imiota Inc.), who in turn purchased a civilian version of the Hummer from a civilian dealer of the AMVC General Corporation named Boomershine Hummer in Smyrna, Georgia. He wanted assurance that the floor of the vehicle could withstand an exploding land mine. The Hummer 4-passenger station wagon was fitted with bullet-resistant glass and ballistic fabric and steel. The roof and floor areas were armored to Level III-A. The vehicle contained defensive gun ports which became operative only if weapons penetrated the body of the car. $170,000 was paid for the Hummer which was armored in accordance with National Institute of Justice standards.[39]

Liberia made it clear that the ultimate recipient of the Hummer was the president. All applications for shipment listed as the end-user "His Excellency Charles G. Taylor, President of Liberia." The Liberian representatives asked the dealer whether there were any problems in connection with exportation of the vehicle to Liberia via Abidjan, Ivory Coast. On January 6, 1998, Rich Marcom of Boomershine-Hummer wrote: "I did double-check on the Export Restrictions, and again there is no problem with a Civilian Hummer that has been Armor Plated." Based on this information, the car was delivered in a container to the port at Savannah, Georgia. On February 21, 1998, the vehicle was seized at the port by U.S. Customs officials who stated that the Hummer would not be released until a State Department export license had been secured.

At the request of the Liberian Government, the U.S. counsel then contacted Brian Browne, the Liberian desk officer at the U.S. Department of State, and asked for its assistance in obtaining the necessary waivers. Because of the thickness of the armor plate, the vehicle technically was classified as a "munition," and since the arms embargo that was placed upon Liberia by the United Nations during the seven years civil war never had been lifted, importation by Liberia of a "munition" would be considered a violation of the arms embargo.[40] Mr. Browne informed the U.S. counsel that State could not proceed with his request since Customs apparently had to first resolve a criminal investigation on the issue.

Mr. Browne then asked the lawyers at the U.S. State Department to contact U.S. Customs to determine the status of the alleged criminal investigation. They reported that U.S. Customs refused to discuss the matter. The U.S. Representative from Georgia, Newt Gingrich, did not fare any better. He wrote to Customs seeking information regarding the seizure of the car, but, on April 22, 1998, Congressman Gingrich received a letter from

Mary Bensel-Mills, Customs Fines, Penalties & Forfeiture Officer in Savannah, who wrote: "The case is currently under investigation for violation of the criminal laws of the United States, and therefore, no further information may be released at this time." This bureaucratic wrangle lasted for months. Liberia retained an attorney in Atlanta and went to court over the matter.[41]

Later it became apparent that the "criminal matter" was Liberia's technical violation of the Arms Export Control Act which gives the President of the United States the authority to control and require licensing for the export of "defense articles and services". 22 U.S.C. section 2794(3)(A) defines "defense articles" as "any weapon, weapons system, munition, aircraft, vessel, boat or other implement of war." The judge, B. Evant Edenfield of the United States District Court for the Southern District of Georgia, said that Liberia's ignorance of the law (the need to obtain an export license) was not a legitimate excuse. He also noted that, prior to seizure of the Hummer, the vehicle had been classified by the Office of Defense Trade Control as a "military armored vehicle" because of the level of armoring. It was clear the vehicle was not intended for any other use than protection of the President of the Republic. Yet the judge cited 22 C.F.R. section 120.3 which says that, in evaluating an article's classification, "the intended use of the article or service after its export is not relevant." Thus, the judge had no choice but to find for the Government and against Liberia. Despite the U.S. State Department's knowledge that the car was to protect the Liberian president, they did not offer assistance.

Because the U.S. Department of State refused to grant a waiver, the judge upheld the seizure of the vehicle. Technically (because of the thickness of the armor plate) it was in violation of the arms embargo which banned the import of "munitions." If the U.S. State Department had granted a waiver, their action would not have violated the United Nations arms embargo.

Although the Liberians acted in good faith and never attempted to disguise or conceal what they were doing and for whom the vehicle was purchased, the president of Liberia did not get the vehicle to use up-country. The United States government kept the car and the money—the Liberian officials could not retrieve the $170,000 they paid. Not only was the government penalized, but Gerald Cooper, who authorized the purchase but handled none of the details, was subsequently informed by the British that, because of the incident, he either must waive his immunity and answer their questions or leave the country. Liberia's U.S. counsel tried to determine why they were interested in this matter and, although no one put anything in writing, he received an unofficial explanation by the British that it was done because of a request from the Americans.[42] The U.S. State Department denied any involvement.

British customs officials attempted to question Mr. Cooper in regard to the U.S. incident, but Liberia declined to waive his diplomatic immunity. The U.S. counsel wrote to the U.S. Embassy in London to ascertain what precipitated this action. On March 29, 1999, John Martinez, Customs attache at the U.S. Embassy responded to his request stating, "Her Majesty's Customs and Excise is conducting a parallel investigation to the U.S. Customs Service investigation concerning the attempted exportation of an armored Hummer vehicle from Savannah, Georgia to Monrovia, Liberia." Mr. Martinez referred counsel's inquiry to B. J. Crossey, Britain's Senior Investigative Officer of Her Majesty' Customs and Excise. Despite the talk of a criminal investigation, it came to naught, as indicated in a letter from the U.S. Department of Justice dated February 3, 2000. It stated that, "the U.S. Attorney for the Southern District of Georgia has never had an open criminal investigation..." and "the Northern District of Georgia U.S. Attorney's office did at one time have an open file on this matter. However I have now been advised by the U.S. Customs case agent that the Northern District of Georgia has closed its file, thus declining to go forward."

Mr. Crossey wrote his response on April 4, 1999, and said,

> I can confirm that HM Customs & Excise are conducting an investigation...The investigation concerns an alleged breach of the United Nations Arms Embargo...It is not the policy of HM Customs & Excise to divulge how or why we commence our investigations but we are duty bound to investigate any alleged breaches of sanctions that have a UK nexus...I hope this has been of some assistance.[43]

This incident reflected the U.S. State Department policy towards the Taylor-led government in Liberia. Even the minor matter of an automobile to protect the life of the president of Liberia was a contentious isssue for the countries.

US PEACE CORPS

The U.S. Peace Corps is one of the finest and most altruistic manifestations of the nation's international diplomacy. Begun by the Kennedy Administration, one of the countries it served successfully during the early 1960s was Liberia. Until the military coup of April 12, 1980, the republic had the largest cadre of Peace Corps volunteers on the African continent. In December of 1998 in conversation with the U.S. counsel to Liberia, President Taylor asked if the United States would revive its Peace Corps involvement in Liberia. He felt it would be a dramatic example of the U.S.'s genuine interest in the welfare of his country— an example that the Liberian populace actually could see.

Accordingly early in 1999 the U.S. counsel initiated a discussion with Mark Gearan who was the head of the Peace Corps and made the formal request. Mr. Gearan told him that he was amenable to revisiting the subject of Peace Corps presence in Liberia, as long as he received a letter from the Liberian Foreign Minister asking for that step to be taken. On February 26, 1999, Monie R. Captan, the Foreign Minister of the Republic of Liberia wrote to Mr. Gearan formally making the request. Counsel also sent a letter to Gearan on March 8, 1999, in which he wrote:

> I do hope you will look favorably upon this request. Every time I go to Liberia, the youngsters there plead with me to ask the United States to help them by providing teachers so they can learn skills that will qualify them for good jobs and allow them to help the democratic tradition flourish and grow in their country. Please note that I make this request of you in a <u>pro bono</u> capacity.

Based on the initial communications it appeared a favorable decision was forthcoming.

But, on April 25, 2000, the U.S. counsel received a letter from the new director of the Peace Corps, Mark L. Schneider, in which Schneider wrote:

> In response to your inquiry concerning a possible return by the Peace Corps to Liberia, *the present civil conflict* precludes the reestablishment of a program in Liberia in the near future. We will continue, however, to watch the situation in an effort to determine the time and conditions under which Peace Corps activities could be resumed in Liberia.

Liberia was troubled about his reference to "the present civil conflict." There was none at that time. The administration felt the the director of the Peace Corps and his staff should be aware that the civil conflict had ended in 1997. The counsel wrote again to Mr. Schneider pointing out the factual error and asked that he reconsider Liberia's request. Schneider never replied, and the Peace Corps did not return to Liberia.

One could understand that the Peace Corps made a mistake about conditions on the ground in Liberia. But, once Liberia addressed that error and established the facts, the only reason for not restoring the program would be the U.S. policy regarding Charles Taylor, as formulated by the State Department, or the CIA, or elsewhere within the U.S. government.

FOOD FOR LIBERIAN CHILDREN

Shortly before leaving office, President Clinton decreed that the U.S. government should spend $300 million on a test program to provide school lunches to children overseas in underdeveloped countries. Former Senator George McGovern, who for years has been involved in the Food for Peace program, said: "The basic idea comes down to 'why not one decent meal every day for every kid in the world?' How can you be against that?" More than 8 million children were expected to benefit from this creative and generous program.

Liberia decided to apply for this program. On September 26, 2000, the U.S. legal counsel wrote to Dan Glickman, then Secretary of Agriculture, to ask that the children of Liberia be made eligible for this new program which was being administered by his department. Unlike the issues described above, the food program request took place after the U.S. and the United Nations expressed their concern about President Taylor's role in the conflict in Sierra Leone.

In response to the possible impact of the charges against Taylor, U.S. legal counsel to Liberia wrote—

> Whatever our problems with the leadership of a given country, the people should not be made to suffer. By providing school lunches for Liberian children, the United States would demonstrate dramatically its humanitarian concern for the poor and the hungry. There are many NGOs that could be used to assure that the school lunch aid is delivered directly to the schoolchildren.

This letter did not receive a response. When counsel checked with the Department of Agriculture, he was told merely that Liberia was ineligible for the program.

In its decision, U.S. policy failed at a chance to win the hearts and minds—and stomachs—of a friendly people in desperate need. By contrast, the United Nations World Food Programme (WFP) in Liberia provided full food aid rations to thousands of internally displaced Liberian and Sierra Leonean refugees. By September of 2002, the caseload of displaced people had risen to 126,427.

The pattern of inconsistent policy by the United States government toward the people of Liberia was criticized by humanitarian aid groups who had taken roles in trying to help alleviate the suffering of the people. Rory E. Anderson, Africa policy advisor at World Vision U.S. testified at Africa's Weak States: U.S. Policy Options in Liberia, Hearing of the Senate Subcommittee on Africa, June 11, 2002:

> Despite the expansion of a regional humanitarian crisis in the MRU, U.S. humanitarian assistance to Liberia has declined by 82% over the past 5 years.

Since 1998, total U.S. government assistance to Liberia, including food aid, has declined to the following levels:

FY1998 – $37,786,000

FY1999 – $16,049,000

FY2000 – $17,529,000

FY2001 – $8,199,000

FY2002 – $6,519,000

This drastic decline in humanitarian assistance demonstrates unfortunate trends: (1) humanitarian assistance in the Mano River Union is a zero sum game, which means that there are only winners and losers—we take from Liberia and give to Sierra Leone, rather than having a balanced, regional approach to humanitarian assistance. And (2) policy makers in the U.S. have incorrectly politicized humanitarian assistance to Liberia. Instead, it is better to separate humanitarian assistance from our political strategy with Charles Taylor. Humanitarian assistance, especially when it is channeled through local and international relief agencies, has proven to be an effective tool for building strong civil society actors that can democratically challenge the political establishment while rebuilding societies and economies damaged by war. These are a long and medium-term investments, with long-term pay-offs. Starving an already volatile region, or unevenly distributing aid—i.e., investing in Sierra Leone, and not in Liberia or Guinea, simply creates a merry-go-round of violence and displacement, shifting war from one country to the next.[44]

One excuse that often was given by U.S. policymakers was that the U.S. was afraid to send money to Liberia for fear that it would end up in the pockets of Charles Taylor and his cohorts. In response the legal counsel pointed out that the training of security forces, the training of the army, the resumption of the Peace Corps volunteers, food for children, and insurance guarantees for business investment do _not_ involve money transfers. They involved in-kind services and goods. The arguments were to no avail.

In fact, the U.S. State Department has asserted repeatedly that Taylor has amassed a personal fortune by exploiting the resources (diamonds, gold, and timber) of his own country. The claim is that Taylor keeps his fortune in Swiss banks. In response Taylor made a commitment to waive his right of privacy at any bank in the world to prove that he has not taken advantage of his countrymen to line his own pockets. On January 23, 2001, Reuters reported that "Liberian President Charles Taylor...has called for a UN probe into his bank accounts and offered to resign if diamond funds are found." Neither side proved or disproved their claim.

THE LIBERIAN EMBASSY, WASHINGTON, DC

The Liberian Embassy in Washington is located on Sixteenth Street NW. During the years of civil war in Liberia (1989–1996), it was unoccupied as there was no *de jure* government in the country. The U.S. State Department's Office of Foreign Missions is charged with the responsibility of protecting foreign embassies located in Washington. Yet someone firebombed the chancery, and the charred building sat empty for seven years. Understandably residents in the immediate vicinity of the Embassy were distressed at the terrible state of disrepair.

By U.S. law, foreign embassies are exempt from local (District of Columbia) property taxes. Nevertheless, in 1994 the D.C. Department of Finance and Revenue removed the Liberian Embassy from the roll of exempt properties and put it back on the tax rolls of the city dating back to October 1, 1991. Mr. Richard C. Massey of the Office of Foreign Missions at the Department of State could not explain why the District imposed taxes retroactively to 1991. At the same time, however, State supported the District's intention to ignore the exemption rule and put the property back on the tax rolls. On September 20, 1994, Mr. Massey of the State Department wrote the following to the D.C. Department of Finance and Revenue:

> Due to circumstances beyond the control of the Liberian authorities, the chancery has not been repaired and remains unoccupied. The Department of State has been in contact with the Liberians to urge them to restore the property and use it again as their chancery. However, due to the five (sic) year civil war, it is unknown when an elected government will be installed and can undertake the renovations . Nonetheless, taking into consideration the period of time that has elapsed since the fire, the Department will not object to the building being restored to the tax rolls of the District of Columbia pending commencement of its renovation.

By the time Ambassador Diggs arrived in 1998, the District of Columbia claimed taxes due from 1991 through 1997 in the amount of $67,690.69. The State Department agreed to let the District of Columbia auction off the property with a tax sale scheduled for July 1, 1998. But neither the D.C. Government nor the State Department were prepared for the newly appointed Liberian Ambassador to the United States, Rachel Gbenyon Diggs, who was determined to save her country's embassy.

After meetings were held between Ambassador Diggs and the State Department, Mr. Massey advised counsel for Liberia (the author and his law partner Kenneth Schaner) that if the Ambassador was sincerely interested in restoring the building to its former use as a chancery and showed good faith by submitting an application and plans for a building permit, he would issue a letter to the D.C. Department of Finance and Revenue to restore the exemption. Mr. Massey also indicated that if Liberia was willing to pay some of the back taxes, he would work with the Ambassador to attempt to get the remainder of the back taxes waived by the City. Ambassador Diggs took up the challenge and had the appropriate applications prepared and plans for rebuilding drawn.

The real problem for Ambassador Diggs, however, was finding the money to actually rebuild the Chancery. After doing extensive research, she learned that, although the United States always had paid a considerable amount of rent for the property it used in Monrovia as the U.S. Embassy, that rent had not been paid at all for a number of years. The creative Ambassador Diggs proposed a swap: exchange the back rent the U.S. owed in Monrovia for a commercial bank loan or line of credit in the U.S. that would be used to rebuild the chancery. The parties agreed, and the project commenced. On September 29, 2000 the newly renovated Liberian Chancery located at 5201 Sixteenth Street. NW (across from the Carter Barron Amphitheater) was dedicated with the Foreign Minister of Liberia Monie R. Captan as the dedication speaker. Ambassador Gbenyon Diggs had prevailed.

US FUNDING AND THE BROOKE AMENDMENT

When traveling through the streets of Monrovia after the civil war and the 1997 election, one saw building after building destroyed, or riddled with bullets. One found an entire city without electricity (except for the fortunate few who had their own generators, and other people who hooked up televisions to their car batteries to watch a program occasionally), a non-functioning communications system, a lack of potable water, homes destroyed, and roads made unpassable because of huge bomb craters. To rehabilitate the capital, Liberia looked first to the United States, its putative patron, and then to the international community.

The United States responded that, aside from humanitarian relief (primarily food) provided by the U.S. Agency for International Development (USAID), there could be no bilateral aid from the United States government because of the Brooke Amendment. The Brooke Amendment was named for Edward Brooke (R-Mass.), the first African-American member of the United States Senate since reconstruction. The amendment is contained in Section 512 of the 1999 Foreign Operations Appropriation Act. It reads: "No part of any appropriation contained in this Act shall be used to furnish any country which is in default during a period in excess of one calendar year in the payment to the United States of principal or interest on any loan made to such country by the United States pursuant to a program for which the funds are appropriated under this Act: Provided, That this section and section 620(q) of the Foreign Assistance Act of 1961 shall not apply to funds made available in this Act or during the current fiscal year for Nicaragua, Brazil, *Liberia*, and for any narcotics-related assistance for Colombia, Bolivia, and Peru authorized by the Foreign Assistance Act of 1961 or the Arms Export Control Act." Note that the language cited above specifically excluded Liberia from the operation of the Act. That language was approved by the U.S. House of Representatives but it was cut out in the Senate, as well as in the Conference. President Clinton vetoed the bill and sent it back to the Congress. But again, the Congress declined to reinstate Liberia's waiver.

In a letter dated October 29, 1999 to Representative Ed Royce, chairman of the Subcommittee on Africa of the Committee on International Relations, in the U.S. House of Representatives, Ambassador Rachel Gbenyon Diggs wrote:

> It has come to our attention that Liberia will no longer benefit from a waiver of the Brooke Amendment under the FY 1999-2000 Appropriations Bill. You may be aware that Liberia has benefitted from an automatic waiver over the past several years as a war-torn country...The consequences of the non-renewal of the waiver would be detrimental to efforts toward reconstruction, strengthening of civil society capacities, and could only undermine our struggles toward a sustained democracy and national stability...In a recent letter from Secretary Albright to President Taylor, she stressed that the United States looked forward to working with him and other leaders in the region to build the peace and stability that is desperately needed to recover from the devastation wrought by nearly a decade of civil war...

Still no waiver was granted to Liberia.

The Brooke Amendment, as it applies to Liberia, states that if a country is in default for more than a year in repaying principal or interest on loans from the United States, that country is ineligible to receive any further foreign aid.

The irony is that these "loans" originally were made by the U.S. to the corrupt Samuel Doe government during the Cold War. The money went into the pockets of Doe and his cronies, and was not used for the Liberian people. Following the democratic election held in August of 1997, the Taylor administration inherited massive internal and external debts.

Only $17,000 was in the national treasury when Taylor assumed office. According to the U.S. State Department (Bureau of Democracy, Human Rights and Labor, January 30, 1998), "the Taylor administration inherited an external debt estimated at over $2 billion and over $230 million in domestic debt."[45] Why should the poor people of Liberia be penalized because the previous government of Samuel Doe squandered millions and millions of dollars? Why should they have to repay the $500 million that the U.S. gave to Samuel Doe, much of which ended up in his own pocket? One of the key issues for which African leaders argue is debt forgiveness. At the very time Liberia needed to rebuild, the U.S. policy was harsh in its failure to grant Liberia a waiver from the Brooke Amendment in the Foreign Operations Appropriations legislation for fiscal years 2000 through 2003. There are, however, some limited statutory authorities or exceptions which allow certain funding obligations to be made for humanitarian purposes by the U.S. Agency for International Development, and some money has been forthcoming from that source. But nothing substantive has been made available for the desperately needed reconstruction of the country, or such elemental needs as potable water, roads, electricity, and telecommunication.

It was, and still is clear, that Liberia is a Highly Indebted Poor Country (HIPC). Yet the United States policy contended that Liberia was not eligible for the HIPC debt forgiveness program that is available to 26 other HIPC countries (including $300 million for the Democratic Republic of Congo) on the grounds that Liberia does not have a commitment to economic reform and a pledge to increase domestic funding of health and education programs. Liberia has such a commitment but lacks the funds to implement their programs, and sought money from the HIPC program meant to address that problem. There was, and is, a further repercussion from the decision that Liberia is ineligible for U.S. aid. It not only affected U.S. help but meant that the Paris Group (an informal group of nations that tries to help underdeveloped countries) was unlikely to support international assistance for Liberia unless the United States took the lead.

Former U.S. Deputy Assistant Secretary of State Howard Jeter made the point that, if the U.S. were to give substantial aid to Liberia, the other members of the international community would withhold funds on the grounds that Liberia was the responsibility of the United States alone. U.S. legal counsel to Liberia maintained that this was specious reasoning—that, in fact, just the reverse was the case, to wit: unless and until the United States, by providing funding to Liberia, signaled to the international community that this was a cause worth supporting, the other countries would not pay their fair share to Liberia. If the United States helped, they would then help.[46]

It was ironic that the Brooke Amendment was used to deny post-conflict African nations U.S. aid because they were unable to repay loans made by the United States to corrupt dictators during the Cold War. Since the United States could not send aid to Liberia after the 1997 election, it could act only through multilateral agencies such as the World Bank and the International Monetary Fund (where the United States has a major voice). The U.S. position influenced the international community's decision *not* to help Liberia.[47] At one such international meeting, a substantial sum was about to be voted for Liberian reconstruction. Eyewitnesses said that Deputy Assistant Secretary of State Howard Jeter came late to the meeting and told the participants that the United States opposed the funding for Liberia. This caused Liberia's Finance Minister Elie Saleeby (who was largely responsible for the economic recovery in Ghana and was trying to do the same for Liberia) to literally burst into tears after Howard Jeter "killed" the international assistance package the international community was prepared to give Liberia.

As further evidence that U.S. opposition to the Liberian government decreased other nations' willingness to aid Liberia, one may contrast the treatment by the United States and the international community of the Sierra Leone crisis as opposed to the Liberian crisis. In 2001, the United Nations granted 80 percent of the $60 million requested by Sierra Leone to help that country, with Britain and the United States being the main contributors. But only $1 million in aid went to Liberia in 2001. There was no bilateral aid from the U.S. to Liberia in 2002 and the U.S. convinced other donor nations not to contribute to Liberia. On February 20, Reuters reported the following:

> Ordinary Liberians are suffering as foreign donors shun Liberia because of opposition to its government, a senior UN official said Wednesday. UN assistant emergency coordinator Ross Mountain said fighting between government troops and rebels had displaced 60,000 people, but international help had been lackluster. 'We recognize some countries are not on the best of terms with the government of Liberia but what we are talking about here is support for the Liberian people, irrespective of political considerations.'[48]

A proposal made by Mr. Saleeby's successor as Finance Minister of Liberia, Nathaniel Barnes, a young, well-educated and capable public servant, called for a summit conference of post-conflict countries. Two sections of his paper deserve consideration here. The first summarizes the characteristics of a post-conflict country. They are:

- High external debt and arrears;
- Withdrawal of international technical and financial assistance (other than short term emergency assistance and food aid);
- Destruction of critical public services (including water and electricity);
- Destruction of social infrastructures (schools, hospitals, clinics);
- Destruction of physical and economic infrastructure (roads, bridges, airports);
- Increased danger from land mines;
- Exodus of skilled labor and depletion of existing human capacity both in the public and private sectors;
- Capital flight;
- Loss of investor confidence;
- Loss of database;
- Widespread absence of accountability and transparency in governance.

The second section lists the consequences of conflict for the post-conflict countries which include:

- Increase in the proportion of the population living below the poverty line;
- Increased child mortality;
- Increase in under-age pregnancy and the number of children having babies of their own;
- Increased incidence of child abuse and rapes;
- Increase in number of single parents and female headed households;

- Child-soldiers;

- Increased number of street children and vagrancy;

- Increased drug and substance abuse;

- Increased incidence of HIV/AIDS/STD;

- Breakdown of normal support systems in the African context;

- Increased danger from land mines;

- Widespread unemployment.

The above is a perfect profile of Liberia immediately after the seven year civil war. Mr. Barnes then said:

> Addressing these ills requires a different strategy, and definitely more resources than ordinarily required for poverty reduction. It calls for a greater speed of implementation, and a genuine dedication to reconstruction, peace building, and rehabilitation. It also calls for greater sympathy on the part of development partners.

With this profile of post-conflict Liberia, one may understand the frustration of its citizens. The comments of Susan E. Rice, U.S. Assistant Secretary of State for Africa, written to a long-time supporter of Liberia, Retired U.S. General Robert G. Yerks, raise additional issues with U.S. policy toward Liberia:

> The International Monetary Fund (IMF) has worked with the Government of Liberia to implement a number of reforms in the economy that could lead to increased international assistance in development projects, and attract international investments, so necessary to Liberia's reconstruction. The IMF recommends action on *three key economic issues*: the rice monopoly, the petroleum monopoly, and compensation of Mobil oil for losses suffered in 1996.[49]

One understands the importance of eliminating monopolies and protecting the business interests of foreign investors. But with its entire nation destroyed, its people starving, and the entire infrastructure in need of rebuilding, the Liberian government found it incredulous for the Assistant Secretary of State of the United States and the IMF to insist that Liberia, as a "key economic issue," first reimburse Mobil Oil for losses it suffered in1996 before the international community would grant aid.

The citation of one more paragraph from the Barnes proposal for a summit conference on post-conflict nations addresses this issue;

> Countries that have gone through conflict situations typically have huge debts, which they probably were unable to service during the conflict period, particularly if the conflict lasted for years. This results in the accumulation of arrears. With the devastation inflicted by the conflict, the economy cannot generate resources immediately after conflict to resume debt servicing. The result is further accumulation of huge arrears and lapse into non-accrual status with major creditors, eliminating ability to borrow to finance post-conflict reconstruction and rehabilitation. Such countries may find it difficult to enter into contention for relief or assistance under special international initiatives such as the HIPC (Highly Indebted Poor Countries) Initiative because of

their debt overhang. Even when they enter the process, it is difficult for them to make appreciable progress toward the decision and/or completion points because of the severe challenges to be met at the same time, and the magnitude of their need for immediate resources to finance massive rehabilitation, reconstruction and poverty alleviation simultaneously. While it is true that the international community during and immediately after conflict provides substantial emergency relief, this is usually in the form of humanitarian aid or short-term emergency assistance dominated by consumables rather than items for reconstruction and rehabilitation. They also tend to taper off quickly. The numerous emergency situations arising today task available resources or may be affected by the emergence of other emergency situations elsewhere. The result is that some countries may be more fortunate than others in attracting more resources or for slightly longer periods of time.

NOTES

[1] Personal communication with State Department official.

[2] Personal communication with State Department official.

[3] Bureau of Democracy, Human Rights, and Labor, U.S. Department of State, *Liberia Country Report for Human Rights Practices for 1998*, Washington, D.C. Released February 26, 1999. Available at <http://www.state.gov/www/global/human_rights/1998_hrp_report/liberia.html>.

[4] Personal communication with the Honorable Olara A. Otunnu, United Nations Special Representative of the Secretary-General for Children and Armed Conflict.

[5] Stephen Ellis, *The Mask of Anarchy: The Destruction of Liberia and the Religious Dimension of an African Civil War,* London: Hurst & Company, p. 109.

[6] Baffour Ankomah, "How Nigeria Prolonged Liberia's Agony," *New African*, September 1997, p. 14.

[7] Republic of Liberia, *Presidential Papers. Vol. I*, Liberian Department of Public Affairs, 1998, p. 30.

[8] Ibid. p. 31.

[9] Kenneth R. Timmerman, *Shakedown: Exposing the Real Jesse Jackson*, Regnery Publishing, 2002, p. 304.

[10] Vernon Loeb, "Rumsfeld's Flying Circus: When it Comes to Going Fast, Far and Frequently, The Defense Secretary is Way Out Front," *Washington Post*, May 3, 2003, Style section, p. C1.

[11] Correspondence to President Charles Taylor, communication to author.

[12] Office of the Secretary of Defense, International Security Affairs, Office of African Affairs, *Critical Factors in Demobilization, Demilitarization and Reintegration: An Analysis of Ethiopia, Liberia, Mozambique and Zimbabwe*, Washington, D.C. p. 2.

[13] Ibid., p. 9.

[14] Ibid., p. 113.

[15] Ibid., p. 17.

[16] Ibid., p. 18.

[17] Ibid., p. 20.

[18] Ibid.

[19] Ibid.

[20] Ibid., p. 116.

[21] Ibid., p. 37.

[22] Ibid., p. 40.

[23] Personal communication with President Charles Ghankay Taylor.

[24] Personal communication with Howard Jeter, U.S. Deputy Assistant Secretary of State for African Affairs from June 1999 to July 2000.

[25] David Halberstam, *War in a Time of Peace*, p. 225.

[26] "Liberian Daily News Bulletin," Star Radio, January 2, 2000.

[27] Nora Boustany, "Diplomatic Dispatches," *Washington Post*, January 22, 1999.

[28] Tiawon S. Gongloe, *Testimony on the State of Emergency, Sanctions and Arms Embargo*, Statement to the Senate of Liberia, February 27, 2002. The Perspective (online newsmagazine). Posted March 7, 2002, at <http://www.theperspective.org/gongloe.html>.

[29] Personal communication with Ambassador Rachel Diggs. The author includes himself in this group due to his participant role.

[30] Personal communication with Honorable Grace Minor.

[31] Personal communication with Howard Jeter.

[32] Ibid.

[33] Ibid.

[34] Emily Wax, "At the Heart of Rwanda's Horror General's History Offers Clues to the Roots of Genocide," *Washington Post,* September 21, 2002; Page A1 Section: A.

[35] Halberstam, p. 273

[36] U.S. Agency for International Development budget for FY 2002, 2003, and 2004, International Military Education and Training, p. 71.

[37] What is OPIC? "All of OPIC's guaranty and insurance obligations are backed by the full faith and credit of the United States of America." <www.opic.gov/WhatIsOPIC/whatis3.htm>.

[38] Interview of Ambassador Rachel Gbenyon Diggs, February 11, 2002, Nashville, Tennessee.

[39] Overseas Private Investment Corporation, Program Handbook, pp. 4-6.

[40] 21st Century Armored Car Corp., Manufacturers Verification of Armored Modification to Hummer 4-Passenger Station Wagon, February 26, 1998; Application for Permanent Export of Unclassified Defense Articles, February 26, 1998.

[41] Letter from Mary Bensel-Mills, Fines, Penalties & Forfeiture Officer, Department of the Treasury, United States Customs Service to Congressman Newt Gingrich, April 22, 1998.

[42] Personal communication with U.S. Embassy in London, England.

[43] Ibid.

[44] June 12, 2002 testimony by Rory Anderson posted by the Office of Public Policy and Advocacy of World Vision United States, Washington, D.C. at <http://www.worldvision.org/worldvision/wvususfo.nsf/stable/globalissues_criticalissues_liberia>.

[45] Personal communication with Howard Jeter.

[46] Personal communication from NGO representatives.

[47] Reuters news wire, February 20, 2001.

[48] Susan E. Rice, letter to General Robert Yerks, September 8, 1999.

CHAPTER 5
US EMBASSY IMBROGLIO

ATTACK AT THE UNITED STATES EMBASSY

An event took place on September 18, 1998 that further strained U.S.–Liberia relations. The United States claimed that Taylor's forces, specifically including his Police Chief Joe Tate, attacked the U.S. Embassy and killed some U.S. personnel. At the State Department those in charge of Liberian policy were appalled and demanded that President Taylor apologize to the U.S.[1]

Let us examine the charge carefully. As described before, Roosevelt Johnson, a Krahn, served as an official in the Finance Ministry under President Samuel Doe. During the civil war, Johnson headed the anti-Taylor faction known as ULIMO–J.

Once he became president, Charles Taylor was urged by the U.S. State Department to include some of the opposition leaders in his cabinet. He did so, and named Roosevelt Johnson as Minister of Rural Development. Johnson and his followers moved to an area of Monrovia known as Camp Johnson Road. It became an armed Krahn enclave and no one could pass through the area without being stopped and searched. In effect, Roosevelt Johnson set up his own city-state within Monrovia, which is an open city. The situation became intolerable to the residents of the capital city. This led Taylor to remove Johnson from his cabinet. But to preserve good relations with Johnson and the Krahn ethnic group, he named him as Liberian Ambassador to India.[2]

Shortly thereafter Johnson suffered a mild stroke and asked Taylor for financial help to travel to the United States for medical attention. Taylor gave Johnson $46,000 to cover the cost of his treatment. Despite Taylor's largesse, the Liberian government received reports that Johnson was in the United States raising funds for an attack on Taylor.[3] While in the States, Johnson accused the Taylor government of killing five of his fighters. There was much uproar between the Taylor government and Johnson's supporters over the charges. The tension eased when the fighters were found unharmed in Banjul, The Gambia.

On August 10, 1998 Johnson returned to Liberia, and along with his ULIMO–J supporters, again took up residence at Camp Johnson Road. Residents and motorists complained of the renewed harassment by Johnson's men. Businessmen and property owners with legitimate claims were prevented from resettling on Camp Johnson Road. Ordinary residents in the area abandoned their homes out of fear and intimidation.

President Taylor made clear his concern over Johnson's activities but said he hoped to meet with Johnson and resolve their differences. Johnson asked for a meeting with President Taylor which was granted for August 28, 1998 at the Executive Mansion. Members of the clergy and leaders of the Krahn community also were invited. Johnson never appeared.

As matters worsened, on the evening of September 18, 1998 intelligence reports indicated that a move to topple the government was underway. Roosevelt Johnson was heard over the radio net saying: "We have 200 men and we are marching all the way to Congo Town to get rid of that damn Charles Taylor man." Several Liberian citizens were abducted by Johnson's men and held hostage as human shields. At 6:30pm, Johnson's men forced their way into The Pepper Bush, a supper club that was about to host a party attended by many government dignitaries. Brandishing cutlasses and rifles, Johnson's men injured 12 people. Miss Naomi Teahway was abducted as a hostage, as was Emmanuel

Gardiner, Taylor's Budget Director. Both of them confirmed overhearing several telephone calls between Roosevelt Johnson and the American Embassy in Monrovia. Johnson told his captives that he was negotiating a possible rescue plan for him and his men to be coordinated by ECOMOG and the U.S. Embassy in the event they were over run by government forces.[4] Although he had shown restraint until this incident, President Taylor finally ordered the government forces to retake the Camp Johnson Road, which they did, at a cost of at least 52 deaths and 49 wounded.

President Taylor addressed the nation on radio, informing the public that he had exercised great patience in handling the conflict but finally had to act, and that the owners of homes on Camp Johnson Road which Roosevelt Johnson had appropriated could return to their homes and normal activities since the operation had ended. Further, the President reassured the citizenry that this was not an ethnic matter, that many Krahn citizens were part of the Taylor government and that they assisted in the effort to remove Roosevelt Johnson from his armed enclave in the middle of the city.

Later Taylor sent some members of his Joint Security Force to occupy a house he had obtained from the Jallah family on Camp Johnson Road in order to conduct surveillance on the activities of persons in the area. At about three o'clock in the afternoon, as the security people were taking up their posts, they were fired upon by Johnson's fighters and driven back. The Johnson group then set up illegal roadblocks in their area. Throughout the night they fired rifles and rocket propelled grenades. The citizens of the area panicked and sought refuge from the indiscriminate shooting.

Early in the morning of September 19, a group of Roosevelt Johnson's men left Camp Johnson Road and headed toward the Barclay Training Center (BTC, where the Armed Forces of Liberia—the AFL—were quartered) and the Executive Mansion. At that point, the government Joint Security Force was ordered to engage the advancing forces of Roosevelt Johnson. Several members of the AFL were gunned down. The Joint Security Forces said that they had monitored calls from Johnson announcing his intention to assault Government facilities including the Executive Mansion and the President's residence. After a fierce battle at the BTC, the Joint Security Force, supplemented by reinforcements from the Military Police, dislodged the Johnson people. They fled toward Mamba Point, the location of the U.S. Embassy.

Roosevelt Johnson and a group of his followers arrived at the gates of the American Embassy. The Police Chief Joe Tate arrived shortly thereafter and consulted with John Bauman, the Chargé d'Affaires of the Embassy. Tate radioed the Justice Minister that the co-conspirators were trying to enter the embassy. According to the Liberian government, Tate then left. According to the United States, Tate first whispered orders to his men to attack. (Tate vehemently denied this). A Liberian police officer attempted to arrest one of Johnson's armed fighters who ran toward the embassy. An embassy guard who was outside the gate tried to obstruct the arrest. At that moment a second Liberian police officer came to assist and was shot and killed by the Embassy guard. Fighting broke out among the security forces of the government, armed loyalists of Roosevelt Johnson, and U.S. embassy guards. The U.S. later claimed that the Liberians had killed two Americans. The United Nations Mission report rejects that claim. Two U.S. Embassy staff were injured, but they were hired security personnel and not Americans. Johnson and 24 of his men were taken into the U.S. Embassy for sanctuary. The U.S. insisted that it rejected their pleas for sanctuary and, unbeknownst to the Americans, they slipped into the embassy. That statement did not seem credible. One who has visited the U.S. Embassy in Liberia knows that no person can sneak in undetected. The entry has iron gates and a guardhouse manned by U.S. Marines. A more credible explanation was that the U.S. allowed Roosevelt Johnson and his men to enter the U.S. Embassy. Although there is a video camera mounted to the building to monitor visitors, the tape of that particular event somehow disappeared.[5]

Thereafter the United States angrily demanded an apology by the Liberian government for "attacking the U.S. Embassy." Ambassador Diggs and the U.S counsel to Liberia discussed the matter with the U.S. Department of State. The U.S. and Liberian views diverged greatly, however, both sides agreed to work together to find the truth. In a spirit of accommodation, Diggs and counsel suggested that a joint investigation be undertaken. Initially the U.S. agreed; they began discussion of the Terms of Reference. At this point, Ambassador Jeter was called out of the meeting. When he returned, he said it was inappropriate for the U.S. to participate in an investigation, thus making the exercise irrelevant. Shortly thereafter in Liberia, the counsel went to view the bullet holes in the U.S. Embassy for which the Liberians supposedly were responsible, but found none. John Bauman (the U.S. Chargé d'Affaires who had a flair for the melodramatic—he reportedly walked around the Embassy wearing a metal helmet), who saw everything that happened, was suddenly whisked away from his post and never seen in Liberia again. His testimony never was taken.

The United States then closed the embassy and said it would not open it again until it received an apology from the Liberian government. The negotiators argued that first there should be an investigation and, if it proved that the Liberians were in the wrong, an apology would immediately be forthcoming. The U.S. rejected that view and demanded an apology first. The compromise was a letter from the Liberian government stating that if the facts turned to be as the U.S. claimed, they would apologize.[6] Soon the international community raised questions about "possible human rights abuses during the shoot-out." President Taylor's position was that this was a false accusation against his government, since the U.S. arrived at its conclusions without a full investigation of the facts. Accordingly the government of Liberia requested a United Nations information-gathering mission to look into the situation. The UN agreed, and a mission worked in the area from May 7 to 25, 1999.

UNITED NATIONS INFORMATION-GATHERING MISSION

The lengthy report of the UN Mission tended to confirm most of the allegations of the Liberian government. For example, the report stated:

> Independent eyewitness accounts stated that Roosevelt Johnson and several hundred of his supporters had literally colonized the Camp Johnson Road area of the city and operated there with a certain measure of 'protection' from ECOMOG forces. Government Security Forces...seldom ventured into the enclave. The Camp Johnson Road area virtually became 'a state within a state,' and there were frequent exchanges of gun fire between government security forces and supporters of Roosevelt Johnson.[7]

The report did not cover the so-called "attack" on the U.S. Embassy, saying only that it "was seen as a bilateral issue which had been mutually settled between the Government of the Republic of Liberia and the United States of America."

The report referred to Roosevelt Johnson's testimony: "He claimed that he and his supporters in the area did not have any offensive weapons except for seven pieces of weaponry kept for their personal security." However the Mission concluded that Johnson was not telling the truth and indeed that "the duration of the gun battle indicates that both government forces and Roosevelt Johnson's supporters were in possession of a sizeable quantity of arms and ammunition."

Three other conclusions of the UN Mission are included here. The first dealt with the immediate cause of the events. It refers to,

> an expanding enclave in the Camp Johnson Road area, occupied almost exclusively by Roosevelt Johnson's supporters, most of them belonging to Johnson's Krahn ethnic group and described by various government and other testimony depositors as unruly and arrogant bullies who inhibited access to the area even by the government security and other officials, and was a provocative challenge to the sovereign authority of the government over the country as a whole The Government decided to confront the challenge posed by Roosevelt Johnson and his supporters by asserting authority over the area.

It should be noted that one of those "unruly and arrogant bullies" who somehow "slipped into," and was given asylum by the U.S. Embassy on September 18, 1998 was Joe Wylie. Wylie becomes the top Military Advisor to the rebel group known as LURD which is terrorizing the Liberian people. Second, regarding President Taylor, they wrote:

> President Taylor has openly complained that ECOMOG tried to conduct business as if it was a parallel government in Liberia, which, if true, could not, according to him, be tolerated by the legitimate and popularly elected government of Liberia.

Finally, and most important, the report of the United Nations Mission concluded:

> While the Members of the Mission are fully aware that it is not within the terms of their mandate to make any recommendations or pass any judgement, they feel impelled to mention a recurrent theme voiced by virtually all their interlocutors. It is the grave concern felt all around that the international community, particularly Liberia's donor countries, should not abandon Liberia; rather, that they should return to Liberia and extend badly needed assistance in the country's efforts to undertake the daunting task of reconciliation, reconstruction and development after a debilitating civil war. The Mission's interlocutors strongly pleaded that the ordinary people of Liberia should not be punished for whatever wrongs their leaders may be rightly or wrongly accused of.

The United States rejected the advice of the mission, cut off most aid (other than food) to Liberia, and urged other nations to do likewise (as also discussed in Chapter 4). The international community followed the U.S.'s lead. The unwarranted accusations of the United States against the Liberians had devastating consequences to the reconstruction effort. Specifically, at the Paris Donor Meeting of April 8, 1998 the international donor community committee approved—but did not pay out—$220 million in support of the first phase of the Government of Liberia's National Reconstruction Program. A communique from the donor countries stated:

> Following the security incidents of September 18, 1998, which seemed to throw into doubt the return of sustainable peace to Liberia, donors postponed

consideration of all new funding pending an international independent inquiry. The planned multi-donor assessment mission also was postponed.

Then, seemingly in support of the conclusions regarding the incident at the U.S. Embassy, the donor nations issued the following statement:

> Following conclusion of the inquiry and review of its report at a donor meeting convened in Washington to coincide with the 1999 Annual Meetings of the World Bank and the International Monetary Fund, it was decided to go ahead with the organization of the donor assessment mission, as agreed in Paris, as a basis for considering new support.[8]

Accordingly, a multi-donor assessment mission visited Liberia from November 15 to 19, 1999. At the conclusion of their visit, they stated: "The mission confirmed that, by and large, progress had been made in the implementation of the first phase of the National Reconstruction Program, in spite of financial and human resource constraints."

Other findings of the group:

- E.U., USAID, and the Netherlands aid thus far to the Health, Education and Agriculture ministries was being utilized "with much positive impact.

- Positive results have been attained in the areas of resettlement and the rehabilitation of war-damaged infrastructure.

- The mission recognized that the overall security situation in the last two years had improved although ongoing apprehension remains.

- The general security situation is no longer a major impediment to the social and economic development of the country, as confirmed by GOL, NGO's and the private sector.

- "Given that insecurity in one country has spillover effects on the entire West Africa sub-region, the mission commended the positive role played by President Taylor of Liberia in the negotiations leading to the Lome Peace Agreement, and urged the Liberian government to continue its current efforts to help maintain sustainable peace in the region.

- The mission welcomed the recent efforts by the GOL and the Judiciary to restore the effectiveness of the court system and confidence in the rule of law.

- The mission commended GOL (the Government of Liberia) for establishing a program for good governance which could be a springboard for its anti-corruption efforts.

- Respect for human rights has recently been bolstered by the reinstitution of training programs at the Liberian National Police Academy. There is also evidence that disciplinary actions are being taken to address the culture of impunity in the security forces.

- The mission recommends the intensification of the dialogue with GOL focused on poverty alleviation and economic growth...identification of possible sources of funding support for the needs of GOL in training, restructuring and rationalization of the security forces with the assistance of the donor community [note that the U.S. had denied any ICITAP assistance to help train the security forces]; identification of possible sources of funding for the capacity building needs of the GOL with the assistance of the donor community; and the establishment of an active privatization program supported by donors in the context of increased participation of the private sector in Liberia [note that the U.S. had refused to grant Liberia OPIC assistance in that regard].

No American reader of the press ever read this assessment of Liberia's progress because it never was printed. At the same time the U.S. Department of State publicly berated the Liberian government and emphasized its violations of human rights.

On March 13, 2002, the Associated Press reported that,

President Charles Taylor pardoned 21 top government officials and military officers jailed in a violent 1998 uprising in Liberia in the alleged attempt to force him from power. The 21, all members of the late Samuel Doe's ethnic Krahn tribe, had been convicted of treason after a three-day outbreak of fighting in Liberia's capital in 1998. The officials and officers had been accused of siding with former Liberian warlord Roosevelt Johnson, whose forces engaged government troops in running battles in the streets of Monrovia at the time...Johnson and some of his supporters sought refuge in the American Embassy after the uprising, and were flown out of the country...Taylor called it proof of his 'commitment to true reconciliation' after the West Africa nation's devastating civil strife of the 1990s.

NOTES

[1] Meeting between Ambassador Rachel Gbenyon Diggs, U.S. legal counsel to Liberia (author) and U.S. Deputy Assistant Undersecretary Howard Jeter and the Liberian Country Officer.

[2] Republic of Liberia, *Presidential Papers. Vol. I*, Liberian Department of Public Affairs, 1998, p.57.

[3] Ibid., p.57.

[4] Ibid., p.58.

[5] Personal communication with U.S. Embassy officials in Monrovia.

[6] Personal communication with Liberian Ambassador Rachel Diggs.

[7] United Nations, "Report of the United Nations Information Gathering Mission to Liberia, May 7–5, 1999," released 18 June 1999, p.12.

[8"] Communique of Multi-Donor Assessment Mission to Liberia (November 15–19, 1999)," p.1.

CHAPTER 6
REGIONAL RELATIONSHIPS AND SANCTIONS

On the west coast of Africa lie two other small countries whose fates are inextricably intertwined with the fate of Liberia: Sierra Leone and Guinea. As previously discussed, Sierra Leone was colonized by Great Britain and Guinea colonized by France. Together the three are known as the Mano River Union.

CHARLES TAYLOR AND SIERRA LEONE

From 1991 to 1999, civil war engulfed Sierra Leone. The goals of the competing forces were power, revenge, and control of the country's rich diamond fields. In recent years that bloody battle crossed national borders to Liberia and Guinea. Only when the media reported, and more importantly, showed horrifying pictures of the atrocities that were perpetrated in Sierra Leone did the world pay attention to the war crimes and human rights violations. The combatants, who mutilated children and adults by amputating their limbs, were universally condemned as barbaric.

Charles Taylor supported the Revolutionary United Front (RUF), the major faction in Sierra Leone that sought to topple the government. Despite his protestations to the contrary, evidence suggests that President Taylor took diamonds smuggled out of Sierra Leone by the RUF, sold those diamonds on the international market, and used a portion of the proceeds to purchase weapons, which he then supplied to the RUF. At some point Taylor stopped aiding the RUF and assisted the Sierra Leonean peace process that attempted to end the horrors and restore order to the country. Analysts have disagreed as to when Taylor ceased supporting the RUF; there are some indications that it ended earlier than the U.S. contended. Ultimately, Charles Taylor's role in the Sierra Leone civil war led to his indictment "for his acts and omissions" by the Special Court of Sierra Leone. The document was signed March 7, 2003, but not disclosed until June 4, 2003, when President Taylor was in Akosombo, Ghana; he was attending the start of the peace conference that was to resolve the armed conflict between the government of Liberia, and the rebel groups, Liberians United for Democracy (the LURD), and the Movement for Democracy in Liberia (MODEL), his departure from the presidency, the establishment of an interim government, and elections for a new president and administration. The 17-count indictment states in part in paragraph 20:

> To obtain access to the mineral wealth of the Republic of Sierra Leone, in particular the diamond wealth of Sierra Leone, and to destabilize the State, the ACCUSED provided financial support, military training, personnel, arms, ammunition and other support and encouragement to the RUF, led by FODAY SAYBANA SANKOH, in preparation for RUF armed action in the Republic of Sierra Leone, and during the subsequent armed conflict in Sierra Leone.[1]

Although the warrant and indictment were delivered to the Ghanaian government, Ghana's president declined to arrest and transfer him to the United Nations Special Court for Sierra Leone in Freetown (the capital city). Further details of this incident and its aftermath are discussed in the Epilogue.

MOMOH AND TAYLOR HOSTILITIES

In 1990 President Momoh of Sierra Leone inserted himself indirectly into the civil war in nearby Liberia by rejecting Charles Taylor's request for safe haven and refusing to support his effort to topple the corrupt and murderous Liberian reign of Samuel Doe. Instead Momoh sold his support to Samuel Doe. By these actions, he precipitated the basis for later actions against him. The most important development was Taylor's punishment of Momoh by sponsoring a group of Sierra Leonean exiles, called the Revolutionary United Front (RUF), led by Foday Sankoh, a former army corporal, who opposed the Momoh government.

According to the New York Times (January 31, 1999):

> Mr. Sankoh...founded the Revolutionary United Front in 1991, saying he was disgusted with the mismanagement and corruption of successive civilian governments. (He)...directed his guerillas from the bush. He has been seen in the outside world only a few times and is said to inspire religious devotion among his followers, an unknown number of whom are now fighting on his behalf and demanding his release.[2]

In the early 1960s, Sankoh served under the UN flag in the Belgian Congo. He is said to have never forgiven the United Nations for "allowing" the assassination in 1961 of Congolese Prime Minister Patrice Lumumba, whom Sankoh cites as a revolutionary inspiration for Africa. Former U.S. Ambassador to Sierra Leone John Hirsch wrote: "Whether the RUF is to be understood as a revolutionary group or a gang of criminals, the significant fact has been its staying power and the remarkable loyalty of its cadres to Foday Sankoh."[3] Either because of Sankoh, or in spite of him, his followers later perpetrated horrors that shocked the world.

In 1991 Taylor's NPFL found itself under siege by the newly formed ECOMOG (the military force of ECOWAS, the Economic Community of West African States, which was, for all intents and purposes, controlled by Nigeria). According to Ambassador Hirsch,

> Sierra Leonean RUF elements were fighting alongside NPFL forces in Liberia. When President Momoh allowed ECOMOG to use Lungi International Airport in Sierra Leone as an assembly point for Nigerian fighter planes (in range of NPFL positions), and dispatched Sierra Leone Army forces to join other ECOMOG units in Liberia, Taylor retaliated by supporting the Revolutionary United Front's incursion into Sierra Leone, including the provision of arms and ammunition.[4]

Taylor was not the only person seeking revenge against what he perceived to be the betrayals of Momoh. One finds a motive for Sankoh's actions in the period of 1968 to 1985, when Siaka Stevens governed Sierra Leone. Stevens turned Sierra Leone's fragile democracy into a one-party state and corrupted the army, the judiciary, the police, the educational system, and politicians of all stripes, according to Ambassador Hirsch. The country was well on its way to insolvency when Stevens handed over power in 1990 to his chosen successor, General Joseph Momoh. John Hirsch explained:

> Contrary to the conventional wisdom, control of Sierra Leone's alluvial diamond fields was not the motivating factor for the RUF invasion of 1991. Sankoh had been imprisoned in the 1970s for a foiled coup attempt against Siaka Stevens, and was thirsting for revenge against Momoh, his (Stevens') chosen successor...Exploitation of the alluvial diamond fields has been a major factor, however, in the war's continuation. For the RUF, the Kailahun district in eastern Sierra Leone became the command center for its operations; for Taylor, it was important to maintain a close relationship with the RUF as he

(Taylor) fought against other Liberian factions in his quest for control in Liberia.[5]

With this complicated background, the relationships were formed for very different reasons. Ambassador Hirsch says of the Momoh regime:

> The government hit bottom when it stopped paying schoolteachers and the educational system collapsed. The growing population of unemployed rural young men in the 1980s was to become the RUF's rank and file in the 1990s. The emergence of the RUF was a reflection of the state's failure to provide education, vocational training and economic opportunity to a whole generation of youths who grew up seeing no future for themselves.[6]

However one assesses the RUF—or the thousands of mercenaries fighting on all sides of African wars—author James Baldwin's perspicacious comment in his 1963 book, *The Fire Next Time,* applies: "The most dangerous creation of any society is that man who has nothing to lose." Baldwin's words should act as a global alarm bell. As the Sierra Leone conflict showed, abject poverty and the absence of opportunity were the breeding grounds of violence, as a group of unemployed young people became rebels.

By 1991, Momoh's government had disintegrated—it could not even provide its troops with food. In 1992, a group of young officers, led by 26-year-old Captain Valentine Strasser, staged a coup which ousted Momoh. The new President Strasser pledged to end corruption, but within two years everyone realized that his junta had lost control of its troops, which pillaged whole cities, factories and mining operations. The New York Times reported that the young officers enriched themselves in the country's diamond mines—"tapped since by the Government and the rebels to finance their war effort."[7]

Over the objections of the junta, a national election was held in 1996 and Ahmad Tejan Kabbah became president. In the months leading up to the vote, a broad range of Western diplomats and UN officials, and most particularly the U.S. Ambassador to Sierra Leone, John Hirsch, encouraged and generated the resolve that sent thousands of Sierra Leoneans to the polls.

Despite its support for the election of Kabbah, the international community, after the vote, remained aloof from Sierra Leone. They expected Kabbah to transform Sierra Leone into a functioning state, although there had been no organized government for many years. Read the words of Joseph Opala, an American anthropologist who lived for 17 years in Sierra Leone (part of it with the U.S. Peace Corps). Opala was the founder of the Campaign for Good Governance that led to the 1996 elections in Sierra Leone, and now is an adjunct professor at James Madison University in Virginia:

> Once it was clear the election had succeeded, hundreds of people gathered spontaneously outside the U.S. embassy to express their gratitude. The lone white American in the crowd, I had never been prouder of my country, or its ambassador...today, I am crying once again—but this time tears of rage and sorrow. Rage at the international community's failure to follow through, and sorrow at what has now happened. Since that hopeful day in 1996, Sierra Leone has endured the continued slaughter of thousand of its citizens and the mutilation of thousands more...some 500 UN peacekeepers were kidnaped by the thugs who were invited into the government by diplomats from other nations, including my own. I firmly believe this madness would have stopped long ago if the international community had recognized the situation in Sierra

Leone for what it was—not a civil war, but civil chaos, following the collapse of government—and had been willing to take the appropriate action.[8]

With regard to Kabbah, Opala wrote:

> The entire political elite, including most of Kabbah's cabinet, were all corrupt— and worse, inept. Kabbah began discrediting himself almost immediately. Although 40 percent of his people were then living in refugee camps, he saw no reason to visit them. He waited months to announce his agenda, and when he did, it was a wish list of impossible dreams…The international community pledged millions in aid, but Kabbah could not even manage to submit the paperwork necessary to obtain the funds.[9]

On May 27, 1997, the Armed Forces Revolutionary Council (AFRC) was joined by the RUF and staged a coup that toppled the Kabbah government and held the capital for nine months. After the coup, the AFRC suspended the constitution, banned political activities and public meetings, and invited the rebel fighters of the RUF to join the junta. A West African force composed primarily of Nigerians returned Kabbah to power in February of 1998. Angered after the government's public execution in Freetown of 24 soldiers involved in the 1997 coup and the death sentence handed down against their leader Foday Sankoh (it later was lifted as part of the Lomé Accord), the rebels, joined by the new Armed Forces Revolutionary Council (AFRC), again terrorized Freetown in January of 1999. They murdered and raped their way across a city of million people, and in the process hacked off the limbs of thousands of inhabitants. In July of 1999 diplomats from the United States, Britain, the United Nations and several African nations brokered a peace deal with the rebels. Sankoh and his followers were granted positions in the government and amnesty for their crimes in exchange for an agreement to disarm. Yet, in May of 2000, the RUF kidnapped and disarmed some 500 U.N. peacekeepers. In characterizing Kabbah, Sankoh, Strasser, or Momoh, the question was not good versus bad—but rather bad versus worse. While the international community portrays Kabbah as a competent president, the facts speak to the contrary.

John L. Hirsch, Vice President of the International Peace Academy and U.S. Ambassador to Sierra Leone in 1995–1998 concluded in 2001 (in an article written for "Survival," a publication of the International Institute for Strategic Studies), that "various strategies over the past four years—first to defeat the RUF, then to include it in an expanded government, and subsequently to place its leadership before an international war tribunal— reflect the uncertainty and vacillation of the international response."[10]

Because the U.S. State Department was well aware of the historic relationship between Charles Taylor and the RUF, it asked Taylor if he could exercise his influence with Foday Sankoh to help gain the release of the U.N. hostages. Taylor agreed to try and indeed succeeded in obtaining the release of the 500 U.N. prisoners. Privately the State Department expressed its appreciation to Taylor—but never publicly.

On October 20, 1999, the Department requested its embassy in Liberia to deliver a message from Secretary of State Madeleine Albright to President Taylor. The embassy was cautioned that "no signed original will follow." They did not allow Taylor the chance to demonstrate publicly that he received approval of the U.S. government for his actions. The text of the message from Secretary Albright included the following language:

> Dear Mr. President:
>
> I would like to extend my sincere appreciation and gratitude to you for the critical role you have played recently in supporting the peace process in Sierra

Leone. Your work in promoting dialogue among key players and persuading the rebel leaders to return to Freetown is an important contribution to the implementation of the Lomé accord...While I regret that I am unable to visit Liberia on my trip later this month, I want to thank you for your recent support of regional peace.[11]

This message never was made public, and, concurrent with its issuance, the State Department continued to castigate Liberia as the main supporter of the RUF.

In discussing the disconnect between what was said publicly versus privately, Howard Jeter, U.S. Deputy Assistant Secretary of State, commented that President Taylor's action in convincing the RUF to release the 500 U.N. hostages proved that he was "in" with the RUF. If Taylor had refused to help the U.S. in convincing the RUF to free the hostages, he would have been accused of siding with the RUF. By actually facilitating the release of the hostages, he was accused of siding with the RUF. Taylor had a "damned if you do and damned if you don't" position.

The RUF initially was a movement organized to oppose a corrupt government—but later members of the RUF were responsible for some of the worst human rights violations imaginable, namely the mutilation and amputation of limbs of thousands of Sierra Leoneans, including many innocent children. Yet, even as that carnage took place, the Lomé agreement, which gave the RUF a stake in the Sierra Leone government, was signed in Togo in July of 1999 with the support and encouragement of the United States government.

The inclusion of Foday Sankoh in a new government and the granting of amnesty for the atrocities committed by him and his followers offended many. Even more surprising was the provision that gave Sankoh's men control of the diamond mines which many felt was the real cause of the civil uprisings in Sierra Leone. U.S. Secretary of State Madeleine Albright defended the U.S. policy that approved of the Lomé Accord, and which gave the RUF the right to control the diamond mines. On October 19, 1999, Karl Vick of the Washington Post wrote about Secretary of State Albright's visit the previous day to Sierra Leone at the start of a six-country African tour:

> At her next stop in Freetown, the capital, Albright met with leaders of the rebel forces who committed the atrocities during eight years of chaos and killing that have left this West African country in shambles. They are reviled figures who nevertheless have received amnesty and are headed for senior government positions by dint of a peace deal that U.S. officials helped broker. The Secretary, who would not be photographed with the rebels, defended giving them immunity, calling it the price of a peace so desperately needed after a struggle for power in which severing limbs was a common rebel tactic. But even as she took pains to bolster the fragile accord—the rebels have not begun disarming as promised—Albright also acknowledged that it fails to satisfy a fundamental yearning for justice...As part of the peace deal, Foday Sankoh, leader of the rebel Revolutionary United Front, was named head of a commission that will determine the fate of the country's diamond mines...Albright met briefly with Sankoh, and the other major rebel leader, Johnny Paul Koroma, at the residence of the U.S. Ambassador.[12]

Human Rights Watch said: "...U.S. policy toward Sierra Leone failed to attract high level attention within the administration. Most U.S. officials continued to defend the amnesty under Lomé, despite the February report by David Scheffer, ambassador at large for war crime issues, who reported the ongoing atrocities and abuses, and acknowledged the inadequacy of mechanisms for accountability."[13] Mary McGrory, writing in the Washington Post on April 20, 2000 described the Lomé Accord as "insane" because it included "blanket amnesty to warlords and the handing over of the country's greatest treasure, its diamonds, to those same warlords."

UNITED NATIONS INTERVENTION

The United Nations in 1999 appointed a Panel of Experts to go to the region and report back to the body on the situation in Sierra Leone. Its report confirmed that the international community, specifically including the U.S., had put the fox in charge of the chicken coop. The U.N. report said: "The Lomé Peace Agreement appointed Foday Sankoh Chairman of a Commission for the Management of Strategic Mineral Resources (CMRRD)"…meaning the diamond fields.[14] But the original RUF interest in diamonds took place years earlier, in 1997, when Foday Sankoh was imprisoned in Nigeria. The UN report stated:

> Until 1995…the RUF diamond mining and digging was probably done on a sporadic and individual basis. By 1995, however, the RUF and its patrons were clearly taking a much greater interest in the diamond fields of the Kono District, and had to be removed forcefully at that time by the private military company, Executive Outcomes, a South African mercenary group. From then on, the RUF interest in diamonds became more focused, especially with the 1997 imprisonment of Foday Sankoh in Nigeria.[15]

Most observers of the Sierra Leone scene agree that it was a mistake to let Executive Outcomes cease its activities, especially when the UN peacekeepers took over and demonstrated an almost total lack of effectiveness in dealing with the RUF. Executive Outcomes allegedly was terribly expensive, and no country was willing to put up the money to continue their contract. In terms of cost effectiveness, this was, to say the least, a short-sighted decision. Ambassador Hirsch says that "President Kabbah's precipitate decision in January 1997 to have Executive Outcomes leave the country…proved a fatal mistake."

After Foday Sankoh returned to Freetown in 1999, "he signed numerous agreements with international business firms…in the name of the CMRRD Commission and in the name of the RUF." The UN Report stated:

> In November, 1999, for example, Foday Sankoh received a visit from Chudi Izegbu, President of the Integrated Group of Companies based in McLean, Virginia…They discussed…a major investment in the Koidu diamond kimberlites…and they exchanged test messages in a code which would allow them to disguise names…like 'diamonds' and 'gold.'[16]

The UN Report also said:

> In March 2000, Damian Gagnon of the U.S. company, Lazare Kaplan International (LKI), visited Foday Sankoh, and in a subsequent letter to Sankoh, LKI Chairman Maurice Tempelsman [who most Americans know as the long-time companion of Jacqueline Kennedy] said that Gagnon had reported 'a commonality of views between you and this company on the possibilities of LKI entering the Sierra Leone diamond business in a manner beneficial to all the people of that country as well as our company.'[17]

This took place contemporaneously with the accusations that Foday Sankoh oversaw the hacking off of limbs of Sierra Leonean children. Yet there were no press reports about these U.S. companies doing business with Sankoh when any enterprising reporter easily could have obtained the UN report which was a public document.

The UN Report stated that "Michel Desaedeleer, a U.S. based, self-employed Belgian, made contact with the RUF...during the summer of 1999 and...by October he and John Caldwell, President of the Washington, D.C. based U.S. Trading & Investment Company, had worked up an arrangement with Foday Sankoh which would give them authority to broker rights to all of Sierra Leone's diamond and gold resources for a ten-year period."[18]

There was no conclusive evidence that any of the above companies were involved in the diamonds-for-weapons trade. According to the UN Panel of Experts, they were doing business with Foday Sankoh at the very time his RUF compatriots were committing atrocities...and at a time when the United States government, as well as the United Nations, were urging nations, companies and individuals not to engage in trade in "conflict" diamonds or, as the media dubbed them "blood diamonds."

The UN Panel of Experts Report, however, made clear that many countries were involved in this illicit trade. For example, the neighboring country of Guinea. "...RUF diamonds have been traded in Guinea. There are reports of one-off deals in which RUF commanders have traded diamonds for supplies, and sometimes for weapons, dealing with individual, mid-level Guinean military officers acting on their own account."[19] Yet the U.S. State Department, while condemning Liberia, said nothing about Guinea's complicity—and indeed regularly has sent financial assistance to Guinea.

The UN Report describes the presence of "40 separate diamond dealers, many of them Lebanese" in the diamond center of Kenema in Sierra Leone. "It is...likely...that these diamonds are being smuggled out to neighbouring countries."[20]

The New York Times on June 4, 2000, in a story with the headline "How U.S. Left Sierra Leone Tangled in a Curious Web" reported that

> at the State Department, an administration official said, three high-ranking officials—Harold H. Koh, U.S. assistant secretary of state for human rights; David J. Scheffer, the ambassador at large for war crimes; and Julia V. Taft, the assistant secretary of state for refugees—recorded their opposition to giving Mr. Sankoh a role in the government...'Bring Sankoh into the government? Make him the head diamond counter? What were we thinking?' said another American official.

On May 9, 2000, Senator Judd Gregg of New Hampshire wrote an OpEd article that condemned the Lomé Accord, when he wrote:

> Inexplicably, our diplomats gave the RUF at the negotiating table all the things it could not capture on the battlefield. The Lomé Accord granted total amnesty to the RUF, promised reintegration of the RUF into the Sierra Leonean army, assured the RUF of several cabinet seats in the 'transition' government, left the RUF in control of the diamond mines, and invited RUF leader Foday Sankoh to participate in the UN-sponsored elections. It was surrender at its most abject...The West abandoned (the people of Sierra Leone) to their fate.[21]

Then second, Senator Gregg condemned Charles Taylor.

> Let me start with an unhappy truth. There can be no peace in Sierra Leone until the strongman of neighboring Liberia, Charles Taylor is brought to

heel…Liberian leader Taylor and his criminal gang must go; every feasible effort ought to be made to undermine his rule."[22]

The New York Times commented further:

> …(T)he British were conspicuous as the one Western power willing to shore up the faltering United Nations peacekeeping force. To many, their presence merely emphasized the absence of the United States, which last year was a major backer of the peace agreement that granted amnesty to a brutal warlord, Foday Sankoh, and even brought him into government.[23]

Charles Taylor was consistently accused by the United States of sending weapons to Sierra Leone, and bearing responsibility for the use of these weapons in the horrific human rights violations. Yet other parties supplied weapons to Sierra Leone. U.S. Secretary of State Colin Powell stated his position in remarks to the press while visiting Bamako, Mali on May 23, 1001: "Certainly Charles Taylor cannot take all the responsibility for the problems in the regions, but I think he bears a large portion of the responsibility."[24] Secretary Powell mentioned other parties, but did not name them specifically, instead maintaining his focus on Taylor's role.

The London Sunday Times on January 10, 1999 published an article, titled, "British Firms Arming Sierra Leone Rebels." The story read:

> Two British firms are at the centre of a suspected sanctions-busting operation in which weapons have been supplied to rebels in Sierra Leone. Last night it emerged that the companies have secretly flown tons of guns and ammunition to Africa. Aircrew involved in the operations say that the weapons have ended up with rebels (RUF) battling to overthrow the government of President Ahmed Tejan Kabbah…Sky Air Cargo of London and Occidental Airlines, which is part-owned by a British pilot, are using aging Boeing planes to transport AK-47 rifles and 60mm portable mortars. The trade could breach the United Nations embargo on arms to Sierra Leone. The two companies have also supplied arms to rebels fighting to overthrow President Laurent Kabila in the Congo…The revelation will embarrass Robin Cook, the foreign secretary. Last year Sky Air Cargo was named as one of the companies that helped to fly AK–47 rifles to Kabbah's forces as part of a countercoup to restore him to power. That equipment, bought in Bulgaria, was supplied by Sandline, a company of 'military consultants' claiming to have the support of the British government. Cook and other ministers were later cleared of knowingly breaking sanctions but the affair damaged Cook.

Despite these reports of British involvement, no link was made in the media that parties in Great Britain were responsible for the mutilation of civilians.

On July 12, 2000 the President of Sierra Leone, Tejan Kabbah, denied reports by Mark Doyle of BBC that the Sierra Leone police had documentary evidence to prove that President Charles G. Taylor had supplied weapons to the Revolutionary United Front (RUF). President Kabbah told journalists at the Roberts International Airport that the accusation that President Taylor delivered weapons, including a rocket launcher and a forty-barrel artillery, to the RUF of Foday Sankoh is "false and baseless propaganda intended to divide the sub-region." He said that the BBC was making those allegations in her own interest and not his government's. The Sierra Leonean president pointed out that, even though there was a crisis in Sierra Leone, Liberia had a large role to play in the effort to restore peace. Interestingly, President Kabbah's statement contradicted the accusations that would later become part of the indictment against Charles Taylor.

On July 17, Thomas Pickering, U.S. Under Secretary of State for Political Affairs, visited President Taylor in Liberia. After his meeting Mr. Pickering spoke at an airport press briefing before his departure. He said the U.S. government "unfortunately" believed that Liberia's role in Sierra Leone had been "negative" and that there were "strong indications that Liberia has become the primary patron and benefactor of the RUF (Revolutionary United Front) rebels." The Panafrican News Agency continued:

> Pickering said Taylor had shown that he has influence with the RUF (by Taylor having arranged the release of the 500 UN hostages) and must use that influence to bring about an early return to the peace process and an end to the conflict in Sierra Leone.[25]

Then Pickering said: "If Liberia cannot play this role, then clearly there will be consequences very severe for our bilateral relationship and, I believe, the entire international community relations with Liberia. So we hope for action, and action now."[26] Shortly thereafter, the United Nations, at the insistence of the United States and Great Britain, imposed sanctions on Liberia.

The major accusation against Charles Taylor was that he received diamonds that the RUF mined in Sierra Leone, and sold them to purchase arms which were then sent back to the RUF. The U.S. claimed that it had proof that this happened. Taylor vehemently denied the charge. The U.S. legal counsel to Liberia requested to see the proof of the charges from Susan Rice, but the request was denied. Counsel asserted that, if what the United States claimed was true, and that information was divulged (as was done later in the case of Al Qaeda's role in terrorism, and Iraq's possession of weapons of mass destruction), pressure could be brought upon Taylor to stop an arms-for-diamonds swap. Citing the need to protect its sources, and the interest of national security, the United States never revealed the evidence for its accusations.

The issue of Charles Taylor's involvement with the RUF in Sierra Leone was difficult to unravel. First, as to diamonds, it was estimated that the volume mined by the RUF ranged from $25 million to $125 million per year. It was very small in relation to the global annual output of diamonds (2 million carats from Sierra Leone versus 250 million carats worldwide), yet enough to support the RUF's military effort. The UN Panel of Experts Report acknowledged that "diamonds have always been smuggled out of Sierra Leone, the bulk through Liberia. This historical fact is not in dispute...Historically, Liberia was the route of choice primarily because of its use of the United States dollar as its official currency."[27] In paragraph 86, the UN report said: "A Liberian is said to be President Taylor's representative in Kono (a diamond center), with a mandate to supervise diamond operations." "(T)here have been frequent disputes over the diamonds, and RUF couriers travel in fear of being robbed by rogue Liberian NPFL (National Patriotic Front of Liberia) fighters." The Panel then concluded in paragraph 87:

> Because of time constraints, the Panel could not go into details of ways and means through which RUF diamonds are moved out of Liberia, however there is sufficient evidence to prove that this trade cannot be conducted in Liberia without the permission and the involvement of government officials at the highest level. In Liberia, *uncorroborated stories* refer to high-level go-betweens, senior government officials, and financial transactions made in Burkina Faso, South Africa, the United States and Lebanon.[28]

In paragraph 88: "Liberian officials thrive on their country's reputation for weak administration, its crippled infrastructure and its 'porous border'. In fact, however, very little trade, whether formal or informal, takes place without the knowledge and involvement of key government officials." Finally, in paragraph 141, the UN Panel of Experts acknowledges that diamonds alleged to come from Liberia might not come from there at all: "The statistical anomalies...demonstrate that the Liberian name, and most likely the names of other countries, has been widely used by individuals and companies wishing to disguise the origin of rough diamonds."[30]

Certain sections of the report are less credible than others. In paragraphs 126 and 127, the report speaks of "an intimate Liberian connection with these deceptive diamond transactions" and then adds this sentence: "The name of retired U.S. Army General Robert A. Yerks occurs frequently in discussions about Liberian diamond transfers."[31] General Yerks is a decorated hero who devoted much of his time <u>pro bono</u> to helping the people of Liberia. In 2001 he was nominated for the Nobel Peace Prize. The general was shocked and outraged by this slur on his name. General Yerks, in his letter to the President of the UN Security Council said:

> I unequivocally state that I never have been, am not now, nor would I ever be involved in such a dastardly activity. I have trouble even visualizing anyone having a motive to so link me. The implication is reckless and baseless. I have worked for peace in Liberia since 1991 as a private citizen...My peace efforts were completely pro-bono, intended only to repair relations between the Republic of Liberia and the United States and to improve the quality of life of the fine African people.[32]

It was inconceivable that a man of his moral and ethical probity would be connected with illicit diamond trade. General Yerks confronted the Security Council and demanded a retraction. They had no evidence to back up their charges, and they finally did retract and apologize in writing. The use of hearsay by the Panel of Experts caused some skepticism regarding the report.

The Panel described the situation regarding weapons and the RUF.

> Systematic information on weapons-smuggling in the region is non-existent, and information which could be used to combat the problem on a regional scale—through ECOWAS or through bilateral exchanges—is generally not available. Few States in the region have the resources or the infrastructure to tackle smuggling, a situation that creates opportunities for the smuggling of weapons across all major borders in the region.[33]

The report stated that the AK–47 Kalashnikov rifle is the weapon of choice in Sierra Leone (Paragraph 171).

> Although a Russian design, the AK–47 is today produced in so many countries, in so many variants, that a thorough study of model numbers, serial numbers and factory markings would be required in order to determine their precise origin. After this, it might be possible to determine the supply trail of the weapons, but even this would be complicated by the fact that many may have been bought on the open market, and may be second- or even third-hand weapons.[34]

Essentially the UN had no evidence on the source of the arms.

Charles Taylor's involvement with the RUF with respect to weapons is also discussed. Paragraph 180, stated:

> The personal connection between President Charles Taylor and Foday Sankoh goes back ten years to their training in Libya, to their combined efforts on behalf of Blaise Campaore in his seizure of power in Burkina Faso, and to Sankoh's involvement in Charles Taylor's struggle as head of the NPFL to take power in Liberia in the early 1990s. These events are well documented, and President Taylor told the Panel that he was a close friend of Foday Sankoh. President Taylor denies unequivocally, however, that he or his government have provided any training to the RUF, any weapons or related materiel, any Liberian facilities or territory for staging attacks, or a safe haven.[35]

Then in paragraph 182:

> The Panel, however, found unequivocal and overwhelming evidence that Liberia has been actively supporting the RUF at all levels, in providing training, weapons and related materiel, logistical support, a staging ground for attacks and a safe haven for retreat and recuperation.[36]

The Report then cited its "proof," given by "...many former RUF leaders have confirmed this in oral testimony and in writing." Or

> '...sufficient corroborative documentary evidence in the form of written reports of RUF commanders to Foday Sankoh is also available.' 'The panel received information...' on the presence of Ukrainian, Burkinabe, Nigerien (this refers to Niger, not Nigeria), Libyan and South African nationals in Liberia for training purposes...Early in 1999, a significant improvement of tactics and use of weapons by the RUF rebels was noted in Sierra Leone. It was more than a coincidence that this happened immediately after foreigners started training these elements in Liberia.'[37]

"In addition, the police interrogation statements of some arrested RUF officials...confirm the presence of foreign mercenaries, including South Africans and Ukrainians training and fighting alongside the RUF." Sanctions were imposed upon Liberia. "There are innumerable accounts in RUF written reports...of high-level RUF meetings with President Taylor." "The Panel has found conclusive evidence of supply lines to the RUF through Burkina Faso, Niger and Liberia."[38]

On January 26, 1999, Liberia vehemently denied the charges in a document entitled "Liberia's Response to allegations of her involvement in the Sierra Leone civil war" and dismissed such accusations as "an international conspiracy spearheaded by the United States and Britain in an attempt to internationally isolate, economically destroy and politically destabilize the government of the Republic of Liberia."[39]

The document stated:

> The Liberian Government has gone beyond mere denials and has proposed numerous options by which the allegations of her involvement could be disproved including, among other things, the constitution of a joint UN/ECOMOG border patrol contingent to monitor troop movements, and the setting-up of an international board of inquiry by the United Nations Secretary-General to investigate these accusations.[40]

Neither the border patrol suggestion, nor the international board of inquiry suggestion was adopted. As to the former, the State Department said it was impossible to monitor the border between the two countries.

The Liberian document continued:

> At the core of the onslaught against Liberia is the demonstrated failure and unquestionable inability of the United States and Britain to evidentially prove their allegations against Liberia. Despite repeated challenges to authenticate their claims, the British and Americans have only relied upon rumors, speculations and a massive disinformation campaign intended to internationally isolate, economically strangulate, and diplomatically destroy Liberia…Interestingly, the Americans and the British have depended only on the unsubstantiated accounts of Sierra Leonean government officials, especially her Foreign Minister, James Jonah, a well-connected veteran of the United Nations system, who meticulously uses his connections in the world body to scape-goat Liberia by deliberately ignoring the irrefutable evidence of American and British complicity to destabilize Sierra Leone by the use of private firms and individuals.[41]

The Liberians further contended that, when President Momoh was in office,

> he approved a military partnership between the Sierra Leonean national army and the so-called ULIMO movements which consisted of Liberians who were opposed to Charles Taylor from the very beginning…and that these are the Liberians now fighting on both sides in Sierra Leone.[42]

It is doubtful that many people have taken the time to wade through the voluminous report of the UN Panel of Experts. One who does must agree there are questions concerning the authentication of some claims made in the report. Still the United States headed the effort to maintain all penalties on Liberia, despite President Taylor's work in helping to broker a Sierra Leone peace agreement.

Had the U.S. government fully supported the Nigerian-dominated ECOMOG force in Sierra Leone in ensuring a comprehensive disarmament and demobilization, followed by elections, the problem in this West African nation would not have occurred. But the failure of the West to commit support for the ECOMOG force in favor of a UN force, led to the pullout of the ECOMOG, setting the stage for armed renegades to overrun the understaffed and under-equipped UN peacekeeping force. The Nigerians' involvement in Sierra Leone was very costly to them, and when Olusegun Obasanjo became the President of Nigeria in May of 1999, he pledged to pull out. At that point the U.S. and the international community should have expanded the number of African nations involved in the ECOMOG contingent and underwritten their involvement—but they did not.

This pattern repeated itself in the context of other rebel uprisings. At the end of 2002, the government of Côte d'Ivoire found itself under attack from a rebel force and called upon ECOMOG, the West African regional peacekeeping group, to help. Nigeria is the largest contributor to ECOMOG. But on December 18, 2002, Nigeria announced that it would not send troops to Côte d'Ivoire. Nigeria's Information Minister Jerry Gana told BBC that his government reached that decision

> because it spent US $8 billion in Liberia and approximately US $8 billion in Sierra Leone, and that no compensation has been received so far. He indicated that the United States and Great Britain governments should have been at

the forefront of the collaboration with the United Nations to see how to provide some compensation in the form of debt waiver to the Nigerian Government[43]

adding, "Liberia and Sierra Leone are progenitors of the United States and Great Britain respectively."

On January 28, 1999 the Washington Post carried an editorial, titled, "The Horror in Sierra Leone." It contained the following paragraph:

> The only thing that stands between Sierra Leone's civilians and the brutal rebel force is an alliance of West African troops led by Nigeria. Since its ill-fated intervention in Somalia, the United States has encouraged precisely this kind of solution: Africans helping Africans. Yet this is not an easy mission for the Nigerians, with economic troubles of their own and a continuing democratization process that will lead to pressures to withdraw troops from foreign entanglements. They cannot possibly do the job without sustained financial, logistical and political support from the United States. And how much has the United States budgeted to support the force this year? A laughable $1.3 million.[44]

Contrast this figure with a New York Times story on January 31, 1999 reporting that "...some diplomats have suggested that (the costs incurred by Nigeria) might reach as high as $1 million a day."[45] Meaningful support never was given. To make matters worse, a question arose as to whether the $1.3 million ever was received. The testimony of Nathan Jones of International Charter Incorporated (ICI) of Oregon whose company provided helicopters to evacuate wounded civilian in Sierra Leone gave a relevant comment: "...$1.3 million in logistics aid to ECOMOG, the West African peacekeeping force, sat hostage to bureaucratic ineptitude—approved, appropriated and untouched. Without the funding, my company's helicopters sat grounded while Freetown burned."[46] Later an additional $1.7 million in logistics support was promised by the U.S. government for ECOMOG, an amount that was tragically short of the $15 million needed for the rest of 1999. In comparison, it cost $150 million to evacuate U.S. citizens from Liberia in 1996, while the U.S. ignored the tribulations of the Liberian people under attack.

On February 3, 1999, the Congressional Black Caucus sent a letter to President Clinton stating that,

> Sierra Leone is now, by all accounts, worse than Kosovo with 2,700 killed in January alone...These atrocities have reached crisis proportions and we believe that while ECOMOG is the primary peacekeeping force on the ground, the U.S. government can and should also assist the areas of humanitarian concern.

As David Halberstam commented in his book, *War in a Time of Peace*:

> Rwanda was, in the eyes of many nonwhite critics of Western geopolitics, the quintessential example not just of the indifference of Americans and Europeans to the problems in Africa, but of the double standard used in Washington and other Western capitals to judge the value of African lives compared with Western or Caucasian ones. The West, or at least part of it, they believed, agonized over events in Bosnia, violence inflicted on Europeans by Europeans, but was almost completely unconcerned about violence inflicted on Africans by Africans."[47]

There was no question that the Taylor government gave assistance to the RUF. The real question was whether this support continued during the period of Sierra Leone's most serious travails. The government of Liberia said, "No." The United States said, "Yes."

On February 19, 1999, the Liberian Ministry of Foreign Affairs, headed by Monie Captan, a Liberian diplomat highly regarded by the international community, issued an official statement on the Sierra Leonean crisis. It contained the following language:

> Liberia is sensitive to the international concerns that have been expressed regarding its alleged complicity in the Sierra Leonean crisis. The Government of Liberia is cognizant of the adverse affect that this state of affairs is having on the maintenance of peace, unity, stability and progress in Liberia, the ECOWAS sub-region and the larger international community. At the same time, the Government is outraged by the nature and level of atrocities attending the war in Sierra Leone. The use of children as soldiers and the maiming of fellow Sierra Leoneans are unconscionable. This malevolent human tragedy must be stopped.

> The Liberian Government recognizes the efforts of ECOWAS to restore and maintain peace in the Sub-region, and as a member of the Committee of Six, wishes to restate its support for the ECOWAS Peace Plan for Sierra Leone.

> In this regard, the Government of Liberia reaffirms its recognition of the elected Government of President Ahmed Tijan Kabbah as the legitimate Government of Sierra Leone. The Government of Liberia states further that it has not and will not support, nor be a party to any attempt to destabilize the Republic of Sierra Leone or any other country.

> As a democratically elected Government, the Government of Liberia has not and will not support any attempt by insurgents, including the Revolutionary United Front (RUF) and the Armed Forces Revolutionary Council (AFRC) or other armed dissidents to destabilize or remove the legitimate Government of Sierra Leone from office."[48]

The Liberian statement identified what it considered as a root cause of the charges that Liberia is helping the RUF. It said: "The Government of Liberia has consistently argued that Liberian citizens have been used as mercenaries in the Sierra Leonean conflict by successive governments of Sierra Leone, the RUF/AFRC, the Kamajors and ECOMOG.

> The Government of Liberia notes the existence of legal instruments that prohibit its nationals from serving as mercenaries. These instruments include international conventions and protocols, particularly the Non-Aggression and Security Cooperation Treaty between countries comprising the Mano River Union. Most importantly, Chapter Eleven of the Liberia Penal Code, Subsection 11.13 on Mercenaries, provides for life imprisonment or the death penalty for convicted mercenaries.

> In view of this notation, the Government of Liberia has repeatedly called on its citizens to disengage from the conflict in Sierra Leone and return home."[49]

Liberia then called for a period of voluntary repatriation of mercenaries, followed by imposition of criminal penalties on those who fail to return home.

The U.S. Embassy in Monrovia welcomed the Liberian government's initiatives on Sierra Leone, especially the call for Liberian mercenaries to return home. On February 23,

1999 the Acting Chargé d'Affaires Donald Peterson described the measures as a good attempt.

These various statements highlight what is common knowledge in the region, namely that West Africa is awash with mercenaries, both from the area and from elsewhere.

If all the above seems confusing and unclear, it is because there was no easy solution to this and to so many of the world's problems. Each one—whether Rwanda, or Kosovo, or East Timor, or Somalia—had a complicated dynamic of its own, and there was no such thing as a simple answer. H. L. Mencken once wrote that,"for every complicated problem, there is a simple solution...and it is usually wrong". Such was the situation in Sierra Leone. After many years of watching these frightening and inhumane wars, the author has concluded that either the international community must involve itself in a massive way at the beginning of the trouble, or else it will have to wait until all the participants finally tire of fighting, and the people of a country demand an end to the warfare. In the meantime, however, the civilian populace suffers inordinate hardships. Machiavelli said it well: "When trouble is sensed well in advance it can easily be remedied; if you wait for it to show itself, any medicine will be too late because the disease will have become incurable."

On November 14, 2000 Reuters carried the story of a new Sierra Leone cease-fire pact "that could lead to a truce in the West African country's 9-year-old civil war." It quoted Jeremy Greenstock, Britain's ambassador to the United Nations, as saying that "Liberian President Charles Taylor, who helped negotiate the truce, appeared to be serious in seeking an agreement."

President Taylor finally did precisely what the U.S. had asked of him, but threatened Liberia with new sanctions. Would not this have been the time to encourage Taylor to continue to act in a constructive manner? U.S. policy in this instance was counter-productive to our national interests, and the interests of Liberian citizens..

A curious incident was used by the United States to further demonize the Taylor government, which involved Sam Bockarie (known as the "Mosquito"), the former ground commander of the RUF and one of the most vicious fighters in the RUF organization in Sierra Leone. When the U.S. and Britain were trying to broker a peace agreement with the RUF, the U.S. State Department privately asked Charles Taylor if he would take Sam Bockarie to Liberia and keep him there while negotiations proceeded (Bockarie had broken with Foday Sankoh and was a disruptive influence in Sierra Leone). Taylor agreed and kept Bockarie under "house arrest" in Liberia. The international press ran stories that Sam Bockarie's presence in Liberia was proof of Taylor's complicity with the RUF. The U.S. never stated publicly that it was they who asked Taylor to take Bockarie. On February 16, 2001, the Liberian government announced the departure from the country of Sam Bockarie. Stories circulated that he remained in Liberia, again as proof that Taylor was in league with him. Even the U.S. said that Bockarie was in Liberia and that Charles Taylor had the burden to prove that he was not. On May 6, 2003, Liberian military officials announced that

> Gen. Bockarie, 40, was shot and later died of his injuries following a shoot out between Liberian troops and his loyal forces in the Liberian border town of Bin-Houn, Nimba County, May 6, 2003. The report further indicated that he attempted crossing into Liberia with arms after he reportedly killed Ivorian rebel leader Felix Doh. Following his death the war crime tribunal in Free Town demanded that the Liberian government turn over the body of Bockarie to it for forensic test. But the Liberian authorities said that they

would rather turn over the corpse to the Sierra Leonean government instead of the court.[50]

The article (June 2, 2003) also stated that "the bickering between the Liberian government and Sierra Leone's war crime court over the corpse of former rebel leader, Sam Bockarie, has been settled as the authorities in Free Town have finally received the body."

UNITED NATION SECURITY COUNCIL SANCTIONS

In February of 2001, the United Nations Security Council met to act upon the recommendation of the Panel of Experts that sanctions be imposed upon Liberia. At the time, diplomatic circles reported that Russia, France and China were opposed to sanctions. Mali, another member of the Security Council, expressed reservations about the sanctions on the grounds that the Americans and the British had not presented "hard facts" to warrant any such action against a country coming out of the ruins of a civil conflict. France said that it viewed calls for punitive action against Liberia "negative." The French Ambassador, after a meeting with President Taylor, said that his country was not requesting a punitive approach but rather it favored an "incentive" approach to the matter. Discussions dragged on for months, but finally, despite these objections, the United States and Great Britain campaigned strenuously for sanctions to be imposed, and, as usual, they got their way.

In May of 2001 the United Nations Security Council imposed sanctions on Liberia (to be reviewed every six months thereafter), consisting of a one-year embargo on diamond exports and a ban on travel by senior officials. It also extended an arms embargo imposed in 1992 in the midst of Liberia's civil war which never was removed even after the national election of 1997 (UN resolution 1343). After the sanctions were imposed the United Nations sent a team to Monrovia to determine whether Liberia was respecting UN demands to stop its support for the rebels in Sierra Leone. On July 6, 2001, Reuters reported that "Sierra Leone has been largely peaceful since a November cease-fire which has allowed deployment of UN peacekeepers to rebel-held areas and the start of disarmament." Significantly, Reuters went on to say that, at that very time "Liberia is battling an insurgency it says is backed by neighboring Guinea, an ally of Sierra Leone's government."

By September of 2001, it became clear that, as a Reuters headline stated, "U.N. Liberia Sanctions (are) Hurting the Wrong People."[51] The story quoted the spokesman for UNICEF, MacArthur Hill, who said that the sanctions only were hurting "the ordinary population, women and children." He went on to say: "We know fewer children are going to school, while healthcare and education facilities are constantly deteriorating. Mr. Hill said that finger-pointing at Liberia as a "pariah state" by Western countries—the United States and Britain in particular—had slowed, if not halted, badly needed international aid flows. "We launched a consolidated appeal for funds earlier this year—and got nothing," he said. Once again Reuters reported: "While guns appear to have fallen almost completely silent in Sierra Leone since a ceasefire agreement last November, fighting has moved to the north of Liberia—where dissidents have been battling Taylor's troops for more than a year." One cannot be blamed for surmising that the real motivation of the U.S. and Britain in cutting off arms with which the government of Liberia could defend itself against rebel attack was to encourage those rebels in their attempt to depose by force a democratically elected government.

In December of 2001, out of concern for the welfare of the citizens of Sierra Leone, the Paris Club of donor nations wisely agreed to restructure that country's public external debt, canceling about $72 million in debts in order that more money could be put into priority areas such as health, education and agriculture. In other words, frustration over the civil war did not deter the international community from trying to meet the basic needs of the people of Sierra Leone. Yet no such generosity was extended to Liberia primarily because the U.S. opposed any such help.

January 18, 2002 is the date on which the war officially ended and peace came to Sierra Leone. On that date, Tejan Kabbah declared in the local Krio language before a jubilant crowd..."War don don", meaning the decade-long conflict that devastated Sierra Leone had officially ended. Kabbah shook hands with his former enemies, the rebel group known as the RUF (Revolutionary United Front), and weapons collected from 47,000 fighters from both sides were symbolically burned as patriotic music played. It was a scene one could hardly have imagined just a few short months before. It occurred to a significant degree because of the involvement of a 13,000 strong force of United Nations peacekeepers backed by the Sierra Leonean government army, newly trained by the British, and because Great Britain stepped up to its responsibility for Sierra Leone.

In March of 2002 (months after the war in Sierra Leone was over), the UN Secretary-General appointed a panel to verify Monrovia's compliance with the UN resolution to end its support to Sierra Leonean dissidents. In welcoming this panel, Robert Lormis, the public affairs officer of the Liberia Ministry of Foreign Affairs, said that Liberia wanted the sanctions lifted because the reasons for which they were imposed no longer existed. He said that Liberia did not act in any way that warranted sanctions against the government. People, he said, are suffering as a result of the sanctions, adding that Liberia had gained a bad name and was losing business. The ban on diamond exports, he added, was hurting small-time local miners, while public hospitals and schools were being inadequately run. Liberia also was unable to defend herself adequately against armed dissidents. "What little money we manage to scrape, we use on defense," he said.

On March 5, 2002 Foday Sankoh appeared in court in Freetown, Sierra Leone to face murder charges, the first time he had been seen in public since his arrest in May of 2000.

The UN panel, in April of 2002, recommended that the Security Council retain sanctions against Liberia, while acknowledging that Monrovia no longer was fueling a civil war in Sierra Leone. The Reuters report said that the UN panel faced a "dilemma" since the Sierra Leone government had declared that the decade-old civil war had ended and the RUF had been transformed into a political party.[52] But they added that a hard core of RUF members now served as mercenaries on both sides of the Liberia/LURD war. The panel called the rebels attacking the Liberian government a "motley bunch". Significantly the UN Panel said that "the remnants of the RUF resident in Liberia...pose no direct threat to the stability that has returned to Sierra Leone."

The UN Panel also suggested that the travel ban against 129 Liberians should be reduced to "cabinet members, key government officials and officials...that have violated the UN Sanctions."[53]

Mark Doyle of BBC said of the latter: "This recommendation can be seen as a compromise between the Liberian government's position that the travel ban is unfair, and the view of countries such as the U.S., the UK and Sierra Leone which think the travel ban is an effective "stick" to wield against Mr. Taylor."[54]

The Panel of Experts also said that a ban on the diamond trade (at the most 10 to 15 million dollars a year) could be lifted if Liberia set up a credible certification system for its diamonds. It did. The UN didn't lift the sanctions (see Chapter 8, Diamonds).

On April 28, 2002 the Associated Press reported President Taylor's comments regarding the impending renewal of sanctions on Liberia. "...Taylor told hundreds of people attending a church service at a packed public hall: 'they don't want Charles Taylor here. They want a puppet they can manipulate', he said during a speech that was repeatedly interrupted by cheering and applause. 'In most countries where there is war there is massive humanitarian assistance, but that is not the case with Liberia' he said. 'You see our people dying and burning in their villages, our young girls are being raped...but people say there is no war here.'"[55]

On May 6, 2002, as predicted, under pressure from the United States and Great Britain, the UN Security Council, in resolution 1408, extended sanctions against Liberia for another 12 months—including an arms embargo, travel ban for officials, and a prohibition on the import of diamonds—deciding that Liberia had not fully complied with Council demands that it halt its support for the Revolutionary United Front (RUF) and other armed rebel groups in the region.

This action took place despite the fact that there had been no record of armed hostilities in Sierra Leone *for more than seven months,* and indeed on May 14th a national election was held in Sierra Leone and President Kabbah won an overwhelming victory (the RUF did not even field a candidate to oppose him). The UN action totally ignored the views of UNAMSIL (the United Nations Mission in Sierra Leone) which said that "it has no reason to believe that the RUF has received military or related support from the Liberian Government during the period under review."[56] It ignored the report of the ECOWAS Mediation and Verification Mission which visited Liberia from 27 March to 3 April and concluded that "the Government has expelled all RUF rebels from Liberia and no longer has either direct or indirect contact with that organization."[57] The UN Mission also found

> that there are no assets or financial resources of RUF in the territory and the Government is not engaged or involved in the illegal trafficking of arms, and has not solicited arms from any third party. Further, the Government has banned importation of rough diamonds from Sierra Leone and has taken measures to establish a certificate of origin regime.[58]

UN Secretary-General Kofi Annan drew attention to Liberian government efforts to improve its relations with its Mano River Union partners since the adoption of the last sanctions resolution. He recalled the February 27 Summit Meeting of the Heads of State of the Mano River Union countries held in Rabat under the auspices of King Mohammed VI of Morocco aimed at finding a lasting solution to the crisis in the Mano River Union basin.

Despite all of the above, the sanctions against Liberia were extended for another year. Counselor Benedict Sannoh speaking before the National Endowment for Democracy in Washington on April 9, 2002 said:

> While it is true that the sanctions imposed by the UN Security Council are primarily directed at President Taylor and his Government, it has indirect repercussions on the lives of ordinary Liberians. The imposition of sanctions have had a chilling and negative impact on the bilateral relations between Liberia and several other countries from which it traditionally receives economic and development aid. It is through these bilateral programs that Liberia has in the past addressed its economic and social development agenda, such as light, safe drinking water, schools, health care, roads and communications among others. Such economic aid is all the more imperative for a country emerging from war, with most of its infrastructure, economy and institutions virtually destroyed. The development indicators for Liberia

are very grim: A United Nations Development Programs (UNDP) human development index ranks Liberia at 174th out of 177 developing countries; the literacy rate is less than 35%; the life expectancy at birth is pegged at 43 years; and over 85% of its population lives in abject poverty. It appears to me that with the imposition of sanctions, many of Liberia's traditional partners have scaled down, and in some cases cut off, all bilateral assistance to Liberia that would have otherwise inured to the benefit of the masses...(T)he international community seems to project the view that once sanctions have been imposed on Liberia because of the alleged conduct of their president, the fate of the Liberian people has become irrelevant and immaterial. As a staffer on the House Foreign Relations Subcommittee put it, 'The fate of the ordinary Liberian is linked to the fate of Charles Taylor.'

The United States should decide that the fate of three million people be given primacy in the formulation of its policy.

In UN resolution 1408, the Security Council "looks forward to the full implementation of the international certification scheme proposed by the Kimberly Process as soon as possible recalling its concern at the role played by the illicit trade in diamonds in the conflict in the region."

In that same resolution the UN, for the first time, extended the arms embargo to all armed groups in the region, including the LURD, but its directive was more hortatory than effective.

The New Liberia newspaper on May 10, commenting on the sanction extension, wrote: "The grassroots population is the one who are feeling the pinch of the high prices, the lack of jobs, the sky rocketing exchange rates, the hunger, despair and shame of hardship. The Liberian people know that they are the victims and UN or big power propaganda cannot deceive them."

On June 14, 2002, the former Chief Justice of Liberia and current chair of the Catholic Justice and Peace Commission of Liberia, Frances Johnson-Morris attended a conference of civil society organizations from the Mano River countries in New York sponsored by the New York based International Peace Academy. She said that "the end of the war in Sierra Leone acknowledged in January by the UN showed the grounds for sanctions no longer existed. To continue with sanctions would only amount to increasing the suffering of the people", she said. She also described the ongoing rebel war in the North and West of Liberia as a distraction from the task of national reconciliation and reconstruction. The insurgency, she said, has caused suffering for displaced people and human rights abuses.

For most Liberians living in a country with an unemployment rate of 85%, there are few opportunities; businessmen say conditions are getting worse as the government gradually runs out of cash. "It's all down to money. There is no money in this country" says a businessman who works in shipping.

> The only things coming in are donated humanitarian relief and second-hand cars. Liberia has loan arrears of $176 million at the African Development Bank alone, the second highest after the war-ravaged Democratic Republic of Congo. Senior bank officials say they are optimistic about resolving Congo's back payments but Liberia is branded as hopeless for the time being. All this because of the sanction regime and the chilling affect it has on international assistance to Liberia.[59]

The sanction regime, particularly its ban on the importation of arms, has resulted in rebel groups attempting to remove the democratically elected government by force of arms. United Nations Emergency Relief Coordinator Kenzo Oshima, on December 5, 2001, expressed alarm about the deteriorating humanitarian situation in Liberia's northwestern Gbarpolu county following attacks by the LURD dissidents that have put thousands of civilians at risk. Oshima issued a statement saying: "The displacement of 1,413 people by these attacks has nearly doubled the population of the Bopolu IDP camp, strained its already inadequate resources, and created serious security and health risks for all those seeking refuge there."

According to the release put out by the UN Office for the Coordination of Humanitarian Affairs, Mr. Oshima "condemned the attacks and joined other humanitarian organization in calling on the Liberian Government to take measures to ensure protection of civilians and relief workers. He added that humanitarian agencies operating in Liberia lacked sufficient resources and may have to cease operations at the end of the year and called on donors to fund the 2002 inter-agency humanitarian appeal for Liberia."

It was not just the pro-Taylor people who called for an end to sanctions. Bacchus Matthews, who ran against Taylor in 1997, said:

> People are starving because of the sanctions. It's a confidence-impacting measure which undermines the investment climate and discourages investors...Every company is down-sizing. Importers will tell you that the figures are dropping substantially. The price of everything is going up, but nobody's buying, so nobody's importing.[60]

Yet U.S. Assistant Secretary of State for African Affairs, Walter Kansteiner, told the United States Senate in June of 2002 that "greed and lack of good governance" were the root causes of Liberia's "present deplorable state of affairs."[61] As demonstrated in earlier chapters, if the United States had assisted the mineral-rich country to recover from its civil war—if it had encouraged the international community to pitch in, as they have in almost every other post-conflict country in the world, there would be a decent economic climate and a chance for the people to live normal lives.

The U.S. bewails the fact that there are mercenaries throughout West Africa, many of them Liberian. If you were a young person who could not get a job, might you not look to anyone who could pay you a salary, even if it meant fighting in other country's wars? Yes, there are Liberian freelance mercenaries throughout West Africa. But there also are South African mercenaries, Nigerian mercenaries, and Burkina Faso mercenaries. The U.S., however, only has taken action against Liberia.

There is a great despair evident in the Liberian people—both on the part of those in high office and those poor people who live off the land just to survive. The President Pro Tem of the Liberian Senate is a woman named Grace Minor. Senator Minor had this to say about the UN sanctions:

> As a mother and one who, like most other Liberians, has nowhere else to go and live, I am filled with apprehension and near helplessness because I believe that the uncertainties and dangers which imminently face Liberia are more enormous and calamitous than we ever have experienced. I refer specifically to the current war in Liberia and the UN imposed Arms Embargo and Sanctions. It seems like a deliberate and calculated plan maybe designed by powerful countries in the United Nations to have us perish as a people and a

nation. My reason for believing this is the refusal of the United Nations Security Council to lift the Arms Embargo and Sanctions on Liberia in the midst of a war being waged on the people and government of Liberia by LURD emanating from neighboring Guinea. Never before in the history of Liberia have we experienced such a vicious treatment as a Government and people. Liberia has had her dark days but none as desperate as depriving her of self defense when her territory is under serious attacks by dissident forces (LURD) as the result of which thousands of our citizens are dying daily and languishing in displaced and refugee camps in and out of Liberia with nothing being done by the United Nations to bring the hostilities to an immediate end. It is worth noting that LURD has capitalized on the United Nations' arms embargo and sanctions to persistently wage war on the people of Liberia and that the refusal of the UN to lift its imposed arms embargo and sanctions, in the midst of war, contravenes Article 51 of the United Nations Charter and hence have committed an injustice upon the government and people of Liberia. It is common knowledge that the imposition of UN sanctions and embargoes emanate from Liberia's alleged support to the RUF of Sierra Leone. Yet the United Nations continues to turn a blind ear and deaf ear to Guinea's support to LURD which has culminated into the mass suffering and displacement of children, women and the elderly...It is about time that our longtime and traditional big brother, the United States of America, comes to the aid of Liberia in these difficult times especially when Liberians are perishing in the hundreds daily due to the present war being waged against our democratically elected government.[62]

The continuation of sanctions seemed to contradict the statement contained in the UN Information-Gathering Mission to Liberia of May 7 to 25, 1999, citing "the grave concern felt all around that the international community, particularly Liberian donor countries, should not abandon Liberia; rather they should return to Liberia and extend badly needed assistance in the country's effort to undertake the daunting task of reconciliation, reconstruction and development after a debilitating civil war." This never has been done.

Recently Dr. Emmet A. Dennis, professor of cell biology and neuroscience and Vice President of Rutgers University called upon the United Nations Security Council to reexamine its sanction policies against member states so innocent people are not victimized. Dr. Dennis, who is of Liberian descent and is the founding director of the Liberian Institute for Biological Research, in an address to the 41st commencement convocation of Cuttington University College in Monrovia, said: "I'm always baffled by the efficacy of sanctions...Historically, it seems to me that for the most part, sanctions frequently harm the innocent." He called upon the UN Security Council to "lift components of the present sanctions that directly or indirectly harm the innocent Liberian population and review its policy on punitive sanctions such that the innocents are held harmless."[63]

But on July 14, 2002, Al Kamen, writing in the Washington Post, said:

> The United Nations, supported by the Clinton administration and now the Bush administration, has imposed various sanctions on the murderous thugs running Liberia, including chief thug Charles Taylor and his cronies, for supporting the vicious hand-chopping rebels in Sierra Leone.

In contrast to this blanket indictment of the people who govern Liberia, it should be noted that the head of the Central Bank, Elie Saleeby, for example, is a noted economist who is given much of the credit for having revived the economy of Ghana before coming to Liberia to try and do the same. Monie Captan, the Foreign Minister, is a superb diplomat who has won the praise and respect of the international community. It was biased and misleading to categorize the entire government as a bunch of "thugs," when there are many able and dedicated people, some of whom belong to opposition political parties, who work for their country.

Complicated events too often are painted in black-and-white terms, especially by the media. For example, in the Sierra Leone situation, Charles Taylor is the "bad guy" and Tejan Kabbah is the "good guy." As recently as April 11, 2002, Philip Neville, editor of the Standard Times in Freetown, Sierra Leone and winner of the World Press Review's International Editor of the Year Award in 2000, wrote:

> There is already evidence that Kabbah is easily influenced by [Libyan President Colonel Muammar] Gaddafi. After September 11, at the request of Gaddafi, Kabbah immediately canceled a solidarity march at the U.S. Embassy in Freetown. The question on the lips of most Sierra Leoneans is why President Kabbah would enter into a relationship with an individual who provided training ground, finances, and weapons for the Revolutionary United Front (RUF) leader Foday Sankoh's massacre of thousands of innocents. The fear is that their close friendship is fueled by shared religious fanaticism.

Following his election, Kabbah named a new 22-member cabinet. According to BBC, "contrary to expectations, the new cabinet includes neither political opponents nor former rebels who dropped their guns to participate in the elections."[64] Kabbah won re-election with 70.6 % of the vote and his party won 83 of the 112 seats in parliament. While the U.S. was enraged when it learned that Charles Taylor had support from Gaddafi, it apparently did not have similar concerns when Tejan Kabbah did the same. Taylor, after his election, formed a coalition government that included former opponents, but Kabbah did not. Yet the United States has continued to oppose the one and support the other.

The May 2001 UN sanctions included "a travel ban on senior members of the Liberian government and military and their spouses, as well as any other individuals providing financial and military support to armed rebel groups in countries neighboring Liberia, as designated by the UN Sanctions Committee."[65] If the United States had welcomed Liberian officials to come here and meet with governmental leaders, international banking leaders, and others, there would have been an opportunity for dialogue leading to a constructive effort to promote transparency in the conduct of the Liberian government, in exchange for U.S. and international help for rebuilding the war-torn country. By keeping the decision-makers of the Liberian government out of the U.S., while at the same time allowing opposition leaders and rebel leaders to roam the halls of Congress and the State Department freely, the unintended consequence of its policy was the loss of the United States' reputation for even-handedness. This in turn reduced its opportunity to achieve peace in Liberia.

On November 26, 2002, the UN Security Council left sanctions against Liberia in place for another six months. Reuters reported that "council diplomats have expressed fears that lifting the sanctions could prompt fresh flows of arms into a region with a history of instability, even though the fighting in Sierra Leone has ended and Liberia's illicit diamond trade has pretty much dried up."[66]

On February 3, 2003, following the First Extraordinary Session of the Assembly of the African Union (AU), a coalition of African countries, chaired by President Thabo Mbeki of South Africa, appealed to the United Nations Security Council to reconsider its decision on the sanctions imposed against Liberia. However, with an impending war against Iraq occupying the attention of the UN and the world, the chances of serious attention being paid to Liberia are remote at best.

It is acknowledged by all parties that the war in Sierra Leone ended on January 18, 2002. Yet one year later, on January 16, 2003, President Bush issued an Executive Order continuing the U.S. national emergency with respect to Sierra Leone.

The original order (Executive Order 13194) declaring a national emergency with respect to Sierra Leone was issued on January 18, 2001. Four months later, on May 22, 2001, the President issued another Executive Order 13213 "which expanded the scope of the national emergency to include actions of the Government of Liberia in support of the RUF and prohibited the importation of all rough diamonds from Liberia." Now, one year after the war in Sierra Leone ended, President Bush stated: "Because the actions and policies of the RUF continue to pose an unusual and extraordinary threat to the foreign policy of the United States, the national emergency...must continue beyond January 18, 2003. Therefore...I am continuing for 1 year the national emergency with respect to Sierra Leone and Liberia."[67]

To further demonstrate the effect of U.S. policy against President Taylor, it prevented him from attending peace conferences intended to resolve the problems of western Africa. Under the terms of the travel ban sanction against Liberia, no one on the list of 129 people is allowed to travel outside the country unless so permitted by *all* the members of the United Nations Security Council. Mr. Taylor was allowed to travel in early February to Paris for French-brokered talks aimed at ending a civil war in neighboring Ivory Coast. He also was allowed to travel to Ethiopia in January to attend an African Union Summit. In February, 2003, however, President Taylor was invited to attend a Franco-African regional peace summit in Paris, which was attended by heads of state and representatives from 52 African countries; only Somalia, which has no recognized government, was not invited. But President Taylor could not participate because a single member of the Security Council refused to grant him a waiver to travel: the United States of America. On February 19, 2003 Taylor was forced to cancel his travel plans. As Agence France-Presse wrote: "The president's decision to cancel his visit comes in the wake of objections raised by the United States in the United Nations Security Council."[68] On the one hand, the U.S. constantly urged Taylor to do everything possible to restore peace to Liberia and the region, but did not allow him to attend a regional peace conference designed for that purpose.

On May 6, 2003 the United Nations Security Council voted once again a one-year extension of the sanctions against Liberia: arms embargo, travel ban on senior Liberian officials, and a prohibition on the import of Liberian diamonds.[69] They also imposed a new 10-month ban on the importation of timber from Liberia. In past years, the United Nations Security Council imposed these sanctions on Liberia *because of* the report of its appointed Panel of Experts.[70] But in May of 2003 the United Nations Security Council imposed them *in spite of* the report of its Panel of Experts. Here are the specifics contained in that April 24 Report:

> "The Panel documents the support of Guinea for LURD fighters in Liberia.
> Guinea is used as a supply route for arms and supplies...Guinea by supporting

LURD is violating the embargo" (Summary, paragraphs 3 and 9). Despite this information, the Security Council made no attempt to impose sanctions against Guinea, while continuing to penalize Liberia. If Liberia cannot obtain arms, it cannot defend itself against the rebel attacks which continue unabated throughout the country.

"President Taylor in March openly declared that Liberia would import weapons for self-defence and the (Liberian) Government has provided the Panel with a list of weapons it has procured" (Summary, paragraph 5). Liberia's position is that, by the terms of Article 51 of the United Nations Charter, it has the right to defend itself against outside attacks, and acts accordingly.

"It is clearly the objective of the Government to stamp out the illegal trade in diamonds and a scheme is being coordinated by the Ministry of Land, Mines and Energy to implement the Kimberley Process Certification Scheme. Progress has been made in this regard but only an end to the internal conflict can guarantee success" (Summary, paragraph 6). Yet the UN has placed an embargo upon only Liberia's sale of diamonds. In the meantime Liberia finds itself in a Catch-22 position: the UN wants Liberia to participate in the Kimberley Process; but the plenary session of the Kimberley Process group says they cannot allow Liberia to participate in the process until the UN lifts its sanctions (Business Day. No independent monitoring for Kimberley process, May 5, 2003, p.2). This places Liberia in a stalemate position.

Although the Security Council has renewed the travel ban against members of the Liberian government, the Report states unequivocally "that the original rationale for the travel ban is no longer applicable." (Summary, paragraph 9.) It should be noted that, at the same time the travel ban was renewed, the Military Advisor of the rebel LURD force was allowed to come to the United States to lobby his cause and raise money while the democratically elected head of the country was and is refused admission to the United States.

Most blatant of all is the Security Council's actions vis-a-vis Liberia's alleged relationship with the RUF. The Panel of Experts report first sets forth the demands that were made upon Liberia as the conditions for removing the sanctions (Introduction, section B, paragraph 19 (a)(b) and (c)), to wit:

1. "Expel all RUF members from Liberia and prohibit all RUF activities in its territory;

2. "Cease all financial and…military support to RUF…";

3. "Freeze funds or financial resources or assets that are made available…for the benefit of RUF…"

The Panel then concluded (paragraph 20) as follows: "The Panel can no longer establish any direct link between these demands and what is occurring in Liberia today. The Revolutionary United Front Party in Sierra Leone is a legitimate party and the Panel has found no evidence of links between RUF in Sierra Leone and former field commander Sam Bockarie and his followers!"

The Panel of Experts concluded (Summary, paragraph 9) "that the basis for the imposition of the sanctions against Liberia needs to be reassessed because violence and conflict are spreading across the region and are generated not only by Liberian forces."

Why, then, did the UN Security Council totally ignore the recommendations and conclusions of its own appointed investigatory group? For two reasons. First, because the Council was not given sufficient time to examine the Panel of Experts report before it was asked to vote on extending the sanctions against Liberia. And second, because the United States and Great Britain placed great pressure upon the Council to continue the sanctions, regardless of contrary views expressed privately by other Council members (author's off-the-record conversation with an Ambassador to the United Nations who was privy to these deliberations).

The causes of the horrors that have beset Sierra Leone in recent years are many, some of them self-inflicted wounds by a succession of corrupt governments. Britain, the international community, regional Africa peacekeeping groups, Liberia, the United Nations and the United States all bear a share of the responsibility. While it is clear that Liberia did help the RUF, the real question is when Charles Taylor ceased that help. It is all too convenient to place all the blame on Liberia and ignore the many opportunities missed for ending the Sierra Leone war and helping its people. Liberia has become the whipping boy behind whom all the other malefactors in this tragedy have hidden, and the imposition and retention of sanctions against Liberia is the diversion that places all the blame on only one of the players in the Sierra Leone tragedy.

THE MANO RIVER UNION

For many years there have been attempts to establish a bond among Liberia, Guinea and Sierra Leone because of the common identities of so many of their peoples. Known as the Mano River Union, this attempt at mutual cooperation never really materialized.[71] While the U.S. State Department urges the parties to reconstitute the Mano River Union, in practice it is taking steps to make that impossible. If the U.S. would cease training troops in Guinea and sending in arms that are being used in LURD's battle against the Liberian government, the Mano River Union could become a reality.

INITIATIVES IN THE TWENTY-FIRST CENTURY

At President Taylor's initiative, the leaders of Liberia, Guinea, and Sierra Leone, who had hostile relations for too long, decided to take matters into their own hands and try to end their dispute. The U.S. had nothing positive to say. The three presidents of the Mano River Union Basin countries (Taylor of Liberia, Kabbah of Sierra Leone, and Conte of Guinea) met in late February, 2002 in Rabat, Morocco and resolved to end the long-running border conflicts between their countries; to set up joint border patrol units; to prevent the proliferation of small arms; and to end the problems of dissidents, armed groups and other paramilitary groups involved in attempting to destabilize the region. The United States government was less than enthusiastic about this historic, welcome, and significant development in West African relations. In fact, Mark Bellamy, U.S. Deputy Assistant Secretary of State (the principal deputy), instead of encouraging the Morocco initiative, described Taylor's significant role in promoting Mano River Union solidarity as a "charm offensive."[72] His statement reinforces the analysis that the U.S. State Department consistently did not recognize anything that the Taylor Government did as positive.

On March 5, 2002, just six days after the Morocco Agreement, Walter Kansteiner, U.S. Assistant Secretary of State for Africa, told the Voice of America that the United Nations soon could slap new sanctions on Liberian President Charles Taylor and his closest associates. As it has happened so many times in the course of U.S.-Liberian relations, the

United States missed an opportunity to encourage a positive course of action taken by the Liberian Government. Furthermore, instead of commending and encouraging this constructive step, the U.S. Ambassador to Liberia, Bismarck Myrick, knowing full well that the Liberian government was under attack from a rebel force known as the Liberians United for Reconciliation and Democracy (LURD) which had been trying to unseat the Taylor government by force since 1999, stated on March 1st: "To help prevent further fighting and suffering by the Liberian people, the United States challenges President Taylor to establish the conditions necessary for peaceful political competition and change to occur." In other words, the Ambassador in effect maintained that it was *Taylor's* responsibility that he was being attacked by the LURD—a conclusion defying reason and reality.

On the same day, March 5, 2002, even one of Taylor's political opponents in Liberia, Dr. Togba-Nah Tipoteh, the standard-bearer of the Liberian People's Party (LPP) who will contest Taylor for the Presidency in the next election, embraced Charles Taylor and commended him for the success of the Morocco Talks held among the Mano River Union leaders. The LPP leader said that, because the President had done the right thing by attending the talks, it was important, as a matter of principle, to commend him.

In stark contrast to the tepid response of the United States, on February 26, 2002, the European Union assured the Three Heads of State of its full support in their search for a peaceful development of the Mano River region. On February 28 the UN Security Council welcomed the summit pledge of the three West African heads of state to seek peace on their common borders. To prove that the Morocco accord involved actions, not just words, on April 20, 2002, Liberian and Guinean security forces launched tandem deployments along their shared border, thus implementing in reality the agreements they had signed in Morocco.

The Mano River Union is a realistic approach to stabilizing a significant portion of West Africa. It requires the support of the international community and the cessation of activities that serve to divide the three countries, rather than unite them.

CONCLUSION

On May 8, 2001 when no longer representing Liberia, the author, as a concerned citizen who maintained his interest and support for the people of Liberia, wrote a letter to Walter Kansteiner shortly before he re-entered government as U.S. Assistant Secretary of State for Africa under the George W. Bush Administration. The two previously had discussed Liberia when Mr. Kansteiner worked with General Brent Scowcroft's private consulting group. This letter summarized the subject of the Mano River Union and sanctions as a function of U.S. foreign policy.

Dear Walter:

While you are still a "civilian," I thought it might be useful to send you some brief thoughts on U.S. policy toward Liberia in light of what has happened in the last few days (sanctions).

First, despite our State Department's continuing insistence that it is not trying to undermine the Taylor government, its actions belie that sentiment. By cutting off almost all aid and refusing to condone military attacks against Liberia from adjoining countries, the U.S. and Britain appear to be spearheading an effort to bring down a democratically elected government without any thought as to what will happen if they succeed. If the Liberian government falls, the former warlords who have been militarily attacking Liberia from safe havens in Guinea will return to Liberia and civil war once again will ensue...after 3½ years of peace...and anarchy will prevail. Is this the result we want? Do we really want to reward military force and repudiate the democratic process? Do we want to further destabilize all of West Africa?

Why are U.S. military advisors admittedly in Guinea for "training purposes"? Why did the IMF just commit 80 million dollars of "humanitarian aid" to Guinea while, at the same time, it and the rest of the world community, in response to U.S. and British requests, have cut off practically all aid to Liberia? When a summit conference recently was held in Abuja under the auspices of President Obasanjo of Nigeria to help solve the unrest among members of the Mano River Union (Guinea, Sierra Leone and Liberia), the Presidents of Sierra Leone and Liberia attended, but the President of Guinea refused to participate in that peace conference. Liberian dissidents are operating freely out of Guinea, attacking Liberia border cities and towns—yet the U.S., to my knowledge, has not uttered a word in protest against this action...and instead strongly supports an arms embargo against Liberia so it cannot properly defend itself against armed attacks.

Second, with regard to the sanctions which were imposed by the UN at the instigation and insistence of the U.S. and Britain, our State Department insists that those sanctions will not penalize the Liberian people. I submit that that is untrue. As an example, thousands of Liberians currently employed in mining indigenous industrial-quality diamonds now will be put out of work, adding to the country's 85% unemployment rate.

Further, in announcing the sanctions, the UN Secretary-General significantly did *not* say that there was credible evidence that the Liberian government had failed to take the actions demanded of it in order to stave off those sanctions (severing ties with the RUF, grounding air flights, etc.). Instead, despite Liberia's insistence that it had complied fully with the UN requirements, all Mr. Annan cryptically said was that there was "not sufficient verifiable evidence" that the RUF (and Sam Bockarie in particular) had left Liberia. At the same time, he did not offer any evidence that the RUF leader *does* remain in Liberia. The only way to prove that someone has *not* left your house is to prove that he is still there. This has not been done.

In conclusion, if the U.S. and Britain are unhappy with the actions of the Liberian government, the way to change that conduct is to 1) engage the government; 2) help the people who are in dire straits; 3) condemn those who are attempting to change the government through force of arms; and 4) encourage the further development of diverse political parties and institutions so that the national elections scheduled for 2003 can act as a referendum for the actions of that government, and the people of Liberia—not the U.S. and Britain—can freely decide who they want to lead their country.

Thank you, Walter, for taking the time to listen to my viewpoint.

Warmest personal regards.

> Always sincerely,
> /s/ Lester S. Hyman"

No answer was forthcoming from Mr. Kansteiner.

These questions go to the very foundation of United States policy toward Liberia. Why has the United States failed to encourage Liberia when it has acted constructively? Why has it consistently wielded the "stick" at a time when enlightened diplomacy would call for "the carrot and stick", that is: reward a country when it has acted well, and penalize it when it has acted poorly? Why has it failed to come to the assistance of the people of Liberia who are suffering? Chapter 12 examines what the United States might do to reverse its failed policy in the future.

NOTES

[1] The Special Court for Sierra Leone, "The Prosecutor Against Charles Ghankay Taylor also known as Charles Ghankay MacArthur Dapkpana Taylor Indictment." case No. SCSL-03-1, 7 March 2003, p. 4.

[2] Norimitsu Onishi, "What War Has Wrought: Sierra Leone's Sad State," *New York Times*, January 31, 1999, Late Edition-Final, Section1, p. 6, Col. 3.

[3] John L. Hirsch, "War in Sierra Leone," *IISS* (International Institute for Strategic Studies) Quarterly, Volume 43, Number 3, Autumn 2001, p. 150.

[4] Ibid., p. 147.

[5] Ibid., p. 150

[6] Ibid., p. 147

[7] U.S. Overseas Loans and Grants, Military Assistance Loans and Grants, U.S. Agency for International Development, Fiscal 2003 and Fiscal 2004 budgets for Guinea.

[8] Joseph Opala, "What the West Failed to See in Sierra Leone," *Washington Post*, May 14, 2000, B1.

[9] Ibid. p. B2, Col. 1.

[10] Hirsch, IISS Quarterly, Autumn 2001, p. 146.

[11] Madeline Albright letter to Charles Taylor, October 20, 1999. Courtesy of the recipient.

[12] Karl Vick, "Sierra Leone's Unjust Peace: At Sobering Stop, Albright Defends Amnesty for Rebels," *Washington Post*, October 19, 1999, p. A12.

[13] Human Rights Watch, "Africa: Sierra Leone: The Role of the International Community," *World Report 2001*, Washington, D.C., 2001, <http://www.hrw.org/wr2k1/africa/sierraleone3.html>. Janet Fleischman, Africa director of HRW said: this: "...another indication of the U.S. being unwilling to invest the political capital to ensure that a sustainable peace could be arrived at by incorporating the broader issues of human rights."

[14] United Nations, "Report of the Panel of Experts appointed pursuant to Security Council resolution 1306 (2000), paragraph 19, in relation to Sierra Leone. Part one-Diamonds. Section I. Sierra Leone diamonds, E. Foday Sankoh's post-Lomé diamond business," p. 19, paragraph 90.

[15] Ibid., "B. Diamonds in the RUF," p. 16, paragraph 67.

[16] Ibid. "E. Foday Sankoh's post-Lomé diamond business," p. 19, paragraph 93.

[17] Ibid., p. 19, paragraph 94.

[18] Ibid,. p. 20, paragraph 96.

[19] Ibid., "D. How the RUF move diamonds out of Sierra Leone," p. 18, paragraph 82.

[20] Ibid., paragraph 83.

[21] Judd Gregg (U.S. Senator), "A Graveyard Peace," *Washington Post*, May 9. 2000, OpEd, p. A31.

[22] Ibid.

[23] Norimitsu Onishi with Jane Perlez, "How U.S. Left Sierra Leone Tangled in a Curious Web,"

New York Times, June 4, 2000, Late edition-Final, Section 1, p. 6, col. 3.

[24] Secretary Colin Powell, Press Remarks with Foreign Minister Sidibe, Bamako, Mali, May 23, 2001 <http://www.state.gov/secretary/rm/2001/3013.htm>.

[25] Peter Kahler, "U.S. Convinced of Liberians Negative Role in Sierra Leone," *PanAfrican News Agency*, July 17, 2000.

[26] Ibid.

[27] Report of the Panel of Experts appointed pursuant to Security Council resolution 1306 (2000), paragraph 19, in relation to Sierra Leone. Part one, Section I., D. How the RUF move diamonds out of Sierra Leone, p. 18, paragraph 81.

[28] Ibid., p. 19, paragraph 87.

[29] Ibid., p. paragraph 88.

[30] Ibid., Section II. International diamond statistics and transit countries, D. Conclusions on statistics and transit countries, p. 26, paragraph 141.

[31] Ibid. C. Case studies: Liberia, Gambia, Guinea and Côte d'Ivoire, p. 25, paragraphs 126, 127.

[32] Letter from General Robert Yerks to President of UN Security Council, Ambassador Kishore Mahbubani of Singapore, January 2001; letter from General Yerks to President of the UN Security Council, Honorable Sergei Lavrov of Russian Federation, December 28, 2000.

[33] Report of the Panel of Experts appointed pursuant to Security Council resolution 1306 (2000), paragraph 19, in relation to Sierra Leone. Part two, Weapons, Section I. Weapons and the RUF, A. Background, p. 31, paragraph 171.

[34] Ibid., B. Sources of RUF weaponry within Sierra Leone, p. 32, paragraph 177.

[35] Ibid. Section II. Liberian support to the RUF, A. General, p. 32, paragraph 180.

[36] Ibid., paragraph 182.

[37] Ibid., paragraph 183.

[38] Ibid.

[39] Liberia's Response to Allegations of her Involvement in the Sierra Leone Civil War, presented by the Deputy Minister of Information, J. Milton Teajay, London, United Kingdom, January 26, 1999, p. 2.

[40] Ibid., p. 1.

[41] Ibid., p. 1.

[42] Ibid., p. 5.

[43] Stanley McGill, in Monrovia, and Nigeria Information Minister Jerry Gana, *BBC Network Africa,* interview, December 18, 2002.

[44] "The Horror in Sierra Leone," *Washington Post*, January 28, 1999, p. A26, Editorial.

[45] Norimitsu Onishi, "What War Has Wrought: Sierra Leone's Sad State," *New York Times*, January 31, 1999, Late Edition-Final, Section 1, p. 6, col. 3.

[46] Testimony of Nathan Jones, International Charter Incorporated, Oregon, n.d. The company, that consists of former U.S. Special Forces, receives Pentagon contracts to work in high-risk conflict areas.

[47] Halberstam, *War in Time of Peace*, p. 273.

[48] Official Statement of the Government of Liberia on the Sierra Leonean Crisis, Ministry of Foreign Affairs, February 19, 1999, p. 1.

[49] Ibid., p. 3.

[50] Peter V. Cooper, "Free Town Receives Rebel Leader's Body—As 'Dead Mother' Surfaces in Monrovia," *AllAboutLiberia.com*, June 2, 2003 <http://www.allaboutliberia.com/june2003/230602n6.htm>.

[51] Silvia Aloisi, "U.N. Liberia sanctions hurting wrong people-UNICEF," *Reuters English News Service*, September 1, 2001, p. 1.

[52] Irwin Arieff, "UN experts back extension of Liberia sanctions," *Reuters*, April 17, 2002, p. 1.

[53] Ibid., p. 1.

[54] Mark Doyle, "Liberia sanctions renewed," *BBC News*, April 18, 2002, at <http://news.bbc.co.uk/2/hi/africa/1937807.stm>.

[55] Jonathan Paye-Layleh, "President Taylor says he expects U.N. to extend sanctions against Liberia," *The Associated Press*, April 28, 2002, p. 1.

[56] "Security Council extends sanctions on Liberia for further 12 months, unanimously adopting resolution 1408 (2002)," *M2 Presswire*, May 7. 2002, available at <http://m2.com/m2/M2Archive.nsf/UserSearch/85256B00004976D185256BB1006ED642?opendocument>

[57] Ibid., citing report of ECOWAS Mediation and Verification Mission of 27 March 2001, p. 3.

[58]. David Clarke, "Business struggles in lawless Liberia," *Reuters English News Service*, June 23, 2002, p. 1.

[59] Ibid., p. 1.

[60] Ibid. p. 2.

[61] UN Office for the Coordination of Humanitarian Affairs 2002. "Mano River Union: one of the world's worse crises, says USAID," June 13, 2002, citing U.S. Assistant Secretary of State for African Affairs Walter Kansteiner testimony before the United States Senate "the previous Tuesday."

[62] Statement of Hon. Grace Beatrice Minor, Senior Senator of Montserrado County. Republic of Liberia lauding United Nations Secretary-General Kofi Annan and others for their far-sighted approach to amicably resolving the Liberian crisis, Monrovia, Liberia, n.d.

[63] Moses M. Zangar Jr., Monrovia; "Educator wants UN examine sanctions policy," p. 1, n.d.

[64] "New cabinet for Sierra Leone," *BBC News*, May 22, 2002. See <http://news.bbc.co.uk/2/hi/africa/2002526.stm>.

[65] Security Council resolution 1343 (2001), March 7, 2001, Part B., Section 7(a), p.2. See <http://ods-dds-ny.un.org/doc/UNDOC/GEN/N01/276/08/PDF/N0127608.pdf?OpenElement>

[66] "UN leaves sanctions on Liberia another six months," *Reuters English News Service*, November 26, 2002, p. 1.

[67] The White House, Office of the Press Secretary, Notice: Continuation of the National Emergency with Respect to Sierra Leone and Liberia, President George W. Bush, January 16, 2003.

[68] "Liberia's President Taylor cancels attendance at Paris summit," Monrovia, *Agence France-Presse*, February 19, 2003.

[69] Edith M. Lederer, UN Security Council extends sanctions against Liberia for a year, *Associated Press*, May 6, 2003.

[70] Report of the Panel of Experts appointed pursuant to paragraph 4 of Security Council resolution 1458 (2003), concerning Liberia, April 24, 2003.

[71] UN Security Council workshop on the Mano River Union, July 18, 2002. Discussion paper, p. 1.

[72] Charles W. Corey, Washington File Staff Writer, U.S. Department of State, International Information Programs. "Liberia's Ability to Foment Regional Trouble," speech by William Mark Bellamy before the United States Institute of Peace in Washington, D.C., December 11, 2002, p. 2.

CHAPTER 7
ARMED INCURSION

Since 1999 the group known as the Liberians United for Reconstruction and Democracy (LURD) has carried out armed attack against the government and people of Liberia. They stated that their intent was to remove Charles Taylor from power. The LURD rebels consist of some of Samuel Doe's forces, anti-Taylor groups and remnants of the RUF from Sierra Leone. Agence France-Presse described LURD as "a ragtag force of children and disenchanted and for the most part ill-educated veterans."[1] Their leader is Sekou Damate Conneh of the Mandingo ethnic group who is said to be a relative of the president of Guinea.

THE LURD INVASION 1999–2003

One of the major criticisms of the Taylor government was that it failed to serve the needs of the people of Liberia. Among the multiple factors for the failure of the Taylor regime to render services to the Liberian citizenry are: 1) Liberia's huge debt inherited from previous administrations; 2) the insufficient financial and security assistance from the international community; 3) the use of the country's limited resources for the procurement of arms to repel the armed attacks of the LURD rebels. As MacArthur Hill, UNICEF spokesman, stated:

> The new wave of fighting, coming hot on the heels of a devastating seven-year civil war which ended in 1997 with Taylor's election, meant that even basic services could not be provided in Liberia. Liberia is a country at war. The government is spending all its resources on war.[3]

Liberia protested to the international community, including the United States, that Guinea was harboring and arming the LURD rebel forces.[3] A Human Rights Watch report of May, 2002 discussed the direct link between the LURD and the government of Guinea. It reported Guinea's logistic, financial and military support to the rebels:

> Evidence indicates that this support is being given with the knowledge and support of high-ranking Guinean officials. The LURD leader Sekou Conneh, a Liberian Mandingo, has access to Guinean President Lansana Conté through his wife Ayesha Conteh, who has been the president's spiritual advisor since she foretold a 1996 coup attempt. Human Rights Watch interviewed some fifteen LURD recruits from Sierra Leone, who, after arriving in Conakry (Guinea) by boat, described being picked up at the wharf by men in military uniform...Most described being transported across Guinea to Liberia in military convoys, where they received new uniforms and guns, said by their commanders, to have come from Guinea...In view of the close links between the Guinean government and the LURD rebel forces in Liberia, the participation of Guinean troops in the U.N. peacekeeping mission in Sierra Leone, UNASMIL, should give cause for concern.[4]

On June 30, 2002, Cheikh Oumar Diarra, deputy executive secretary of ECOWAS said that its military delegation's findings confirmed that the rebels were receiving external support, a clear breach of the regional community's moratorium on the importation, exportation and manufacture of light weapons. The report concluded that the rebels were well equipped and better resourced than the Liberian government forces. "We are facing a situation," he said, "where we have the rebels receiving support on the one side, and, on the other side, the government, under embargo, is receiving no support." The Executive Secretary of ECOWAS, Mohamed ibn Chambas insisted that the region would under no circumstances accept a violent transfer of power anywhere in West Africa. "We will use any means, including force, to re-establish the democratically elected government, and we made that clear to LURD."

The relationship between the United States and Guinea was also decried by the Taylor regime and others. The U.S. through the U.S. Agency for International Development (USAID), which had been merged into the U.S. State Department, provided Guinea with money to train its army. For example, in the FY 2003 budget, USAID requested $250,000 for "International Military Education and Training" to Guinea, and in the FY 2004 budget, the USAID request for Guinea was $350,000.[5] According to press reports, the United States later conceded that the LURD dissidents possessed powerful U.S. military equipment originally supplied to the Guinean government to build up its defense system.[6] A UN panel wrote that "different LURD factions got new supplies of arms and ammunition. LURD strongholds and positions can only be re-supplied by road from Guinea, Côte d'Ivoire and Sierra Leone…"[7]

As reported by Human Rights Watch:

> Although the U.S. has expressed concern about the human rights situation in Guinea in its human rights report to the U.S. Congress, (in its 2001 human rights report on Guinea, the U.S. State Department noted: 'Extrajudicial killings; disappearances; use of torture, beatings, and rape by police and military personnel; and police abuse of prisoners and detainees. Soldiers, police, and civilian militia groups killed, beat and raped citizens, as well as refugees from Sierra Leone and Liberia.') the U.S. has not made public statements expressing concern about Guinea's role in supporting the LURD incursion.[8]

Despite the criticism of U.S. policy and actions regarding Liberia, LURD, and Guinea, once LURD emerged as a force, the United States refrained from criticizing the rebel group, while still exerting pressure on the Taylor regime through the UN imposed sanctions and denial of most U.S. aid. The U.S. was joined by Great Britain, which opposed the Taylor regime because of its support of the RUF in Sierra Leone and allegedly guerilla groups elsewhere in West Africa. The U.S. and Britain both used their massive influence in the UN Security Council to maintain the arms embargo against Liberia. Citing the reports by the UN assessment teams to Liberia, the U.S. justified its actions in pushing for the extension of sanctions against Liberia. For example, it alleged that Liberia violated the sanctions by purchasing large supplies of weapons and ammunition from Yugoslavia in June, July, and August of 2001.[9] The shipments were obtained through a dealer in Belgrade.

The policies of the U.S. and the international community regarding the institution of an arms embargo against the Taylor government actually contravened Article 51 of the United Nations Charter that states "nothing in the present Charter shall impair the inherent right of individual or collective self-defense if an armed attack occurs against a Member of the United Nations…" The actions of the U.S. and international community toward Liberia were tantamount to support for an attempt at military subversion of democracy, and denial of a democratic nation's right to self-defense. Note that in Bosnia where Milosevic's forces attacked the government, the U.S. policy was different. According to David Halberstam in *War in a Time of Peace*, "(Paul) Wolfowitz thought that American participation in the arms embargo toward Bosnia was absolutely appalling. It was morally unacceptable to permit the aggressor the luxury of arms but to deny those under attack the ability to defend themselves." Halberstam concluded that:

> Because of the arms embargo, we were not even able to let decent people defend themselves. That went against the American grain, he (President Clinton) believed. Hell, he said at one meeting, if Americans were fighting against brutal oppressors, and the most powerful countries in the world kept them from getting arms, he'd have been damn pissed.[10]

Although the United States did not condemn the actions of LURD, or support the end of sanctions, other parties did. In March of 2002 Agence France-Presse reported that Nigeria's President Olusegun Obasanjo opened talks in Abuja (the capital of Nigeria) in an attempt to bring about a peaceful resolution in Liberia.[11] ECOWAS was the host for the conference that was intended to bring both sides together to work out their problems. The Liberian government delegation was led by Agriculture Minister (now Planning Minister) Roland Massaquoi. Also attending were former Liberian heads of state Ruth Perry and Amos Sawyer, as well as leaders of political parties and business figures. Agence France-Presse wrote,

> Real hope for progress was dim as a team from the rebel Liberians United for Reconciliation and Democracy (LURD) which opposes Taylor's regime in the west African country, did not turn up...Liberian rebel spokesman Charles Bennie...explained that his group was boycotting the talks because they paved the way for discussions with Taylor. The LURD refuses to deal with him... 'If we are left with no alternative, our forces will take Monrovia and arrest that common criminal Taylor,' Bennie then said.[12]

The Organization of African Unity called upon the United Nations to lift the sanctions on the grounds that they were harming ordinary Liberians, but the Security Council rejected that plea on May 5, 2002.[13]

Contrary to its name, the LURD rejected both reconciliation and democracy. The LURD committed atrocities during their attacks. For example, on May 8, 2002, the BBC reported: "Before leaving the town (Zoum Wesso), the rebels slit a woman's throat and burned three men alive, all in the presence of children who seemed to wonder what kind of a world they were living in." On May 15, 2002, Kofi Annan, secretary general of the United Nations said: "I condemn all attempts by LURD and any armed factions to take power by force." In May of 2002 the LURD abducted a Catholic priest in Tubmanburg. On June 20, 2002, the rebels kidnapped five Liberian nurses from a UN–sponsored medical clinic that was serving as a refugee camp. On July 26, 2002, the LURD rebels crossed into Sierra Leone and abducted 18 villagers.[14]

In testimony before the UN Security Council in July of 2000, Monie Captan, foreign minister of Liberia, gave yet another example of the LURD's viciousness.

> The last attack has led to the destruction of reconstructed and renovated buildings and private property in the northern provincial capital of Voinjama. Many civilians have been killed, farms destroyed and another harvest season lost. The reparation of some 32,000 refugees to Liberia by the UNHCR has been suspended as a the result of the armed incursion. Liberia could never be a facilitator of such mayhem. Indeed, Liberia is a stakeholder in the peace and security of the sub-region...(T)he United Nations should desist from using embargoes against legitimately elected governments in violation of their

inherent right under the United Nations Charter to act in self-defense in the face of armed aggression.

Opposition political parties in Liberia (the True Whig Party, Free Democratic Party, Liberian People's Party, Unity Party, United People's Party, National Democratic Party of Liberia, and All Liberia Coalition Party, among others) opposed the LURD, because of LURD's failure to use the democratic process to gain state power.[15] Acting in concert, an organization known as the Collaborating Political Parties of Liberia (CPP) urged its members and supporters "to resist at all costs the unconstitutional attempt of attaining state power through the barrel of the gun by the dissident Liberians United for Reconciliation and Democracy (LURD)."[16] The political parties called upon the LURD to disengage from its military campaign and bring its claims through the political process.

In a speech before the Liberian senate, Tiawon S. Gongloe, a prominent Liberian attorney, spoke of the LURD attacks. He said:

> All well-meaning Liberians must condemn the aggressors, the LURD rebel group. The action of LURD is diabolic, criminal and shows no remorse of conscience for the ordinary Liberians who have experienced so much pain and suffering over the years, for the quest of a few Liberians for power. There is only one way to power in Liberia and that way is the consent of the people of Liberia expressed through the electoral process. The electoral process is the only path that the Liberian people have chosen for forming a government. Political power according to our Constitution is inherent in the people. And power, according to our Constitution, is not to be taken or seized, but to be freely given or bestowed through the process of elections and appointments, all of which are products of consensus building and various means of persuasion, not coercion. It is against our Constitution to use force to gain power. I therefore call upon the rebels causing mayhem and terror in our land to ceasefire and bring their grievances to the table for discussion…All Liberians had the chance to participate in the electoral process in 1997 and freely elected a government of their choice. Whatever the differences are with this government, every effort should be made to ensure that a free, fair and transparent electoral process is pursued in 2003.[17]

An April 26, 2002 release from the U.S. Embassy in Liberia took quite a different position:

> The United States condemns recent Government of Liberia actions to suppress freedom of expression and freedom of the press…These actions, allegedly justified in the name of some perceived threat to national security, in fact create a climate of intimidation and uncertainty that undermines efforts at national reconciliation. The U.S. Embassy release continues: In condemning renewed fighting during his March 12, 2002 statement to the press, Ambassador Bismarck Myrick observed that 'Political change at the point of a gun is not acceptable; it must not be Liberians' only option'" But Myrick continued: "The Ambassador urged President Taylor to take specific steps to create a climate for peaceful political dialogue and change."

The above statement contradicted the facts, because the LURD, unlike the 18 opposition political parties, disavowed peaceful use of the political system to bring about democratic change, and initiated attacks against the Liberian government as the sole means to depose Charles Taylor.

After Ambassador Myrick ended his tour of duty, he gave an interview to his hometown newspaper, *The Virginian Pilot* (Norfolk, Virginia) on October 29, 2002. His comments illustrated Mr. Myrick's true attitude. Referring to the LURD attacks on the Liberian government, the story said that "the renewed fighting came as no surprise to Myrick. 'This is the outcome of a society that does not allow an open political space.' In the same interview, "Mr Myrick said...Taylor's intolerance has Liberians intimidated... 'If they said anything critical of the government, they were subject to being arrested, beaten up and run out of town.'" An analysis of the press and political parties, discussed in later sections of this book, show that Mr. Myrick's sweeping statements were exaggerations. Dissent existed, and still exists, in Liberia, through mass media and political opposition. But, more important, the former ambassador seemed to not grasp the fact that the LURD was never interested in "open political space." It declined from the start to participate in the political process, and was criticized for that position by the other Liberian opposition groups, who were certified political parties. It had, and has, only one goal in mind: remove Taylor from power militarily.

By September 2002, when the Liberian forces appeared to have successfully repelled the LURD attacks after almost four years of fighting, U.S. State Department officials privately described the LURD as a "terrorist organization" (but publicly declined to use that term).[18] On September 16, 2002 the BBC reported that the LURD rebels said: "We are not prepared to hold talks with Mr. Taylor and we will not negotiate with him."

On September 18, 2002 the Liberian government removed its soldiers from the streets of Monrovia, five days after lifting a state of emergency it imposed the previous February when LURD dissidents encroached on the Liberian capital. The soldiers were placed in the streets since August 24, 2002. According to the Panafrican News Agency,

> Though Washington welcomed the lifting of the state of emergency, it urged Taylor to take concrete actions to improve human rights, and create an enabling environment for presidential and general elections next July (sic). A statement from the US Embassy here also asked for the release of all those detained in connection with LURD...activities.[19]

This request came at the very time LURD recommenced its armed attacks against Liberia.

In a November 6, 2002 press statement, Tarty Teh, LURD's chief political representative, stated, with the approval of Moses Jarbo, general coordinator for the organization that, "LURD has not wavered in its determination to remove Charles Taylor by force." On November 19, 2002 the fighting continued and the LURD rebels claimed that they were in control of the northern district of Kolahun by virtue of the capture of the town of Foya.

Some U.S. diplomats stated that the LURD was a figment of Charles Taylor's imagination—that he created the fiction that he was under attack as an excuse to rearm.[20] Taylor responded in a radio address on May 9, 2002:

> Those who have been telling the world that there is no war in Liberia will now see that this democratically elected government is under attack, and that powerful nations of the world continue to deny Liberia the right under Article 51 of the UN Charter to defend herself. How many dead bodies—how many rapes—how many displaced refugees need these critics see before they open their eyes to the facts?

The Human Rights Watch organization in New York on LURD in its May, 2002 report stated:

> ...(T)he LURD does not appear to have a defined political program, other than to remove Charles Taylor from power. The organization has been plagued with internal power struggles, political rivalries and corruption, and there also appears to be some division between the Guinea-based political side of the movement, and its field based military commanders. There seems to be little clarity or consensus on key political issues, such as whether or not to seek a negotiated settlement with the Taylor government, or what kind of government should replace Taylor in the event of a LURD military victory. In March 2002, at peace talks brokered by the Economic Community of West African States (ECOWAS) in Abuja, Nigeria, LURD did not send official representation that could speak on behalf of the group.

> Some observers accused the Taylor government of exaggerating the LURD threat in order to divert attention from the failure of its domestic policies, and to justify its call for the lifting of United Nations sanctions imposed in May of 2001. Some sources have alleged that certain attacks carried out closer to Monrovia and attributed to LURD by the government may actually have been either fabricated attacks by government forces or the result of skirmishes between government security and militia forces. The absence of a credible and articulate LURD leadership has contributed to a blanket dismissal of the LURD's existence by some Liberia-based international observers, who explain away the rebel group as "roaming bandits" or the result of fighting between different sections of the government's forces. It is clear, however, on the basis of research undertaken by Human Rights Watch in Liberia and neighboring countries, that the LURD is an organized fighting force, and does pose a real threat to peace and security in Liberia.[21]

> Several LURD combatants told Human Rights Watch that, while they were ordered not to abuse civilians' rights, some abuses, notably rape and looting were regularly overlooked. They also admitted abducting young men and forcing them to join LURD forces, but denied recruiting child soldiers. While scores of young men reportedly joined the LURD voluntarily, forced conscription by the LURD was nevertheless the most frequently reported abuse received during Human Rights Watch interviews.[22]

The Liberian government continued to plead with the United States to cease its support of Guinea, which has used American money to underwrite the LURD's campaign of terror against the Liberian people. On March 27, 2003 the State Department responded to the petition, announcing: "Inflammatory statements by senior Liberian government officials regarding U.S. policies and presence in Liberia could only incite violence against American interests."

DISPLACEMENT OF CIVILIANS

The UN reported that the fighting in Liberia has led to the multiple internal displacement of hundreds of thousands of Liberians and to the exodus of 200,000 into other countries. "Liberians live in constant fear of the LURD." In an address on April 9, 2002 before the National Endowment for Democracy (NED) in Washington, D.C., Counselor Benedict F. Sannoh, a professor of law and the executive director of Liberia's Center for Law and

Human Rights, spoke of the effect of the LURD attacks upon the people of Liberia. He said:

> Rebel attacks, whatever way one may want to characterize it, are inherently brutal and violent. Those against whom the war is directed are the least to face the brunt of the suffering. Instead, innocent people, the elderly, women and children are the real victims; some get killed by the bullets or by the starvation, deprivation and denial occasioned by the conflict, while others are injured and maimed. Properties are destroyed, and the inhabitants are forced to flee from the only place they know as home, either internally as displaced persons or externally as refugees..."

Action against the LURD became more important; on October 29, 2002—one day before the UN was to consider action against the LURD—the rebels launched another attack in northern Liberia. The UN Office for the Coordination of Humanitarian Affairs issued this information in a press release that described the rebel group as "fighting to topple Charles Taylor since 1998." The attacks occurred in the Lofa County area of Liberia. The World Food Programme said that "should movement intensify it might result in a dramatic explosion of the current caseload" (the numbers of internally displaced persons in the refugee camps on the outskirts of Monrovia already had reached 183,900), adding that "food harvests which normally start in October were expected to be poor this year because fighting had disrupted farming."[23] Deutsche Press Agentur quote President Taylor as confirming that "government positions have been receiving sustained attacks from LURD forces." Taylor added that the LURD forces had been re-armed with troop carriers, heavy guns and sophisticated weapons by the Guinean government in order to "wreak havoc on Liberian territory after government forces drove the terrorists across the border several weeks ago."

Emily Wax of the Washington Post on January 8, 2003, writing from the Ivory Coast, told of the impact of the rebel attacks against the government of Liberia. Wax reported:

> Emma Sekah, a 13-year-old girl with braided pigtails, covered her ears. An angry crowd gathered around her. She grabbed her 5-year-old brother, who was howling hysterically. They looked in all directions to run away. But there was nowhere to go.
>
> They had come here (the Ivory Coast) three years ago from Liberia. Now they were uprooted again, among thousands of people fleeing Ivory Coast's civil war, taking refuge in a school tucked deep in a rubber plantation, just miles from the front lines of combat between rebels and government forces.
>
> As Emma and her brother cowered before the crowd, a tall, thin man wearing a T-shirt emblazoned with the face of President Laurent Gbagbo and the orange, white and green national flag shouted, 'Get out of here!' The crowd pressed in closer. 'Leave the Ivory Coast!'
>
> Emma began to cry. When she fled Liberia, she was running from rebels— teenagers with sunglasses, pink wigs and hunting rifles. They ransacked her village, so Emma and her family fled to Ivory Coast, Liberia's West African neighbor.
>
> Today, Emma and thousands of other Liberians are running again. They are without food and water. Pregnant women are dehydrated; their lips are white from relentless thirst.

To Emma and the others, the rebels now fighting in Ivory Coast seem very much the same as those who attacked her village in Liberia —and some are. Liberian fighters in the west of Ivory Coast, many of them teenage mercenaries, are the latest to join one of the three main rebel groups battling the government. All the rebel groups want Gbagbo to step down. He has refused…"Just get us back to Liberia," Emma said. "Just someone take us back."…Now thousands of Liberians and Ivorians are hoping to go to Liberia to escape Ivory Coast's increasingly violent civil war.

…Two weeks ago, the rebels—Liberian teenagers—came to her house with rifles. They stormed in, just as they did a few years ago. The boys with guns demanded rice and money and fired rounds into the air, frightening her family. She grabbed her five-year-old brother and they followed the rushing crowd.

It all happened so fast. Now she cannot find her mother. She has no food or money and her brother keeps crying, and she has no idea how to calm his fears… 'Now I am suffering. I don't know what to do…'[24]

It is also important to comment on the U.S. policy toward Liberians who fled the civil war, and the more recent rebel conflict. From 1989, thousands have entered the United States as refugees, some of whom sought asylum. In 1990, the U.S. Congress established a procedure for the Attorney General to extend Temporary Protected Status (TPS) to "eligible nationals of designated countries (or parts thereof)." TPS is authorized by Section 244 of the Immigration and Nationality Act for "aliens who are nationals of countries that are subject to ongoing armed conflict, an environmental disaster, or extraordinary and temporary conditions," "or aliens of no nationality who regularly resided" in the designated country" who meet certain conditions. An alien who was a convicted felon, a persecutor, terrorist or with other security-related issues, or criminal related grounds is not eligible. The status allowed the registered person to work, but did not lead to permanent residency. A process for applicants to request fee waivers was also authorized. Permission for travel outside the U.S. was required, called "advanced parole," as continual residency was also a requirement to maintain the protected status.[25]

As a result of Liberians' plight, the U.S. Attorney General (AG) first designated Liberia as a TPS on March 27, 1991 (corrected on June 26, 1991) Both the U.S. Department of State and the Immigration and Naturalization Services (INS), formerly in the U.S. Department of Justice (and now part of the Department of Homeland Security, as the Bureau of Citizenship and Immigration Services) conducted reviews of the conflict that were used in the AG's determination. Liberian nationals were also given Deferred Enforced Departure (DED) status, which is "designated by the Office of the President of the United States of America, as a constitutional power to conduct foreign relations." The process for DED is by Executive Order or Presidential Memorandum. Due to the nearly 14 years of conflict in Liberia, the U.S. attorneys general in successive administrations granted a total of five extensions, between January 24, 1992 and March 1, 1996, an extension and redesignation on April 7, 1997, a termination on March 31, 1998, a redesignation on September 29, 1998, a second termination on July 30, 1999, and a designation on October 1, 2002.[26]

Vocal public support from Liberians and their supporters in the humanitarian and political spheres, among others, was required to maintain these designations. The prolonged need for TPS was directly due to the failed policies that had prolonged the civil war, and allowed the emergence of the two rebel factions who wished to depose Charles Taylor. A press release issued on August 16, 1999 by Congressman Patrick K. Kennedy announced that he

> ...today wrote to President Clinton to urge him to grant an immediate extension of the Temporary Protected Status (TPS) for Liberians currently residing in the United States.

> Kennedy cited the recent outbreak of violence in the war-ravaged African nation as the major reason why the U.S. should continue to grant TPS to thousands of Liberians living in the U.S. for the past eight years. TPS is scheduled to expire on September 30, 1999.

> 'It is clearer than ever that Liberia is a nation that is no longer equipped to accept the return of their refugees from the United States,' wrote Kennedy to Clinton. 'Extending TPS would be a lifesaving measure to the thousands of Liberians here in the U.S. who were lucky enough to flee the fighting of their nation's civil war, a war it would appear never really ended. This horrendous outbreak of violence shows us, as Americans, that returning Liberians from our shores to their war-torn homeland could be, for all practical purposes, a literal death sentence.'[27]

President Clinton determined that

> Over the past 10 years, many Liberians have been forced to flee their country due to civil war and widespread violence. From 1991 through 1999, we have provided Liberians in the United States with Temporary Protected Status because of these difficulties. Although the civil war in Liberia ended in 1996 and conditions have improved such that a further extension of Temporary Protected Status is no longer warranted, the political and economic situation continues to be fragile. There are compelling foreign policy reasons not to deport these Liberians at this time, including the significant risk that such a decision would cause other countries in West Africa to repatriate involuntarily many thousands of Liberian refugees, leading to instability in Liberia and potentially threatening peace along the Liberian border.

> Pursuant to my constitutional authority to conduct the foreign relations of the United States, I have determined that it is in the foreign policy interest of the United States to defer for 1 year the deportation of any Liberian national who is present in the United States as of September 29, 1999, except for the categories of individuals listed below.[28]

DED was also extended by President Bush on September 28, 2000, and September 25, 2001. The latter expired September 29, 2002.

The U.S. policy that contributed to Liberia's failure as a state, has made it virtually impossible for Liberians to return to their country. As immigrant blacks adjusting to a new country, they have been subject to a variety of socioeconomic ills—underemployment or unemployment, racism, hostilities from other U.S. residents to due to cultural differences—that has affected the welfare of families and communities. Yet the population as a whole is dedicated to making a successful life, while assisting family members left behind in Liberia. In June 2001, Melissa Bowman wrote an Op-Ed for Brown University News Service, in Providence, Rhode Island:

The Liberian population is spread throughout the United States, with the largest concentrations in Texas, Minnesota, Massachusetts, Philadelphia, Washington D.C., New York and Providence, R.I. In many states, they have organized community associations where they discuss the situation in Liberia and adjustment to the United States. Like other refugee populations, the Liberians retain close ties to their home countries while also participating fully in U.S. society. In fact, as a country originally founded by freed American slaves and as the United States' strongest ally in Africa, Liberia has always had a special relationship with this country.[29]

Due to the ethnic basis nature of the Liberian conflict, what will happen to those who fear reprisals should they be forced to return, and who wish to remain in the U.S. permanently has emerged as a policy and legislative issue. Bowman continued:

While there are currently bills in both the House and Senate proposing the granting of permanent status to those Liberians who arrived in the United States after March 1991, HR1806 and S656 will require vocal public support to pass. As a matter of life and death, what happens to these people is in no way a partisan issue. Democrats and Republicans coming together around these bills would demonstrate that the value of freedom and America's reputation as a safe haven is not divided along party lines.[30]

Finally, because of the complexity of the INS registration process, many individuals have required assistance in registering for TPS. This was customarily given by Liberian professionals and community leaders, religious groups, non-profit organizations, attorneys who specialize in immigration matters, and other parties. In 2003, the Department of Justice estimated that, for the period from October 1, 2002 to October 1, 2003, "(T)here were approximately 15,000 to 20,000 nationals of Liberia who are eligible for registration.[31]

ARMS PROLIFERATION

Observers and analysts have stated that the flow of weapons in West Africa is uncontrollable and impossible to detect.[32] Liberia Foreign Minister Monie Captan in his July, 2000 presentation before the UN Security Council. Minister Captan said:

The control of the illegal trade in arms would require the concerted efforts of the international community in monitoring the production and sale of arms and ammunition by arms-producing countries. If the international community could muster the political will, an arms registry databank could be established with data directly supplied by the manufacturer upon sale to member states. This would provide an ideal arms tracking and identification mechanism.

But the major powers—including the United States—rejected the scheme for fear of reducing their sale of arms to underdeveloped and developing countries.

In July of 2000 the New York Times reported that,

more than 170 nations reached consensus on a watered-down plan to combat illegal small-arms trafficking after the United States threatened to block agreement if language to restrict civilian gun ownership and limit weapon sales was included.[33]

The story continued that

the United States made clear from the outset that it would...reject any measure barring governments from supplying small arms to 'nonstate' actors, such as rebel groups. In the final make-or-break negotiations, the United States said it could not support consensus unless language calling for governments... 'to seriously consider legal restrictions on unrestricted trade and ownership of small arms and light weapons' was dropped and the United States view prevailed.[34]

"The U.S. should be ashamed of themselves," said South African envoy Jean Du Preez. "We are very disappointed."[35]

The Catholic Justice and Peace Commission condemned in the strongest terms the dissident attacks. They warned the rebels to take a cue from the recent Sierra Leone elections in which the war weary people of that country demonstrated their aversion to violence through the ballot box.[36]

The Panafrican News Agency reported on July 10, 2002 that the government of Burkina Faso, which in the past had been a strong and significant supporter of the Taylor government, now had distanced itself from Monrovia and no longer supplies arms to the Liberian government. A highly placed former American official commented on that information and the charges that the United States government was "pressuring" Burkina Faso to take that action.[37] He said the following: "It's not 'pressure'...it's out and out threats...if Burkina Faso does not cut off Taylor completely, the U.S. will see to it that Burkina Faso gets no more World Bank assistance." This same person expressed the belief that the United States and Great Britain were backing the LURD—that they were providing the Guineans with arms and vehicles and then looking the other way as those arms and vehicles were sent to the LURD from Guinea, a country with a terrible human rights record. He pointed to the fact that the United States was training Guinean soldiers and doing anything and everything it can to get rid of Charles Taylor.

EMBARGO ON LURD

On October 30, 2002—three years after the LURD began its military attacks on Liberia—the United Nations considered an arms embargo against the rebels. On that date, the UN Office for the Coordination of Humanitarian Affairs issued a press release, which stated that a UN panel of experts has recommended that an arms embargo be maintained against the Liberian government and extended to all armed actors, including rebels of the Liberians United for Reconciliation and Democracy (LURD)... " Note that this was merely a recommendation. The UN took no action at the time.

Finally, on November 26, 2002, the UN Security Council issued a statement extending the arms embargo to LURD. Ambassador Wang Yingfan of China, November's Security Council president, said that "prohibitions on the sale and supply to Liberia of arms and related materials...applies to any recipient in Liberia, including all non-state actors such as the LURD." There was, however, no mention of how to enforce the ban. At the same time, the Security Council once again accused Liberia's government of buying weapons in violation of a UN arms embargo and left sanctions on Liberia in place for another six months (until May of 2003). The Council did not respond to Liberia's contention that Article 51 of the United Nations Charter gives them a right to defend themselves against continued attacks by the LURD.

On November 27, 2002, the Liberian government asked ECOWAS to help arrange peace talks between the state and the LURD rebels. This request resulted from the meeting Taylor held in Monrovia with Senegal's president Abdoulaye Wade who is serving as the ECOWAS chairman. The UN Office for the Coordination of Humanitarian Affairs reported that,

> humanitarian sources said Liberia wanted the war to end to allow for peaceful presidential, parliamentary and chieftaincy elections that are slated for next year. On Monday, Taylor reaffirmed that the elections would take place as scheduled.[38]

Radio France Internationale also reported on this development:

> Since the beginning of the rebellion in 1999, this is the first time President Taylor is appearing so determined to hold a dialogue with the rebels. The move was a pleasant surprise for the civilian population, which had lost hope. This is a victory for President Wade, who, thus, is forming part of the solution to the sufferings of the Liberian people. Many Liberians reacted on national radio and television to thank the incumbent ECOWAS chairman.

However, the LURD refused to attend any talks with Charles Taylor or with any group that might lead eventually to talks with Charles Taylor.

GUINEA RESPONSE TO ALLEGED LURD TIES

On February 19, 2003 the British Broadcasting Corporation (BBC) aired an interview with the Foreign Minister of Guinea Francois Lonseny Fall by correspondent Christophe Boisbouvier. The interview dealt with Guinea and its relationship to LURD vis-a-vis Liberia:

> (Boisbouvier) You (the Foreign Minister of Guinea) will be chairing the Security Council in March. Will you be able to free yourself from the Iraqi obsession and do something else at the United Nations?

> (Fall) Yes of course. We are planning to submit several African issues. We are also planning a large ministerial debate on the proliferation of arms and the use of mercenaries, which constitutes a real threat and a concern for everyone.

> (Boisbouvier) But Lonseny Fall, you know that an accusing finger is pointed at you as well. Guinea is accused of fueling the civil war in Liberia by supporting the LURD rebels against Charles Taylor.

> (Fall) Yes, those who are saying this are saying it. But the problem of Liberia is not Guinea. We have always made it clear that the problem of Liberia is an internal issue.

> (Boisbouvier) So you are not refuting the charges of backing the LURD.

> (Fall) We are not backing the LURD at all…The LURD is not the only group that is against President Taylor…85 per cent of Liberian politicians are in exile. We wish all Liberian politicians to return home so that political life returns to normal. This is our wish for Liberia.

> (Boisbouvier) You will not be unhappy if Charles Taylor steps down, will you?

> (Fall) If this can lead to the restoration of peace in Liberia and the subregion, of course."

In one other exchange the subject discussed Guinea and U.S. interaction:

(Boisbouvier) But Francois Fall, the pressures by a country as powerful as the U.S.A. on poor countries like Guinea must be very strong at the moment. (Here they are talking about Guinea's position vis-a-vis a UN resolution to force Iraq to disarm.) Will you be able to resist such pressures and refuse to vote with the Americans?

(Fall) ...Concerning the pressure you are talking about, everybody is talking about it. But so far, we have very good relations with the US mission at the United Nations and with the US government...

(Boisbouvier) ...Is the United States promising economic assistance to you?

(Fall) We have a very balanced stance on major issues and we think we are always acting in a totally independent manner. I do not think that Guinea's policy will be based on money matters.

US CONTAINMENT POLICY

In its fiscal year 2004 performance plan, the U.S. State Department noted that:

> To help protect Sierra Leone from external threats, the United States will seek to contain Charles Taylor in Liberia using a mixture of bilateral and multilateral diplomacy (e.g., sanctions, Kimberly Process, etc.), and primarily through Economic Support Fund (ESF) programs designed to lay the foundation for his succession following the next round of elections.[39]

Even before the official publication of the performance plan (March 2003), this policy was in practice. Rather than condemn the LURD rebel offensive, Deputy Assistant Secretary of State Mark Bellamy, (in a release from the U.S. Department of State International Information Program) said at a December 9 forum held in Washington (which was attended by top-ranking members of LURD, including Joe Wylie, the self-styled military advisor of the group which is not covered by the U.S. travel sanctions against Liberian government officials): "Another 'major factor' which has served to restrain Charles Taylor's efforts to meddle in the region...has been the insurgency carried out against the Taylor government by the Liberians United for Reconciliation and Democracy (LURD)."[40] Mr. Bellamy added: "The United States does not in any way support the armed activities of this organization." At the same time he called Liberia a "failed state" and referred to the Liberian government and its president, Charles Taylor, as follows: "This is a regime whose attributes more closely resemble...a gang than...a government. This is a leader whose behavior is more closely akin to a gang leader than that of a president." Mr. Bellamy finished as follows:

> The United States does not have a duty or a moral responsibility to get rid of Charles Taylor. We have a duty and responsibility to contain him, to pressure him and to work with democratic forces in Liberia to empower them and enable them to get rid of Charles Taylor and we will do that.

Mr. Bellamy's remarks condemning President Taylor and his government were printed in the Monrovia newspaper, The Guardian, on December 17, 2002.

Shortly after U.S. Principal Deputy Assistant Secretary of State Mark Bellamy made his public comments that the LURD attacks were helpful in "containing" Charles Taylor— thereby giving a green light to more violence—the LURD recommenced its attacks and, on December 20, 2002, they retook their former northern Liberia headquarters of Bopolu and the diamond-rich town of Weasua. Their next target was the town of Tubmanburg. Once again, innocent Liberians were killed, injured and displaced.

IMPETUS FOR PEACE ACCORDS

President Taylor, according to the Associated Press, on February 5, 2003 once again urged the rebels to join him in peace talks sponsored by the other West African leaders. The talks were to be sponsored by the 15-country Economic Community of West African States (ECOWAS) and held in Bamako, Mali. Taylor also urged the rebels to lay down their arms, form a political party, and compete in national elections set for October 14. Instead of encouraging this attempt to bring peace to Liberia, the U.S. was occupied with sending military advisors to the Ivory Coast.

Later the same day (February 5, 2003) the LURD ignored President Taylor's proposal for ECOWAS brokered talks and instead issued a press release which read in part:

> ...After several days of preliminary discussions, and being responsive and sensitive to the pleas of many Liberians both at home and abroad, the LURD is asking the ICG, the Inter-Religious Council of Liberia (IRCL), and the Movement for Democratic Change in Liberia (MDCL)...to call on the Taylor government to negotiate directly with the LURD in bringing an end to the on-going military confrontation in our country. While we will lay down no preconditions to negotiation, we want to have a big say in where the meetings may be held. /s/ Gen. Joe Wylie, Senior Military Advisor & Member of the National Executive Council (LURD).

This appeared to be a somewhat disingenuous invitation since President Taylor, on at least two occasions in recent months, had asked the LURD to negotiate, which they had refused. Since the Movement for Democratic Change (MDCL), among others, was headed by Taylor's political opponents, Ellen Johnson-Sirleaf, Charles Brumskine and Harry Greaves, they were not neutral persons, as ECOWAS would be.[41]

On February 21, 2003, Agence France-Presse reported that the ECOWAS peace talks were scheduled to be held in the Malian capital of Bamako on March 9 and 10. Meanwhile the ICGL met in New York on February 28 to advance its mission for peace in Liberia. On the other hand, LURD redoubled its attempts to bring down the Liberian government.

On January 1, 2003 the National Islamic Opinion Leaders of Liberia categorically condemned the military struggle of the Liberians United for Reconciliation and Democracy (LURD) against the peace deserving people of Liberia. The group said "it believes that the barrel of the gun is not the answer and the prudent way forward in ascending to political power in the country." Their statement urged the LURD to disengage from their military campaigns and begin to constructively engage the government "through dialogue and reconciliation since in fact reconciliation can be symbolically found in the acronym of the LURD." At the same time, the Liberian Islamic leaders called upon the United States "to quickly and sincerely emulate the good examples of Great Britain and France in Sierra Leone and Ivory Coast respectively by helping to foster genuine peace and stability."[42]

Reuters, on February 18, 2003, quoted the Liberian Defense Minister as saying that "rebels fighting to oust Liberian President Charles Taylor are battling government troops on four fronts...Tubmanburg, Gba, in and around Zorzor and around the Kolahun area." The Reuters story added: "Some Western diplomats say they believe Liberian armed forces, often made up of private pro-Taylor militias, sometimes fake rebel attacks to allow them to loot and spread fear." Giving the lie to these unnamed "Western diplomats," the United Nations put out a release the same day which said:

> An inter-agency mission dispatched over the weekend reported that large areas of western Liberia have fallen under rebel control. In Monrovia at the weekend, we had reports that the rebels have pushed to around 20 kilometres outside the city...However by yesterday we were told that the government forces had repulsed the rebels and the city was calm.[43]

NOTES

[1] Emmanuel Goujon, "Conneh: Liberia's top rebel leader who see himself as president," *Agence France-Presse,* September 18. 2002, p. l.

[2] Silvia Aloisi, "U.N. Liberia sanctions hurting wrong people-UNICEF," *Reuters English News Service*, September 1, 2001.

[3] Note Verbale from the Ministry of Foreign Affairs of Liberia to the Embassy of the United States in Monrovia, Liberia, October 23, 2000.

[4] Human Rights Watch. Africa Division, "Back to the Brink: War Crimes by Liberian Government and Rebels: A Call for Greater International Attention to Liberia and Sub Region," Vol 14, No. 4(A), May 2002, p. 10.

[5] U.S. Overseas Loans and Grants, Military Assistance Loans and Grants, U.S. Agency for International Development, Fiscal 2003 and Fiscal 2004 budgets for Guinea.

[6] "LURD possesses U.S. weapons," *The New Liberia Newspaper*, June 11, 2002. citing a Radio France Internationale (RFI) report.

[7] Irwin Arieff, "Liberian arms deals laundered through Nigeria," *Reuters English News Service*, October 14, 2002, p. 1.

[8] Human Rights Watch, p. 13–14.

[9] Report of the Panel of Experts appointed pursuant to Security Council resolution 1306 (2000), paragraph 19, in relation to Sierra Leone.

[10] Halberstam, *War in a Time of Peace*, p. 141.

[11] Awoniyi, Ola, "Nigeria hopeful of peace in Liberia," *Agence France-Presse,* March 15, 2002, p. l.

[12] Irwin Arieff, "Liberian arms deals laundered through Nigeria," *Reuters English News Service*, October 14, 2002, p. 1.

[13] Alphonso Toweh, "Fighting intensifies in central Liberia," *Reuters*, May, 7, 2002. p. 1.

[14] Sherriff Z. Adams, "Rebels Release Catholic Priest to Inter Religious Council," the News, *allAfrica Global Media*, May 29, 2002, p. l. <http://allafrica.com/stories/200205290298.html>; "UN urges Liberian rebels'to release five nurses," *Reuters English News Service*, July 21, 2002, p. 1.

[15] "Interview with William Hanson, Senior Spokesman of LURD," *The Perspective*, May 15,2002, p.2, <www.theperspective.org>.

[16] "Resist unlawful attempts, CPP tells members," The News, *allAfrica Global Media*, p. 1, February 18, 2002, at <http://allafrica.com/stories/200202180121.html>.

[17] Tiawon S. Gongloe, address before the Liberian Senate, February 27, 2002.

[18] Personal communication between the author and State Department official.

[19] "Government withdraws soldiers from streets of Monrovia," *Panafrican News Agency (PANA) Daily Newswire*, September 18, 2002, p. 1.

[20] Personal communication with State Department official; "Bitter fighting as rebels attack key Liberian town," *Agence France-Presse,* May 9, 2002, quoting Charles Taylor.

[21] Human Rights Watch, "Back to the Brink." Vol.14, No.4(A), May 2002," p.7.

[22] Ibid.

[23] UN Office for the Coordination of Humanitarian Affairs, "Fighting resumes in Lofa County," October 29, 2002, p. l, citing World Food Programme.

[24] Emily Wax, "In Peril, Liberians Look Homeward: War in Ivory Coast Leaves Thousands Displaced Again, *Washington Post*, January 8, 2003, A13.

[25] Immigration and Naturalization Services (INS) (now Bureau of Citizenship and Immigration Services)."What is Temporary Protected Status?" <http://www.immigration.gov/graphics/services/tps_inter.htm#whatistps>.

[26] INS, "Liberia, Temporary Protected Status." <http://www.immigration.gov/graphics/services/tps_LIBE.htm>.

[27] U.S. House of Representatives. "Kennedy Calls Upon Clinton to Extend Temporary Protected Status for Liberians," Press Release, August 16, 1999, <http://www.house.gov/patrickkennedy/pr990816.html>.

[28] The White House Office of the Press Secretary (New Orleans, Louisiana) September 27, 1999 Memorandum for The Attorney General Subject: Measures Regarding Certain Liberians in the United States <http://www.reliefweb.int/w/rwb.nsf/0/8fa13409b6fd3756852567fa00768edc?OpenDocument>.

[29] Melissa Bowman, "Liberians fear of being denied refuge is a real one," <http://www.brown.edu/Administration/News_Bureau/2000-01/00-147.html>

[30] Ibid.

[31] U.S. Department of Justice. "Attorney General Designates Liberia Under The Temporary Protected Status Program." September 27, 2002. Press Release.

[32] UN Security Council, Panel of Experts Report, 1999. paragraphs 171, 172 and 176.

[33] "Nations agree to limit sales of illicit arms," *New York Times*, July 22, 2001. Late Edition–Final, Section 1, p. 10, col. 6.

[34] Ibid.

[35] Colum Lynch, "Nations Reach Pact on Trade of Small Arms," *Washington Post*, July 22, 2001, p. Section 1, A17.

[36] "LURD Listen to the Voice of Reason," *AllAbout Liberia.com*, July 6, 2001, <www.allaboutliberia.com/editorial91.htm>.

[37] Personal communication with former State Department official, July 26, 2002.

[38] UN Office for the Coordination of Humanitarian Affairs, Taylor urges ECOWAS to arrange talks with LURD, November 27, 2002, p. l.

[39] U.S. Department of State, "FY 2004 Performance Plan," Bureau of Resource Management, Office of Strategic and Performance Planning (RM/SPP), U.S. Department of State, Number 11042, March 2003, p. 47. Available at <http://www.state.gov/m/rm/rls/perfplan/2004/>.

[40] Charles Corey, Washington File Staff 'writer, U.S. Department of State. International Information Program (www.usinfo.state.gov.). Principal Deputy Assistant Secretary Bellamy addresses Liberia forum, December 11, 2002, pp. 1–3.

[41] Bodioh W. Siapoe, "Liberian Woman Eyes Presidency: Forms Another Movement in America," Coalition of Progressive Liberians in America (COPLA), n.d., <www.copla.org/mdcl.htm>.

[42] "National Islamic Leaders Condemn LURD, Appeal to U.S.," *AllAboutLiberia.com*, January 23, 2003. <http://www.allaboutliberia.com/jan2003/230107n7.htm>.

[43] Alphonso Toweh, "Liberian minister says fighting on four fronts," *Reuters*, February 18, 2003.

CHAPTER 8
NATURAL RESOURCES

DIAMONDS

As in the section on Sierra Leone regarding aid to the RUF, one may not suggest that Liberia was not involved in the diamond trade with Sierra Leone; the country has done so—legally—for many, many years. Regarding the *illegal* sale of diamonds, many countries of the world are complicit; while shielding complicity of certain countries from public view, worldwide scrutiny has highlighted the problems in several African nations, and especially the Taylor administration's violations of UN sanctions against the sale of diamonds from conflict nations. The United States, the main proponent of the UN sanctions, implemented its own sanctions prohibiting trade in diamonds from Liberia.

Diamonds have served as the "banker" for many of the civil disruptions in Africa. In 1982 an investigative reporter named Edward Jay Epstein wrote a book, titled *The Rise and Fall of Diamonds,* which delineates the history and importance of diamonds. In the words of the publishers (Simon and Schuster),

> the compelling, in-depth story of the creation, maintenance and imminent shattering of a brilliant illusion: the belief that diamonds are scarce and consequently of great value, inherently desirable for their beauty and as lasting tokens of wealth, power and romance. But the tiny carbon crystals that make up diamonds are neither scarce nor of great intrinsic value; in fact, until now, their supply has been ingeniously controlled to ensure that their market worth remained high. Even the demand for diamonds itself was artificially created and is part of...an immense international yet centrally controlled system that has lasted for nearly a hundred years.[1]

Beginning in 1870 when huge diamond mines were discovered near the Orange River in South Africa, the British financiers who had organized the South African mines realized that their investments would be endangered if the market became deluged by a growing flood of diamonds. So they formed a cartel known as the De Beers Consolidated Mines Ltd. It was incorporated in South Africa and took control of all aspects of the world diamond trade. As Edward Jay Epstein wrote:

> In London, it operated under the innocuous name of the Diamond Trading Company. In Israel it was known under the all-embracing mantle of 'the syndicate'. In Antwerp, it was just called the CSO—initials referring to the Central Selling Organization (which was an arm of the Diamond Trading Company). And in Black Africa, it disguised its South African origins under subsidiaries...At its height, it not only either directly owned or controlled all the diamond mines in southern Africa, it also owned trading companies in England, Portugal, Israel, Belgium, Holland and Switzerland...By 1981 De Beers had proved to be the most successful cartel arrangement in the annals of modern commerce.[2]

Epstein continued:

> Through the brilliant financial maneuvers of Sir Ernest Oppenheimer, the diamond cartel had succeeded in gaining control of virtually all the diamond

mines in the world by the early 1950s. It had made its arrangements with the governments of South Africa, the colonial administrations in Angola, the Congo and Sierra Leone…It was fully backed by the British, Belgian and the French governments, and it was recognized by every other government concerned as the official channel for the diamond trade.[3]

De Beers has made the diamond industry competitive and profitable. Diamonds are precious items for which people will pay huge sums of money. A number of African countries, that are rich in diamonds, have used this wealth to finance whatever adventures state or non-state actors wished to pursue.

The sale of illicit diamonds has fueled many of the civil wars in Africa, the Congo, Angola, and Sierra Leone are prime examples.[4] As with so many other issues, however, the major powers have focused their attention on only one part of the problem: the actions of countries that mine and sell the diamonds. Every effort was made to shield the other half of the equation: the countries that bought the diamonds. But just as in the drug trade, the buyers were just as complicit as the sellers. Great Britain is the largest seller of diamonds in the world, many of which come from its former colony in Africa, Sierra Leone.[5] As we examine the diamond trade in Sierra Leone, and the historic route of sale through Liberia, one must ask the question: who was responsible for trading in what has become known as "blood diamonds"? Since the diamonds were smuggled, the sellers could not use reputable dealers but instead relied upon middle-men with questionable business practices. These unsavory characters in turn sold the diamonds in the world's major diamond capitals, such as Belgium, South Africa, Israel, Britain, etc. Belgium, for example, is the world's main importer of diamonds. If a diamond company was approached by one of the middle-men with the so-called "blood" diamonds, the buyer knew very well that the diamonds were likely smuggled.

A report on the diamond trade by Partnership Africa Canada, a coalition of Canadian and African nongovernmental organizations, urged Belgium to end its attraction for organized crime syndicates.[6] The report said that "by accepting Liberian exports of diamonds as legitimate, the international diamond industry actively colludes in crimes committed or permitted by the Liberian government."

In addition to the official channels described above, there were unofficial channels that the diamond cartel, back in the 1950s, did not control: the smuggling routes that, according to Epstein, "led from the diamond mines and diggings in southern and western Africa to entrepots such as Monrovia and Beirut."[7] Sir Ernest Oppenheimer, the head of De Beers, hired the former head of Britain's MI-5 (its counter-espionage service), Sir Percy Sillitoe. Oppenheimer explained to Sillitoe that "the smuggling of diamonds not only deprived De Beers of the value of the stolen diamonds, but far more serious, it threatened to undermine the monopoly prices for diamonds that De Beers had established."[8] Sillitoe was to identify the individuals who illegally bought and sold the diamonds and then "turn" them into double agents for the cartel. Sillitoe soon learned that "the cartel's problem was not the trickle of diamonds being stolen from the South African mines but the flood of diamonds that were smuggled out of west and central Africa every year."

Note one of Sillitoe's conclusions as reported by Epstein in his book:
In central and west Africa…most diamonds were 'mined' from stream beds that meandered over tens of thousands of miles of jungle. To recover these diamonds, natives needed only a shovel and a pan. Even though the governments had granted concessions to various

diamond mining companies associated with De Beers, and had in theory banned anyone else from digging for diamonds, it was in practice impossible to enforce these regulations.[9] Fifty years later the United Nations Panel of Experts came to the same conclusion. "The problem," continued Epstein,

> was particularly difficult in Sierra Leone, where the river banks were littered with diamonds...At night, gangs of 'pot-holers', as they were called, would dig up the river banks and disappear at daybreak with the diamondiferous gravel. The pot-holers would then either sell their diamonds to Lebanese traders or directly to Mandingo tribesmen who, in turn, smuggled them across the long open border to Liberia. By one means or another, it was estimated that more than half of Sierra Leone's diamonds were sold in Monrovia as 'Liberian' diamonds.[10]

To return to the 1950s, Sillitoe concluded that he could not do business with the "pot-holers," so he decided to concentrate on the Lebanese middlemen. He recruited a group of intelligence agents posing as independent diamond buyers. They let it be known that they would pay high prices for large numbers of diamonds. The British government then authorized Sillitoe and his men to use hard currency to buy up smuggled diamonds. Then, through surveillance and intercepted mail,

> they traced the traffic from the diamond fields of Sierra Leone through the entrepots of Liberia to the wholesale markets in Belgium. It turned out that reputable European merchants, who were also customers of the cartel, had been surreptitiously financing the African smugglers and one of the principal buyers of the smuggled goods was the (then) Soviet Union, which critically needed industrial diamonds to retool its factories.[11]

Sillitoe hired private armies of mercenaries to ambush the diamond caravans formed in the jungle on the route that led through the swamps from Sierra Leone to Liberia known as the "stranger's trail." His informants told him about the exact movement of the diamond shipments in order to facilitate his ambush. Then he turned over the diamonds to a De Beers subsidiary. Because many of these ambushes were bloody affairs and the risk of smuggling diamonds had increased, the Lebanese dealers began to sell their contraband diamonds in Sierra Leone. De Beers then established a string of buying offices in Sierra Leone. "Each buying office was no more than a corrugated iron hut with a barred slit through which De Beers' agent did business with the Lebanese traders and the pot-holers."[12] In this way De Beers controlled the traffic in smuggled diamonds. Sillitoe completed his work on behalf of DeBeers in 1957.

This problem has continued unabated. When the U.S. and the UN accused Liberia of dealing in Sierra Leonean diamonds, it was impossible to differentiate between the involvement of the government, and the traditional middlemen. The latter, mainly either Lebanese or Mandingo, often smuggled diamonds independently from Sierra Leone to Liberia, and hence to the diamond capitals of the world. There are also countries which, for tax-savings purposes, falsely describe their diamonds as "Liberian."

In 1968, Sierra Leone was severely criticized for doing business with the diamond cartel. In response, the government created a state-owned diamond company called Dominico to which all the diamonds found in the country had to be sold. Then, according to Edward Jay Epstein, half of the diamonds were sold by Dominico to a London corporation which in turn sold the diamonds to De Beers.

The remaining half was in theory at least sold to three independent American dealers—Maurice Tempelsman, who received 27 per cent, Lazare Kaplan, who received 3 per cent, and Harry Winston, who received the other 20 percent. In reality, however, both Tempelsman and Kaplan resold their share to the Diamond Trading Company in London, which effectively gave the cartel control of 80 per cent of the Sierra Leonean diamonds. Winston, who like Kaplan and Tempelsman was a major customer of the cartel, was temporarily permitted to sell his 20% share in New York.[13]

This arrangement worked out well until a group of Lebanese tradesmen decided that they no longer would tolerate being cut out of the lucrative diamond trade. On November 13, 1968, a group of masked gunmen held up a shipment of diamonds destined for Freetown. They obtained a private plane at the airport in Freetown and flew the diamonds to Europe where they were sold for an estimated $10 million to a consortium of diamond dealers. The cartel's investigations showed that the Sierra Leone police had allowed the bandits to leave Sierra Leone and concluded that there was corruption high up in the Sierra Leonean government, which was in league with the disgruntled Lebanese diamond traders.

The cartel decided to do business with the Lebanese and chose the single most powerful Lebanese entrepreneur in Sierra Leone, Jamil Mohammed. It took away the 20% "cut" previously granted to Harry Winston and gave it to Mohammed on the condition that Mohammed sell the diamonds back to the cartel at a substantial profit. "The net effect of this new arrangement was that the cartel received nearly 100 per cent of Sierra Leone's diamonds…"[14]

De Beers made similar deals with President Mobutu Sese Seko of Zaire in which all Zairian diamonds were sold to a privately held corporation which in turn delivered the diamonds to De Beers' Diamond Trading Company in London. A similar deal also was arranged in Angola.

For 300 years, diamonds from around the world have been graded, sorted and classified in Antwerp, Belgium (King Leopold of Belgium started the infamous "scramble for Africa" at the end of the 19th century). Antwerp has four of the world's 21 diamond exchanges and does a turnover of $23 billion a year. Christopher Dickey wrote in the July 10, 2000 issue of Newsweek that:

> Diamond traders…do million-dollar deals with a handshake…But the other side of the diamond fellowship is secrecy that verges on *omerta.* Organized crime also loves handshake deals. In the mid–1990s a Pakastani allegedly used a diamond business to launder huge quantities of drug money. Russian bureaucrats charged with embezzling $180 million worth of gold and diamonds went to Antwerp to cash their diamonds.

Diamonds that come from conflict areas (such as Angola, Congo or Sierra Leone) are called by the British "blood diamonds." They account for less than 4% of the 860 million diamonds polished last year.[15] But diamonds cannot be distinguished as coming from one country or another. In other words, they can't be "fingerprinted"; however, the middle men who sell the diamonds can be identified. Diamonds are the cornerstone of the economies of South Africa, Namibia, and Botswana.

De Beers today controls perhaps only 50% of the worlds' diamond trade.

> They used to try to buy up all the rest—whatever their source—to control prices. But the system started to break down in the 1990s as producers in Canada, Australia, Russia and elsewhere refused to go along...As international pressure grows, handshakes are less common than finger-pointing among diamonds' big players.[16]

Although the focus of the international press on Liberia could lead one to believe it was the greatest source of the trade in illegal diamonds, the estimated value of illegitimate diamonds traded in the Congo annually is $400 million, contrasted with $138 million (World Bank estimate) in Liberia and Sierra Leone.[17] Notwithstanding, the U.S. has continued to send large amounts of financial aid to the Congo, while sanctioning Liberia and sending little aid.

The charge against Liberia was, 1) that it took Sierra Leone diamonds provided by the RUF, sold them abroad, and used the money both to buy weapons for its own use (presumably to defend Liberia against the LURD armed attacks) and for the RUF; and 2) that Liberia has failed to develop a certification program to identify diamonds that it exports for sale.

On July 31, 2000 Monie Captan, Liberia's foreign minister, and Jenkins Dunbar, the minister of Lands, Mine & Energy, appeared in New York at a hearing of the Security Council called to assess the role of diamonds in the Sierra Leone conflict pursuant to UN Resolution 1132 (1997). Minister Captan said at that hearing:

> The Government of Liberia, before the passage of Resolution 1306, required the processing of an application for precious commodity export permit which required a declaration of origin of precious commodities, including diamonds. The application form, which has been in use in Liberia for several years, will be distributed to this assembly. Additionally, and in support of the measures taken by the international community, the Liberian government has introduced a Certificate of Origin regime, specifically for rough diamonds; a copy of this Certificate form will also be distributed to this assembly. With the introduction of this regime, the Liberian Government will call for buyers to only purchase diamonds from Liberia that are certificated by the Government and can be verified by Liberian Embassies, and specifically our Embassy in Brussels and the Liberian Consulate General in Antwerp.

Thus, Liberia did have a diamond certification program, although not one that the United States and the UN apparently accepted as adequate.

Minister Captan continued in his statement, and said:

> ...(T)he measures taken by the Liberian Government will only be effective with the cooperation of the buyer countries. Also essential is the assistance of the international community and the United Nations Secretariat, in the provision of resources to develop the capacity of the Liberian Government to effectively monitor and control the diamond trade in its territory. The Government of Liberia, in its Reconstruction Plan presented to the Donors Consultative Meeting held in Paris in December 1997, under the aegis of the World Bank and the United Nations, solicited support for the effective expansion of government authority throughout its territory under its local governance program. The response of the international donor community

for this program was negligible, despite the breakdown of the local governance program after the 7-year civil war in Liberia, and the Government's continued appeal for assistance for human resource development and capacity building. Liberia needs the technical empowerment to monitor and control the complex illicit trade occurring within its territory and the West African sub-region as a whole. Small poor countries just do not have the capacity to tackle the complex syndicates of illicit trade on their own.

Minister Captan then raised a compelling question, relative to the Lomé Accord and its extension of control of Sierra Leone's diamond fields to RUF rebels. He said:

> In the absence of the Sierra Leonean Government control of its diamond mines , one is constrained to ask the question, 'which diamonds has the Government of Sierra Leone been certificating?' Are rebels (in July of 2000) selling their diamonds to brokers who take these conflict diamonds to Freetown and legitimize them through the payment of taxes and export fees to the Government of Sierra Leone? The Government of Sierra Leone has reported an increase in its diamond revenue since its introduction of the Certificate of Origin regime despite the fact that rebels continue to control the country's mining regions…Isn't it the intention of the Security Council, that as members of the international community, we take collective measures to ensure that rebels do not earn income from conflict diamonds to purchase arms to continue armed struggle against a legitimate government?

Captan maintained that control of the diamond regions of Sierra Leone by legitimate authorities could be achieved through the deployment of peacekeepers in the diamond region. He described the complexity of the diamond trade in the sub-region as follows:

> Liberia's border with Sierra Leone is 250 kilometers (about 155 miles) long; that the border is mostly dense tropical forest with footpaths linking villages from both sides; that a large volume of cross-border trade occurred between the two neighbors before 1990 with traders using the footpaths and existing motor roads; that the regions bordering Liberia and Sierra Leone are diamond bearing…; that between 1965 and 1989, Liberia's total export-production of diamonds amounted to 11.4 million carats; that during the civil war in Liberia, diamonds were mined by various armed factions and sold into neighboring countries without the knowledge of the authorities; that the same situation is also occurring in Sierra Leone; that diamond trading in the sub-region is mainly through smuggling involving international brokers to evade government taxes.

Despite the facts set forth above, the United States demanded that Taylor patrol the border between Liberia and Sierra Leone. But when Liberia asked the UN to help monitor the border between the two countries, the UN answered that the border is too long and porous for effective patrols.[18] The contradiction—it can or it cannot be controlled—was not resolved.

> It is also important to note that according to De Beers, most so-called Liberian diamonds entering Antwerp actually come from Russia in order to avoid the .3 per cent import levy that Belgium charges on non-African goods." So-called Liberian diamonds entering Belgium do not require documentary evidence of origin, and therefore the methodology of using Liberian imports

into Antwerp as a measure of calculating Sierra Leonean production is undoubtedly questionable and inaccurate."[19]

Industry complicity was an issue. U.S. Congressman Tony Hall (D-Ohio) stated that "rebels could not have turned their contraband into ready cash without this industry's complicity."[24] BBC stated in its July 6, 2000 news report that the diamond "pipeline"— "from mines in Africa, North America and Russia to the sparkling gems in your local jeweler's—is long and complex, with gems passing through literally dozens of hands." The industry's reluctance to control the buyers, as well as the seller, likely stemmed from financial interests: $6.8 billion of uncut stones are produced internationally, then turned into 67 million pieces of jewelry worth $50 billion dollars. BBC concluded: "If the main cutting centres in Belgium, Israel, India and the United States could be obliged only to accept diamonds of clear origin, conflict diamonds could be squeezed out of the industry."

Minister Captan's argument to the UN also advanced another important perspective on the diamonds issue for Liberia and other diamond-producing nations:

> It is quite unfortunate that international attention was only aroused by the linkages of illegal diamond trading to conflicts and not to the many years of exploitation and outright theft of the precious mineral resources of poor countries. If Liberia today supports the actions of the Security Council, it is not only because illegal diamond trading can fuel conflicts, but also because of the tremendous deprivation of our resources by the powerful and affluent buyers.[20]

Although Foreign Minister Captan always observed diplomatic etiquette, he was extraordinarily frustrated that the UN and the United States in particular, insisted that Charles Taylor smuggled diamonds, but gave no proof. In that regard, BBC's West Africa correspondent, Mark Doyle, in a July 18, 2000 story on the diamond trade, wrote: "What is curious is that if Britain or the United States do have evidence to prove Liberia's involvement, why do they not publish it?" Doyle put that question to Walter Greenfield, the Chargé d'Affaires of the U.S. Embassy in Liberia:

> What we have said is that there are many reports out there that allege that the Government of Liberia is involved through illicit diamonds and the flow of weapons and we are concerned by them." Doyle comments: "Is that the kind of evidence that warrants cutting off all outside aid to the three million Liberian people, so many of whom live in poverty and misery?[21]

Liberian President Charles Taylor was asked the same question and answered Doyle:

> When someone gets up and says that Liberia is involved in diamond smuggling and gun-running like a movie—you've got to be joking. But what we have said is, with all of the western intelligence—for God's sake. These people have satellites focused on Sierra Leone. Could someone please bring me one photograph of a convoy going?[22]

If Taylor lied, why did not the United States refute his denials? The traditional answer was that "we never reveal information that might compromise our intelligence gathering capacity and our informants."[23] However, many Americans remember that President John F. Kennedy faced down the Russians by showing on U.S. television the satellite photos of Russian missile facilities in Cuba. When President George W. Bush asked the world to join the U.S. in fighting the Taliban, he made public intelligence that revealed their activities.

In 2003 the U.S. turned over intelligence material to the inspectors in Iraq. Secretary of State Colin Powell, on February 5, 2003 appeared before the UN Security Council with maps, aerial photographs and recordings of phone taps to make the case that Iraq possessed weapons of mass destruction. If public proof was given in these cases, the question remained: Why not in the case of Liberia and Sierra Leone?

BBC's Mark Doyle concluded that "proof is hard to get" that Liberia is smuggling out Sierra Leone diamonds in exchange for arms to the RUF. The so-called Sierra Leone secret police files which purport to describe the movement of guns and diamonds between Sierra Leone and Liberia were suspect. "These interesting documents remain allegations, not proof," said Doyle. They purported to implicate both Liberia and Burkina Faso. Interestingly, Liberia bore virtually all criticism, and little or nothing was said about the actions of Burkina Faso. Diamonds are relatively easy to smuggle because of the difficulty in identifying their geographic source. There is less difficulty in identifying illicit diamond traders from legitimate ones, but the buyers of the diamonds in Antwerp, New York, Tel Aviv and Bombay (the major diamond centers of the world) and elsewhere ignore that issue. As a rule, they have purchased diamonds, no matter where they come from or who sells them.

There was an international response to problem of conflict diamonds, fully supported by the U.S., the UN, and the diamond industry, to stop the fradulent certification and trade of raw conflict diamonds. Initiated in South Africa in May 2000 and developed through a series of meetings, it was implemented January 1, 2003 as the Kimberley Process Certification Scheme (KPCS).[25] The Kimberley Process was designed to benefit "nations affected by rebel activity...financed by trade in conflict diamonds" and "the broader diamond industry" by providing "a consistent and stable framework for the trade..."[26] The implementation document, listed more than 70 participating countries and regional governments. The certification procedure includes these requirements:

> Each Participant should ensure that:
>
> (a) a Kimberley Process Certificate (hereafter referred to as the Certificate) accompanies each shipment of rough diamonds on export;
>
> (b) its processes for issuing Certificates meet the minimum standards of the Kimberley Process as set out in Section IV;
>
> (c) Certificates meet the minimum requirements set out in Annex I. As long as these requirements are met, Participants may at their discretion establish additional characteristics for their own Certificates, for example their form, additional data or security elements;
>
> (d) it notifies all other Participants through the Chair of the features of its Certificate as specified in Annex I, for purposes of validation.[27]

If all nations in the diamond trade participate, monitor, and comply with KPCS, it would stop the sale of falsely labeled "conflict" diamonds.

In conjunction with the Kimberley Process, greater industry self-regulation and the imposition of sanctions or penalties by countries on the 13,000 traders of both rough or finished diamonds who violate the new provisions, could further limit the laundering of gems. Another constructive move would be oversight of the country's diamond industry by the Belgian government, instead of relying on the private Diamond High Council (De Beers in another guise).

On April 25, 2003 President George Bush signed into law the Clean Diamond Trade Act, the legislative measure taken in conjunction with the U.S. adoption of the Kimberley Process. In Section 2. Findings, the Act states issues involved with the conflicts in Sierra Leone, the Democratic Republic of Congo, and Angola, and the prohibition of U.S. trade in Liberian diamonds (the only country against which the U.S. has imposed sanctions). Section 8, Enforcement indicates that civil penalties "not to exceed $10,000 may be imposed," and

> (2) whoever willfully violates, or willfully attempts to violate, any license, order, or regulation issued under this Act shall, upon conviction, be fined not more than $50,000, or, if a natural person, may be imprisoned for not more than 10 years, or both; and any officer, director, or agent of any corporation who willfully participates in such violation may be punished by a like fine, imprisonment, or both.

> (b) IMPORT VIOLATIONS- Those customs laws of the United States, both civil and criminal, including those laws relating to seizure and forfeiture, that apply to articles imported in violation of such laws shall apply with respect to rough diamonds imported in violation of this Act.[28]

The enforcement is the responsibility of U.S. Customs and Border Protection and U.S. Immigration and Customs enforcement.

As indicated in the report from the Kimberley Process 2003 plenary meeting, Liberia expressed its intent to become a participant. But the UN sanctions still in place against the trade of diamonds from Liberia must be lifted before it can achieve this goal:

> The Participants in the Kimberley Process Certification Scheme (KPCS) met in Johannesburg, South Africa from 28 to 30 April 2003, to deliberate on matters pertaining to the implementation of the KPCS, which started on 1 January 2003. Fifty-one (51) states and one Regional Economic Integration Organisation, the European Community, are currently participating in the Kimberley Process Certification Scheme...

> The Plenary also considered the Republic of Liberia's indication that it would like to become a Participant in the KPCS. In view of the existing United Nations Security Council embargo against trade in diamonds with Liberia, an application to become a Participant may only be considered once the diamond trade embargo has been lifted. The Liberian Government has invited the Kimberley Process to send a review mission to Liberia as soon as possible.[29]

On February 18, President Taylor sent a letter to the president of the United Nations Security Council, with copies to Secretary-General Kofi Annan, the chairman of the African Union, Thabo Mbeki, and the chairman of ECOWAS, John Kufuor, explaining that since Liberia had met the requirements set down by the UN, and since hostilities in Sierra Leone had ended, there no longer was any basis for the UN to continue sanctions against Liberia. One section of President Taylor's letter is worthy of note. It deals with the UN's demand for a diamond certification program. President Taylor wrote:

> (T)he Government of Liberia contacted the High Diamond Council in Brussels seeking assistance in establishing its diamond certification regime. The High Diamond Council initial reaction was one of willingness pending the acquiescence of the Security Council. The Government sought out and

obtained the acquiescence of the Security Council, reverted to the High Diamond Council, which surprisingly expressed reluctance in providing its assistance to the Government of Liberia. The Government reported this development to the Panel of Experts on Liberia which later reported to the Security Council sanctions Committee on Liberia after their investigation they had discovered that the United States Ambassador accredited to Belgium had called the high Diamond Council and dissuaded it from providing any assistance to the Government of Liberia…nevertheless the Government of Liberia has completed its diamond cerificate regime with the technical assistance of a South African firm.[30]

After giving other examples of U.S. interference, Mr. Taylor concluded that these cases

present a very disturbing and frustating paradox because while Liberia is exerting every effort to comply with the demands of the Security Council, the United States, a permanent member, has acted to undermine Liberia's compliance while advocating the continuation of sanctions on Liberia.[31]

TIMBER

Between 1997 and 2003, the other most controversial revenue-producing industry in Liberia was logging. Liberia's timber, of exceptionally high quality, is sold all over the world. The reactions to the management of Liberia's timber industry have greatly differed from the government position. One is reminded of Rashomon in which two people see the same event but come to totally different conclusions as to what actually happened.

Generally speaking, the international environmental community has been appalled by what they believe is the destruction of one of Africa's last remaining rain forests. Internal opponents of the government have claimed that the profits from the logging industry go into the pockets of President Charles Taylor. They have also asserted that foreign workers were used in the timber industry and there have been no benefits to the people of Liberia.

The government sold timber abroad to produce revenue but insisted that it was not clear-cutting the forest but rather replanting in an environmentally correct manner. It stated that the money produced was used to pay Liberian workers, keep the country's economy afloat, and support the army as it defended itself against attacks by the LURD rebels and other anti-government forces.

Liberia's Forest Development Authority (FDA) is the sole body in Liberia charged with allocating timber concessions and gathering revenues. It estimates that Liberia's forests total 11.8 million acres and are home to more than 2,000 varieties of plants of which less than 240 are considered as rare wood. The FDA says that the potential stock of saleable timber species is estimated at 81.3 million tons. Most of the timber is exported to Europe, notably France, and to Asia, mainly China and Indonesia.[32]

In 2000 China imported 303,377 cubic metres (11 million cubic feet) of Liberian wood, France 105,126 cubic metres and Indonesia 25,444 cubic metres.[33] The varieties included the coveted mahogany and local hardwoods. Global Witness reversed these figures when it stated that France buys 37.07% of total Liberia exports; Italy is at 19.17%; Turkey at 15.07%; China at 7.77%; and Indonesia at 6.31% of total exports.[34]

In 2001 the FDA said that 52% of the production in Liberia was managed by the Oriental Timber Company (OTC), a Malaysian-based company, which exported 61% of the timber products of the country.

In June of 2001 the FDA, in collaboration with the Oriental Timber Corporation, put on nursery over 4,320 varieties of tree species, which covers 200 acres of reforestation farmland adjacent to the Cestos Bridge, connecting Grand Bassa and Rivercess counties. These are species that can be used for plywood, paper production, and timber.

Agence France-Presse (AFP) reported on August 10, 2002 that

> the increase in logging and the revenues earned from wood are related to the upsurge in fighting, British-based watchdog organization Global Witness has said. 'The Timber provides funds which contribute to perpetuate the armed conflict in the region,' Global Vision director Patrick Alley told AFP in London. Citing an annual report of Liberia's central bank, Global Witness said the 'wood of war' fetched the state 49 million dollars between January and May 2000...United Nations sanctions on major Liberian products do not include wood. The sanctions were imposed because of Taylor's perceived support to rebels in neighboring Sierra Leone who ended their brutal war in January."

The OTC recently invested 45 million dollars in Africa's largest plywood factory in the eastern port city of Buchanan.[35] In the debate over Liberia's forests, that was a very good thing for the people, but a very bad thing for the environment.

In January of 2002, the Government of Liberia signed a Memorandum of Understanding (MOU) with the Conservation International Foundation of California, an organization dedicated to the conservation of biodiversity worldwide by demonstrating that humanity and nature can live in harmony. The parties agreed "that the GOL is committed to establishing a biologically representative network of protected areas covering at least 30% of the existing forest area, representing about 3.7 million acres."[36]

The agreement would preserve the Lake Piso Nature Reserve (76,025 acres), the Cestos-Senkwehn National Park (226,595 acres), the Wologezi National Park (197,690 acres), another portion of the Wologezi National Park (176,491 acres), the Mt. Nimba Nature Reserve (56,000 acres), and extension of the Sapo National Park (321,000 acres) all in the year 2002. These are the short-term provisions of the agreement.

The medium term actions include, among others, the "identification and designation of core protected zones within current logging concessions."

Long-term actions (within 5 years) include "complete establishment of protected area network covering...3.7 million acres.

There are reports that the U.S. Ambassador to Liberia John Blaney held meetings meeting with environmental experts, Liberian government officials, and the OTC leadership in an attempt to bring these agreements to fruition.[37]

Despite this commitment to preservation of national parks, environmental groups such as Global Witness, which is a United Kingdom NGO (non-governmental organization) "recommend that the United Nations Security Council impose sanctions on Liberia's timber exports which they claim help finance the war in neighboring Sierra Leone and along the border with Guinea." according to the London Financial Times.[38] The newspaper quoted a western diplomat who commented in September 2001 that "we are at the beginning of the end game in Sierra Leone. I don't think the Security Council is going to want to turn up the ratchet on Liberia."

Environmental groups continued to focus on Liberia for its practices. Kofi Annan, the secretary-general of the United Nations on September 3, 2001 warned that any attempt by the world body to include rubber, timber, air transportation or shipping would further worsen the humanitarian crisis in Liberia. Mr. Annan's initial report stated that, any restrictions imposed on the weak Liberian economy, which depends quasi entirely on the export of traditional primary products and continues to be highly vulnerable with the ongoing political instability and the fighting in the North, would have a negative impact on employment, populations support and government revenues.

In September of 2001, Global Witness charged that Liberia used the revenue from the sale of logs "to fuel war in West Africa." At the same time, President Taylor announced that he was returning 100% of all timber revenues to local areas to finance development. Approximately $1 million was earmarked for Sinoe, Grand Gedeh, River Gee, Maryland and Grand Bassa counties. Rivercess was to receive $500,000. The funds were to be taken directly from taxes paid by the timber industry in those countries.

However it is worth noting that Global Witness, in a briefing paper to the United Nations Security Council in January of 2001 stated:

> Certainly there is no reliable data or estimate as to the amount of revenue that President Charles Taylor is gaining as a result of the Liberian timber industry because to date very limited research has been carried out on the subject. For this reason it is not possible to give figures and it is clear that there is urgent need for reliable research to be carried out. However, a wide number of observers have noted that the forestry sector provides the bulk of President Charles Taylor's funds...According to sources, he uses this income to provide the RUF with funding, arms, training and logistical support.[39]

Translated into simple English, Global Witness did not know anything definitive about either the revenues from timber or for what the monies were used.

Global Witness' also gave description of Gus van Kouwenhoven, who runs Oriental Timber Company (OTC), the premier logging company in Liberia and his relationship with President Charles Taylor.

> In 1999 OTC...made a deal between Mr. Kouwenhoven and President Charles Taylor. As part of this deal, Mr. Kouwenhoven became OTC Chairman, OTC would conduct field extraction, control the port of Buchanan and the construction of roads of benefit to the Liberian people. According to sources, OTC paid President Charles Taylor USD 5 million up-front; it is likely that this was in exchange for tax-exemption and exclusion from controls and regulations.[40]

With the data from anonymous sources to substantiate its claims, Global Witness, concluded that "it is undeniable that the timber industry in Liberia has funded and continues to fund regional and national insecurity." Also in January, 2001 Global Witness claimed that "commitments to invest in a plywood factory and reforestation have not been realized." Global Witness stated OTC is responsible for "clear-felling, extracting all species, and leaving little or nothing behind. This renders forest renewal practically impossible and is in most cases illegal."

Yet on February 1, 2001, Agence France-Presse reported:

> a $40 million wood-processing factory operated by the Indonesian-based logging concern, Oriental Timber Company, has been officially opened in Liberia. The plywood factory, located in Buchanan...is considered the largest in Africa and employs 2500 workers...The factory has six production plants

with 122 generators providing electrical power...With the opening of the plywood factory, the OTC now boasts a 5,000-strong workforce, making it the largest employer in the country's private sector.

At the opening ceremony, Gus Kouwenhoven said that Global Witness had claimed that OTC 'was pretending to be building a plywood mill, that we had plans but no actual intention of doing so. Today we are proving that they were wrong.'

The Bush administration used its own research and the reports of Global Witness, and other environmental groups, to formulate U.S. policy towards Liberia's timber operations. Published July 1, 2001, a U.S. State Department Bureau of Intelligence and Research fact sheet, titled, *Arms and Conflict in Africa*, stated the following:

Several reports have suggested Liberian timber exports increasingly are used to finance and smuggle weapons, further facilitating Taylor's ability to evade UN sanctions directed against Liberia's exchange of conflict diamonds for arms.

On August 10, 2001, The Wall Street Journal reported:

The State Department weighs sanctions against Liberia for permitting clear-cutting of its rainforest by a Malaysian company. Bush officials, already chagrined over reported human rights violations, say one possibility is a United Nations-backed naval blockade.

Africa: The Road to Conflict Resolution, a Foreign Press Center briefing in Washington, D.C., on November 18, 2002 was conducted by the U.S. Assistant Secretary for State for African Affairs, Walter H. Kansteiner. He answered a query on the amount of pressure put on the Taylor administration and gave a response that highlighted the U.S. policy towards Liberia relative to the revenue from timber:

Oh, I think I would disagree with that. I think there is pressure. In fact, it was interesting that they felt the pressure so much that they bought a six-page spread in *The Washington Post*, so I thought that was interesting. But no, I think there is pressure. I think the pressure that the diamond sanctions have had has clearly produced some results; that is, we've cut off some of that revenue stream.

Timber sanctions. We continue to press for increased timber sanctions against Liberia at the United Nations.

You know, we're putting together these series of mechanisms where you ring-fence the revenues of the ship registry or of the timber, in particular. And we could look at other sources of revenue, too, but the ring-fencing then enables an objective third party to come in and basically audit. What does Liberia do with these timber proceeds? Where are these timber proceeds going? And, in fact, it audits it in an effort to make sure that those finances and the cash flow does not go to disrupting the neighbors, but goes to what it should go to: education, health, and all of the many needs that the people of Liberia have.

In view of the negative reports and possible sanctions, the Chairman of OTC responded to the charges and said:

> We...categorically deny that either OTC, nor any logging company for that matter in Liberia, is involved in clear felling of tress so as to extract the logs that are wanted...Such a venture is so wasteful and expensive that it is being pursued only by those involved in real estate and developing.[41]

The OTC President also said he personally had taken United Nations and European representatives to the foreign region being operated by his corporations to show them some of the operations. Not one of them was a timber expert but they were

> surprised to see that the reality on the ground was not as they had been informed...They were unable to define which areas were worked and which were not, as the worked forest and the un-worked looked exactly the same with the exception of the roads and spur roads that were built in the worked forest.[42]

Mr. Kouwenhoven said that OTC has planted 200,000 trees as part of its reforestation program. In direct contrast, Tim Birch of Greenpeace said: "There is no sustainable logging anywhere in Liberia...It's effectively a mining operation."[43]

In February of 2001, Alexander Peal, who, in 1986 founded the Society for the Conservation of Nature in Liberia (SCNL), Liberia's first and only NGO dedicated to conserving the country's spectacular bio-diversity, was awarded the prized Whitley Award for International Nature Conservation. A high profile conservationist, Dr. Peal said that Liberia is home to two or three of the remaining intact blocks of Upper Guinean rainforest, which are of incalculable value given the poor condition of the forests in the remainder of West Africa. He also said that only in Liberia are the forests largely in good condition.[44] They comprise an estimated 43% of the remaining Upper Guinean rainforest and are a reminder of what was once a vast forest cover stretching from Ghana across to Sierra Leone.

As a contrast, in May of 2002 the Enron Corporation won the promise of $200 million of U.S. federal financing for a 390-mile natural gas pipeline from Bolivia to Brazil through the Chiquitano Dry Tropical Forest. With that pledge of $200 million, Enron built its pipeline directly through South America's largest remaining undeveloped swath of dry tropical forest, a region rich with endangered wildlife and plants. The pipeline, completed late in 2001, and its service roads have opened the forest to every kind of environmental damage. The Washington Post reported:

> Perhaps most stunning, however, to many federal employees who reviewed the project, was how Enron persuaded a U.S. agency, the Overseas Private Investment Corp., to support the pipeline, even though the agency was charged with protecting sensitive forests such as the Chiquitano. 'It shouldn't have been done,' said Mike Colby, a former Treasury Department senior environmental adviser and now a corporate consultant. 'The forest had been declared by the World Bank...one of the two most valuable forests in Latin America. And OPIC chose to ignore that. They were so driven to reach these unsupportable conclusions because they wanted to finance the project at all costs.[45]

After the project was completed, OPIC wrote to Enron that, because it failed to achieve the environmental measures included in the deal, it was canceling the $200 million loan. But it was too late...the damage already had been done. No one suggested that the United States be sanctioned for what it had done to Latin America.

Liberia, in the absence of substantive foreign economic aid, expanded its logging operations, either in an environmentally sound or unsound manner, and provided thousands of jobs for its people and huge amounts of revenue to meet the country's needs. Yet, Liberia, unlike its neighboring countries, had worked to preserve its forests. However, because of the Taylor administration's reported use of revenue from timber to purchase weapons and support conflict in the West Africa region, the UN Security Council added a 10-month sanction that banned the import of Liberia's timber on May 6, 2003.[46]

NOTES

[1] Epstein, Edward Jay, *The Rise and Fall of Diamonds*, Simon and Schuster, 1982, book jacket.

[2] Ibid., p. 12.

[3] Ibid., p. 143.

[4] James Rupert, "Diamond Hunters fuel Africa's brutal WMS," *Washington Post*, October 16, 1999. p. A21; "The Gems of War," *Newsweek*, July 10, 2000, p. 18; Tina Rosenberg, To prevent conflicts, look to commodities like diamonds, *New York Times*, July 15, 2002.

[5] Epstein, p. 33.

[6] Ibid., p. 143.

[7] Ibid., p. 144.

[8] Ibid., p. 144.

[9] Ibid., p. 147.

[10] Ibid., p. 147.

[11] Ibid., p. 148.

[12] Ibid., p. 149.

[13] Ibid., p. 150 .

[14] Ibid., p. 152.

[15] *Newsweek Magazine*, "The Gems of War," p. 22.

[16] Ibid., p. 22.

[17] Ibid., p. 20.

[18] Personal communication with State Department officials.

[19] Monie R. Captan, Liberian Foreign Minister, "Statement of the Government of Liberia at the United Nations Open Hearing to assess the role of diamonds in the Sierra Leone conflict pursuant to UN Resolution 1132 (1997) concerning Sierra Leone," p. 3; Desmond Davies, "What price diamonds?," *West Africa magazine*, June 26, 2000, p. 10.

[20] Ibid., p. 3.

[21] Mark Doyle, "Liberia's Diamond Links," *BBC* (World: Africa), July 18, 2000.

[22] Tony P. Hall and Frank Wolf, "Diamonds and Dictators," *The Washington Post*, January 5, 2000, OpEd p. A19; Charles W. Corey, The Washington File, Office of International Information Programs, U.S. Department of State, U.S. lawmakers to introduce "conflict diamond" legislation, February 14, 2001.

[23] Ibid.

[24] Personal communication with Susan Rice, U.S. Assistant Secretary of State for Africa.

[25] Kimberley Process Certification Scheme (KPCS), "The Kimberley Process promoting prosperity diamonds: Background,"<http://www.kimberleyprocess.com/background.asp>.

[26] Kimberley Process Certification Scheme (KPCS), Preamble, at <http://

www.kimberleyprocess.com/documents.asp>

[27] Ibid.

[28] Honorable George W. Bush, "Statement by the President: I have now signed into law H.R. 1854, The Clean Diamond Trade Act...,". White House, Office of the Press Secretary, April 25, 2003. The President must implement regulations to carry out the Kimberley Process Certification Scheme.

[29] Kimberley Process 2003 Plenary Meeting, report, 28 to 30 April 2003, see <http://www.kimberleyprocess.com/>.

[30] Excellency Charles G. Taylor, "Letter to H.E. Gunter Pleuger, President, United Nations Security Council regarding sanctions and the diamond certification regime," February 18, 2003.

[31] Ibid.

[32] Emmanuel Goujon, *Agence France-Presse*, August to, 2002.

[33] Ibid.

[34] "Uncontrolled logging in Liberia wreaks all-round havoc," *Agence France-Presse*, June 27, 2001.

[35] "New wood processing plant opens in Liberia," *Agence France-Presse,* February 1, 2002.

[36] Memorandum of Understanding between the Government of the Republic of Liberia and the National Environmental Commission of Liberia, January 17, 2002.

[37] Personal communication with Tyler Christie of Conservation International, May 22, 2002.

[38] Carola Hoyos, "UN urged to put sanctions on Liberia's timber exports," *Financial Times* (London), September 6, 2001.

[39] Briefing to the UN Security Council by Global Witness, "The role of Liberia's logging industry on national and regional insecurity," January 24, 2001, p. 2.

[40] Ibid., p. 5.

[41] The Analyst newspaper, Monrovia, Liberia, February 4, 2002. p. l.

[42] Ibid.

[43] "Greenpeace exposes global crisis in last ancient forests," Greenpeace, February 25, 2002. press release, p. 1.

[44] "Conservationist Alexander Peal wins international award," *PanAfrican News Agency*, February 8, 2001, p. 1.

[45] James V. Grimaldi, "Enron pipeline leaves scar on South America," *Washington Post,* May 6, 2002, p. 1.

[46] UN Security Council, "Security Council Extends Sanctions Against Liberia until May 7 2004, Unanimously Adopting Resolution 1478 (2003): Also Places 10-Month Ban on Import of Liberian Timber," 6 May 2003.

CHAPTER 9
HUMAN RIGHTS, THE PRESS,
WOMEN, AND SOCIAL ISSUES

HUMAN RIGHTS

The best way to guarantee human rights is to prevent human wrongs. Yet that maxim is not easy to fufill. Liberia has suffered a devastating seven-year civil war, in which human rights were violated by parties on all sides. This happens when people are at war. Now the citizens of Liberia are innocent pawns in yet another uprising, where violent opposition groups, in their attempts to remove the President from power by force of arms, committed heinous acts of violence upon Liberian citizens. The government responded to those attacks by engaging in violent tactics. In attempting to defend itself against the LURD (and later MODEL), the government was suspicious of any individuals or group which appeared to be sympathizers. Thus, the Liberian government precipitously arrested and detained persons suspected of aiding, in particular, the LURD terrorists. These actions brought condemnation, largely through the media, from human rights groups in Liberia and worldwide. In response to that criticism, the Taylor administration temporarily shut down newspapers and radio stations suspected of giving comfort to the enemy, in the name of fighting terrorism; human rights activists in turn condemned the government's violation of the right of free speech.

Compared to many other nations around the world, Liberia's human rights record was not the worse. Examples of human rights violations were in the tens or hundreds, unlike some other nations, which have violations in the tens of thousands and hundreds of thousands. In many cases the U.S. looked the other way and gave substantial assistance to nations with a far worse record. However, Liberia was penalized for its human rights record and denied aid.

Liberia, unlike many other countries that do receive support and assistance from the United States in the name of the fight against terrorism, allows a relatively free press, opposition political parties (18 parties in a population of 3 million people), and independent members of the legislature, who speak both for and against the government in power.

Still journalists (see subsequent section on the press) and "human rights activists" have been arrested and detained for uttering views that are critical of the Taylor government and directly or indirectly supportive of the LURD and MODEL. Government security forces have been guilty of individual cases of harassment and killings. But there never has been the kind of "ethnic cleansing" that marked the U.S.–supported regime of Samuel Doe, which killed and tortured thousands of Liberians not of Doe's Krahn tribe. The compelling question that remained was: did the Taylor government order, or know about, these incidents on the part of Liberian security force members?

One of the paradoxes in Liberia is that the Catholic Archbishop of Liberia, Michael Francis, has consistently criticized the government, both in private and in public, for preventing freedom of speech; yet he himself never has been stopped from expressing his beliefs. Through all of the fighting and violence over the years, Archbishop Francis courageously has remained at his post, ministering to the people of Liberia while other leaders have fled the country. On December 2, 2001, Bishop Francis, in a pastoral letter read in churches across the capital city of Monrovia, accused the government of arbitrary arrests and hampering press freedom, citing a recent decision to prevent the church-run Radio Veritas from broadcasting on shortwave frequencies. "We see daily how our people are being treated and their rights violated with impunity," said Bishop Francis. "Citizens have been murdered and up until now their murderers have not been brought to justice."[1]

Two days after Archbishop Francis made the anti-government remarks cited above, the BBC monitored the pro-Taylor Radio Liberia International, which stated that "the Government of Liberia welcomes Archbishop Michael Francis's criticism about current conditions in Liberia and invites him to use his vast experience and resources to help solve the problems."

The government controlled radio station then said: "The government reminds Bishop Francis that free speech, free movement and freedom of expression continue to thrive under the Taylor administration such that even with this type of criticism by the bishop, he is not molested by anyone."[2]

The prevalence of human rights violations differ in degree and number. The ethnic cleansing carried out by Slobovan Milosevic in Kosovo, Bosnia and Serbia was on a massive level, with hundreds of thousands of people murdered in a campaign of annihilation directed and carried out by the government. The same is true in Rwanda (where the U.S. did little or nothing to prevent those massacres). In the central African countries of Rwanda, Congo, Uganda and Burundi, as many as 1.5 million people have been slaughtered during the past 20 years. These atrocities are entirely different in scope and cause. Countries coming out of civil conflicts are expected to implement democratic self-governance and yet still have instances of abuse. One must recognize a concept of proportionality in these matters. Richard Holbrooke, former U.S. Ambassador to the United Nations called Charles Taylor "the Milosevic of Africa." It leads one to Clark Clifford's remark in a different context (the U.S. versus Grenada): comparing Milosevic with Taylor is like pitting Notre Dame against the Sisters of Mercy football team. Judging by the same standards that the U.S. applies to Liberia, the U.S. is a violator of human rights and has been so accused by human rights groups over the years.

An editorial on December 27, 2002 in The Washington Post, titled *Torture is Not an Option...?* refers to an "eye-opening story" by Post writers Dana Priest and Barton Gelman.

> They report that CIA interrogations of captured Al Qaeda and Taliban fighters employ tactics such as depriving them of sleep, forcing them to assume 'awkward, painful positions' and 'softening them up' with beatings by military police and soldiers. Interrogators may threaten to turn over non-cooperative detainees to brutal foreign intelligence services, and in some instances they have actually done so. Interrogators have also selectively withheld pain medication from those already wounded when captured. On February 6, 2003 the Washington Post reported that four prisoners at the Pentagon's Guantanamo Bay prison for terrorists tried to kill themselves in the preceding three weeks.
>
> Noting previous suicide attempts, the rights group Amnesty International has protested the prolonged detention and the uncertainty the men face about

their future...Some of the men have been held more than a year for interrogation by the military without charges, trial or access to lawyers or their families. The Bush administration has designated the men 'unlawful combatants', saying they are not entitled to the same rights as prisoners of war but are being treated humanely. Officials decline to say exactly how many are held and what their nationalities are, though the roughly 625 men are believed to come from more than 40 countries."

The Post story continued:

The (U.S.) Government denies it is torturing anyone...But what, then, to make of anonymous comments from officials involved in the detentions? One...is quoted as saying, 'If you don't violate someone's human rights some of the time, you probably aren't doing your job'...And while the government denies that its purpose in transferring prisoners to foreign custody is so that other intelligence services can torture them, still another official says, 'We don't kick the [expletive] out of them, we send them to other countries so *they* can kick the [expletive] out of them.

While the United States self-righteously condemns Liberia for beating prisoners suspected of being LURD terrorists or collaborating with LURD terrorists, it does the same thing. Neither is justified. Anyone who tortures prisoners is in violation of international law. But it is hypocrisy for the United States to condemn what it also practices. Instead the United States and Liberia should refrain from such violations of human rights. Anyone who is incensed over the horrors perpetrated on September 11 wants the terrorists brought to justice. But the U.S. investigative agencies and judicial system can do the job without resorting to torture. By giving in to the understandable desire to torture and even kill the terrorists, who so cowardly slaughtered thousands of innocent people at the World Trade Center, the nation injures itself by undermining the principles of democracy that it attempts to promote throughout the world.

Human rights groups, by and large, serve an extremely useful purpose by acting as the conscience of the world and never letting us forget what horrors human beings are capable of wreaking upon fellow human beings. These groups, in their zeal to expose human rights violations, often fail to consider how their actions can become counter-productive.

Roger Winter is director of the U.S. Committee for Refugees, a nonprofit humanitarian organization based in Washington, D.C. Some time ago he wrote an article for the Washington Post (February 22, 1998), titled, "How the Human Rights Groups Miss the Opportunity to Do Good." He made some very interesting and worthwhile points.

Those of us who work as international human rights advocates tend to regard ourselves and our institutions as humanity's conscience and as vigilant protectors of the world's humanitarian ideals. We are fearless in judging others. We should be equally fearless in judging ourselves.

Mr. Winter then said the following:

We in the human rights community are so busy issuing strongly worded reports and ostracizing imperfect new governments that we risk inviting more instability and bloodshed, not less"…"Withholding aid to a struggling young government is the same as pushing for its collapse—which may lead to just the kind of mayhem that human rights groups seek to avoid…(C)ondemning governments—which we do well—is not enough. At times, we need to adopt a more constructive attitude and intervene directly to improve human rights conditions…(P)erfect leadership and capable governing systems cannot spring forth spontaneously in troubled nations that have known only misrule. Our edicts fall on deaf ears unless we shape our message constructively.

(S)ometimes governments are more inexperienced than evil. Central Africa's new leaders have the enormous task of reassembling nations that are among the poorest on earth, ethnically divided, riven with corruption and saturated with arms and shadowy groups willing to use those arms to gain power. National armies are usually untrained and unrepresentative, national treasuries are virtually bare and the political systems have limited experience with democracy. The shooting may have stopped, but a practical state of emergency persists.

Rather than blast these officials for their failures, human rights advocates should use their considerable knowledge to suggest how leaders can achieve better human rights despite limited resources and experience.

The 'rule of law' is the bedrock of human rights, but it can take years to implement after years of dictatorship.

Many of my colleagues regularly urge that new governments be isolated and deprived of foreign assistance until they prove their fidelity to human rights…There may come a time when it is appropriate to reduce or eliminate aid to an incorrigible regime, but it is reckless policy to financially starve new governments when they most need assistance and guidance.[3]

Mr. Winter bewailed the fact that many African leaders "have come to perceive us as political enemies—not because we want to be, but because our tone is relentlessly confrontational and because we seem impatient with anything less than our ideal of human rights perfection and instant political pluralism."[4]

When the Taylor government arrested people it claimed were supporting the rebel LURD group and kept them in custody for long periods of time before bringing them to trial, it was no different from what the U.S. is doing with hundreds of people who are arrested on suspicion of aiding terrorists, kept in jails for long periods of time, sometimes tortured, and too often deprived of legal representation.

In that regard, Senator Russ Feingold of Wisconsin wrote an OpEd piece that appeared in the Washington Post on December 23, 2001:

Who are the people the Justice Department has detained in its investigation into the September 11th terrorist attacks, and why are they being held? I have asked the Bush administration this question repeatedly, but to little avail. The Justice Department has provided scant information about the identities and basis for detention of more than 1,100 people who have been or are currently detained, the vast majority of whom, Justice

Department officials admit, have no link to Sept. 11 or the Al Qaeda terrorist network...in certain cases they have suffered death or serious injury.

Members of Congress and public interest organizations have been told that our effort to oversee the Justice Department's investigation is tantamount to aiding the terrorists. That accusation is not only untrue, it is offensive in a democracy, and a stunning example of the lengths to which some will go to deflect criticism about the way the Justice Department is conducting its investigations...By insisting on keeping this information secret, the department only furthers suspicions that it is doing so to conceal abuses of innocent people.[5]

On May 28, 2002, the Washington Post reported:

U.S. moral authority to criticize human rights abuses abroad has been undermined by the Bush administration's failure to guarantee the rights of foreigners detained in the aftermath of the September 11 terrorist attacks and its 'selective adherence' to international law, Amnesty International charged today. 'In suggesting that national security may require compromises on human rights here at home, the U.S. government risks signaling its allies that 'anything goes' in their own human rights practices," Amnesty said.[6]

A June 26, 2002 release from the very conservative Cato Institute discussing the measures being taken by the United States in fighting terrorism:

We can either retain our freedom or we can throw it away in an attempt to make ourselves safe...No one can deny the fact that if the cycle of terrorist attack followed by curtailment of civil liberties continues, America will eventually lose the key attribute that has made it great, namely freedom...It is therefore both wise and imperative to address the terrorist threat within the framework of a free society...In this dangerous world, freedom is a precious thing that must be vigorously defended.[7]

There are many human rights groups active in Liberia. For example, the Rural Human Rights Activists (RHRAP) Inc., established in 1997, specializes in human rights education in rural areas of the country. The organization's aims and objectives are

to enhance the advancement of public education on human rights in schools, towns, villages, refugee camps, communities and rural Liberia; to educate rural inhabitants about all forms of discrimination especially tribal or ethnic violations; strongly campaign against the culture of impunity, corruption, and to work for the promotion of good governance, democracy, probity and accountability in public life."[8]

This type of constructive human rights education in the long run is effective.

In the 1998 Country Report on Democracy, Human Rights, and Labor for Liberia, the U.S. State Department stated that

The Government created a Human Rights Commission in 1997, but it caused considerable controversy by limiting the commission's investigatory power to future abuses only, restricting its ability to compel testimony or gather evidence, and denying it budgetary support. Four members were named to the commission in 1997. When the Senate finally held a confirmation hearing in July, it rejected two of these four individuals (see Section 1.c.). However, the Senate passed a bill that strengthened the commission by, among other things, giving it the right to subpoena witnesses. The President failed to nominate persons to fill the three vacancies on the commission, and it remained inactive for all of 1998.

On March of 2002 the State Department released its annual report on human rights abuses. Liberia was one of several African nations singled out for criticism. Others included Zimbabwe, Burundi, Sierra Leone and Somalia. The report said that Liberia's

---

There is a tradition of "dash," meaning minor bribes, which is considered culturally acceptable in most third-world countries. It is not considered to be corruption. Let me give you an example. On one of my trips to Africa, I was in Abidjan, Cote d'Ivoire, awaiting an Air Ghana plane to go to Monrovia, Liberia. The airport was jammed with people standing in line for their Boarding Passes. After some two hours of waiting, I finally got my turn at the ticket counter but was waved away with the explanation that the passes were not yet available. Soon, however, I noticed that other people appeared to be getting their Boarding Passes without any problem. I couldn't figure it out. I asked a few people what was going on, and all they would say was: See Vincent. At last I found Vincent who was a polite entrepreneurial young man who said: "I'll get you your Boarding Pass...just give me your ticket and passport and baggage." I was reluctant, thinking I might never see Vincent, my passport, my ticket, or my baggage again. However I was desperate to get on the plane (the next one wouldn't come for another two days) and something in his demeanor made me take a chance that he was honest. So I handed over the documents. He told me to go to the cafeteria upstairs, relax, have something to eat, and he would come call for me soon. I asked how much this service would cost me. He said: whatever you wish to pay. After pressing him to be more precise, he said that most people gave him $30. I handed over the money. Standing directly behind me in line was a clergyman from California, the Reverend Dennis Woodsmall, who was in the country to visit a sister church in Liberia. He, too, had failed to get his Boarding Pass. I suggested that he utilize Vincent's services for $30. "No, I can't do that," he said. "It would be a violation of my religious principles to pay him money." I respected Pastor Woodsmall's convictions and went upstairs. About thirty minutes later, Vincent came to the cafeteria, handed me my passport, boarding pass, and baggage receipts and led me to the First Class waiting lounge. A few minutes later, to my surprise, the Minister came in with his Boarding Pass in hand. I said that I owed him an apology and that "the power of prayer certainly was impressive." He looked at me with a grin and said: "Yes, the power of prayer and thirty bucks!" He had yielded to the third world culture which considers the methods of the Vincents of the world perfectly acceptable and indeed a good way to spread the money around (I assume that Victor shared his "dash" with the man behind the ticket counter). Is that corruption...or culture? If its is the former, how do you stop it? If it is the latter, how do you stop tiny bribes from becoming major bribes?

human rights record remained poor. It said human rights organizations estimated that security forces carried out hundreds of extra-judicial killings during the year. It said that although the Liberian government investigated some abuses, offenders were rarely punished. It said that prison conditions remained harsh and sometimes life-threatening, and that there were about 20 political prisoners still being held. The report also said that the government continued to discriminate against indigenous ethnic groups that had opposed "warlord-turned-president Taylor" during the civil war.[9] According to the Associated Press, the State Department report conceded that "the rebels had also committed serious human rights abuses."[10]

On March 7, the government responded that the State Department report was out of date. Information Minister Reginald Goodridge said: "It appears like a photocopy of previous reports because Liberia has made significant progress in all these areas."[11]

Because of the continuous military forays by the LURD that came closer and closer to the capital city of Monrovia, the Liberian government, on February 8, imposed a state of emergency in the country, and thereafter the government began a crackdown on persons it alleged were aiding or abetting the rebel forces. There seems to be little question that, at times, excessive force was used against these people.

THE TIAWON GONGLOE INCIDENT

The reporting of human rights violations by the government against attorney Tiawon S. Gongloe varied according to the source. On April 26, 2002, in a release issued by the Human Rights Watch, from New York City, said:

> One of Liberia's most prominent human rights lawyers, Tiawon Gongloe, has been brutalized in police custody and is hospitalized as a result. Police guards remain near his hospital bed, and the police director has announced that Mr. Gongloe remains in police custody without charges pending an investigation.[12]

"The government of Charles Taylor is using violence to silence independent voices speaking out about Liberia's deteriorating human rights record," said Peter Takirambudde, executive director of Human Rights Watch's Africa division.

The release continued:

> Although no charges have been brought, Mr. Gongloe appears to have been arrested in connection with a speech he gave at a March 2002 conference in neighboring Guinea on peace in the Mano River Union...The speech dealt with ways in which civil society groups could play a role in the attainment of peace in the Mano River Union, and condemned the use of violence as a means to state power...The same day as Mr. Gongloe's arrest, the government ordered the closure of The Analyst newspaper, which had just printed the speech made by Mr. Gongloe.

> After briefly being questioned, he was stripped nude and placed in police cells in the basement. Two plainclothes police officers in the cell proceeded to severely beat and kick him through the night. They also threatened him, telling him he was a dissident whom they would deal with, and that they would kill him. In the morning, he was taken again for questioning, but was unable to stand or sit as a result of his injuries. Lawyers who had been notified of Mr. Gongloe's whereabouts pressured the police to hospitalize Mr.

Gongloe. Mr. Gongloe is currently at Cooper Hospital where he is receiving treatment. As a result of the torture, Mr. Gongloe has lost some hearing in his left ear, his left eye is swollen and bloodied, and his head and body are badly bruised…Clearly Mr. Gongloe remains at great risk of further police brutality and harassment. President Taylor must immediately end this harassment and intimidation of rights activists.[13]

Agence France-Presse covered the same unfortunate incident, but presented more of the story than did the humans rights group. In an April 26, 2002 article, they wrote:

Human rights lawyer Tiawon Gongloe has alleged that police brutalized him after his arrest earlier this week, press reports said Friday. However, the Monrovia government immediately denied his claim, saying in fact fellow prisoners had beaten him up…Gongloe, who was arrested…for allegedly 'endangering national security' told reporters from his hospital bed that he was beaten by policemen masquerading as detainees…Gongloe, according to news reports, said: 'The police officers who beat me up were cleverly imprisoned with me so as to carry out the act.'…Liberia's information ministry…said Gongloe had been beaten by other prisoners…The incident occurred at about 5:00 am on Thursday…Police sources indicate that there is what detainees in cells call 'prison democracy' —new inmates must comply with demands of those they meet upon arrival. Gongloe's reported refusal to comply led to the fracas, which was quickly brought under control by the police…Police said he was arrested 'to answer questions relating to statements he made recently holding Liberian President Charles Taylor responsible for fomenting instability in the Mano River Union' which consists of Liberia, Sierra Leone and Guinea. They said Gongloe made a speech in the Guinean capital Conakry on March 27, where he purportedly said: 'It is well known that the armed conflict within the Mano River Union started in Liberia and then spread to Sierra Leone and Guinea"…Gongloe, an indefatigable critic of Taylor's government, has had several brushes with the authorities…Taylor's government has attracted sweeping international condemnation for rights abuses but authorities steadfastly deny the charges as propaganda.[14]

Either way, what happened to Counsellor Gongloe was unacceptable. This incident was typical of the human rights violations perpetrated in Liberia during the four years that the LURD rebels have conducted military attacks against the government and its people. There was no excuse for imprisoning people because they expressed their views, nor for beating and injuring people when they were in jail.

At the same time, the government justified its actions as part of its effort to remain in power and resist statements that condemn the government in power or give comfort to the LURD rebellion. It argued that it has a right to detain people who are a threat to national security because of their provocative statements. In most countries where human rights are violated, the world does not often learn of the abuses until years after they occur because the press is muzzled. Yet, in the Gongloe matter, the victim was allowed to speak with reporters and make his accusations. The local Liberian human rights organization, Movement for the

Defense of Human Rights (MODHAR) publicly condemned the arrest and detention.

The accusation in Mr. Gongloe's speech given, not in Liberia, but in Guinea, was that President Taylor fomented the troubles in Guinea and Sierra Leone. At the same time, Human Rights Watch in its May, 2002 report stated unequivocally: "The government of Guinea is currently fueling the Liberian conflict by providing logistic and some financial and military support to the LURD rebels..."[15] Since the relations between Liberia and Guinea were hostile, Mr. Gongloe's speech put him in danger of reprisal from the Taylor government.

In the case of Mr. Gongloe, according to the Associated Press, the police, on May 1, 2002, after Mr. Gongloe completed his hospitalization for the injuries he received while in jail, handed him over to the Roman Catholic archbishop of Monrovia to allow him to recuperate. On March 1, 2003 Counsellor Gongloe attended a Liberian conference held in the U.S. at the University of Maryland. (The author saw that he was restored to good health, despite his ordeal.)

THE HASSAN BILITY AFFAIR

On June 24, 2002 the Liberian government arrested a young journalist named Hassan Bility and, according to The Christian Science Monitor, a reputable source, the government "charged him with plotting to kill Charles Taylor. Human rights and press watchdogs said the arrest is a sham, and a worrying sign of the increasingly repressive nature of the Liberian government. They are voicing concern that Mr. Bility, who edited a major opposition newspaper, The Analyst, may have been tortured to death." Amnesty International stated: "We are seriously concerned that he may have been seriously tortured or killed."[16]

Judge Wynston Henries of Criminal Court "B" ordered the State to produce Bility, but the government failed to produce the three accused, Bility, Mohammed Kamara, and Ansumana Kamara, in court on at least two occasions. Judge Henries then issued a 24-hour ultimatum but the judge's order did not yield any result. The State's lawyers argued that Bility and the others were "unlawful combatants" and that they could not be released to a civilian court. Counsellor Theophilus Gould told the court that Bility and his colleagues should be tried in a military court because, according to him, they engaged in warfare to overthrow the Liberian president. Judge Henries said the repeated failure of government to produce Bility and others was "repugnant to good governance."[17]

The court system spoke in favor of Mr. Bility's rights without interference from the government. In keeping with Liberia's press freedom, the material set forth above appeared in local Liberian newspapers.

President Taylor noted that Mr. Bility and the two Kamaras were in military custody and would be tried by military courts. He, however, clarified that such organizations as the Red Cross would have access to them.

The Christian Science Monitor story said that "going through Bility's private e-mail account last month, the government claims it found 'incriminating letters' from figures such as Damate Konneh, leader of the rebel group LURD...and opposition leader in exile Alhaji Kromah—in which a murder plot was outlined.

> Copies of these e-mails, given to the Monitor by the Liberian government,
> are filled with both code phrases such as 'meet at the usual place and bring

what is needed' and straightforward language such as 'Taylor will soon be dead.' The e-mails also implicate, by name, several other Monrovians, including a driver at the American Embassy."[18]

If these e-mails are legitimate, there is at least a colorable case to be made that Mr. Bility was more than an objective journalist and in fact was involved with the rebels. But that is for a court—whether civilian or miltary—to decide.

"Bility is also a member of the predominantly Muslim Mandingo tribe, to which many of the LURD rebels belong. 'This looks like persecution,' said one diplomat, who, like the others, spoke on a condition of anonymity," wrote the Christian Science Monitor.

> 'Liberia is a whipping boy for the media', says (Liberian) information minister Reginald Goodridge, "but in fact Liberia is exemplary when it comes to freedom of the press." There is a degree of hyperbole here because the truth is that certain newspapers and radio stations have at times been closed down by the government but then later re-opened. "The Minister (Goodridge)," said the Monitor "who has been on friendly terms with Bility for years, says that he was 'shocked' by the charges, but adds that Bility 'has admitted journalism was a cover for his vile activities.'[19]

President Taylor told KISS-FM (his personal radio station) that Bility and those arrested with him are terrorists and would be treated in the same manner in which the U.S. treats terrorists. *The way the U.S. treats suspected terrorists, then, has had the unintended consequence of emboldening other countries to act in a similar manner.*[20]

A July 9, 2002 editorial in the Washington Post dealt with two men (Jose Padilla and Yasar Esam Hamdi)—both U.S. citizens—who were being held indefinitely (Hamdi for 187 days and Padilla for 122 days) by the United States and who the U.S. was "unprepared to charge with crimes and did not permit those detainees access to lawyers." The editorial states that these men

> are imprisoned on nothing more than the government's claim that they are enemy combatants. According to the government, the president alone has the power during wartime to designate people, including citizens, as enemy fighters subject to detention until the end of hostilities…Moreover, the determination of when a war begins and ends is the president's to make, too. To make matters more Kafkaesque, those he designates as enemy combatants cannot meet with lawyers, so even if they had a legal forum in which to challenge his judgment they would have no practical ability to tell their side of the story…The government's adopting such a hard-line position only ensures that a cloud of lawlessness will hover over detentions that need not be controversial…(B)oth Mr. Padilla and Mr. Hamdi are being denied what have long been presumed to be birthrights of American citizens: the right not to be held without the assistance of counsel or on the say-so of a single branch of government. With every day that passes, the needless deprivation becomes more injurious.[21]

These situations were not different from the Bility case. Still, the U.S. Department of State through its spokesman, Richard Boucher, said on July 8, 2002:

The United States shares the concern recently issued by Amnesty International, Reporters Without Borders, and others over the physical safety of journalist Hassan Bility and two others. We condemn the Government of Liberia's failure to follow the rule of law and urge it to comply with a Liberian court order to present these individuals publicly...?

On September 6, 2002, the minister of defense was ordered by the president of Liberia to constitute an appropriate military tribunal to determine the status of all persons arrested and currently held by the military (including Mr. Bility) in connection with the ongoing war in Liberia.

On October 24, 2002, the military tribunal determined that Bility and 10 others were prisoners of war, "given their role in prosecuting an illegitimate war against the government and people of Liberia", according to the Associated Press. At that time, AP stated that "the fighting between rebels and Taylor's forces has displaced about 200,000 people, according to the United Nations Human Rights organizations which accuse both sides of abuse, including rapes, killings and the forced recruitment of civilians." The releases did not discuss the fact that, for four long years, the LURD have been the attackers and the Liberian government forces are the defenders.[22]

The Liberian government then said that it was prepared to allow journalist Hassan Bility and others to be taken out of the country by the United States Embassy. On the question of why the POWs could not be released in Monrovia, Minister Goodridge said there was concern for the safety of Bility and others who could be harmed if they were let out into the streets of Monrovia. Minister Goodridge added that there are a lot of people who are angry over Bility's actions, and the government does not want to be responsible for his security after he is released, saying "he therefore needs a cooling-off period in a third country." The Information Minister clarified that Hassan Bility is not a political prisoner. Mr. Goodridge said that Bility and others were never arrested for political activities or anything that he may have said or published as a journalist, noting that "they were arrested for planning and collaborating in a terrorist war against the Liberian government and people." Bility also was accused of running a terrorist cell in Monrovia for rebels of the Liberians United for Reconciliation and Democracy (LURD).[23]

On December 8, 2002 Mr. Bility was handed over to the U.S. Embassy on condition that the Embassy ensured that he left Liberia. U.S. Ambassador John William Blaney escorted Bility to the airport, where he boarded a commercial flight bound for Ghana's capital, Accra.[24]

Mr. Bility was a featured speaker at a meeting of opposition leaders held at the University of Maryland in the United States on March 1, 2003. When he finished his speech, he walked off the platform and embraced two people: Ambassador Blaney (who had worked so hard for his release) and Joe Wylie (the military advisor to the LURD rebels). While every one of the opposition political parties present renounced violence and pledged to oppose the Taylor government solely through the political process, only Mr. Wylie defiantly told the audience that the LURD would continue to fight militarily to remove Charles Taylor. His remarks were denounced by many of the speakers, including Bishop Michael Francis. One finds it unexplainable that Mr. Wylie freely roams the corridors of powers in Washington (he actually sat at the same table with Ambassador Blaney at the University of

Maryland conference), travel anywhere in the United States preaching his message of violence, and raise money for his military rebel force, while 129 members of the Taylor government and their associates, including the elected President of the country, are forbidden to leave the country and forbidden to come to the United States because of the travel sanctions imposed at the behest of the United States government.

A British journalist named James Brabazon made a documentary film of his travels with the LURD rebels in June and July of 2002. In that film, *Liberia: A Journey Without Maps*, one sees the rebels killing young boys, literally eating the hearts of captured government soldiers, taking all the food from the villagers, driving the civilian population from their homes, and carrying weapons that were provided the rebels by outside parties—and in the midst of this mayhem, the film shows Joe Wylie, the same man who, in 2003, a "human rights activist" embraced.

In stark contrast to Joe Wylie's threats, the new U.S. Deputy Assistant Secretary of State for African Affairs, Ambassador Pamela Bridgewater, said at the same conference:

> Let me reiterate our condemnation of the LURD's 'campaign of violence' and our call for all irregular forces to lay down their arms and work peacefully for change, as the LURD promised in the recent Freetown communique. We also have told the Governments of Guinea, Sierra Leone, and Côte d'Ivoire repeatedly not to support any insurgencies in the region.[25]

The U.S. State Department now publicly condemns the LURD violence. The condemnation was a stark change from the words of Mark Bellamy.

Those who condemn human rights abuses, and those who claim they are necessary for national security, each are selective in their explanations and rarely put the issue into perspective. Stanley McGill (who was twice attacked and robbed, including an incident in June 2003 by armed men in ATU uniforms that was reported by the international media) wrote an editorial that appeared in The NEWS, one of Liberia's independent (neither government nor the opposition) newspapers which analyzed the situation in a balanced presentation. It is printed here:

> The first quarter of this year has witnessed tremendous efforts by the Government and other national stakeholders at ensuring that an environment is created in which our common national agenda of peace, stability, and national growth and development are achievable.

> Some...efforts include...a national religious crusade in search of peace and stability; the collective and collaborative efforts of civil society groupings which cumulated into a positive peace dialogue among leaders of the Mano River Union states including the encouraging participation of Liberians in the ECOWAS sponsored preparatory reconciliation conference held in Abuja, Nigeria.

> Other positive initiatives ...the release from detention of treason and sedition convicts by the Government as well as...a national reconciliation program bureau to mobilize citizens for the proposed Government sponsored reconciliation conference expected in July.

> It is unfortunate that in spite of these positive initiatives, recent events and incidents of undesirable impact appear to be beclouding our national reconciliation and democratic process.

It would seem that whenever a forward step is taken in our national endeavors, we find ourselves in a situation suggestive of taking 50 steps backward.

The prevailing atmosphere…has left many citizens pondering over whether the much needed reconciliation and the strengthening of the democracy process will be achieved sooner than later.

For instance…the arrest by the police of former Chief Justice Frances Johnson-Morris and the physical torture of human rights lawyer Tiawon Gongloe while in police custody are two of the several situations that have overshadowed concerted efforts at establishing peace and stability.

Whatever may have given rise to these incidents, we think they could have been avoided had the authorities exercised a bit more tolerance and flexibility.

The nation is at a crisis point…it has become more imperative that every small step toward reconciliation and the nurturing of the democratic process…be well guided and sustained.

Since it is the Government that has the task in coordinating and spearheading our common national agenda, we urge it to be more tolerant and flexible to ensure that our positive initiatives are sustained.[26]

Mr. McGill's reasoned and constructive editorial is the type analysis one would expect from U.S. diplomats. Instead, representatives of the U.S. government indulge in hypocritical accusations, while withholding all substantial help from the people of Liberia.

With regard to Liberia's record on human rights, it is known there have been many violations. The questions one must ask are: 1) Did the government order arrests of individuals suspected of giving aid to, or collaborating with, the LURD rebels? Yes. 2) Did the government, specifically including President Taylor, order torture or killings? There is no tested evidence, one way or the other, on this issue; and 3) Did Mr. Taylor know about the violations of human rights committed by his armed forces and security forces, and could he have done anything to stop them? Yes, he did know about them, and he could have prevented some, but not all abuse, given the escalation of conflict in the country.

With regard to prisoners kept in detention, more could be done to protect them from fellow inmates or police brutality. But when soldiers are in the field fighting for their lives, it is difficult for governmental officials to govern their conduct from a distance. Nevertheless the attempt should and must be made. Regarding the ATU (Anti-Terrorist Unit), it is fair to say that President Taylor could have done much more to rein in his people.

If the U.S. continues with its current implementation of policies in use to fight terrorism, it will fail to convince others to refrain from doing the same thing.

One can never be an apologist for those who harass, jail, or mistreat people who have spoken their minds, no matter what they say. But one must be consistent in condemning such action. At the same time the Bility case made the headlines, other incidents in Africa took place unnoticed. Niger journalist Abdoulaye Tiemogo was arrested and faced a possible two-year prison term on charges of defaming Prime Minister

Hama Amadou; officials in Togo jailed journalist Basile Agboh after they accused him of defaming the son of Togo's President Gnassingbe Eyadema; and four journalists in Zambia were imprisoned without bail for reporting that Zambian President Levy Mwanawasa has Parkinson's disease. Yet these incidents receive no public attention.[27]

THE LIBERIAN PRESS

This section examines the actions of the press, both in Liberia and in the United States, in reporting events in Liberia. Although people bemoan a total loss of freedom of the press in Liberia spanning the years from 1991 to the present, one can purchase pro-government, anti-government, or independent papers, at least five different newspapers with differing points of view.

As early as March 12, 1999, Felix Downes-Thomas, representative of the UN Secretary-General in Liberia and head of the United Nations Peace-building Support Office, stated that "the basic freedoms of the press, assembly and religion are flourishing in Liberia. The press, especially the print press, is among the most free in West Africa."

Here is a list of some of the Liberian newspapers and their point of view:

- The Inquirer: independent, though some self-censorship

- The Guardian: pro-government

- National: independent but wary

- Daily Times: known as Alhaji Kromah's papers (anti-Taylor); more objective recently

- The News: independent, mostly dissident

- Patriot: President Taylor's own paper

- New Liberia: published by the Ministry of Information

- The New Democrat: generally considered oppositional

- The Pepperbird: paper of the NPP, Taylor's political party

- The Analyst: opposition.

The Liberian media has several newspapers, as well as radio and television stations, with various viewpoints.

Here is a specific example of press freedom in Liberia. The News, as indicated above, is an independent newspaper. On January 22, 2003 it published a story with the headline: "Brumskine Gets Rousing Welcome—Speaks Out on Crucial Issues of Concern." Charles Brumskine is a Liberian attorney who previously served as President Pro Tempore of the Liberian Senate. He was a member of President Taylor's political party, the NPP (National Patriotic Party) but was expelled in 1988 for what was termed "loss of confidence." Thereafter, he went to the United States where he has been living until his return to Liberia on January 21, 2003—but this time as a candidate for president under the flag of the Liberia Unification Party (LUP). He seeks to contest for the presidency in the next national elections.

In so many countries of Africa, neither an opposition party nor an opposition candidate would be allowed. In Liberia there are many. In many other countries the local newspapers would not be allowed to proclaim the merits of opposition candidates. In Liberia, they are.

Here is what the NEWS had to say about Mr. Brumskine:

> ...Counsellor Charles W. Brumskine was welcomed home yesterday from the United States of America by thousands of partisans of the Liberia Unification Party (LUP), sympathizers, well wishers and friends following five years in exile.
>
> People from far and near converged at Roberts International Airport...at about noon where he touched down...Commuters and many residents in Monrovia and its Paynesville suburb nearby stood still when people of all ages lined the highways and streets to see him...Counsellor Brumskine said while he wish (sic) to become the Flag Bearer of LUP, he will encourage collaboration with other opposition political parties for the selection of a single candidate to challenge the ruling National Patriotic Party during the October 14 General and Presidential election...The former ruling party stalwart...commended the thousands of partisans, well wishers, sympathizers and those that lined the highways and streets to give him a rousing welcome.[28]

Liberians have the freedom to join an opposition party, the freedom to run against the incumbent president, the freedom to try and rally the people to his or her cause, and the freedom to write about opposition candidates.

On too many occasions the government has temporarily shut down some of the media for various reasons (giving comfort to the enemy, misstating the facts, failure to obtain license renewals, and the like). One can sympathize with a government that is being improperly described in press reports. But that does not justify violating the freedom of the press. The fact that it is done regularly in other nations of the world still is no excuse for violations of this basic right. When the Liberian government has shut down a newspaper, protests have arisen within and without the community, that cause the President to allow the newspaper or radio station to resume its activities. Constant threat of censorship negatively impacts a free press. The UN Representative for Liberia, Felix Downes-Thomas said there had been incidents where media houses were closed for a brief period of time because they were not abiding by certain government regulations. There had been isolated incidents where security people had beaten up people from the press and the media. Mr. Downes-Thomas explained that these "episodic events" —as grave as they were—were interpreted by some to signify a State-sponsored trend toward gagging the press. "That is just not true," he said. "The problem in Liberia with human rights violations is traceable to the excesses of security forces. Attempts are being made to curb them."

While the U.S. condemned Taylor for harassing the press, it continued its enthusiastic support and embrace of the Putin government in Russia which continuously reined in its press. As an example, on December 25, 2001 a Russian military journalist who exposed nuclear waste dumping by the Russian navy was convicted of treason and sentenced to four years in prison. Yet there was not a word of criticism publicly from the U.S.

Another example: on December 31, 2001, the Washington Post editorialized:

> In the People's Republic of China, which is one of America's new allies in the war against terrorism, a judge recently sentenced Wang Jinbo to four

years in prison…after he reportedly e-mailed to acquaintances articles that were critical of China's Communist government…Russia's democratically elected government similarly wants its fight against Chechen separatists blessed as one more front in America's anti-Osama bin Laden campaign…If any of these countries had a free and vibrant press testing and evaluating the official version of reality, outsiders might feel more comfortable accepting that version…This is where we come back to Mr. Wang…President Vladimir Putin's campaign against the independent media has limited reliable reporting from Chechnya. Governments of these countries ask for the benefit of Americans' doubt as they wage their repressive campaigns. But their unwillingness to open those campaigns to independent reporting automatically tips the scale against their claims.[29]

On the U.S. side, reportage of Liberia has been singularly sparse and uninformed. Washington Post editorials have been consistently vituperative. While Charles Taylor was refused an opportunity to answer the charges made against him on the OpEd page, U.S. legislators, most of whom never had set foot in Liberia, have unlimited opportunity to express their opinions in the Post's columns.

An article written by Thomas L. Friedman of the New York Times was published on January 21, 1996, when he accompanied the then UN Ambassador Madeleine Albright on a tour of four major civil wars in Africa: Liberia, Angola, Burundi, and Rwanda. Thomas Friedman is a pre-eminent foreign policy analyst. He wrote about Liberia just after the civil war had ended. At the time the country was governed by a group of faction leaders leading up to the national election of 1997. Friedman said:

> Liberia, which was founded by American slaves in 1847, is a country in meltdown. It is in the grip of a clique of evil warlords and teen-age gunmen, who rampage the countryside, high on drugs or drunk on moonshine made from sugar cane, where they routinely murder civilians with machetes. It is an African "Clockwork Orange" in which militias don't even pretend to stand for anything other than looting villagers of all they own. Indeed, the militias rarely fight each other. They fight the people. The six-man ruling council, which supposedly runs the country, is made up of three warlords, two political figures, and one powerless man whose title is "Representative of the Civilians." Each of the warlords has his own floor in the executive palace, and each also controls ministries and is in private business…Charles Taylor and Alhaji Kromah, two of the ruling warlords, are eager to be interviewed by CNN and myself. While children with distended bellies haunt the streets, these two look as if they have not missed a meal. Their watches are gold, their shoes brightly polished, their offices cool with air-conditioning. They are peacocks strutting through the graveyard, killers with fax machines…Liberia is a country that will have to liberate itself. We can apply the Band-Aids to reduce the suffering, and we should. But as long as the innocent civilians have only one seat in the ruling council, any major funds poured in here will never get to the people who truly need them.[30]

After reading this article, the author called Mr. Friedman and asked if he would meet to discuss Liberia. During the conversation Tom Friedman very politely said that he didn't want to meet because "to tell the truth, I only was in Liberia for a few hours, and I really don't want to spend any more time on Liberia." One can only consider this particular article an anomaly in his repertoire of well-researched well-reasoned articles published since then. The hope is that reporters will do thorough, on-the-spot research and devote space to the "back-burner" countries. One also may note that often major newspapers assign junior reporters to the smaller countries. As related by a prominent journalist who covers Africa for a major U.S. newspaper, they sit in Abidjan (Ivory Coast) restaurants, compare notes with their compatriots, and never actually go into Liberia.

There is an unfortunate tendency toward "herd mentality" among the members of the press—the need to play it safe by regurgitating the same basic line as their colleagues, especially when they really don't know that much about their subject. David Broder of the Washington Post, one of America's most respected journalists, calls it the phenomenon of the "great mentioner," meaning that when one leading journalist writes about a subject in a certain way, his colleagues, even those of competing papers, tend to repeat the basic line. This approach was best described in a novel by a British author, Sebastian Faulks (*On Green Dolphin Street*). He dealt with the horrible murder of an African American boy, Emmett Till, in Sumner, Mississippi in the late 1950s. It was quite clear that the boy had been brutally murdered by two white men simply because he allegedly had whistled at a white woman in the general store owned by one of the accused. Yet the all-white jury found the two men innocent. Few members of the press had the guts to pursue a story which truly had shocked the world. As Faulks puts it:

> Most journalists...were frightened of being caught out, exposed as naive or ignorant. They were afraid of being telephoned by an editor the following day and asked why their story did not match that of their competitors. They therefore accepted with earnest nods and without question what they were told; they wanted to get the labyrinthine story and all its bizarre details into one of the simply labeled boxes that their editors would understand...The most obvious rivals were therefore, for reasons of common self-interest, the most ardent collaborators. The aim of each of them, in the end, was to report on events in such a way as to render them comprehensible, to remove the strangeness by using recognized and reassuring phrases.[31]

Thus reportage on Liberia and particularly on Charles Taylor inevitably uses words like "rogue state," "warlord," "thug," and "savagery." Very few journalists have the courage and tenacity to dig behind the labels and find the truth. Freedom of the press carries with it a responsibility to be accurate and truthful.

THE DEATH OF VICE-PRESIDENT ENOCH DOGOLEA

In June of the year 2000, Enoch Dogolea, the Vice-President of Liberia, died. Opponents of Charles Taylor, both within and outside of Liberia, claimed that Taylor had murdered his Vice-President. The media reported those stories. It was not until an autopsy report was issued by Dr. Helen Yapo Ette of the Treichville University Hospital that the rumors ended. Mr. Dogolea's death, according to the report, was a natural one, attributable to digestive hemorrhage resulting from complications of hepatocarcinoma (a form of cancer) on a cirrhotic liver. The report said further: "No element or arguments were found that could invoke the direct intervention of any person." The late Vice-President died on June 23, 2000 at 11:00 a.m. at the Clinique Medical in Abidjan following a protracted illness.[32]

WOMEN

Despite the lack of progress in the development of rights for women in Liberia and other African countries, several women have held, and now hold, many of the most important positions in the Liberian government. These are a group of highly intelligent and sophisticated people.

- Honorable Gloria Musu Scott, Chief Justice of the Liberian Supreme Court;

- Honorable Grace Beatrice Minor, President Pro Tem of the Liberian Senate (It is reported that Senator Minor is the first female ever to lead an African parliamentary body);

- Honorable Ophelia Hoff-Saytumah, Mayor of the capital city, Monrovia;

- Honorable Amelia A. Ward, Minister of Planning and Economic Affairs;

- Dr. Evelyn S. Kandakai, Minister of Education;

- Dr. Musuleng Cooper, Minister of Gender and Development;

- Madam Ruth Sando Perry, Chairman of the Liberia Council of State;

- Honorable Neh Tolbert, Liberia's Ambassador to the United Nations;

- Honorable Agnes Taylor, Liberian Ambassador to the IMO (International Maritime Organization) which is part of the United Nations;

- Honorable Rachel Gbenyon Diggs, Liberian Ambassador to the United States;

- Angie Brooks Randolph, the first African woman elected as President of the UN General Assembly.

The list, which could have numerous other entries, indicates the extent to which women lead the Liberian Government.

The background of Rachel Gbenyon Diggs is typical of these women. Ambassador Gbenyon Diggs holds a degree from the University of Geneva. She is fluent in English, French and German and has a working knowledge of Italian and Russian. For 12 years she was a research analyst in the Offices of the Director of International Relations, Strategic Planning, and External Affairs of the World Bank in Washington, D.C. She worked as a member of the core team promoting expanded collaboration between the bank and nongovernmental organizations (NGOs) which led to the creation of a World Bank grant fund for NGOs. She was Staff Assistant in the Office of the Secretary-General of the United Nations Conference on Trade and Development (UNCTAD) in Geneva, Switzerland, and was Chief of Staff to the Minister of Finance in Liberia. From 1997 to 1999, Ms. Diggs served as Liberia's Ambassador Extraordinary and Plenipotentiary to the United States. Ambassador Diggs' education and background is not exceptional in Liberia. There are many women and men who are highly educated and dedicated to serving the needs of the Liberian people as members of the government.

After years of contention among the Mano River Union countries, the women of Liberia, acting in concert, demanded that their government meet with the governments of Guinea and Sierra Leone to stop their internecine disputes, and learn to work together in unity. The UN Security Council, according to Agence France-Presse, on November 7, 2001, "praised the efforts of women's groups in war-torn countries in Africa, notably Liberia, Guinea and Sierra Leone, and urged UN member states to give women a greater part in negotiating peace accords." In recognition and support of the Mano River Union women, Ted Turner (the founder of CNN) made a grant of $6.6 million over a period of 36 months to the UN women's fund (UNIFEM) to help enhance the role of women in conflict resolution and prevention and post-conflict peace building.

The Chargé d'Affaires of the Guinean Embassy in Monrovia, Liberia, on August 23, 2001, said:

> 'The ongoing peace process in the Mano River Union (MRU) is a fruit that came from mothers of this region after a workshop was held in Monrovia.' He said the outcome of the meeting created a room for the women to meet with the three heads of state of the MRU countries of Liberia, Sierra Leone and Guinea. The envoy said that 'we want...to give the glory to MRU Women's Peace Network who started the process.'

President Lansana Conte of Guinea, who initially resisted meeting with his Mano River neighbors, finally agreed to do so at the urging of the women of the member countries. He said (as reported by BBC on September 11, 2001):

> I would like...to thank the women of our three countries. As you know, they are the ones who triggered off this process. Therefore, they deserve our thanks and congratulations...The women have found a way of making me change my mind. I am ready to negotiate...let us get it over so that we can live in peace.

The most visible person in Liberia who sets an example for women throughout the country is the First Lady, the Honorable Jewel Howard Taylor. During the first quarter of 2001, she was appointed by the government to head the National Humanitarian Task Force to help care for internally displaced persons (IDPs) affected by the rebel war. Since that time, she has made innumerable visits to the camps of the IDPs, always bringing food and clothing to distribute. A photograph shows her toting a 100 pound bag of rice at the VOA displaced camp as she distributed relief supplies to citizens fleeing the war zones in Lofa, Bomi and Gbarpolu counties.

In May of 2002 the First Lady addressed the United Nations' Special Session on Children, warning that efforts being made towards child development would be "meaningless" if the issue of debt settlement by Liberia and other African countries is not prioritized for peace and stability. The NEWS newspaper in Liberia reported further on Mrs. Taylor's speech:

> The First Lady told the Global Community that Liberia's high indebtedness and government's inability to pay back age-old debts and loans are obstacles that have led to the increase in general poverty among the population. She also told the forum that the extent of poverty, especially among rural poor

in Liberia, remains very precarious due to the inability of families to adequately feed their children, particularly amidst prolonged and continuous disruption of agricultural activities by warfare. The First Lady said: 'I am saddened by the sorrows of our orphans, forced into shouldering adult responsibilities, prostitution and by our families' increasing inability to meet the dire needs of our war-affected children and to prepare them a legacy for tomorrow's leadership.'[33]

Mrs. Taylor has the ability to explain complicated issues in ways that people can understand. For example, she tells the story of a man walking along a beach where thousands of starfish had been washed up on shore. He noticed a boy picking up the starfish one by one and throwing them back into the sea. When he asked the boy why, the boy replied: "If I don't, they'll die." "But how can saving so few make a difference when so many are doomed?" the man asked. The boy picked up another starfish and threw it back into the sea and replied "It'll make a lot of difference to this one!" She then said:

> I hope that this story will inspire those who need to be actively involved in making our one world better for all the children of the world. For those who need more encouragement, I hope this will give you a fresh burst to help us in this fight for our children.[34]

In March of 1998, the First Lady traveled to Washington and asked to see her U.S. counterpart, First Lady Hillary Rodham Clinton, not to discuss politics or diplomacy, but to share thoughts on how the average citizen, particularly women, could be empowered in Liberia and throughout the world. To her credit, Mrs. Clinton received Jewel Taylor for a 45 minute meeting in the White House. In their discussion, Mrs. Clinton informed Mrs. Taylor of several programs that had worked successfully in other African nations that she had visited. As a result of Mrs. Taylor's interest, Mrs. Clinton sent her the details, that in particular included so-called "microlending programs."

The following is an example of this type of financial assistance. Esther Afua Ocloo of Ghana, as a young woman, turned a gift of less than a dollar into twelve jars of marmalade—which she sold for a profit, and became one of Ghana's leading entrepreneurs and a prominent exponent of the role of women in economic development. As the first chairwoman of Women's World Banking, Ms. Ocloo was one of the pioneers of microlending, the financing of homespun businesses, predominantly run by women, through very small loans, sometimes as little as $50. If a business prospers and the loan is repaid—as more than 98 percent are — then a larger loan is made available. Large lending institutions give microlending institutions like Women's World Banking, big loans of, say, $5 million. The money is then parceled out in small loans, at interest rates slightly higher than normal commercial rates, for enterprises as simple as drying fish. 25 million people, three-quarters of them women, have received microloans in more than 40 less-developed countries.

First Lady Jewel Taylor returned to Liberia inspired by the examples related to her by Hillary Clinton. Accordingly, in addition to micro-lending projects, Mrs. Taylor most recently has focused on health projects (such as rehabilitating the

John F. Kennedy Medical Center which originally was a gift from the United States government to the Liberian people in 1972); social services (by providing monthly rations of food for orphanages and indigent homes for the elderly); aid for ex-combatants (such as medical attention for the wounded at several hospitals and clinics in Monrovia and providing wheelchairs for the disabled); Children's Activities through Child Art Liberia (where, in the 1999 International Child Art Festival held in Washington, D.C., a Liberian child artist, Permanent Wilmot, only 12 years old, gained recognition as the best artist, winning first prize in the international competition); the Annual Christmas Drive (where toys are provided to Liberian children); the Girls in Crisis Program (where the YWCA has been renovated to provide shelter for 60 disadvantaged girls); and the Scholarship and Educational Assistance Program (where the goal is to lower the illiteracy rate in Liberia). These activities of women in Liberia rarely receive the attention of the foreign press.

While people in so many countries are struggling with poverty and disease, the U.S. sometimes takes positions on issues affecting women that are antithetical to that goal. In July 2002, the U.S. administration opposed the international Convention on the Elimination of All Forms of Discrimination Against Women, a document which affirms that women have equal human rights and fundamental freedoms in the political, economic, social, cultural, civil or any other field. According to the Washington Post on July 18, 2002, "the convention has been ratified by 170 countries, leaving the United States in the company of Afghanistan, Iran, Sudan, Somalia, Syria, the United Arab Emirates and Qatar." Harold Koh, a former U.S. Assistant Secretary of State for Human Rights, testified before the U.S. Senate that,

> America cannot be a world leader in guaranteeing progress for women's human rights...unless it is also a party to the global women's treaty...There is nothing in the substantive provisions of this treaty that even arguably jeopardizes our national interests...Its provisions are entirely consistent with the U.S. Constitution and federal and state laws.[35]

David Broder in the July 28, 2002 edition of the Washington Post, said:

> Every administration makes certain compromises...to satisfy important political constituencies. But most administrations draw the line at compromises that cost lives. The Bush administration now has crossed that line—not accidentally but deliberately.

> The decision...to withhold the $34 million United States contribution to the United Nations Population Fund (UNFPA) will cost uncounted women and children their lives. This organization supports family planning and maternal health programs in more than 140 countries, including education programs to prevent HIV and AIDS. Its projects have a proven track record of reducing mortality rates for mothers and infants as well as limiting population growth.

> If historical patterns hold, UNFPA says that the loss of the U.S. contribution—12 percent of its $270 million budget—will translate to 2

million more unwanted pregnancies, 800,000 more abortions, 4700 more dead mothers and 77,000 more deaths among children under 5…When our government allows special-interest pleading to cost lives, it shames us all.[36]

One hopes that the United States will change its position and sign and ratify the treaty.

EDUCATION

Civil disruption in Liberia has devastated the country's educational system. The Ministry of Education, under the leadership of Dr. D. Evelyn Kandakai, has strived to keep the system going under the most difficult of circumstances. There has been massive destruction and looting of physical facilities, instructional materials, textbooks and, above all, displacement and death of trained teachers. This condition has been aggravated by a depressed national economy, lack of investment in the productive and social sector, a high level of unemployment and ongoing conflict in many parts of the country causing major mass movement and displacement of people, many of whom are students and children of school-age.

Despite these difficulties, the Ministry of Education, beginning in 1997, developed and launched several postwar innovative initiatives. Some of those are: 1) the Accelerated Learning Program (ALP) that aims to provide education to over-age children whose schooling was affected by the war and other circumstances; 2) The National Mass Literacy Program (NMLP) which is geared toward reducing the illiteracy rate of 70 per cent; 3) the Assisted Enrollment Program (AEP) which is a Government initiative that provides incentive packages to attract more children to enroll and remain in school; 4) the Girls in Distress Program which attempts to address the educational and training needs of disadvantaged girls; and 5) the Population and Family Life Education-School Health Program which caters to the teaching of health with emphasis on reproductive health and HIV–AIDS education being carried out in partnership with UNFPA. Yet the failure of the international community to help Liberia financially has prevented many of these programs from being implemented fully and effectively.

The statistics set forth below indicate that since the Taylor government came into office in 1997, the number of students in the primary school system increased exponentially. But in the years 2001 to 2003 when the LURD uprising disrupted the country and caused havoc in many areas, school enrollment understandably has decreased.

In 1999 the total enrollment of students throughout the country in pre-primary, primary and secondary schools was 678,673. Legislation has been passed, but not yet implemented because of lack of funds, to provide universal free and compulsory primary education, which will require additional school buildings and teachers who must be trained and paid.

In 1999 the total number of schools nation-wide stood at 3,385. Of this total, 519 were pre-primary facilities; primary facilities totaled 2404; and secondary facilities 462. The condition of schools (including furniture, roofing, windows, chairs, etc.) is still deplorable even though the government and NGOs have renovated many schools throughout the country. Despite this help, it is estimated that close to 50% of the schools still have below-standard facilities for effective teaching-learning activities. Also in 1999 there were 16,205 primary and secondary teachers, but the quality of those teachers is a major concern. In 1989, when the current government took office, about 75% of the teachers in primary schools were only high school graduates.

Let us look at the available statistics for primary school enrollment. In 1998 there were 289,883 children enrolled; in 1999 that figure increased dramatically because of the Ministry of Education and NGO efforts to 507,192 students; and in 2000–2001 the total again increased to 890,419; but in 2001–2002 as the LURD fighting intensified, the number decreased to 794,337 and now is much lower yet as the fighting continues and spreads.

The disparity among counties is striking. Of the 794,337 primary school students in the country, 22.5% came from Montserrado county; 18.9% from Nimba County; but only 2.51% from Rivercess County.

With regard to secondary school enrollment, in 1998 it was 27,682; in 1999 it was 115,453; and in 2000–2001 it was 158,424.[37]

Because of the constant disruptions—namely the devastation and near-anarchy that the LURD attacks are causing throughout parts of the country—it is very difficult to obtain any kind of accurate current figures regarding the number of schools, teacher and pupils.

Cold statistics mask the despair that pervades a society when families cannot educate their children.

In order for Liberia to have a chance at rebuilding its educational system, the international community first must help stop the fighting in the country. The LURD and the government must declare a cease-fire. The LURD must lay down its arms and limit itself to becoming a political movement if it wishes. Only then will conditions be stable enough for the schools to get back to normal. At that point, the United States government should help rebuild the schools, train new teachers (perhaps using Peace Corps volunteers), send over more textbooks, provide salaries for the newly trained teachers until the economy of the country is restored, and let the children learn. Americans know the importance of education—it is the key to success in any open society. For a relatively small expenditure of money, we could guarantee every Liberian child a decent education; yet the dividends would be enormous. An educated electorate has a better chance to develop a responsible, truly democratic government.

HIV AND AIDS

Every day more than 8,000 people throughout the world die of AIDS. Every hour almost 600 people become infected. Every minute a child dies of the virus. 40 million people now are infected with the virus. The vast majority, according to UN Secretary-General Kofi Annan, are in sub-Saharan Africa.[38]

Dr. Peter Coleman is the Health and Social Welfare Minister of Liberia. On June 12, 2002 he startled a conference held at the Liberian Baptist Theological Seminary when he revealed that a study done in eight counties of Liberia showed that the prevalence rate of AIDS had jumped from 4.6% to 8.2% over the two previous years.

The Liberian newspapers reported Minister Coleman, who also is a prominent medical doctor, as saying:

> 'The prevalence rate will continue to rise. Maybe six months from now it will be higher.' 'He expressed the hope that the rate at which the virus is spreading will not be higher if Liberians from every strata of the society

get actively involved in combating and spreading the information on the killer disease.'

The Health Minister attributed the rapid spread of HIV–AIDS in Liberia to existing social and economic factors in the country. He added that social upheaval: instability, turmoil and displacement are all conducive social conditions that are facilitating the spread of AIDS in Liberia.

He warned Liberians to be guarded against discriminating or stigmatizing people infected with the virus. 'The church must rise up and put on its agenda to speak for the rights of AIDS victims.'"[39]

The Deputy Minister for Social Services at the Ministry of Health, Madam Diana Davis, said that the rapid increase of AIDS is fast becoming an economic catastrophe in Africa, and Liberia is no exception.

The Liberians newspapers quoted her as saying: "More than half of those infested with HIV–AIDS world-wide contract the disease by age 25 and typically die before their 35th birthday", thus describing the situation as explosive. The Deputy Minister made the statement when she unveiled an AIDS awareness billboard printed by the AIDS Prevention Promoters (APP) at the Diana E. Davies Elementary School in Mombo Town, Bushrod Island.

The health official also sent an SOS appeal to the international community to provide funds to government and local NGOs to provide more education to our people, especially the youth…She also said that the APP (AIDS Prevention Promoters) has launched a campaign in five communities including New Kru Town, Logan Town, St. Paul Bridge, Ricks and Po-River, and is expected to launch an awareness campaign in twenty different schools in Monrovia and its environs next week.[40]

Minister Coleman expressed his thanks to the Taiwan Roots Medical Peace Corps for its help in revitalizing the health sector, specifically mentioning the donation of 5 million condoms to strengthen Liberia's HIV–AIDS intervention program. The Minister also noted that the government of France had supported Liberia's 3-year national strategic plan of action in the areas of AIDS awareness and prevention.

In January of 2002 Pennsylvania State University in the U.S. announced a collaborative program with some African universities, specifically including Cuttington University in Liberia, to establish a center for research and training on AIDS issues.

On March 21, 2002 the then U.S. Ambassador to Liberia Bismarck Myrick signed a memorandum of understanding between the United State government (acting through USAID) and the United Nations Population Fund (UNFPA) for the presentation of 2,280,000 condoms to Liberia. Interestingly according to Kenneth Davidson, writing in *The Age*, a centrist publication in Melbourne, Australia, at the UN Asian and Pacific Population Conference held later the same year, in December of 2002, in Bangkok (the U.S. was represented because of its ownership of the island of Guam), "the U.S. delegation demanded the deletion of a recommendation for 'consistent condom use' to fight AIDS, even though a Berkeley study found condom distribution to be astonishingly cost-effective, at $3.50 a year of life saved. Anti-retroviral therapy costs more than $1000."[41]

The First Lady of Liberia, Mrs. Jewel Howard-Taylor, on September 5, 2002, urged all Liberians to know their HIV–AIDS status by taking the test "which will enable you to determine your future action." The First Lady inaugurated an HIV–AIDS testing and counseling center at St. Luke's Lutheran Church in the Phebe Hospital Compound in Suakoko, Bong County. She set an example during her visit by having herself tested for the virus.

In light of the spreading HIV–AIDS epidemic in Africa, President of the United States George W. Bush addressed the subject in his 2003 State of the Union speech when he said:

> ...(T)o meet a severe and urgent crisis abroad...I propose the Emergency Plan for AIDS Relief—a work of mercy beyond all current international efforts to help the people of Africa. This comprehensive plan will prevent 7 million new AIDS infections, treat at least 2 million people with life-extending drugs, and provide human care for millions of people suffering from AIDS, and for children orphaned by AIDS. I ask the Congress to commit $15 billion over the next five years, including nearly $10 billion in new money, to turn the tide against AIDS in the most afflicted nations of Africa and the Caribbean. This nation can lead the world in sparing innocent people from a plague of nature.[42]

The question then became whether the words would be backed up with action. On February 7, 2003, for example, the Washington Post reported that

> several new programs that President Bush proposed in the buildup to his fiscal 2004 budget have turned out to be somewhat smaller than they first appeared...In his address, Bush proposed spending $15 billion to combat AIDS overseas over five years. He said $10 billion of that would be in new funds, But his 2004 budget plan called for spending $1 billion—of which $450 million would be new funding, the Office of Management and Budget (OMB) said. The increase was partially offset by a reduced commitment to another foreign aid proposal.[43]

Even $450 million of new funding, however, would be extremely helpful to Africa.

On February 23, 2003 the New York Times pointed out that most of the U.S. money for the AIDS project will *not* go to the global AIDS fund; rather "the White House wants the State Department, rather than the global fund, to control the money." The most plausible reason for having the State Department control the money is to use the funds as an arm of U.S. foreign policy rather than disburse them strictly on the basis of need. That soon became obvious.

Congress prepared the legislation to implement the President's State of the Union speech, announcing in February as reported in the Washington Post that "the money is to go to only 12 countries in Africa, plus Haiti and Guyana. The program will cover prevention efforts, including voluntary testing and counseling; drugs and other treatment for people infected with HIV, the virus that causes AIDS, and care of HIV–infected individuals and AIDS orphans."

The Department of State, in its February, 2003 report on international assistance programs, referring to President Bush's HIV–AIDS initiative, states:

"These funds will be targeted on the hardest hit countries in Africa and the Caribbean with the objective of achieving dramatic on-the-ground results."[44]

The White House verified that President Bush soon will name a Special Co-ordinator to International HIV–AIDS, with Ambassadorial rank, who will be located within the Department of State and report to the Secretary of State. The 12 African countries which will receive American assistance are: Botswana, Côte d'Ivoire, Ethiopia, Kenya, Mozambique, Namibia, Nigeria, Rwanda, South Africa, Tanzania, Uganda and Zambia. Liberia is conspicuously missing from the list.

The test for selecting the countries, according to the White House, is those which are "most affected." It is incontrovertible that Liberia, torn asunder by a rebel war, with a prevalence rate of HIV–AIDS that has doubled in less than two years, and now is probably more than 10%, is one of Africa's hardest-hit countries. Yet Liberia was not on the list of countries eligible for President Bush's AIDS initiative.

NOTES

[1] Jonathan Paye-Layleh, "Liberian bishop accuses government of corruption, rights abuses," *Associated Press*, December 2, 2001, p. 1

[2] "Government reacts to archbishop's pastoral message," *BBC*, December 4, 2001, p. 1.

[3] Roger P. Winter, "How human rights groups miss the opportunity to do good," *Washington Post*, February 22, 1998, p. C2.

[4] Ibid.

[5]. U.S. Senator Russ Feingold, "Name the Detainees," *Washington Post*, December 23, 2001, p. D7.

[6] Karen DeYoung, "Group criticizes U.S. on detainee policy," *Washington Post*, May 28, 2002.

[7] Timothy Lynch, "Policy Analysis, No. 443, Breaking the vicious cycle," CATO Institute, June 26, 2002, p. 17.

[8] Ibid.

[9] Jonathan Paye-Layleh, "Liberia rejects U.S. State Department report, says has made progress on human rights," *Associated Press*, March 1, 2002, p. 1.

[10] Ibid.

[11] Ibid.

[12] Jonathan Paye-Layleh, "Rights group accuses Liberian government after lawyer is arrested and beaten," *Associated Press*, April 26, 2002.

[13] "Leading Liberian rights lawyer tortured by police," Human Rights Watch, April 26, 2002, p. 1, release.

[14] "Detained Liberian rights lawyer alleges police brutality," *Agence France-Presse*, April 26, 2002, pp. 1–2.

[15] "Back to the Brink, Vol. 14, No.4(A)," Human Rights Watch, May 2002, p. 10, at <www.hrw.org>.

[16] Danna Harman, "Africa's dangerous profession: a missing Liberian editor high-lights Africa's treatment of opposition journalists," *Christian Science Monitor*, July 8, 2002, p. 1; "Hassan Bility incommunicado without charge (AFR *34/011/2002*)," Amnesty International, August *2002,* press release.

[17] George Bardue, "Liberia: Bility Faces Military Court," *The NEWS*, AllAfrica

Global Media, allAfrica.com, July 10, 2002; Musue N. Haddad, "An open communication to a detained journalist," ThePerspective, July 25, 2002 <http://www.theperspective.org/opencommunication.html>.

[18] Harman, p. 2.

[19] Ibid. p. 2.

[20] Bill K. Jarkloh, "U.S. against government failure to produce Bility," *The NEWS* (Monrovia), citing President Taylor interview with KISS PM radio, n.d.

[21] "Still no lawyers," *Washington Post*, July 9, 2002, p. A20, editorial.

[22] Jonathan Paye-Layleh, "Military tribunal in Liberia says detained journalist is prisoner of war," *Associated Press*, October 24, 2002.

[24] "Liberia, Government wants Bility, others taken out by U.S. Embassy," *The NEWS* (Monrovia), n.d.

[23] Jonathan Paye-Layleh, "Jailed Liberian journalist handed over to U.S. Embassy, flies out of country," *Associated Press*, December 8, 2002.

[25] Presentations at the "Symposium on Liberia's political future," Movement for Democratic Change in Liberia (MDCL), Nyumburu Cultural Center, University of Maryland, College Park, Maryland, March 1, 2002; letter from Pamela Bridgewater, Deputy Assistant Secretary of State to author dated March 17, 2002.

[26] Stanley McGill, Editorial, *The NEWS* (Monrovia), n.d.

[27] Harman, p. 1.

[28] Bobby Tapson, "Liberia, Brumskine gets rousing welcome," *The NEWS* (Monrovia), January 22, 2003.

[29] "America's Repressive Allies," *Washington Post*, December 31, 2001, editorial page.

[30] Thomas L. Friedman, "Foreign affairs; heart of darkness," *New York Times,* January 21, 1996.

[31] Sebastian Faulks, *On Green Dolphin Street*, Hutchinson, April 2001.

[32] Bobby Tapson, "Dogolea died of cancer, Government releases autopsy report," *The NEWS* (Monrovia), May 31, 2002.

[33] "Liberia, For better and for worse—First Lady remains committed at 40," *The NEWS* (Monrovia), May, 2000, p. 2.

[34] Unpublished speech, n.d.

[35] Karen DeYoung, "Senate panel to defy Bush, vote on women's treaty," *Washington Post*, July 18, 2002.

[36] David Broder, "Deadly Politics," *Washington Post*, July 28, 2002, Section B, p. B7.

[37] The Ministry of Education of Liberia, Fact Sheet, August 24, 2002; MOE/UNDP/UNICEF Consultative Workshop on Free and Compulsory Education in Liberia, November 28, 2002.

[38] UN Secretary-General Kofi Annan, "No letting up on AIDS," *Washington Post*, November 29, 2001, p. A33.

[39] Speech by Liberian Health and Social Welfare Minister Peter S. Coleman, "HIV/AIDS to further spread unless...", n.d., delivered June 12, 2002.

[40] Statement by Madam Diana Davies, "AIDS becoming economic catastrophe," n.d.

[41] "U.S. Ambassador calls for awareness," *The Inquirer Newspaper, Monrovia*, March 21, 2002; "The truth about George Bush's anti-AIDS push," *World Press Review*,

April 2003. citing article by Kenneth Davidson in *The Age*, Melbourne, Australia, February 10, 2003

[42] Hon. George W. Bush, State of the Union speech, January 28, 2003.

[43] Dana Millbank, "Bush budget uses fuzzy math, Democrats say" *Washington Post*, February 7, 2003. p. A4.

[44] U.S. Department of State, U.S. Department of State and International Assistance Programs, February 2003, p. 212.

CHAPTER 10
GLOBAL TERRORISM AND DIPLOMACY

GLOBAL TERRORISM

Global terrorism has become the primary dynamic of this first decade of the 21st century. For the United States, in the interest of national and economic security, the use of American power to fight global terrorism dominates its foreign policy. This represents a dramatic departure from the Cold War era, when America allied itself and funded many of the same terrorists that are now its enemies in the Middle-East, Africa and elsewhere, to advance U.S. policy in the defeat of Communism. The relationship between the U.S. and any country now depends on the U.S. assessment, supported by accurate or suspect intelligence, of whether the country has links to the axis of terrorist groups and countries that foster terrorism. Since September 11, 2001, the U.S. analysis of Liberia was dual; it credited the republic for supporting the fight against global terrorism, then charged Charles Taylor as having links to Al Qaeda. At the same time, the U.S., in Cold War fashion, used the LURD and MODEL rebel groups in its policy to contain Charles Taylor. Both U.S. positions have further impaired U.S.–Liberia relations.

An African academician, Mahamood Mamdani, a native of Uganda, who is the Herbert Lehman Professor of Government and director of the Institute of African Studies at Columbia University, commented on America and terrorism. On January 8, 2002, Professor Mamdani wrote an OpEd piece that appeared in the Washington Post titled, *Turn Off Your Tunnel Vision*. He said that the same events that Africans celebrated as ushering in the end of European colonialism, opened a new phase in the Cold War's center of gravity from Indochina to Southern Africa.

> Official America harnessed, even cultivated, terrorism in the struggle against movements it saw as Soviet proxies. Yes, I do mean 'terrorism', which Washington supports when it backs groups for whom the preferred method of operation is destroying the infrastructure of civilian life. Right up until September 11, America counseled African governments to 'reconcile' with terrorist groups. Since then, that has given way to a demand for 'justice'. But just as reconciliation became a code word for impunity, the danger now is that 'justice' will mean bloody revenge.[1]

He then offered evidence to support his claim:

> The American embrace of terrorism was global—in Angola where the U.S. feared the Popular Movement for the Liberation of Angola (MPLA), which it saw as a Soviet proxy, so we supported the National Union for Total Independence of Angola (UNITA); in South Africa where the Reagan Administration announced a policy of "constructive engagement" with the apartheid regime; in Mozambique where the U.S. supported RENAMO, the Mozambique National Resistance; in Nicaragua (the contras); and in Afghanistan (the mujaheddin). Terrorism distinguishes itself from guerilla war by making civilians its preferred target.

"Even after the Cold War," wrote Professor Mamdani,

the tolerance for terror remained high. The callous Western response to the 1994 genocide in Rwanda was no exception. Nor was January 6, 1999, when Revolutionary United Front gunmen maimed and raped their way across Freetown, Sierra Leone, killing more than 5,000 civilians in a day. The U.S. response was to pressure the government to share power with the rebels.

If the Cold War was an umbrella under which America sheltered right-wing dictators in power and embraced terrorists out of power, the danger is now the temptation to view Africa while preoccupied with a single overriding concern—this time terrorism—and to once again ignore African realities.[2]

In Dr. Mamdani's analysis, Liberia is yet another example of the United States refusing to move against a terrorist group (the LURD) which formed to remove the elected government by military force. Moreover, the U.S. condemned efforts by the Liberian government to arrest and detain suspected collaborators with LURD, and prevented it from obtaining the weapons necessary to defend its citizens against LURD attacks. Since September 11, 2002 the U.S. has arrested and incarcerated indefinitely, without filing charges, hundreds of prisoners (many of them American citizens). The U.S. has called them "terrorists" and denied them the right to consult legal counsel.

One day after the attack of September 11, Agence France-Presse reported that

Liberian President Charles Taylor has strongly denounced the terrorists attacks in the United States. Taylor said in a communique late Tuesday (9/12/01) that he condemned the 'gruesome attacks on the lives of innocent citizens as well as the wanton destruction of properties. The people of Liberia,' Taylor said, 'are in deep sympathy with the people of the United States and wish to identify with them during these hours of national tragedy.'

On September 16, 2001 Liberians offered their sympathy and support to the United States at a prayer service for the victims of the terrorist attacks. The Associated Press reported that President Taylor, at an interdenominational prayer service where the U.S. and Liberian flags flew at half-staff, said: "Your losses are our losses. Your grief is our grief. Today the hands of evil have struck America. Tomorrow it could be any other nation."[3]

U.S. Ambassador Bismarck Myrick thanked Liberia for the support, saying: "We are strengthened by the gesture of the president, the government and the people of Liberia."[4]

On the same day Reuters reported that entrepreneurs had printed pictures of Osama bin Laden for sale in the streets of Liberia, where people's interest was "driven more from fascination than support for his cause."[5] Liberian police chief Paul Mulbah immediately announced that anyone found buying or selling the pictures would be arrested.

Foreign Minister Monie Captan sent a letter to U.S. Secretary of State Colin Powell offering use of Liberian facilities (such as Robertsfield Airport which was used by the U.S. during the Gulf War) that might be helpful to the U.S. in the war against terrorism. The author was unable to verify whether the United States responded to the offer, but on September 9, 2002, when John Blaney was sworn in as the new U.S. Ambassador to Liberia, at the State Department Secretary of State Colin Powell said,

> I wish to express again the gratitude of President Bush and the American people to the government and people of Liberia for their expression of sympathy following the September 11 terrorist attacks. In recent years, the people of Liberia, too, have suffered terrible losses at the hands of hate and so we were especially moved by your gestures of solidarity.[6]

Then he added: "The fighting that has laid waste to Liberia's greatest resource—its people—must end." But there were no U.S. initiatives to restrain the LURD and help make those words come true. Secretary Powell concluded, in words that belied the claims of those in his own Department who said the U.S. no longer cared about Liberia: "America's and Liberia's pasts are closely intertwined. So, too, are our futures. The President and I know, John (Blaney), that you will do your utmost to work with the people and government of Liberia to help them build a future of democracy, prosperity and peace."[7] The U.S. Department of State listed Liberia among the countries who lost citizens in the September 11 attack, and who offered support in the fight against terrorism.

Against this background, let us examine a November 9, 2001 New Republic magazine article titled: *Can Charles Taylor's Apologists Explain His Ties to Al Qaeda?* The author, Ryan Lizza, wrote: "(W)e now know, thanks to a detailed report last week by Douglas Farah in the Washington Post, that something...of great importance happened in Liberia in 1998: Osama bin Laden's Al Qaeda network opened shop there."

Lizza continued:

> According to Farah, one of bin Laden's top aides, Abdullah Ahmed Abdullah, arrived in Liberia and met with one of Taylor's long-time lieutenants, Ibrahim Bah. Together they flew in a government helicopter to meet with a senior commander of the Revolutionary United Front (RUF), the vicious rebel army controlled by Taylor that has controlled the diamond mines of Sierra Leone for the last four years. A few weeks later two Al Qaeda terrorists wanted for the American Embassy bombings in Kenya and Tanzania arrived with $100,000 in cash to buy the first pouch of diamonds from the RUF. Since then, Farah reports, bin Laden has raised millions—perhaps tens of millions—of dollars buying cut-rate RUF diamonds and selling them in Europe.[8]

Although no one suggested that any of the people mentioned in his article met with, or in any way communicated with Charles Taylor, Ryan Lizza drew the following conclusion:

> (N)ow we know that the Liberian dictator is not just a menace to West Africa; he is a menace to the United States as well. That Taylor has ties to Al Qaeda shouldn't be terribly surprising. Since becoming president in 1997, Taylor has run Liberia like a giant criminal enterprise, attracting South African mercenaries, Latin American drug lords, and Ukrainian mobsters to Monrovia. Middle Eastern terrorists were bound to find their

way there…A financial relationship with Charles Taylor no longer just supports a brutal African army terrorizing faraway people; it tacitly supports a terrorist organization dedicated to the destruction of the United States."[9]

The claims in the paragraphs set forth above were incorrect. In 2001 Doug Farah, whose article in the Washington Post was the basis for the New Republic assertions, stated that he never said that Charles Taylor was tied to Al Qaeda.[10] He did say that a Senegalese rebel named Bah smuggled diamonds out of Sierra Leone through Liberia to Belgian diamond dealers, bringing briefcases of cash which somehow ended up with Al Qaeda. Mr. Farah stated that he did not think Taylor knew the identity of the people; nor did he (Farah) believe the RUF had any idea who they were. Only Bah did. Thus, the New Republic article was irresponsible in asserting a connection between Taylor and Al Qaeda.

The New Republic and the Washington Post allegations regarding connections to the "terrorists" dealt with events that took place in 1998, three years before September 11, 2001. In judging actions that occurred before the terrorist attack of September 11, one finds that many nations of the world—including the United States—could be accused of aiding the terrorists. An article in The Los Angeles Times written by the reporter, Robert Scheer, just days prior to September 11 dramatized this point. The headline was: *Bush's Faustian Deal with the Taliban.*

It read:

> Enslave your girls and women, harbor anti–U.S. terrorists, destroy every vestige of civilization in your homeland, and the Bush administration will embrace you. All that matters is that you line up as an ally in the drug war, the only international cause that this nation still takes seriously. That's the message sent with the recent gift of $43 million to the Taliban rulers of Afghanistan, the most virulent anti-American violators of human rights in the world today. The gift, announced last Thursday by Secretary of State Colin Powell, in addition to other aid, makes the U.S. the main sponsor of the Taliban and rewards that 'rogue regime' for declaring that opium growing is against the will of God…Never mind that Osama bin Laden still operates the leading anti-American terror operation from his base in Afghanistan, from which, among other crimes, he launched two bloody attacks on American embassies in Africa in 1998. Sadly, the Bush administration is cozying up to the Taliban regime at a time when the United Nations, at U.S. insistence, imposes sanctions on Afghanistan because the Kabul government will not turn over bin Laden…Our long sad history of signing up dictators in the war on drugs demonstrates the futility of building a foreign policy on a domestic obsession.[11]

To further emphasize this point, one can imagine the reaction if the story reprinted above had appeared on the front page of a major American newspaper, not days before September 11, 2001, but in the days immediately thereafter. There would likely have been an uproar.

On September 12, 2002, the U.S. marked the first anniversary of the previous year's terrorist attacks. As Americans commemorated the event, in Liberia the government and the people held a requiem mass in memory of the victims of that horrible event that shocked the United States and the rest of the world.

President Taylor led an array of government officials to the Roman Catholic Church in Monrovia for a memorial service for the families, government and people of the United States of America. He also declared a holiday to observe the anniversary of the tragedy in solidarity with the American people. The Chargé d'Affaires of the U.S. Embassy in Liberia, Thomas White, attended the service.

In a statement on behalf of the Liberian government, Foreign Minister Monie R. Captan called upon the nations of the world to go beyond mere condemnation and take concrete actions that would reflect the commitment to fight terrorism.

He reaffirmed Liberia's commitment to the global campaign against terror as enshrined in United Nations Security Council Resolution 1373 and explained that, consistent with that resolution, Liberia had adopted comprehensive legislation to meet the new dimensions of terrorism including adoption of financial control regulations, the strengthening of customs and immigration control, enforcement of laws regulating arms traffic and liberalization of extradition of persons suspected of engaging in terrorism.

On October 4, 2002, when the newly appointed Ambassador to Liberia, John William Blaney, presented his credentials to President Taylor at the Executive Mansion, Mr. Taylor said that Liberia would stand shoulder to shoulder with the United States in the war against global terrorism. The President expressed his agreement with the position of the United States and Britain on a new resolution to inspect weapons of mass destruction in Iraq.

It is significant to note that Ambassador Blaney reiterated the special relationship between Liberia and the United States, adding that "Our people, our enterprises, our educational institutions and in fact our dreams are largely intertwined."

Three and a half months later, on December 29, 2002, the Washington Post featured a front-page headline: *Report Says Africans Harbored Al Qaeda; Terror Assets Hidden in Gem-Buying Spree*. There was a sense of *deja vu* in reading the story, as it was a revision of the same story that Mr. Farah wrote in the Post more than a year earlier. Both stories gave the reader the impression that the events reported took place contemporaneously, when in fact the allegation applied only to events that took place from 1998 through mid-2001, before the terrorist attack:

> Al Qaeda's diamond purchases were first reported in The Washington Post 13 months ago," referring to Douglas Farah's story of November, 2001, describing some meetings between a Senegalese man and some RUF leaders that allegedly took place in Liberia as early as 1998.[12]

The lead of the 2002 story was:

> An aggressive year-long European investigation into al Qaeda financing has found evidence that two West African governments hosted the senior terrorist operatives who oversaw a $20 million diamond-buying spree that effectively cornered the market on the region's precious stones.[13]

Yet in the story was the sentence: "Investigators have been unable to trace the diamonds since they left Liberia and Burkina Faso," which certainly somewhat undercut the thesis that there was proof the diamond profits ended up with Al Qaeda.

In the second paragraph of his story, Mr. Farah stated that

investigators from several countries concluded that President Charles Taylor of Liberia received a $1 million payment for arranging to harbor the operatives, who were in the region for at least two months after the September 11, 2002 attacks on New York and the Pentagon. The terrorists moved between a protected area in Liberia and the presidential compound in neighboring Burkina Faso, investigators say.[14]

These are serious charges which Mr. Farah said were based upon a "military intelligence summary," somehow obtained by the Post which

draws on interviews with senior investigators, the intelligence report and documents obtained independently that verify its findings. The Post also interviewed two sources with direct knowledge of certain events, who asked that their names not be used for fear of retribution.[15]

No sources were identified by name given and no countries which allegedly conducted the investigations were named. The article included a response from President Taylor. "Long accused of sanctioning illicit diamond and weapons trading, Taylor and President Blaise Campaore of Burkina Faso deny the charge, which is included in a summary of the joint intelligence findings." Casting doubt upon the validity of one of his sources was Mr. Farah's comment:

Senior European intelligence sources say they have been baffled by the lack of U.S. interest, particularly by the CIA, in their recent findings. The CIA, which in the past has downplayed reports of al Qaeda's connections, declined to comment.[16]

Later in his account, Mr. Farah wrote:

In the weeks after the Sept. 11 attacks, the U.S. Defense Intelligence Agency did try to monitor the two senior al Qaeda operatives supervising the diamond trading, who were known to be hiding in an elite military camp in Liberia. Both men were on the FBI's Most Wanted List of terrorists. The Pentagon prepared a small Special Forces team in neighboring Guinea to snatch the two, but the mission was not carried out because the team could not confirm the targets' identities, according to sources.[17]

U.S. Defense Intelligence Agency could not verify that these so-called operatives were at Camp Gbatala. In that regard, Farah wrote:

'We had multiple, reliable intelligence reports that those two and two others were in Gbatala and we stood a team up for the snatch,' said a U.S. official familiar with the events. 'But in the end we couldn't get the 100 percent identification we needed to pull the trigger and cause a possible international incident. After about a week, the group stood down.'

Mr. Farah's gave other evidence on which he relied to charge that Charles Taylor received $1 million to "harbor operatives." Two-thirds through his article is the description of the incident that is the basis for Mr. Farah's charges, printed here with bracketed comments:

According to the European intelligence summary, in July 2001 [prior to the 9/11 attack], Nassour Aziz Nassour who Farah describes as "a Lebanese diamond merchant" together with "his cousin Samih Osailly and Ibrahim Bah, a Senegalese solider of fortune who has trafficked for years in diamonds and guns across Africa…flew from Beirut to Dubai and picked up $1 million in cash to be given to Liberian President Taylor. Investigators say it is not clear who handed Nassour the money. He then flew to Ouagadougou, the capital of Burkina Faso. By then, the two al Qaeda operatives had returned from Pakistan and, according to the report were staying in the compound of Burkina Faso President Campaore.

Ghailani and Mohammed [two other alleged al Qaeda operatives], the report says, stayed until the summer of 2001 'in the presidential complex in Ouagadougou'…The report said the $1 million was to pay Taylor 'to hide the two al Qaeda operatives in Camp Gbatala,' a military camp in Liberia, near Taylor's private farm, that serves as the base of Liberia's elite Anti-Terrorism Unit and the South African mercenaries who train it."

…Nassour acknowledged the stop in Burkina Faso en route to Liberia but says he never carried $1 million. According to visa files obtained by The Post, Nassour arrived in Monrovia on July 9 (2001), listed as Bah's guest. Sources said he left after a few days because the RUF commanders he had planned to meet had not arrived. He went to Ouagadougou, where he gave a suitcase of cash to a courier [unnamed] to deliver to Taylor."[18]

The Farah story did not quote any source or evidence that confirmed Taylor received the alleged $1 million from the courier.

The Washington Post did not publish the response of the Embassy of Liberia in the United States to the Farah article. The Embassy labeled "false" the allegations purporting to link Liberia to the illicit Al Qaeda money trade. The Embassy release, dated December 30, 2002, stated:

The Liberian Government works with agents of the American intelligence services in Monrovia on a daily basis, providing information. Liberia is firmly supportive of the U.S.–led global fight against terrorism and President Charles Ghankay Taylor has recently signed into law six conventions related to terrorism. With such close collaboration, it is inconceivable that Liberia would or could harbor Al Qaeda operatives.[19]

In his article, Mr. Farah did not address that fact that Liberia worked closely with American intelligence officials in Monrovia (presumably the CIA) in the fight against terrorism. If Liberians were in league with Al Qaeda, it would not make sense for the CIA to work hand-in-hand with the Liberian government.

Based on U.S. intelligence reports and the Farah stories, the President of Liberia was accused of having a link with Al Qaeda. Mr. Farah stated that there was such a link in his story published in 2002. The Republic of Liberia maintained there was credible evidence that Liberia was working with the United States and against Al Qaeda.

TWO US AMBASSADORS TO LIBERIA

Two career diplomats have served as U.S. Ambassador to Liberia since the national election of 1997. The first was Honorable Bismarck Myrick and the second Honorable William Blaney.

Bismarck Myrick joined the diplomatic corps after a 20-year military career. One of his first assignments took him to Liberia as a political officer in the early 1980s (the Doe years). He was principal officer at the U.S. consulate in Durban, South Africa when Nelson Mandela was released from prison in 1990. After serving as Ambassador to Lesotho, he returned to Liberia as Ambassador in 1999. He was the first United States Ambassador named to Liberia since the civil war erupted in 1989.

Shortly after he assumed his post in Monrovia, Ambassador Myrick stated that he was not going to hark back to past grievances, but instead would start with a clean slate regarding the Taylor administration and proceed from there. Soon, however, he was called back to Washington for "consultations" and when he returned to Liberia, his demeanor was far different. As the Virginia-Pilot (Norfolk, Virginia) wrote in an interview with Ambassador Myrick after he had left his post: "As ambassador, Myrick was the most visible point man for a U.S. foreign policy that chastised Liberian President Charles Taylor for running a corrupt regime, abusing human rights and destabilizing his neighbors." It was he who oversaw the imposition of travel sanctions (that exist to this day) so that all members of the Taylor government, as well as Liberians who had anything to do with Charles Taylor (a total of 139 people) were not allowed to leave the country. From then on, relations between Mr. Myrick and the Liberians rapidly deteriorated. The excitement of having an African-American ambassador turned into cynicism, as Mr. Myrick used the same State Department rhetoric as his predecessors when describing President Taylor and his government.

In that same hometown newspaper story, it was said that

> Myrick earned the regime's enmity by practicing what he calls 'people diplomacy', bypassing the government and reaching out to village chiefs, elders, youth groups and women's organization. He gave out small grants for construction of toilets and development of income-generating projects. 'I think it became an annoyance to the government,' Myrick said. 'It highlighted the government's lack of attention to its citizens.'[20]

The government and the people were annoyed, because tiny gestures were the limit of what the United States did for the people of Liberia when the needs were so much greater. The State Department said repeatedly that they did not want to send money to Liberia that would end up in Charles Taylor's pocket. One could not fault Ambassador Myrick for trying to help the people with the limits imposed by U.S. policy. Career ambassadors have extremely small discretionary funds for use in the country to which they are assigned. He deserved credit for the small projects. But his personal gestures merely highlighted the parsimoniousness of the United States government which could have done much more for a country emerging from civil war. During the civil war, the JFK Hospital lay in ruins. The government of Taiwan, and not the U.S., made a grant of $2 million for the renovation of the hospital. Because of Taiwan's help, the JFK Hospital reopened in November of 2002.

The Liberians were delighted to see Myrick leave his post. The official web-site of the government, in July of 2002, in a burst of hyperbole, blared the headline: "Ambassador Bismarck Myrick, the Curse of U.S.–Liberia Relations." The article portrayed Myrick as desperate "to destabilize the Liberian government at all cost...A man who came three years ago with so much promise...is about to leave Liberia a broken, bent and failed diplomat armed with enough venom to poison the Potomac

River."[21] That description was inaccurate. Myrick's initial stated intent and actions were positive. Later, Ambassador Myrick merely carried out the orders of the State Department which opposed Charles Taylor.

When he left his post in Liberia, Ambassador Myrick was given credit by some Liberian newspapers for assisting the empowerment of local grassroots organizations, and trying to interact with the government. One paper wrote: "With all of the wrangling, the Liberian leadership and the American head of mission interacted positively as well. It is recalled that the outgoing U.S. envoy visited President Charles Taylor at the Executive Mansions where they held a closed door discussion for hours."[22]

Mr. Myrick's successor is an experienced American diplomat, Honorable John William Blaney III who served as Deputy Chief of Mission of the U.S. Embassy in Pretoria, South Africa. He also acted as Country Director for Southern Africa at the State Department from 1995 to 1999, and served at the U.S. mission to the UN as Deputy Representative to the Economic and Social Council. Earlier he was a minister counselor in the U.S. Mission in Moscow and served as Economic-Commercial Officer in Zambia.

On July 9, 2002, the Senate Foreign Relations Committee held its hearing on Mr. Blaney's nomination. Mr. Blaney said this to the Committee in his sworn testimony:

> If confirmed, I would apply my experience to facilitate democracy, peace, national reconciliation and *reconstruction* in Liberia. While that may be a daunting task, I look forward to working closely with you in implementing an aggressive, practical and pragmatic policy."[23]

Those were hopeful words indeed. On the day that Ambassador Blaney was sworn in at the State Department, Secretary of State Colin Powell departed from his prepared remarks to say that "there is real hope for Liberia." The signs were positive.

In his Senate testimony, Mr. Blaney conceded a point that the U.S. had denied for years: that it was the conduct of the Doe government, which the U.S. so avidly supported, that caused the civil war in Liberia, not the actions of Charles Taylor in trying to unseat the Doe regime. Mr. Blaney said:

> Americo-Liberians ruled virtually uncontested over the indigenous population until 1980, when the government was overthrown by a group of noncommissioned officers led by Samuel Doe. His refusal to govern democratically created the conditions for the 1989 to 1996 civil war.[24]

On October 4, 2002, Ambassador Blaney presented his credentials to President Charles Taylor in a ceremony at the Liberian Executive Mansion on Capital Hill. The Inquirer newspaper in Monrovia wrote of that day: "The Ambassador of the United States of America is deeply concerned about the well-being of Liberians and will work with the Liberian government and others to stop the ongoing conflict." Despite those good intentions, the "ongoing conflict" continued in 2003 and, based on available information, the United States was unwilling or unable to stop it. In fact, State Department officials such as Mark Bellamy by their words, encouraged the LURD. As it stands, the talk about helping the reconstruction of Liberia has not led to any action.

Ambassador Blaney has tried to help the Liberian people. As he assumed his new post, he disclosed that the United States would contribute US $1 million to the international committee of the Red Cross to help respond to the emergency protection and assistance needs of Liberian conflict victims.

On October 28, 2002 Ambassador Blaney presented a gift of 75,000 textbooks and reference materials to the Ministry of Education at the William V.S. Tubman High School for distribution to learning institutions throughout the country. This was precisely the kind of people-to-people assistance that many individuals urged the United States Government to provide.

Later Ambassador Blaney announced that the U.S. Government, together with American Schools and Hospitals Abroad (ASHA), and the Episcopal Church, was providing grants of $800,000 to Cuttington University College, to provide reliable supplies of electricity and safe drinking water due to war-related destruction to the institution's facilities.[25]

On January 24, 2003, Ambassador Blaney announced a U.S. sponsored $12 million project to "help Liberians at the grass-roots level to participate more fully and strategically in initiating and managing their own social economic development activities and effectively preventing and resolving conflicts at the community level."[26]

Then on February 5, 2003 the U.S. Embassy earmarked U.S. $16,000 for a school project in Sinoe County, including Ambassador Blaney donating footballs for the young people.

While these were laudable constructive attempts to help the people of Liberia, it must be said that they still were "baby steps" compared to the great strides that must be taken to rebuild the country's infrastructure. The United States is capable of doing so much more, either itself or together with the international community. An economic assessment of its situation indicated that Liberia needs hundreds of millions of dollars.

On November 21, 2002 Ambassador Blaney held a press conference to inform the Liberian people of the activities and views of the U.S. Embassy. He said: "One of the most important things I have learned since coming to Liberia is the great hunger for peace in this country. It almost doesn't matter who you talk to, virtually everyone wants peace." Then he said: "The United States wants peace in Liberia, too. The Liberian people have already suffered far too much from war, and the United States condemns the renewal of violence now ongoing in Lofa County."[27] But the Ambassador took an even-handed view of the conflict, instead of condemning the perpetrators of the violence, the issueless LURD group. There were indications that this even-handedness merely emboldened the LURD to continue its violence. Some analysts believe the conflict would end if the United States condemned the LURD's resort to military means to overturn the democratically elected government, and urged them to become a political party that seeks redress through the ballot box, not by bullets.

Soon the hardline appeared. The Ambassador said that the Liberian government should not attempt to search for a scapegoat, such as the U.N.'s "limited" sanctions, in order to explain why major social services, including electricity, health, and education have not been provided. (See Chapter 9.) But Liberia has been cut off from major reconstruction and rehabilitation aid by the U.S. and the international community. Money, not words, was essential to help the people.

At the press conference in November, Ambassador Blaney announced that the United States had joined the International Contact Group on Liberia (ICGL) to try and stop the conflict, but gave little information on the mechanism. The ICGL is an *ad hoc* group made up of representatives from Ghana, Morocco, Nigeria, France, Britain, the United States, the African Union, the European Union, ECOWAS and the United Nations. Its goal is to resolve the conflict in Liberia between the government and the LURD and MODEL. In terms of Liberian participation in the ICGL discussions, Liberia's Foreign Minister Monie Captan was allowed to make an opening statement to the group, then asked to leave.

One view of this development is that the United States was the driving force behind the ICGL (sources have stated its initiation was "amorphous") to promote its strategy for Liberia under the umbrella of other nations, as it did in forcing the United Nations to impose draconian sanctions upon Liberia. However, failure to bring the parties to the conflict into the discussions is a mistake that smacks of condescension. Unfortunate consequences would arise, if the group tried, in effect, to put Liberia into trusteeship, a solution that never was attempted in the Congo or Sierra Leone or Côte d'Ivoire. Why Liberia? Especially because the international community has failed miserably in making any meaningful effort to help Liberia since the end of its civil war, there is a basis for suspicion on the part of Liberians. Since the LURD refused to utilize the political process to solve its grievances, and because it admittedly has no agenda other than removing Charles Taylor from office, any ICGL proposal that suggests power-sharing with the LURD would, and should, be unacceptable to the government and the people. The LURD continued its brutal attacks against Liberian civilians (yet the State Department refuses to call the LURD "terrorists" when their every action defines that term). On February 10, 2003 the LURD seized the Liberian town of Robertsport, 50 miles up the coast from Monrovia, near the border with Sierra Leone. After a fierce battle, the government forces pushed back the rebels to 5 miles west of the town. In direct violation of the UN charter, an arms embargo is still in effect against the Liberian government. As Liberian Defense Minister Peter D. Chea said on February 13 (Reuters): "If we did not have that embargo on us, we would have removed those bandits by now. But we are fighting for survival and if it means using sticks, rocks, stones and metal to stop them from coming, we will do so." At the same time that vicious fighting goes on, Defense Minister Chea said on February 19, 2003, as reported by the Associated Press, that "soldiers caught firing weapons indiscriminately will face at least a year in prison and (he) told generals that forcibly conscripting young men is illegal."[28]

In late December 2002, the Liberian government was still infuriated by remarks given on December 9 by Mark Bellamy, U.S. Assistant Secretary of State for Africa, giving encouragement to the LURD and talking about "getting rid of Charles Taylor." As a result (according to the UN Integrated Regional Information Network) a "demonstration had been called by Liberian leader Charles Taylor in late December during a meeting of his NPP members at the presidential palace in Monrovia. He ordered his party supporters to stage a nation-wide demonstration against what he termed 'the U.S. government support for the rebel Liberians United for Reconciliation and Democracy (LURD).'"[29]

Presenting his New Year's speech on January 2, 2003 at a press conference, Ambassador Blaney talked about the relationship between Liberia and the United States. He said:

> As most of you know, President Taylor is unhappy with some U.S. policies
> toward Liberia. He feels it necessary to call for a peaceful NPP demonstration

against U.S. policies, but not against Americans. Well, I will leave it to President Taylor to explain his reasons for calling for such demonstration, and for his other recent criticisms of U.S. policies. But for our part, we will respond by continuing to do everything we can to help Liberia and its people. In order to do that, we must present our honest views, and sometimes criticize your government when we think it is wrong. That is what really good friends must do instead of pretending that all is well. And yes, we do suggest different courses of action for your government, but too often this advice is not taken. That is what can create or continue problems and suffering, not the United States. Rest assured that we do what we do in order to secure a better future for the Liberian people and for peace. Having said all this, I do admit that I am saddened at the prospect of seeing Liberia demonstrating against America.[30]

Ambassador Blaney told the Taylor government, the LURD, and MODEL: "I must say to all parties of this conflict that the United States expects all parties to the conflict to regard the ICG as the primary institution and focal point for achieving peace." He also made a tough statement, to wit: "Any attempt to shift the focus of negotiations to other venues will be unacceptable" and warned that "the United States will regard any party that attempts to walk away from the ICGL as essentially an opponent of peace." That provocative statement was essentially a take-it-or-leave-it ultimatum. President Taylor's position was that the ICGL had to work along with ECOWAS. To that end, he announced that he would attend the peace conference scheduled to be held in Bamako, Mali.[31]

On January 3, 2003 the press reported Ambassador Blaney's criticism of the tactics of the LURD. He said:

The United States believes that LURD should agree to cease fire and use the political process to advance its objective. The United States Government does not support LURD and urges an end to all military support to LURD from whatever sources.[32]

Despite Ambassador Blaney's statement, the U.S. previously had not acted to stop the LURD. It remained unanswered whether in the future the U.S. and the ICGL, which appeared to be the U.S. acting in another guise, would implement action to support this position.

Due to the planned demonstration, the U.S. Embassy in Monrovia issued a release on January 7, 2003. It stated:

The Government of Liberia has recently made a number of public allegations which have implied that the United States is supporting violent actions against the Government of Liberia and its leaders. These allegations are false...The U.S. Mission...has suspended all visa services as a precautionary security measure.

On January 10, 2003, about 1,000 Liberians demonstrated against U.S. policy toward Liberia. They gathered in the Antoinette Tubman stadium in downtown Monrovia displaying banners which read: "America, we are your children. Stop the terrorist war against us" as they marched along with freedom songs played by the Armed Forces of Liberia's marching band. "American must help us now as the British did in neighboring Sierra Leone and what the French are presently doing now in La Côte d'Ivoire," their statement read. [33]

It seems that both parties—the U.S. Embassy and the Liberian government—overreacted, and indeed both pulled back from their original positions. On February 6, 2003, the Liberian government issued a release emphasizing that all U.S. citizens living in Liberia would continue to live under conditions of peace and security, and the United States Embassy announced it would reopen its Consular Section for normal visa operations, saying that it took note of the Liberian statement reiterating its intent to protect all foreign nationals, including U.S. citizens.

The tone of Ambassador Blaney's remarks were constructive, but one must acknowledge a degree of condescension. Very few ambassadors presume to offer advice to the country where they are posted and then express disappointment when their advice is not taken. That condescension continued with regard to the International Contact Group on Liberia. Nevertheless Ambassador Blaney experienced the same treatment from the State Department as his predecessor. Mr. Blaney tried to engage President Taylor and his government while the "home office" (the State Department in Washington) issued statements that contradicted and undermined his constructive actions. The State Department and the CIA deemed Charles Taylor as "evil," and continually resisted any effort to work with him in a cooperative manner.

Both Ambassador Myrick and Ambassador Blaney intended to forge a constructive relationship with the Liberian government and improve the U.S.-Liberian relationship, particularly by assisting the country in rebuilding its infrastructure. Shortly after assuming their positions, however, likely instructed by the State Department, they became much more confrontational in their approach to the Liberian government. Although the Secretary of State himself expressed great hope for Liberia, his involvement with crises, such as Iraq, Afghanistan, the Middle East and North Korea, occupied more of his time, and lessened his direct involvement on U.S.–Liberian policy. Those responsible for formulating the policy that Secretary Powell approved, largely shared a historic antagonism toward Charles Taylor and instructed the U.S. Ambassador to Liberia to take a hard line.

The State Department called upon President Taylor to "rein in" the Liberian mercenaries who are involved in bordering countries. It was agreed the way to stop Liberian mercenaries from moving into neighboring countries, and the way to stop rebels from other countries to invade Liberia, was to patrol and secure the borders. Taylor repeatedly requested that the United States, the United Nations, and ECOWAS help it seal the borders, but the U.S. rejected his requests and insisted that the UN reject those requests. Because so many mercenaries criss-crossed the borders between Liberia and the Ivory Coast, Charles Taylor and Laurent Gbagbo met in Togo on April 26 and "agreed to deploy a joint force with help from French and West African troops in a bid to end a messy cross-border conflict complicating civil wars in both countries." (Reuters, 4/26/03) The troops were to be deployed on more than 125 miles of the 450 mile border between the two countries. Despite constant U.S. complaints about Liberian rebels fighting in Ivory Coast, the U.S. was conspicuous in its failure to send either send money or troops to help secure the border. The French did both. This failure by the U.S. to act has prolonged instability in West Africa. The U.S helps guard the India-Pakistani border. It helps patrol the North Korea-South Korea border. Why not in Africa?

Judging, not from its words but from its actions to date, the U.S. strategy was: first, continue the imposition of sanctions against Liberia although the conflict in Sierra Leone has ended; second, dissuade the international community from providing monetary help to Liberia to rebuild its infrastructure; third, prevent the Liberian government from purchasing the arms necessary to defend itself against the LURD rebel attacks; fourth, condemn violence but decline to take any steps to prevent the LURD from carrying out its threats to remove Charles Taylor by force; and fifth, work to prevent Charles Taylor from being re-elected in the next elections. Because of the resultant harm done to the people of Liberia, this strategy is anathema to the principles of freedom and democracy that Americans espouse.

THE DEMONIZATION OF CHARLES GHANKAY TAYLOR

When one takes all of the information set forth in this book cumulatively, there is little question that U.S. policymakers have consciously used the image of Charles Taylor as a warlord to their advantage. It started the day he stepped onto the public scene in the early 1980s, and continued with the indictment of President Taylor by the Special Court of Sierra Leone on June 4, 2003. The process of demonization, that used both absurd and believable charges, was complete.

John Lee Anderson, writing in The New Yorker magazine (July 27, 1998), said:

> The gossip includes a story about the President having an employee killed for some transgression, and then filling a bucket with his blood, which was kept under the Presidential bed until Taylor wanted to bathe in it. The diplomatic community is divided about how much of this sort of thing to believe.[34]

Another example of the demonization process was found in the February 16, 2003 PARADE magazine, a popular insert in hundreds of Sunday newspapers across the nation. The headline read: *Who are the world's most inhuman tyrants?* and the story itself was titled: *The 10 Worst Living Dictators.* It was written by David Wallechinsky, a contributing editor to PARADE. Number one was Kim Jong Il of North Korea. Number two were King Fahd and Crown Prince Abdullah of Saudi Arabia (close friends of the United States). Number three was Saddam Hussein of Iraq, and in the number four spot was Charles Taylor of Liberia.

Here is what Mr. Wallechinsky wrote:

> Charles Taylor was the head of Liberia's General Services Agency in 1983, when he was accused of transferring government funds to a private bank account in New York. He fled to the U.S., was tracked down and arrested but escaped during extradition hearings. He reappeared in 1989 at the head of a rebel army that invaded Liberia, touching off a bloody seven-year civil war. In 1997, Liberians elected Taylor president, apparently hoping it would end the fighting for good. But within three years, civil war had returned to Liberia. According to Amnesty International, Taylor's army is responsible for the torture, forced labor and forced recruitment of civilians as well as the use of rape as a war tactic to instill terror.

Henry James once wrote: "Politics is the systematic organization of hatred." When it comes to Charles Taylor, the diplomats seem to have adopted the same approach. The hatred—a word supported by investigation—toward Charles Taylor felt by those few people in the State Department who are charged with Liberian policy, is palpable. Some State Department officials said bluntly, albeit privately, that they despise Charles Taylor.[35] The circumstances that lead to his indictment and expected departure from the presidency, that will be discussed in detail in the Epilogue, support that view.

NOTES

[1] Mahamood Mamdani, "Turn of your tunnel vision," *Washington Post*, January 8, 2002, editorial.

[2] Ibid.

[3] Jonathan Paye-Layleh, "Liberia offers support at prayer service for U.S. terrorism victims," *Associated Press*, September 16, 2001.

[4] Ibid.

[5] "Bin Laden-emblazoned clothing outlawed in Liberia," *Associated Press*, November 12, 2002.

[6] Remarks of U.S. Secretary of State Colin L. Powell at the swearing-in of John W. Blaney as Ambassador to the Republic of Liberia, September 9, 2002, p. 1.

[7] Ibid., p. 4.

[8] Ryan Lizza, "Can Charles Taylor's apologists explain his ties to Al Qaeda?," *New Republic Magazine*, November 19, 2001, (issue date), p. 1, citing Douglas Farah article in Washington Post.

[9] Ibid. p. 6.

[10] Douglas Farah, "Report says African harbored Al Qaeda," *Washington Post*, December 29, 2002, p. 2.

[11] Robert Scheer, "Bush's faustian deal with the Taliban," *Los Angeles Times*, May 22, 2001. Available at <http://www.robertscheer.com/1_natcolumn/01_columns/052201.htm>.

[12] Douglas Farah, "Report says African harbored Al Qaeda," *Washington Post*, December 29, 2002, p. 2.

[13] Ibid., p. 1.

[14] Ibid.

[15] Ibid.

[16] Ibid.

[17] Ibid., p. 2.

[18] Ibid., p. 6.

[19] "Government denies Al Qaeda connection," *The NEWS* (Monrovia), July 23, 2002.

[20] Bill Sizemore, "Envoy back home in Hampton Roads," *The Virginia Pilot*, October 29, 2002.

[21] "Ambassador Bismarck Myrick: The Curse of US-Liberia Relations," *AllAboutLiberia.com*, Opinion, n.d., <http://www.allaboutliberia.com/opinion356.htm>.

[22] "Liberian Civil Society Organizations Jittery As U.S. Ambassador Ends Tour Of Duty," *The Perspective* (Atlanta, Georgia). Posted July 25, 2002 <http://

www.theperspective.org/ambassadormyrick.html>.

23 Federal Document Clearing House, "Testimony of John W. Blaney before U.S. Senate Foreign Relations Committee," July 9, 2002.

24 Ibid.

25 Moses Zangar, "US $800,000 earmarked for Cuttington," *The NEWS* (Liberian newspaper), n.d.

26 UN Office for the Coordination of Humanitarian Affairs IRIN, "USAID launches peace program," January 24, 2003.

27 Office of Public Affairs, "Press conference by John W. Blaney, U.S. Ambassador to Liberia," Embassy of the United States of America in Monrovia, Liberia, November 21, 2002, <http://usembassy.state.gov/monrovia/wwwh112102.html>.

28 Alphonso Toweh, "Liberian minister says fighting on four fronts," *Reuters,* February 18, 2003.

29 UN Office for the Coordination of Humanitarian Affairs, "About 1000 demonstrate against US policy," January 10, 2003.

30 Office of Public Affairs, "U.S. Ambassador to Liberia, John W. Blaney III speach [sic] at a press conference held at the U.S. Embassy in Liberia," Embassy of the United States of America in Monrovia, Liberia, January 2, 2003, <http://usembassy.state.gov/monrovia/wwwhsp010203.html>.

31 Jonathan Paye-Layleh, "Liberia's president calls on rebels to join him for Mali peace talks," *Associated Press*, February 6, 2003.

32 "Liberia: ICG will strive for peace in Liberia,—Amb. Blaney," *The NEWS* (Monrovia). January 3, 2003. Posted to the web January 3, 2003, <allafrica.com/stories/200301030440.html>.

33 Office of Public Affairs, "Suspension of Visa Issuance," Embassy of the United States of America in Monrovia, Liberia, January 7, 2003, <http://usembassy.state.gov/monrovia/wwwhpres0103.html>; UN Office for the Coordination of Humanitarian Affairs, "About 1000 demonstrate against US policy," January 10, 2003.

34 Jon Lee Anderson, "The devil they know," *The New Yorker*, July 27, 1998, p. 4.

35 Personal communication with U.S. State Department official.

CHAPTER 11
NATIONAL ELECTIONS 2003

Under the provisions of the Constitution of the Republic of Liberia, national elections must be held every six years. Accordingly, on October 14 of 2003, a national election was scheduled for the election of the president and the members of the legislature. A number of questions were raised concerning Liberia's elections, that are now postponed (see Epilogue).

First, will there be sufficient security (in view of the fighting in the country, as the LURD continued to attack the government forces) to guarantee that every registered voter cast his or her ballot without fear of intimidation?

Second, what role will the international community play in certifying the election as free and fair?

Third, need there be a national census taken prior to an election, or will it be sufficient to have a period in which the citizens of Liberia registered to vote?

Fourth, qualifications does the Constitution set forth for those running for office? Are those requirements valid?

Fifth, what is the role of the Elections Commission?

Sixth, what role should the United States play with regard to the Liberian elections?

At the beginning of 2003, President Taylor stated that the election would be held as scheduled. Officials of the U.S. government said that they wanted the elections postponed until April of 2004. Since they believed that the likelihood of a Taylor victory in October was high, perhaps they felt that a postponement would give opposition leaders more time to enlist support for their candidacies. The Embassy told people that if Taylor's only opponent in October was Mr. Tipoteh, the United States would not recognize the results of the election.[1]

Some individuals and groups purported that the election would not be fair. The Liberian Catholic Justice and Peace Commission's (JPC) Executive Director Frances Johnson-Morris is one of those persons who anticipated problems. He proclaimed on January 16, 2003 (UN Integrated Regional Information Network–IRIN):

Given the unprecedented multiplicity of armed security agencies in the country, with most of them having no legal status and defined command structures, coupled with their track records of gross human rights abuses, we are inclined to believe that the 2003 elections will be marred by the worst forms of security brutality, molestation, and intimidation of opposition political parties and candidates ever recorded in the country's history.[2]

Mr. Johnson-Morris gave a dire prediction.[3]

In contrast, some members of opposition parties stated that they were in regular contact with the Election Commission and were convinced the elections would be conducted fairly.

THE CONSITUTION AND CANDIDATE ELIGIBILITY

Article 52 of the Liberian constitution deals with the election of the Executive. It reads:

> No person shall be eligible to hold the office of President or Vice-President, unless that person is:
>
> (a) a natural born Liberian citizen of not less than 35 years of age;
>
> (b) the owner of unencumbered real property valued at not less than twenty-five thousand dollars; and
>
> (c) resident in the Republic ten years prior to his election, provided that the President and the Vice-President shall not come from the same County.[4]

The language in Section (c) raises the question of what are the requirements to be a "resident"? Often residency refers to someone who owns property in the country, or pays taxes, or is eligible to vote, and does not imply physical presence. Usually, however, the language that describes that requirement refers to someone who has to be a "resident of" the Republic. Thus, if one meets the residence requirements (property, taxes, etc.) for the 10 years prior to 2003, one would be eligible to stand for executive office. But the language in the Liberian Constitution is "resident *in*" which seems to imply that you actually have to be in the country physically for the 10 years prior to the election. The most pertinent question then becomes: do you have to have been "resident in" the country *continuously* for the 10 years prior to the election? That is unclear. (The United States Constitution, Article II, section 1, states that in order to be eligible for the office of President, one must have been "Fourteen Years a Resident *within* the United States," but, to my knowledge, that clause has not been tested.)

Commenting on the 10-year residency clause, counselor and presidential candidate Charles Brumskine said the issue seems more political than legal. "And every reasonable person knows that it is not a legal issue," he added. It would seem that interpretation of a nation's constitution is strictly a legal issue. Although there were and are political motivations involved in trying to interpret the constitution, the law is what ultimately should prevail. After all, the United States has had a constitution since 1776, but when our country was divided and involved in a civil war in the 1860s, the constitution remained in force—as it did after that war.

According to Brumskine, "if you start from 1997, the 10-year clause will mature in 2007…So it is not until 2007 when we will look back and see who is qualified."[5] It is difficult to understand that argument, since the language of the constitution says in effect that you start in 2003 (the date of the election) and count backward 10 years to 1993. Mr. Brumskine also stressed that Article 52(c) of the Liberian constitution does not say 10 years immediately or consecutively prior to the elections. He is correct in that assessment. However one must ask why he and others waited until just before the election to raise this question, instead of proposing an amendment to the constitution much earlier that would clarify what was meant by the clause. Be that as it may, the question he raises is an appropriate one.

The 10-year rule was put into the 1984 Constitution during the Doe regime:

> The 1984 constitution, drafted under the watchful eyes of the military regime, replaced the old Liberian constitution which was suspended on April 12, 1980. The process of writing a new constitution began on April 12, 1981, when Dr. Amos Sawyer, a political scientist at the University of Liberia was appointed chairman of the National Constitution Committee (NCC). The

25-member body was given the responsibility of drafting a new constitution for Liberia. The NCC completed its work in December 1982, and submitted the new constitution to the PRC (The People's Redemption Council) in March 1983. The next day, the new constitution was published. A 59-member Constitutional Advisory Committee (CAA) was then appointed to revise the constitution. The CAA completed its work on October 19, 1983. On July 3, 1984, the new constitution was submitted to a national referendum and approved

The irony is that the very language that many supported now poses a problem for opposition leaders who have lived in the United States during the past 10 years. Although they would like to contest for the presidency in 2003, according to the constitution they are ineligible to run.

As to the question of "residence," putative candidates who have returned from abroad to contest for the presidency should be required to prove that they maintained their residency in Liberia. That would be done by demonstrating that they either paid income taxes or real property taxes, or both, in each of the years they were away from Liberia. Based upon U.S. experience, there is good precedent for this rationale. In Massachusetts in 2002 Mitt Romney was challenged as a Republican candidate for governor, because he had spent the previous two or three years in Utah heading the U.S. Olympic Committee. A court decided that, because Mr. Romney maintained a home in Massachusetts and paid property taxes in each of the years that he was in Utah, he was eligible as a "resident" to run for governor. He did. He won.

In the national election of 1997 when Charles Taylor was elected president, the 10-year rule did not apply because the international community, insisting upon a speedy national election after the civil war ended, declared the 1997 election to be a "special election" and suspended the normal rules. Conducted under the auspices of the Economic Community of West African States (ECOWAS), it returned the country to constitutional rule. Presumably the normal rules were to apply again in a "regular" election that was scheduled for October of 2003. The U.S. Embassy in Liberia maintained that the election should be considered a "special circumstance" election in which the constitutional rules do not apply. This cavalier dismissal of the constitution of Liberia was troubling to some Liberians.

Two of the most prominent potential election opponents of Taylor are Charles Brumskine and Ellen Johnson-Sirleaf, both of whom have resided in America for a number of years prior to 2003; thus, under the 10-year rule, they may not be eligible. If President Taylor had agreed to waive the constitution for the upcoming national election, he would have been accused of violating the country's constitution, which states in Article 91 that amendments must be proposed in two ways. One way is a proposition by two-thirds of the members of both houses of the Legislature; the second method is by a petition submitted to the Legislature, signed by no fewer than 10,000 citizens, which receives the concurrence of two-thirds of the membership of both houses, and is ratified by two-thirds of the registered voters in a referendum held no sooner than one year after the action of the Legislature. There was insufficient time to invoke the amendment process before an October election. As the incumbent, Taylor could have benefitted by having as many candidates as possible running against him, thus splitting the opposition and making it easier for him to win. But he had said he did not want to be accused of unilaterally overruling his country's constitution.

It is interesting that Archbishop Michael Francis, who regularly disagrees with President Taylor, has expressed reservations about Liberians who fled the country returning to run for president. Although the bishop does not suggest they be banned from running because of the provisions of the constitution, he was quite severe in his judgment of these politicians. When he appeared on September 30, 2002 before the Rotary Club of Monrovia he said:

> We have several persons who want to be president from the north to the south pole, and some people think they are giants…They are not giants. Those of you who are home and making immense contributions to have a better country are the giants…I feel discouraged when people who have not done something good in our country's interest, are glorified as if they are saints…Who will change our country for the best? It is not those abroad and fussing every day on the Internet, but you who are home trying to make our country better.[6]

A solution to the problem of Article 52 Section (c) might have been to refer the matter to the Supreme Court of Liberia and let that body rule on the interpretation. If it was not the intent of the drafters, the Court would rule in favor of allowing candidates to run for president if they met all the residence requirements, but were not in the country continuously for the past 10 years. The only other possibility would be for the Supreme Court of Liberia to rule that, since the 10-year rule was waived in 1997, it could be waived once again in 2003. There were no visible legal underpinnings for such an argument. As far as research shows, none of the opposition parties tried to take the matter to the Liberian Supreme Court.

It should be noted that the U.S. Embassy in Monrovia disagrees with the analysis set forth above. Without citing specific evidence, it maintains that the Supreme Court of Liberia is "corrupt" and would do only what it was told to do by Charles Taylor.

There is the analogy to the U.S. constitution. The requirement for a president is that he or she be at least 35 years of age and someone born in the United States. At one point the economist John Kenneth Galbraith was mentioned as a presidential possibility. But because he was born in Canada, he was ineligible. The same situation applied to Franklin D. Roosevelt Jr. (son of FDR). He was born on Campobello Island in New Brunswick, which, though just across the Passamaquoddy Bay and only two miles from Eastport, Maine, is in Canada. Again, ineligibility.

If President Bush suddenly declared that a person could run for president even if they were not born in the United States, U.S. citizens would object and he probably would be impeached. Why uphold a different standard for Liberia? Yet the U.S. Ambassador to Liberia, John Blaney, announced that unless President Taylor had ignored the 10-year rule of the Constitution, the U.S. would have considered any election held in Liberia to be "fraudulent." That statement is inconsistent with the "rule of law" that the U.S. proclaims. What right does the United States have to demand that the Liberians ignore their own constitution?

PREPARATIONS AND MONITORING

Preparations for the 2003 elections started in November of 2001. At that time, Marty Ryall, executive director of the Republic Party of Arkansas, headed a team that was formed to help Liberia plan for the election. He represented the National Republican Institute, and the group also included representatives from the National Democratic Institute, the

Carter Center, and the International Foundation of Election Systems. The project was funded through the United States Agency for International Development. Mr. Ryall said at the time: "We have one mission, and that's to promote democracy." In 1997 he spent four months in Liberia training 13 political parties on ballot security. He also was an international observer in the first free elections after the seven-year civil war. Mr. Ryall said:

> There are not many phone lines in Liberia. Some places are inaccessible during the rainy season, and you have to fly ballots by helicopter to some areas. It takes a lot of planning to pull off an election like that. That's why you get started two years out.[7]

According to the Associated Press (November 27, 2001) Mr. Ryall said he most remembered the spirit and enthusiasm Liberians displayed in flocking to free elections. This statement of an impartial first-hand witness stands in marked contrast with the State Department "line" that Liberians voted for Charles Taylor out of fear. The AP also quoted Ryall as saying: "I was there and people were lined up for miles…I would hope that the voters here in the United States would go back to (a mentality of) 'this is my privilege and right, and I'm not going to take it for granted.'"[8] In 2002 Mr. Ryall and his group filed their report and recommendations for the forthcoming national election with the State Department/USAID. They have not received a response from USAID since their submission.

In May of 2002, U.S. Deputy Assistant Secretary of State Robert Perry said: "Free and fair elections in October, 2003, conducted on a level playing field, remain key to rejuvenating civil society, promoting regional peace and stability and building internal pressure to open domestic space in Liberia."[9] In July Reuters reported that opposition politicians, civil leaders, human rights campaigners and independent journalists say that the key is first getting the rebels and security forces to stop their attacks, and then bringing in an international monitoring group.

In July of 2002 Reuters reported that

> the West has adopted two broad approaches to Liberia. Diplomats say the United States has taken a view that Taylor is unlikely to change so the best policy is to keep him boxed in and prevent further destabilization of West Africa. Others say the European Union has taken more of a carrot and stick approach, believing that, as Taylor will not just disappear, he should at least be engaged with a combination of diplomatic sticks and financial incentives.[10]

The latter approach is what the author has urged upon the U.S. government for the past six years—to no avail. Reuters further reported that

> diplomats say tentative (positive) signs include the release of political prisoners, an offer to exiled politicians to return, a planned reconciliation conference and the re-opening of independent Radio Veritas, which has a short-wave radio transmitter…Some say the elections could be a catalyst for change from the bottom up, despite the legitimate security concerns of civil leaders, and could put pressure on the government.[11]

In August of 2002 BBC reported that

> Charles Taylor is reaching out to the opposition. The Liberian president has announced a political reform measure that should enable him to end the current deadlock in the country and convince the opposition to take part in

next year's presidential election...He promoted an amendment of the Constitution that enables opposition parties to join the National Electoral Commission. That was the precondition for opposition leaders' participating in the next presidential elections.[12]

On December 20, 2002, the President signed a bill that would increase the number of election commissioners from five to seven, and in a meeting with 15 of the 18 registered parties in the country, he asked them to recommend the names of the two additional people. The President also announced that the Liberian government had provided some funds for the Election Commission (ECOM).[13]

On December 19, the Associated Press said that Taylor had written to the United Nations requesting that a unit of peacekeepers be sent to Liberia to oversee the vote. He also said there would be no restriction on the number of observers, saying that "a man coming to observe can come with his grandma and great-grandma if he likes."[14]

On February 21, 2003 President Taylor welcomed the return of Jimmy Carter to the Liberian election process. Ambassador Gordon Streeb of the Carter Center met with Taylor and said that the Carter Center was ready to lend its support to the electoral process in Liberia. According to the Inquirer newspaper in Liberia, Ambassador Streeb said the "the Carter Center would expect certain international electoral standards to be upheld in the Liberian elections and averred that the credibility of the Carter Center hinges upon their impartiality. Ambassador Streeb informed the President that his institution would be on the ground months prior to the elections so that their participation and observations can be deemed credible." Ambassador Streeb emphasized that "everybody is convinced that the first step to be taken is to bring a halt to the fighting."

In contrast to the criticism of certain State Department officials regarding their attitude toward Liberia, one should recognize the fair and balanced approach taken by Robert Perry, former U.S. Deputy Assistant Secretary of State for Africa. On January 19, 2002 he addressed a meeting in Silver Spring, Maryland of Movement for Democratic Change in Liberia (MDCL) which consisted mostly of opposition Liberian political leaders. Mr. Perry said:

> The United States welcomes the Government of Liberia's promise to conduct free and fair elections and to welcome outside monitors and observers. Recalling our own resilience in holding national elections during our civil war, we challenge the Government of Liberia to abide by its public commitment to hold national elections as scheduled in 2003 at all costs.[15]

However, Mr. Perry no longer is the U.S. Deputy Assistant Secretary.

One of the Liberian opposition leaders rejected Mr. Perry's statement. Amos Sawyer, formerly head of the IGNU government, wrote to Mr. Perry on January 24, 2002 and said:

> ...(T)here has been nothing encouraging in the behavior and performance of Mr. Taylor to give hope that he will allow, contest or accept the results of free and fair elections in 2003. Instead, there is ample evidence that his every act is now calculated to set the context for negotiating domestic and international acceptance of the results of rigged elections.[16]

Dr. Sawyer then suggested the removal of Charles Taylor from the election mix by having the International Tribunal for the Prosecution of Persons Responsible for Serious Violations of International Humanitarian Law indict him for crimes against humanity.

With hundreds of international observers, and the eyes of the world upon him, Charles Taylor had little choice but to conduct a fair election in Liberia in 2003. He could not have "rigged" an election without being exposed for doing so by the opposition and observers. Dr. Sawyer apparently has no confidence in the ability of the people of Liberia to decide for themselves who will be their leader for the next six years. Otherwise he would not suggest that President Taylor be removed by legal means from his democratically elected position—and not by the ballot box.

ROLE OF THE INTERNATIONAL COMMUNITY

One of the remaining areas of contention concerning the 2003 election is to define the appropriate role of the international community. Some of the opposition leaders have demanded that the international community actually run the election. President Taylor adamantly opposed such a solution. He said he welcomes international help in structuring the election so that it is free and fair. Further, he would welcome an international monitoring group such as the one that observed the 1997 election.[17]

Addressing a news conference in Monrovia, Taylor said his government would "not allow any occupational force to come here, like the ECOMOG style, that would disrespect and disregard the authority of this legitimate government. Instead he said that he had requested the United Nations to train about 5,000 Liberian security personnel who would be responsible for elections security.[18]

This tension between "running" an election and "observing" an election became more apparent on January 2, 2003, when the October 14 presidential and legislative elections officially were announced. U.S. Ambassador John William Blaney, despite President Taylor's request to the UN for security personnel, urged the government, according to the AP, "to seek the United Nations' help in organizing the vote. He said 'conditions do not yet exist to permit free and fair elections.' President Charles Taylor, who sought re-election, indicated international observers would be welcome. But (Election) Commission chairman Paul Guah said…they would not be permitted any role in running the elections."19

Having served as a member of the International Observer team for the 1990 national election in Haiti, the author knows that, as an observer, he was able to determine whether people were registered properly, their hands were properly stamped with red ink so they could not vote twice, and the military in any way intimidated voters (physically or psychologically) as they approached the voting booths. He observed every single ballot as it was counted, tallied, and sent to a central counting place where other international observers (including former President Jimmy Carter) were present.[20] Based on this knowledge, the only reason for demanding that outsiders "run" the election would be to demean and disenfranchise the people of Liberia and set rules for the conduct of the election. If the Liberian government in any way tried to "rig" the election, it would immediately be apparent to the observers, who then would announce publicly that it was not a free and fair election. The Associated Press, on January 2, 2003, reported that

> Liberia's election commission…said presidential and legislative polls would be held on October 14 and ruled out any 'foreign supervision', sparking an angry reaction from the United States. The Election Commission's chairman, Paul Guah, said voter registration in the west African country…would be held from April 15 to 29. The final list of candidates will be published on June 20, and campaigning will begin the same day and end on October 13.

'No foreign laws shall prevail in the election process and there shall be no foreign supervision,' he said.[21]

The U.S. Embassy in Liberia objected to campaigning not starting until June, which is in the rainy season, thus hampering the candidates' ability to get around the country.[22] What the Ambassador may not know is that Liberians always have limited campaigning to a period of three or four months (somewhat like the British)—and that elections always have been held in the rainy season without any problem. The election of 1997, which the international community agrees was free and fair, was held in the rainy season and there were neither lights nor electricity throughout most of the country. Yet the determination of the people of Liberia to carry out a clean election prevailed.

The United States should provide maximum assistance to Liberia to assure that the national election is conducted in a totally open and fair manner. This means providing the Liberians with help in registering voters, and in setting up voting systems that allow every registered voter to cast his or her ballot freely and without pressure. It means making sure that all political parties have an opportunity to field candidates and express their views to the electorate through a free press. It means observing, not running, the election process itself. Liberians are quite capable of running their own elections—they already did so in 1997—and there would forever after be a taint of suspicion if the U.S. or the UN or anyone else presumed to run the election. There are many entities which can fulfill the monitoring function. Among them are the Carter Center, the National Democratic Institute and the National Republican Institute. Finally, there must be a full force of international election observers in the country—stationed at election booths throughout the country and watching over the counting of the votes.

COST OF ELECTIONS

If the United States and the international community want an honest, well-run election to take place in Liberia, instead of threatening that they will reject an election which does not meet its requirements as fraudulent, they should help underwrite the activities of the Election Commission so a fair election can be guaranteed. The Liberian government has estimated that conducting a free and fair election will cost $8.3 million. Until recently, the Election Commission (ECOM) received only $192,000 and a 29.9 KVA generator. If the U.S. and the international community are serious about wanting a fair election, all they have to do is invest the money in the Election Commission so it will happen. The U.S. Agency for International Development (USAID), now an integral part of the State Department, lists on its website (as of early 2003 when this was written): "Ongoing programs (for Liberia) for which no new FY2002 or FY 2003 funding is requested" and under which they list programs that require *no* funding: "Successful Democratic Transition, *Including Free and Fair Elections.*" In other words, no USAID help for Liberian elections.[23]

The <u>sine qua non</u> for a successful election in October is a cease-fire between the government of Liberia and the LURD forces. All Liberian and international efforts should focus on that goal.

On February 27, 2003 the Liberian government announced that it had contributed US $600,000 to the Election Commission (in addition to the previous $192,000 contribution) to provide vehicles and other logistics to facilitate the electoral process. On the same day, President Taylor named two of the severest critics of his regime to the Election Commission. According to Agence France-Presse, this was done "to deflect criticism that the body was made up of his stooges…Taylor appointed Mary Brownell, president of the Liberian Womens' Initiative, and James Chelley, both fierce critics of his government…[24]

POSTPONEMENT OF ELECTIONS

By March 2003 it was apparent that the United States and the LURD, as well as some Liberian opposition leaders living in the U.S. who wanted more time to organize, wanted the October elections in Liberia postponed. A postponement of the elections would have particularly benefitted the LURD, by giving them more time to overthrow the government by force. Instead, the U.S. effort should have focused on helping to broker a ceasefire that would stop the mayhem in Liberia, and allow free elections to be held according to the constitutional mandate. A February 28, 2003 release from the United Nations stated:

> …Secretary-General Kofi Annan warned that continued support for Liberian rebels could engulf the whole of West Africa in an economic and humanitarian crisis…The Secretary-General…in a report to the Security Council, noted that, with elections approaching, the Liberians United for Reconciliation and Democracy (LURD) rebel group is determined to seize power by unconstitutional means.[25]

He further said that

> it is clear that LURD enjoys some external military support…The international community should discourage such support, whose only achievement so far has been the massive displacement of innocent civilians, including women, children and the elderly, the deaths of thousands of persons and the wanton destruction of infrastructure and personal property.[26]

Postponing elections would reward only those who ignore the Constitution and believe that force should overrule democracy. All the parties should keep in mind the truism that even the worst civilian government is better than the best military government.

> As we ponder the LURD military war against the elected government, let us keep in mind the sage words of Mark Twain in *The Mysterious Stranger*: …(T)he statesmen will invent cheap lies, putting the blame upon the nation that is attacked, and every man will be glad of those conscious-soothing falsities…and refuse to examine any refutations of them; and thus he will by and by convince himself that the war is just, and will thank God for the better sleep he enjoys after this process of grotesque self-deception.[27]

One should see the LURD for what it is, a vicious terrorist organization.

POLITICAL PARTIES

Looking to the long-term future of Liberia, it is important to say a word about the political parties that will engage in national elections. For most of its history, Liberia was a one-party-state. By 2002, it had 18 certified political parties. Of that group, few appear to be genuine political parties, in the sense that they do not have a clearly articulated political philosophy, or a party platform which spells out precisely what they propose to do for the country if elected, or even a set of rules for selecting their candidates.

There are two mechanisms used to select the candidates for the presidency and vice-presidency of Liberia, known properly as the party standard-bearer and vice-standard-bearer. In the first process which is the one mainly observed, political aspirants negotiate with one or more political parties to serve in these positions, depending more on their political celebrity than their views on issues. This is a personality looking for a party, rather than the party looking for a presidential candidate to best represent its point of view.

An example of the second mechnism is well represented in the New Democratic Alternative Movement for Liberia (the New DEAL Movement) party. It espouses a social democratic ideology, is an ongoing institution, and does not revolves around a single personality for a single election.[28] The New DEAL conducts open democratic primary elections among its members in order to select the candidates it puts forward. Dr.George Klay Kieh Jr. has earned the nomination of this party as standard bearer to contest for president. He currently is chairman of the department of Political Science at Morehouse College in Atlanta, Georgia. The party's vice-standard bearer is Alaric Tokpa, who is a doctoral candidate at Clark-Atlanta University. With their colleagues, they have put together a specific blueprint for governance, in addition to a constitution and code of conduct, and have organizations in the various counties of Liberia, and in the diaspora community in West Africa and the United States. Genuine political parties of this sort hold forth the best hope for the future of Liberia.

The other trend in the political sphere has been the promotion of a merger of several parties to improve their chances in the next election. One such merger is the Committee for the Merger of Liberian Political Parties (CMPP). Its members include the Liberian National Union (LINU), the Free Democratic Party (FDP), the People's Democratic Party of Liberia (PDPL), the Progressive People's Party (PPP), and the All Liberia Coalition Party (ALCOP). The principal leaders are in exile.[29]

NOTES

[1] Personal communication with official at the U.S. Embassy in Monrovia, February 14, 2003.
[2] "Catholic Commission concerned about election security,"UN Office for the Coordination of Humanitarian Affairs 2003, Integrated Regional Information Network (IRIN), January 16, 2003, press release.
[3] Ibid.
[4] Republic of Liberia, Constitution of the Republic of Liberia, Article 52, p.22.
[5] Bobby Tapson, "Brumskine gets rousing welcome," *The NEWS* (Monrovia), January 22, 2003, p. 2.
[6] The Inquirer Newspaper, "Bishop Francis lashes out at exiled Liberians," September 30, 2002.
[7] Personal communication with Marty Ryall, February 8, 2003; James Jefferson "Party director to help structure Liberian election," *Associated Press*, November 27, 2001.
[8] Ibid.
[9] Robert C. Perry, U.S. Deputy Assistant Secretary of State, Keynote address by to the Association of Liberian Journalists in the Americas Conference, National Endowment for Democracy, Washington D.C., May 24, 2002.
[10] David Clarke, "Battered democracy best hope for Liberians," *Reuters*, July 3, 2002, p. 2.
[11] Ibid., p. 3.
[12]. "Opposition party welcomes decision to increase membership of polls body," *BBC*, August 6, 2002, citing Radio France Internationale, Paris, August 6, 2002.
[13] "Government seeks help from UN, others for election," *The Inquirer Newspaper*, December 20, 2002; "Government Provides Funds for ECOM," *The NEWS*, December 20, 2002, (newspaper, Liberia).

[14] Jonathan Paye-Layleh, "President vows to uphold constitutional clause preventing Liberia's exiled leaders from running against him," *Associated Press*, December 19, 2002.

[15] Robert Perry, U.S. Deputy Assistant Secretary of State, Remarks to the National Convention of the Movement for Democratic Change in Liberia (MDCL), Silver Spring, Maryland, January 19, 2002.

[16] "Former interim president Dr. Amos Sawyer responds to U.S. Government," *The Perspective*, January 24, 2002.

[17] "Government seeks help from UN, others for election," *The Inquirer Newspaper*, letter of February 17, 2003 from President Charles Taylor to UN Secretary-General Kofi Annan

[18] Charles Taylor, "Letter to UN Secretary-General Kofi Annan," February 17, 2003.

[19] Jonathan Paye-Layleh, "Liberia sets October 14 general elections," *Associated Press*, January 2, 2003; also "Liberia announces October election, rules out 'foreign supervision'," *Agence France-Presse*, January 2, 2003.

[20] We visited almost every election booth in the country—checked to see that registered voters were entitled to vote—watched to make certain that the military was not pressuring people into voting for one candidate or another—and we stayed up into the wee hours of the morning in every city of the country watching as the ballots were counted by hand and the results announced publicly one by one. And finally our people were stationed in the central election headquarters where the votes would come in from all over the country and tallied. It was an extraordinarily moving experience to see hundreds of thousands of voters, all dressed in their best clothes, proudly walking sometimes miles to get to exercise the precious right of voting. To make certain that people voted for whom they wished, there were not only the names listed on the ballots, but, as well, the pictures of all the candidates. The next morning my partner Steve Horblick and I drove back to the capital of Port-au-Prince from our station-post in Jacmel. The few radios available in the country were reporting the overwhelming victory of Father Aristide. People poured out of their homes and huts, streaming into Port-au-Prince for a celebration.. Our car was inundated with happy, shouting people who had, for the first time in their lives, voted in a free election. Finally all of us on the Mission (which included former Speaker Jim Wright, former Secretary of Defense Robert MacNamara, and former UN Ambassador Andrew Young) met with President Carter at our hotel. Each person reported to Carter on what we had observed and, based on all the reports, he was able to announce that it was a free and fair election.

[21] Jonathan Paye-Layleh, "Liberia sets October 14 general elections."

[22] Jonathan Paye-Layleh, "U.S. Embassy suspends some operation in Liberia amid row with Taylor," *Associated Press*, January 7, 2003.

[23] U.S. Agency for International Development, "Activity Data Sheet, FY2000 Performance Tables," <www.usaid.gov/pubs/cbj2002/afr/lr/669.001.html>. "Successful Democratic Transition including Free and Fair Elections," April 2003 < www.usaid.gov/democracy/afriliberia/html>: 669-001.

[24] "Taylor names critics of government to poll body ahead of October vote," *Agence France-Presse*, February 27, 2003.

[25] "Liberian Conflict could engulf all West Africa in crisis, Annan warns," United Nations, February 28, 2003, <www.un.org/Docs/journal/asp/ws.asp?m-S/2003/227>.

[26] Ibid.

[27] Mark Twain, *The Mysterious Stranger*, January 1, 1910, short story.

[28] Personal communication with George K. Kieh Jr. and Dougbeh Nyan; the New DEAL Movement constitution and by-laws of the party; <www.newdealmovement.com>; Moses M. Zangar Jr., "New Deal's Aspirant Skeptical about Alliance Politics in Liberia," *AllAfrica.com*, January 23,2003.

[29] "Politicians, Parties to Boycott 2003 Elections Under Taylor," *Liberian Orbit*, Minneapolis, <http://www.liberiaorbit.org/lonewscmppboycott.htm>, Posted January 27, 2003.

CHAPTER 12
CONCLUSION

In his presentation of the 2002 Eliot S. Berkley lecture to the International Relations Council on October 29, 2002, Mark Grossman, U.S. Under Secretary for Political Affairs, articulated the themes that will shape America's foreign policy for the 21st century:

> I want today to focus on six broad themes that I believe will shape the future of American foreign policy for a new era...These themes—the global war on terrorism, globalization, free markets, democracy, cultural and national identity, and American power—define today's international landscape...[1]

This framework is useful for analysis of the main factors that have influenced U.S. foreign policy toward Liberia from the last decade of the 20th century to the start of the 21st century.

US POLICYMAKERS

The appropriate people interviewed at the White House and National Security Council, the U.S Department of State, the CIA, and the U.S. Congress did not reveal who makes policy on Liberia. No one purported to know. Was it the Department of State—or the National Security Council—or the Congress—or the CIA? In discussions assistance to Liberia with anyone in the higher echelons of the State Department, he or she mysteriously pointed a finger in the direction of Capitol Hill—and stated one should talk with U.S. Senator Jesse Helms. They implied that the administration was willing to do much more to help Liberia, but could not do so because Jesse Helms was vehemently opposed. In other private conversations, people stated that Senator Helms had been a great supporter of Samuel Doe, carried a grudge against Charles Taylor for opposing the Doe government, and used his power to pull the rug from under Taylor. This translated into withholding aid.[2]

Why did the U.S. Department of State defer to Senator Helms? First, because he was the powerful chairman of the very powerful Senate Foreign Relations Committee which oversaw the operations of the State Department (thus not a man with whom to fight). Second, any State Department career official who was nominated for an ambassadorial post (such as Howard Jeter when he was selected to serve as U.S. Ambassador to Nigeria) had to be confirmed by the Senate Foreign Relations Committee. The people involved could not afford to "cross" Jesse Helms. Today the committee chairman is Senator Richard Lugar of Indiana, whose has a reputation as a man of immense learning and experience, who judges issues on the merits, not personal likes or dislikes. Yet the opposition to Charles Taylor that emanated from the State Department remained as vitriolic as it was under Mr. Helms, and the policy toward Liberia has not changed.

US NATIONAL INTEREST

Every nation acts in its own national interest in the implementation of its foreign policy. In order to determine whether helping Liberia is in the U.S. national interest, one must first define the term.

In the classic text on the subject, *In Defense of the National Interest*, by Hans J. Morgenthau, published in 1951, Morgenthau wrote:

> The choice is not between moral principles and the national interest devoid of moral dignity, but between one set of moral principles divorced from

political reality, and another set of moral principles derived from political realism.[3]

Whenever the United States is faced with a foreign policy issue, the threshold question must be: is the proposed action in "the national interest"? However, there are disagreements within and without the government, when one tries to define what exactly constitutes the national interest of the United States. Lyndon Johnson commented that the challenge for a president is not *doing* what's right but rather *knowing* what's right. The Wilsonian line of thinking emphasized the morality of any action; the Kissinger line of thinking emphasized pragmatics. Political thinkers have shown that in practice a blend of the two was the chosen course.[4]

One questions that seems to least concern those who make foreign policy decisions is this: what are the effects on U.S. national interest by *not* becoming involved in a particular dispute? Would not a measured response, early on, help the U.S. avoid having to make a much greater commitment later ? Much written here about Liberia revolves upon that very question. After the election of 1997 if the United States had immediately given substantial aid to Liberia to rebuild its infrastructure and institutions, Liberia would not have faced another civil war in which the United States has becoming increasingly involved with no clear road-map to peace.

Assuming one concludes that intervention in a particular country is in the U.S. national interest, the next hurdle is to decide whether its involvement will result in a favorable outcome. To leaders such as U.S. Secretary of State Colin Powell (at least before the Iraq initiative), the American military never should be deployed unless there is a defined objective, an understanding of what constitutes success, and a plan for how to extricate once the U.S. objective is met (an exit strategy).

Another area of inquiry is whether the U.S. should work alone, or act as part of a group. Should the nation encourage the United Nations to take the lead—act through alliances such as NATO—or give financial and technical support to regional peacekeeping groups such as ECOWAS in Africa (The Economic Community of West African States)? If the action to be taken is military in nature, the U.S. should act multilaterally; when the involvement is in the form of financial and technical aid, the U.S. should act both bilaterally and multilaterally so the people of the recipient country know that it is the United States which has helped them.

One other major problem is domestic politics. What do the various constituencies in the United States think of a prospective commitment of resources or, worse yet, troops? Regretfully foreign policy has not been a political issue that resonates with American voters except in a situation where the U.S. is directly threatened or attacked (the actions of Al Qaeda, characterized as dastardly by most Americans), or where there is a large U.S. constituency that feels directly affected (Cuban-Americans regarding the Castro government; Irish-Americans on Northern Ireland; or Jewish-Americans and Arab-Americans regarding the Israeli-Palestinian issue). At present, there is no large organized African-American constituency for foreign policy issues affecting Africa. One would hope that such a force will develop in the future. Because of the extraordinary global importance of U.S. posture vis-a-vis Iraq, foreign policy well may become a vital issue for the U.S. electorate in the 2004 presidential election. But there is no such issue of overriding importance when it comes to Africa. The American people are not interested. Congress is not interested. (More than 100 members of the House of Representatives, who make decisions about the United States' role in the world, do not possess passports, which means that they never have traveled outside the country. That is astounding. This author contends a lack of first-hand knowledge about the world should be a disqualifying factor for anyone seeking national office.)

What, then, does Africa mean to the United States in terms of national interest? First and foremost, oil. Nigeria is the largest producer of oil. Hence the U.S. tends to overlook corruption and violations of human rights as long as it get its flow of oil. Is that right morally? No. Is it pragmatic? Yes. Does the U.S. looking the other way have harmful consequences? Yes.

Olusegun Obasanjo was elected president of Nigeria (for the second time) in February of 1999. Aid to that country has jumped from $7 million a year to more than $200 million since then. The stakes are especially high in Nigeria. With 120 million (est. 1999) people and huge oil and natural gas reserves, the country has the potential to drive an economic revival in all of West Africa. It is also one of the few African states where the United States has a real strategic interest. Oil from Nigeria and Angola account for about 16 percent of America's supply, a figure projected to rise to more than 25 percent in the next decade."[5]

On July 5, 2002 Agence France-Presse reported:

> The United States will provide $3.3 million in law enforcement and drug-control assistance to Nigeria, the American Ambassador, Howard Jeter, said. The country, Africa's most populous, is plagued by violent crime and politically motivated thuggery and has become a center for heroin smuggling and international fraud. Mr. Jeter said the money would be used to train drug officials, equip the police to fight financial crimes and human trafficking and provide modern facilities to government agencies involved with law enforcement and drug control.[6]

Yet Howard Jeter, when he served as U.S. Deputy Assistant Secretary of State for Africa refused any such aid for Liberia. Why? The suspicion is because Liberia had no oil. Interestingly, Liberia recently confirmed that it has discovered substantial off-shore oil deposits and that it is just a question of time before that oil is brought on line. Geological and seismic studies have identified some 12 oil wells along the Liberian coastline. Advances in drilling technology have made it financially feasible to extract oil from ocean depths of 5,000 to 10,000 feet, opening up fields off the coast of West Africa that would be more safely insulated from sabotage than upon Middle East sources. Presumably negotiations are underway between the government of Liberia and international oil companies to see who can give Liberia the best deal. What will the U.S. say to Liberia then? One view is that the U.S. suddenly and magically will revise its policy on Liberia. Aside from the cynical view, it is astonishing what a little oil will do to improve the image of a country and its leader.

Five percent of the world's population lives in the United States, but it burns 25 percent of the world's daily consumption of oil. According to the New York Times on October 21, 2001, "American cars and sport-utility vehicles (SUVs) consume 10 percent of that amount." The United States is the world's largest oil consumer. Since its need for foreign oil is insatiable, the U.S. makes concessions or overlooks violations of human rights that presumably would not otherwise be made in the case of oil-producing countries. The South African newspaper, Business Day, reported on December 10, 2002:

> The West African oil rush is in full swing...The rate of discovery of new oil reserves in Africa has been the fastest in the past five years, according to the U.S. Corporate Council on Africa. Most of these new proven reserves have been found around the Gulf of Guinea...Walter Kansteiner, the U.S. State Department's top Africa official said at the recent Corporate Council on Africa's West Africa Oil and Gas Forum in Houston, Texas, that he considered West African oil of "strategic importance" but that the United States had no "detailed battle plan" to extract oil from West Africa.[7]

It would seem to make common sense that, for the U.S. to avoid relying on foreign oil, it should 1) develop alternative energy resources; 2) impose automobile standards that reduce the need for so much fuel; and 3) embark upon an energy conservation program here at home.

David Halberstam wrote:

> The rise of nationalism, indeed tribalism, in several parts of the world and ethnic anger over arbitrary boundaries would cause the outbreak of bitter, unusually cruel fratricidal violence and, in time, masses of refugees flowing across international borders. These were "teacup" wars, as the writer and defense expert Les Gelb called them. The issues they presented evoked not so much any immediate question of American national security as a question of American goodness and generosity of spirit and a long-term view that the less killing there was, the safer the globe was for everyone. If military commitments were made, they tended to be seen by the Pentagon as values-driven commitments, not national security commitments.[8]

What could Africa mean to the United States? The largest untapped market in the world for goods and products. But in order for there to be customers in Africa, there needs to be an alleviation of the poverty and disease that is endemic to that continent. It also means that there must be stability—companies ordinarily will not invest in a country so long as there is a lack of stability. Paradoxically, when members of the U.S. Congress oppose grants to African countries to rebuild their infrastructure, they really are depriving American businesses of potential contracts. People do not realize that most grants are structured so that the money never gets into the hands of the recipient African country but instead goes directly to the American company to pay for the goods and services provided to the foreign nation. So when the U.S. says that X country received Y millions of dollars in foreign aid, usually that means that the Y dollars went to American companies. That is a win-win situation.

What does this mean in terms of U.S. national interest? It means that the United States should be more generous in its aid to African countries for two reasons: 1) because it is morally correct—the U.S. is a wealthy, generous, and caring country which easily can afford to give more financial assistance than it now does to its friends abroad; and 2) it is pragmatic to help a country develop its resources because a) the grants the U.S. gives will be spent on American goods and b) when recovery has been achieved, the citizens of the recipient country will become customers of the United States for all sorts of goods and services. Equally important the earlier the U.S. helps post-conflict countries, the less it will spend later on when entire regions are in turmoil. Both the moral and pragmatic view of national interest should prevail—or as Hans Morgenthau would say—moral principles derived from political realism.

This is the conclusion. Helping Liberia is in the national interest of the United States of America.

A WORD ABOUT AFRICA

Sanford J. Ungar in his book *Africa* wrote:

> From colonial times to the present, the United States has almost ignored the African continent, maintaining a childlike innocence about the second largest land mass in the world, 11,635,000 square miles with a population now estimated to be almost 550 million. Those parts of the continent that did attract American interest—Egypt, for example—were really part of another

world, the more obvious fascinating Middle East. When American attention was diverted occasionally to the rest of Africa, it was temporary, faddish, disorganized, and often obtuse. Even the fact that at least 12 percent of the American people trace their roots to Africa made little difference until recently.

There are now more than 50 independent countries in Africa, but most Americans would be hard-pressed to name half a dozen...Indeed Africa, for some Americans, is one vast exotic place, perhaps a single gigantic country, where wild animals roam and where the people cannot resist killing and perhaps even eating each other.

...(O)nly a small minority of Americans...pay careful attention to Africa. They find a continent of rich, varied cultures and enduring civilization— indeed, the birthplace of humankind as we know it. They recognize plenty of trouble and turbulence, but also see a source of vast human, economic, mineral and agricultural potential.[9]

On April 1, 2003, the U.S. Ambassador to Nigeria Howard F. Jeter spoke in Lagos at a reception in honor of the publication of Chief Opral Benson's biography. He eloquently described the "good" and the "bad" of West Africa.

About 40% of Africa's population resides in West Africa. Its enormous mass is made up of rich, fertile lands that can support this huge population of over 250 million people. The region has tremendous mineral resources, most of which are yet to be explored or exploited. It has a vast coastline, teeming with abundant marine resources. West Africa encompasses the Gulf of Guinea, which has the largest reserves of oil and natural gas on the African continent. It is also the cradle of great African civilizations, great African kingdoms that existed in the past. The African diaspora, with its progeny dispersed throughout the world, but particularly in the United States, the Caribbean, and Latin America also emanates from this region. The energy, intellect, and raw talent of West Africa's people are second to none; and the region's cultural diversity is rich and alluring. West Africa ought to be prosperous and powerful, the engine of growth and prosperity for the rest of the continent. Its voice should be heard and respected in the highest councils of the international community, and it should be on the cutting edge of international diplomacy. Most important, West Africa should be...a force for good, a beacon of hope for the down-trodden, a model of democracy-in-action, a defender of justice and human rights, in Africa and beyond. So much promise; so much potential...

However, the portrait of the region we see is much different, the reality is far from the ideal, what ought to be simply isn't. Our West Africa of today is too often mired in conflict and poverty; resources are wasted and squandered; and old autocrats too often refuse to give way to new, enlightened, and democratic leadership; national potential—economic, social and political— are unrealized. West Africa remains the land of 'ought to be', and the hopes and dreams of those who love this continent are shattered and unfulfilled. More often than not, too often, we weep for this region.[10]

More than 4 million people (Africans and their descendants) were enslaved here in the United States between 1619 and 1865.[5] America today has almost 35 million citizens of African descent, and more than 30,000 Africans studying here in the United States. In the year 2000, trade with Africa approached $30 billion. The United States is the continent's leading foreign investor. The International Monetary Fund (IMF) has reported that "GDP growth in Africa picked up substantially in the second half of the 1990's, underpinned by a renewed commitment to sound economic policies." Another IMF study concludes that "private investment has a significantly stronger, favorable effect on growth than does government investment."[11] Since 1990, more than 30 African countries have held free elections, and the overwhelming majority have launched economic reform programs. Secretary of State Colin Powell has said: "Africa matters to America, by history and by choice."

In a perceptive view, Susan Rice, who was Assistant Secretary of State for African Affairs from 1997 to 2001, responded to the Bush Administration's global response to terrorism:

> …Two critical pieces are missing from our comprehensive strategy. First and most urgent, we must help those countries in Africa and elsewhere that have the will to cooperate with us in the war on terror but lack the means. It's not enough simply to say to the world: 'You are either with us or against us;' there are many countries that cannot defend their own citizens from terror, much less America's.
>
> We need to invest tens of millions of dollars annually to help a large number of African countries control their borders, improve intelligence collection, strengthen law enforcement and build effective judicial institutions.
>
> Second, over the long term, we need to change the conditions around the world that breed terrorism…Africa is an incubator for the foot soldiers of terrorism. Its poor, young, disaffected, unhealthy and undereducated populations often have no stake in government nor faith in the future…That is why we must view it as our fight, not just the developing world's, to close the gaps between rich and poor.[12]

While supporting Ms. Rice's analysis, one would have hoped that U.S. actions under her watch matched those optimistic words with regard to Liberia. But, in her tenure as Assistant Secretary of State for Africa, she implemented none of the measures described above when it came to Liberia.

There also is a downside to the analysis of Africa. These statistics reveal the problems that the continent faces.

• Sub-Saharan Africa's economic growth rate, 1.5%, is the world's lowest. The region's 548 million people have a combined GNP of less than $150 billion, roughly the same as Belgium and its 10 million people. Food production is 20% lower than it was in 1970, when the population was half the size it is now.[13]

• Only 37% of sub-Saharan Africans have clean drinking water. There is one doctor for every 24,500 people.

• Population is growing at the rate of 3.2% annually, versus 2.1% for Latin America and 1.8% for Asia.

• Average life expectancy is 51 years—12 fewer than for Indians or Chinese.

• Half the world's refugees are African, most of them fleeing drought or civil war or both.

• According to World Bank projections, sub-Saharan Africa's population will rise from 548 million today to 2.9 billion by the year 2050, only 50 years from now.

During the Cold War, the Soviet Union and the U.S. poured millions and millions of dollars into Africa but little of it went for development—most went to prop up pro-western or pro-communist surrogates. When the Cold War ended, so did the flow of money. The superpowers no longer cared about Africa.

Companies look for cheap labor, stability and infrastructure. Capital and operating costs in African countries are 50% to 100% higher than in South Asia, where the return on investment is nine times greater. Twenty-five years ago, the regions were even.

Many African countries discourage agriculture. This is a mistake. Countries should develop and diversify agriculture, both to feed their own people and to export product abroad.

There are two deadly races in Africa: economic growth against population, and basic education against ignorance.

The "informal sector" ignores the government. The UN International Labor Organization (ILO) estimates that the informal sector employs 59% of sub-Saharan Africa's urban labor force.[14]

Ethnic and religious rivalries have had a destabilizing effect in Africa. Nationalism, a concept that can supercede such rivalries, has been difficult to promote and maintain. Some leaders do try to promote nationalism as a unifying force. One such leader, Prime Minister Hage Geingob of Namibia says:

> I like to tell the children at home that we are building a house, a house which is very complicated, a Namibian house. We are using bricks as the building blocks and cement and mortar to put the bricks together. The bricks are our different tribes—the white tribes, the black tribes, the yellow tribes—held together by the cement which are our laws and Parliament. After we have built this Namibian house, our people will plaster the wall. And after you plaster the wall and you paint it—any color—you don't see individual bricks any more. You only see the wall. That's what we are aiming at. Now that house, that wall, when it is still wet, will collapse if you push it too hard. But when you give it time to firm up, it will withstand that pressure. So that's what we are doing in Namibia.[15]

The external world's interest in Africa threatens to become merely charitable—a matter of humanitarianism. This will be a moral test for the West.

One of Condoleeza Rice's defining ideas (at least until Afghanistan and Iraq) contrasts sharply with the attitude expressed above by Susan Rice. She believed that the U.S. military should refrain from what she and President Bush disparaged as "nation-building" or what supporters of that idea call helping nations develop democracy and rule of law. In Rice's view, the world's greatest democracy cannot, and should not, do for strife-riven people what they can't do for themselves.[16] Two days later everyone's world changed, as did Ms. Rice's who now espouses nation-building in Afghanistan and in Iraq—but not in Africa.

Spending by the United States government on development assistance in Africa has declined in the past decade. Development aid to sub-Saharan African nations peaked in the early 1990's at just over $800 million a year, dipped to $675 million in 1996 and in 2000 was about $738 million. By comparison a single small country, Israel, received about $900 million in economic support and Egypt about $760 million according to the

Congressional Research Service. The Republican majority in Congress repeatedly cut the president's budget requests for Africa and so far has failed to approve an administration proposal to forgive about $475 million in African debt.[17]

In an address to a White House Conference on Africa held in 1994, President Clinton said that "we need a new Africa policy based on the idea that we should help the nations of Africa identify and solve problems before they erupt." However neither President Clinton, nor his predecessors and successor, have had the political will to carry out this stated goal. It is high time that we back up our brave words with concrete deeds.

In the short run, when one hears the word "Africa," one envisions only sickness, hunger and fighting. In the long run, Africa represents one of the world's last great markets. Those countries which have shown a constructive interest in the Continent will be at the forefront in capitalizing on that market. Most countries, like so many corporations these days, look only at the next quarter and rarely at the next decade.

Even the ultimate pragmatist, Henry Kissinger, believes that the United States has an historical, if not moral, obligation to help Africa. In his book *Does America Need a Foreign Policy*, Dr. Kissinger wrote:

> Absent a strategic adversary threatening the continent or an unfriendly African nation seeking hegemony, there is no strategic rationale for a new African policy." So far Kissinger the pragmatist is speaking, but he continues: "If the term 'world community' has any meaning, it must find an expression in Africa. And history does impose an obligation on America to play the major role in organizing and sustaining such a multilateral effort, The most pressing task must be to ease Africa's suffering and defeat its epidemics. The long range need is to reduce Africa's political conflicts, help reform its political system, and, on that basis, bring Africa into the globalized world.[18]

UNINTENDED CONSEQUENCES?

By signaling its withdrawal of support from President Tolbert of Liberia, the unintended consequence of U.S. policy was to embolden Samuel Doe and his men to brutally murder Tolbert and take over the government by force.

By giving total support to Doe even after he repudiated the democratic election that he lost, and despite his record of mayhem, corruption and his inability to govern, the unintended consequence of U.S. policy was to encourage Charles Taylor to lead a movement to unseat Doe.

By denying Taylor entry into Monrovia and the right to become President after he had secured 95% of the country, the unintended consequence of U.S. policy was to plunge Liberia into seven years of devastating civil war.

By failing to assist in the rehabilitation and reconstruction of Liberia after the free and fair election of 1997, the unintended consequence of U.S. policy was to prevent the restoration of Liberia's economy and cause untold suffering to her people.

By granting respectability to the RUF through support for the Lomé Accord and placing them in charge of the diamond fields, the unintended consequence of U.S. policy was to reinvigorate the RUF and thus prolong the horrors of the Sierra Leone war.

By imposing and re-imposing draconian sanctions upon Liberia, the consequence, intended or unintended, of U.S. policy was to give a green light to the LURD rebels to try and unseat the elected government by force, while, at the same time, imposing additional hardships on the innocent citizenry of Liberia.

By calling Liberia a "failed state" and approving the LURD rebels' efforts to "contain" the Taylor government, the *intended* consequence of U.S. policy has been to isolate Liberia, reduce its help from the international community, and reinvigorate the LURD's campaign of terror that has wreaked havoc upon the innocent civilian population, all in the name of U.S. determination to remove by any means the democratically elected President of the country. The *unintended* consequence of U.S. policy, however, has been to arouse the anger of the Liberian people toward U.S. efforts to tell them who should govern their country, an anger that has made U.S. policy counter-productive. In other words, Charles Taylor's image was often strengthened, not weakened, by the heavy hand of the U.S. policymakers. Not all the problems in Liberia are Taylor-made.

When people are starving, without work, unable to feed and house their families, surrounded by soldiers shooting at one another, and forced to flee their villages or country, they do not worry very much about the form of their government, or the identity of the person in charge of their country's affairs. Only when there is peace and stability can one have a reasonable expectation that the democracy can flourish and an informed electorate can choose the best person to lead their country.

In Liberia there is massive instability. Both the United States and the United Nations had the power to bring an end to its major cause, the LURD insurrection, soon after it started. But as long as the U.S. and the UN deferred and allowed the mayhem to continue, the rebels were encouraged to continue their military offensive and a second rebel group, MODEL, joined them. If they had succeeded, the country would have plunged into anarchy which, like a dread virus, could spread throughout West Africa. The U.S. did not admit its own power in such a situation. The Liberian people treasure their historic relationship with the United States and admire the American people. If the U.S. had helped the people of Liberia and showed no tolerance for the bloodshed that pervaded the country, peace would have returned throughout the country. The unintended consequence of the U.S. policy of disengagement from the civil insurrection in Liberia was to delay what the U.S. claims it wants: a truly democratic election.

If the United States wishes to improve the quality of the government in Liberia, it should do so only through the free will of the people of Liberia. The U.S. should assist the citizenry by helping to rebuild the infrastructure of their country, alleviate poverty and sickness, and help provide new investment which in turn provides new jobs. If the people of Liberia realize that the United States truly is helping them, instead of only condemning their government, they will respond more to the United States' suggestions as to the identity of the men and women who lead Liberia into the future.

When one reviews the information presented in this book, one must conclude that the United States, from the day Charles Taylor announced his intention to depose the despotic Samuel Doe, used all of its power to block him from assuming the presidency. After he was inaugurated, the U.S. denied the three million citizens of Liberia significant help in rebuilding their country and its institutions.

The United States is the greatest nation on earth, iand ts citizenry are the best informed, most generous, and the freest on this planet. Americans traditionally have done their best to help people around the world who are not as fortunate.

Americans are not perfect, however, and sometimes make mistakes. By and large, the U.S. government means well. But there are elements within the government that sometimes act irresponsibly, and out of the public limelight where there is no oversight. To try and justify their deeds, they engage in what only can be described as campaigns of disinformation. This unfortunately is what has happened in the case of Liberia.

This book was not written to condemn the United States government. It is, rather, designed to expose the abuses in U.S. policy toward Liberia. The evidence is set forth that, out of pique and even revenge, the CIA and parts of the State Department have systematically convinced the American people that the current government of Liberia is bloodthirsty, corrupt, and irresponsible in order to rationalize its refusal to help the nation in its time of need. But the U.S.can alter its policy in a constructive manner.

WHAT SHOULD THE UNITED STATES DO?

In an OpEd article in the Washington Post on June 10, 2003, titled, *Aid for the Enterprising*, U.S. Secretary of State Colin Powell wrote:

> Half the human race—3 billion people—still lives on less than $2 a day. More than 1 billion do not have safe water to drink. Two billion lack adequate sanitation. Another 2 billion have no electricity. These aren't numbers but men, women and children who wake up each day to hunger, disease and despair. Lifting humanity out of poverty is one of the greatest moral challenges of the 21st century.[19]

Secretary Powell then argued for Congressional funding support for the Millennium Challenge Account (MCA) proposed by President Bush on February 5, 2003. It "would provide the largest increase in U.S. development assistance since the Marshall Plan…From 2006 onward, we would invest $5 billion per year in the MCA…MCA would target only countries that govern justly, invest in their people and encourage economic freedom." Using Secretary Powell's test, few countries in Africa would be eligible for such aid, even if the MCA program is passed and implemented by the Congress. The real question is how to empower the people of a country so that they can elect governments that will govern justly and promote economic freedom. In other words, this is the chicken-and-egg problem. Bad governments won't get aid under the MCA program; but only aid first (First Aid) will help people get rid of bad governments and bring about good governance.[20]

By contrast, on the same day as Secretary Powell's article, David Ignatius wrote a column for the Post, titled, *Turning Africa Around*, which defied the "conventional wisdom." He found:

> For believers in a global market economy, Africa is the confounding exception. In a world of rising trade flows and economic growth, Africa is going backward…Africa's problem is not that it has too much connection to the global economy but too little. It needs more globalization, not less. In simple, financial terms, Africa doesn't attract enough foreign capital to finance its development needs. Africa has about 10 percent of the world's population, but in 2001, it received only about 1 percent of the world's foreign direct investment.[21]

"Global aid agencies such as the World Bank and International Monetary Fund have been trying emergency therapy for a generation, but none of it will work until Africa has the capital to generate growth and development on its own. Then, at last, the virtuous cycle can begin." Mr. Ignatius then pointed to the work of the Commission on Capital Flows to Africa, sponsored by the Corporate Council on Africa in partnership with the Institute for International Economics, and headed by James A. Harmon, former chairman of the U.S. Export-Import Bank. In a report about to be issued, the Commission "will outline a 10-year program for putting the African economies into forward gear, rather than reverse. The group stresses putting globalization to work as a reality, rather than a slogan." Here are a few of its recommendations:

All products from Africa should enter the United States duty-tree and quota-free (Ignatius wrote: 'That's discriminatory and unfair to other nations, but so what? Africa needs some positive discrimination.')

The United States should negotiate free-trade agreements with individual African countries and a free trade zone within southern Africa; and[22]

"Most important," wrote Mr. Ignatius, "the Commission will urge that over the next 10 years, U.S. taxes would be zero for repatriated profits on new investments in Africa by U.S. companies." Ignatius continued:

That would instantly make investing in Africa more attractive. The Commission estimates that if coupled with local African tax reforms, an overall reduction in business of 10 percentage points could lead to a 20 percent to 40 percent increase in non-energy investment in Africa—or an extra $800 million to $1.6 billion annually. For every dollar lost to the U.S. Treasury, the commission calculates, there would be a benefit to Africans of five dollars. That's the kind of tax cut I can get excited about—one that benefits poor children in Africa.[23]

That is the "macro" picture for Africa. But what of Liberia in particular? What are the "micro" steps that can be taken that can improve the integrity of the government and the quality of life of the people of Liberia?

One key question remains: what specifically should the United States do now and in the future? In the short term, it is in the national interest to help bring peace and stability to Liberia now so that a meaningful free election can take place. It is *not* in the national interest to tell the people of Liberia who they can or cannot, should or should not, vote for. The goal is to help the Liberians establish an atmosphere in which they can vote for the candidate of their choice without fear of intimidation or coercion. After certification of a genuinely free and fair election—which the United States and the international community can help guarantee—the United States and the international community must then move quickly to provide all the assistance that previously has been denied the country. The United States should do everything within its power to do what it should have done six years ago: help the three million citizens of Liberia to rebuild their country's infrastructure and institutions so Liberia once again can become a beacon of democracy on the African continent.

The United States should provide the funds and technical assistance to Liberians which is necessary to assure that the next national elections are scrupulously fair. It should support a UN force coming into the country for the sole purpose of guaranteeing security for the election, and with the power to repel any groups that try to disrupt the election by force of arms. An international observer team should go to Liberia for the election and they, and only they, should be the judge of whether the elections are free and fair. The Liberians should run their own election.

In advance the U.S. should agree, and state publicly in advance, that it will recognize and deal with whomever the people of Liberia freely elect as their next president. Then do just that: engage the Liberian government. That does not mean trying to micro-manage the government. It does not mean telling Liberians who may serve in government posts. It means working closely with whomever they choose to manage their government.

For too long, the United States has used only "the stick" in dealing with Liberia, when common sense tells one that the only way to get positive results is to use a "carrot and stick" approach. In other words, reward the country through meaningful assistance when it acts in a free and democratic way—penalize the country when it abuses those rights. It's time that we provided genuine assistance to help the country rebuild its infrastructure and operate efficiently. That never was done after the devastating seven year civil war. It must be done now.

The U.S. should ask the United Nations to lift all the sanctions against Liberia. Liberia, for its part, must pledge not to interfere in the internal affairs of any other country except in its own defense. A methodology should be agreed upon to test whether Liberia is sending arms or military assistance to other countries in violation of that pledge.

The U.S. no longer should treat Liberia disproportionately to other nations in the world, which have perpetrated far worse violations of human rights, and yet still receive massive U.S. financial assistance.

In the longer term this is what the United States should do:

1. Seek a Congressional waiver of the Brooke Amendment so the U.S. can re-establish a bilateral relationship with Liberia and send aid to that country directly instead of only through multilateral alliances.

2. Promote a debt forgiveness program as we have done for so many other countries around the world, contingent upon Liberia opening up its books and displaying transparency in its financial affairs.

3. Encourage the international community to provide financial assistance to Liberia, with America setting the example for generosity and concern.

Make Liberia eligible for OPIC coverage so that American businesses thinking of investing in Liberia can do so with some guarantee of indemnification through OPIC insurance; and encourage U.S. businesses to invest in Liberia so long as proper business practices are employed on both sides.

4. Send a Defense Department team to train the Liberian army in return for Liberian guarantees that child soldiers no longer will be allowed in the armed forces.

5. Send an ICITAP team to train Liberia's security and police forces in return for the Liberians agreeing to dismiss and penalize anyone in those organizations who violates human rights.

6. Send financial aid to augment the salaries of judges so the legal process can be saved from corrupt influences (judges in Liberia currently receive about $30 a month salaries, yet they are asked to rule impartially on multi-million dollars cases; as one might suspect, some of these judges are subject to outside influence).

7. Support a UN and/or ECOWAS peace-keeping force being available at all times to put down any rebellion that is based upon force, while supporting the right of anyone to oppose the government peacefully through the political process.

8. Through loans or grants, assist the government in rebuilding buildings, providing electricity and potable water and telecommunications throughout the country, including access to the Internet.

9. Allow the Peace Corps to return to Liberia.

10. Invite the leadership of Liberia to come to the United States for meetings with Administration officials at the highest levels (up to and including the

President of the United States) where a clear understanding can be reached that the U.S. will provide substantial help to Liberia so long as Liberia conducts itself in democratic ways (that means not harassing the press, not closing down Liberian owned and operated radio stations and respecting the right of free expression for all of her people).

11. Help Liberia develop a market economy for an era of international capital flows and global competition.

12. Send agricultural experts to help the people, particularly in the up-country areas, learn to be self-sustaining in food production.

13. Help establish industries that take advantage of Liberia's natural resources and do not just export Liberia's precious natural assets without allowing manufacturing facilities that give them added value.

14. Help Liberians make the John F. Kennedy Hospital a first-rate medical institution for the country and offer support for medical facilities throughout the country, including providing medicines and particularly drugs to combat HIV–AIDS.

15. Send in sufficient food and medicine through USAID to alleviate the worst pockets of hunger and disease in the country, so long as these gifts are labeled "From the people of the United States of America to the people of Liberia."

16. Constitute a task force made up of the U.S., (perhaps along with the French and British) ambassadors to Liberia, Guinea, and Sierra Leone that will meet on a regular basis with the foreign ministers of those countries, in order to revive an active and cohesive Mano River Union. I also would recommend that serious consideration be given to adding Côte d'Ivoire to the Mano River Union (even though that country does not actually abut the Mano River) since the four countries, taken together, can control the destiny of western Africa.

17. Send a truly high level U.S. delegation (ideally Secretary Powell) to the inauguration of whomever is elected president of Liberia in the next election as a signal that the U.S. is ready to do its part to help the country, provided that the Liberians agree to do their part to run an open and honest government.

18. Implement the African Growth and Opportunity Act (AGOA) passed by the U.S. Congress to cover Liberia. The bill allocates U.S. $500 million as loan assistance for trade exchanges, industrial development and services. Its goal is to accelerate Africa's full integration into the global economy, increase trade and commercial links with the rest of the world, and alleviate extreme poverty.

19. Help augment the salaries of school teachers who are so essential to the future of Liberia, and send more textbooks to the country's schools.

One can properly ask: why should the U.S. help Liberia? What's in it for the nation? The answer falls into two categories: altruism and self-interest:

1) On the altruistic side, Liberia was founded by the United States and has been its partner in Africa ever since. Liberia has sided with the United States

whenever asked. It's time that the U.S. returned the favor and helped its friend.

2) On the self-interest side of the ledger:

- If the U.S. makes Liberia the showcase of democracy on the African continent, America's position and reputation will be enhanced;

- For every grant of money made to Liberia, there usually are requirements that the money be spent in purchasing U.S. products for use in Liberia (such as telecommunications, electricity needs). American companies make money while the Liberian people are helped;

- There is a huge amount of offshore oil in Liberia, as well as enormous untapped iron ore, gold, and diamond resources. If the U.S. helps Liberia rebuild, it will be favorable toward U.S. bids to develop and purchase those natural resources;

- Africa is potentially one of the largest undeveloped markets in the world. By establishing a base in Liberia and encouraging U.S. investment there, it can be used as a hub to open up commercial opportunities throughout Africa.

Immediately after September 11, Liberia was one of the first countries to contact the U.S. to offer its assistance. During the Gulf War, Liberia made available Robertsfield, its international airport, as a jumping off place for American troops…and indeed the U.S. took up the offer and used it accordingly. With the war against terrorism, Liberia once again has pledged all of its resources to help the U.S. Isn't it time the U.S. does something for Liberia?

Liberia is a small country with a population of about 3 million citizens. It would not take a huge amount of U.S. money to revive the country and its economy. The peace dividends from such an investment would be huge, both to Liberia and to the United States' reputation in the world community—and especially on the African continent.

Finally, the United States must shift its focus away from the President of Liberia and concentrate primarily on the needs of the three million citizens of Liberia who revere the United States of America.

CONCLUSION

After a seven year bloody civil war, Liberia held a free and fair democratic national election in 1997, so certified by almost 500 international observers including former U.S. President Jimmy Carter. The Liberian people elected Charles Taylor as their President with an overwhelming 75.3% of the vote.[24] Relative peace ensued in that little nation of three million people. However, the U.S. attempted to micro-manage the new Liberian government, refused to acknowledge the special relationship that existed between the U.S. and Liberia, did little or nothing to help Liberia rebuild its infrastructure which had been largely destroyed in the civil war, and later cut off almost all aid (except some limited humanitarian assistance through the U.S. Agency for International Development). Later, because of charges by the U.S. and Britain that President Charles Taylor of Liberia aided the RUF, the United Nations Security Council, again at the behest of the U.S. and Britain, slapped onerous sanctions on the country, thereby penalizing the innocent citizenry and driving the country further into poverty and despair.

Starting in 1999 a group of rebels, the LURD and MODEL, employed military force to try to remove President Taylor from office. The United States failed to stop this terrorist group from destabilizing not only Liberia, but as well, its neighboring countries. Quite to the contrary, through the public statements of the U.S. Deputy Assistant Secretary of State, the United States encouraged the rebels. The United States helped train the Guinean army and has sent them arms which ended up in the hands of the LURD rebels. In the United Nations, the United States, together with Great Britain, maintained an arms embargo against Liberia that did not allow it to obtain the weapons necessary to repel the terrorist rebel force. The LURD killed, tortured, and displaced thousands of innocent Liberian citizens. The U.S. should pressure countries (such as Guinea) to cease harboring and supporting rebel troops. The United States should condemn (as the British did in Sierra Leone and the French now are doing in Ivory Coast) any military campaign to unseat a democratically elected government, and provide assistance to guarantee free and fair national elections in Liberia.

The United States' history with Liberia, since its founding in 1822, has been one of alternate paternalism and neglect. Either of these would be better than the existing current outright enmity. Liberians freely chose Charles Taylor as their president and should not be made to suffer for his alleged sins.

By their actions, the British helped defeat the rebels in Sierra Leone. By their actions, the French are helping to defeat the rebels in Côte d'Ivoire. By its *in*action, the United States helped the rebels defeat the democratically elected government in Liberia.

It is time for the United States to re-evaluate its policy toward Liberia. It is time for the country to be constructive and not destructive in its actions toward Liberia. It is time for the U.S. to show its "cousins" in Liberia the generosity and concern for which the American people are famous.

Liberia is roughly the same size as the State of Tennessee; their populations are about the same. But while the annual budget of Liberia is approximately $70 million dollars, the annual budget of Tennessee is about $20 *billion* dollars which is *300 times larger* than that of Liberia. On a per capita basis, that amounts to $5,714 per person in Tennessee and only $30 per person in Liberia. Think of what a difference that makes in serving the needs of the people.[25]

If, however, the United States is not prepared to offer immediate and substantial help to Liberia, it should not meddle in Liberia's affairs nor hinder other nations from helping Liberia, which hesitate to help for fear of offending the U.S. That is the very least the U.S. owes to Liberia.

At the beginning of this book, I cited a quotation by James Thurber: "Let us not look back in anger; nor forward in fear, but around us in awareness."

It is time for Liberians to give up their internecine squabbles and "look forward" to a future where all factions in the country can unite for the good of the whole by promoting Liberian nationhood.

It is time for the international community to "look around in awareness" of the desperate needs of the people of Liberia, and extend the same helping hand that has been offered to so many other post-conflict nations.

The author found it ironic that the United States refused to help rebuild Liberia's infrastructure after its seven year civil war ended in the democratic election of a new regime, while today it proposes to do just the opposite in Iraq. On February 28, 2003, Steve Hadley, Deputy National Security Advisor to President Bush stated in an OpEd article:

> We will…work to rebuild Iraq's infrastructure, which for years has been
> mismanaged and neglected. Early efforts will include restoring electricity and

clean water, as well as addressing the immediate need for medical care and public health.[26]

Substitute the word "Liberia" for the word "Iraq" and you see what the U.S. should have done in1997—but didn't. Note that Liberia still does not have country-wide electricity and clean water.

The author hopes that the reader—as well as American opinion leaders in and out of government—will gain a new awareness of the United States relationship with Liberia and resolve to do better for this nation that the U.S. founded and with which it has such a long historic relationship.

NOTES

[1] Marc Grossman, U.S. Under Secretary for Political Affairs, "American Foreign Policy for the 21st Century, Remarks to the Kansas City International Relations Council, Kansas City, Missouri," U.S. Department of State, October 29, 2002. As prepared, <http://www.state.gov/p/14810.htm>.

[2] Personal communication with member of the U.S. Senate Foreign Relations Committee.

[3] Hans Morgenthau, *In Defense of the National Interest*, Alfred Knopf, 1951.

[4] Jack C. Plano and Roy Olton. *The International Relations Dictionary.* 4th ed., Santa Barbara: ABC-Clio, 1988; observations based on the historical treatises of Lyndon Johnson, Woodrow Wilson, and Henry Kissinger.

[5] U.S. Department of State, "Background Note: Nigeria", <http://www.state.gov/r/pa/ei/bgn/2836.htm>; Human Rights Watch, "Africa Overview: Nigeria: The Role of the International Community," *World Report 2000*, May 2001.

[6] "Nigeria: Crime-fighting aid from U.S.," *Agence France-Presse*, July 5, 2002.

[7] Business Day, South Africa, December 10, 2002

[8] Halberstam, *War In a Time of Peace*, p. 74.

[9] Sanford J. Ungar, *Africa:...*, Simon & Schuster, 1985, p. 20.

[10] Howard Jeter, U.S. Ambassador to Nigeria. Speech delivered at the Shell Muson Center, Lagos, Nigeria, April 1, 2003 as released by the Public Affairs Office of the U.S. Embassy, Nigeria.

[11] Exxon Mobil, "Africa: a wealth of opportunity," *Washington Post*, November 1, 2001.

[12] Susan Rice, "The Africa Battle," *Washington Post*, December 11, 2002, p. A33.

[13] "Africa: The Scramble for Existence," *Time Magazine*, September 7, 1992, p. 30.

[14] Ibid., p. 38.

[15] "Namibia seeks economic gains to match political success," *Africa News*, August 3-16, 1992, 8.

[16] Condoleeza Rice, *Washington Post* magazine, September 9, 2001.

[17] "Africa: Foreign Assistance Issues," CRS Issue Brief for Congress, No IB95052, updated February 19, 2002. Available at <http://fpc.state.gov/documents/organization/9037.pdf>.

[18] Henry Kissinger, *Does America need a foreign policy?*, Simon &. Schuster, 2001, p. 201.

[19] Colin L. Powell, "Aid for the Enterprising," *Washington Post*, June 10, 2003; p. A21, section Editorial.

[20] Ibid.

[21] David Ignatius, "Turning Africa Around," *Washington Post*, June 10, 2003,

[22] Ibid.

[23] Ibid.

[24] Terrence Lyons, *Voting for Peace*, Brookings Institution Press, 1999, p. 57.

[25] State of Tennessee, State Budget, p. A-10. <www.state.tn.us/finance/bud/bud/0304/0304/buddoc.pdf>.

[26] Steve Hadley, "The plan for a postwar Iraq," *Washington Post*, February 28, 2003.

EPILOGUE

This volume has examined the relations (economic, social, cultural, political, ideological, and military) between the United States and Liberia from the dawn of the 19th century to the preent. It has described the beneficial aspects and pitfalls that are inherent in this relationship, and sets forth a "Road Map" for its overall improvement. As the harshness of the U.S. policy to contain and isolate Charles Taylor reached a critical juncture, Liberia's already desperate state of political stalemate, institutional paralysis, and violent conflict, erupted into virtual chaos. At that crucial moment, as Liberia teetered on the cusp between deliverance and disaster, a significant development took place, giving the war weary Liberian people a ray of hope.

In early May of 2003, President Charles Taylor signaled to the U.S. that he was prepared to make significant concessions, including his agreement not to stand for re-election, if only the international community, spearheaded by the United States, finally would focus on the impending disaster and move boldly to end the civil war. As awareness of President Taylor's offer spread, urgent requests to the State Department to act upon this welcome initiative were made by interested parties, such as the Carter Center, the International Contact Group for Liberia (ICGL), the United Nations, and Liberians of all political viewpoints. In the face of this barrage of concern, the United States government at long last became seized with the Liberian issue, the highest echelons of the State Department became involved, and events moved quickly.[1]

Almost at the same time, in a May 6 press release, the U.N. Security Council urged President Taylor, and the rebel factions of LURD and MODEL to enter into peace negotiations. It cited the upcoming meeting of the ICGL (its third working session) that was scheduled for May 12, 2000, at the Council of the European Union, in Brussels, Belgium.[2] At the meeting, ICGL scheduled reconciliation talks, within the framework of an ECOWAS mediation process, for June 2, in Accra, Ghana. All parties to the Liberian conflict, Liberia's opposition political parties, the leaders of many African countries, and a high-level U.S. delegation were to attend. General Abdulsalami Abubakar, former Head of State of the Federal Republic of Nigeria, was appointed as the mediator.[3] Due to security concerns and other issues, the date was changed to June 4 and the venue to Akosombo, a city approximately 40 miles from Accra.[4] (The talks later alternated between Accra and Akosombo).

During the intervening period of time, rebel forces and government troops engaged in vicious fighting, and Liberian citizens were caught in the crossfire. In his May 25, 2003 article in the Washington Post, Colum Lynch reported that "The conflict has driven more than 200,000 Liberians from their homes and forced more than 300,000 to flee the country, according to UN estimates." [5]

Still, the peace conference began in a spirit of reconciliation. The parties to the dispute indicated their readiness to make concessions. Those who had a stake in the proceedings and observers hoped that its deliberations would result in unanimous approval for an immediate cease-fire, followed by disarmament of all combatants, the agreement of President Taylor not to stand for re-election, the creation of an interim government, and the presence of an international peacekeeping and stabilization force leading to a national election for a new government.[6]

Charles Taylor addressed the delegates in Akosombo and told them that he would step down if he were seen as an obstacle to peace in Liberia. "If President Taylor is seen as a problem, then I will remove myself," Taylor said. "I'm doing this because I'm tired of the people dying. I can no longer see this genocide in Liberia." After Taylor's statement, Mohammed ibn Chambas, Executive Secretary of ECOWAS, said the commission was encouraged by the statement "because it offers a genuine chance for a peacefully negotiated settlement of the Liberian crisis."[7]

But a legal bombshell was tossed that threatened to undermine the peace conference. David Crane, the chief prosecutor of the Special Court for Sierra Leone, on the morning of June 4, announced that he had "indicted Liberia's President Charles Taylor for his alleged role in crimes committed during Sierra Leone's civil war," and called upon the President of Ghana to turn Mr. Taylor over to the court.[8]

However, instead of complying with Mr. Crane's expectation, President Kufuor arranged for Charles Taylor to leave Ghana aboard his personal plane so he could return to Liberia. At the same time, Ghana's Foreign Minister Nana Akufo-Addo said: "I believe the action by the prosecutor in unsealing the indictment at this particular moment has not been helpful to the peace process." Reuters reported that

> after the indictment was served, there were rumors in Monrovia that Taylor had been arrested and panic gripped the capital. Civilians raced to their homes, shops and banks closed and soldiers spilled onto the streets. Military sources in Monrovia said the U.S. Embassy had contacted Vice President Moses Blah and told him to take over because Taylor would not be returning from Ghana…the U.S. Embassy was not immediately available for comment.[9]

Mr. Crane condemned the Ghana president for not arresting President Taylor and turning him over to the Court.[10] As Bola A. Akinterinwa wrote in an article in the Nigerian press cited below,

> The warrant cannot but create bad blood among West African or African leaders as a whole. It is very unAfrican for an African leader to release another African brother to his enemies. The principle of African hospitality goes beyond extending friendly hands shake and warm welcome to guests. Essentially, the principle is predicated on protection and security of the guest first…Thus, in the context of Charles Taylor, was the Ghanaian leader expected to arrest Charles Taylor while playing host to him? This is where there is a point of fundamental difference in African traditions and Euro-American ways of life. African hospitality does not mean acquiescing to criminal activities. It does not mean condoning it or implying a rejection of the warrant of arrest. It simply means that another appropriate context and forum be found for the enforcement of the warrant of arrest.[11]

The indictment of Charles Taylor appears to have been a part of United States policy toward him. On February 12, 2003, Dr. Timothy W. Docking, an African affairs specialist for the United States Institute of Peace testified before the Subcommittee on Africa, House Committee on International Relations. His testimony was in conjunction with the testimony of Walter Kansteiner, U.S. Assistant Secretary of State for Africa. Although the hearing was on the "Prospects for Peace in the Ivory Coast," Dr. Docking addressed the Liberian situation. He stated that "(s)ince the late 1990s, American foreign policy toward West Africa has been dominated by efforts to contain and isolate the Taylor regime in Liberia…" Dr. Docking recommended that "we…should …intensify our dialogue with the French over Liberia and encourage them to toughen their policy toward the Taylor regime." He also advised the United States should consider "(d)eveloping a short-term contingency plan to exploit the possible indictment of Charles Taylor as a war criminal by the Sierra Leone's Special Court…"[12]

In its June 4 report, Irwin Arieff, Reuters news correspondent, revealed that

> Sierra Leone's special court had approved Taylor's indictment March 7 but kept this secret until Taylor took a rare trip outside Liberia, traveling to Ghana's capital Accra for peace talks with rebels who have been fighting to topple him since 2000…The court…gave the Ghanaian authorities a warrant for Taylor's arrest and urged them to turn him over.[13]

Since March 7, President Taylor had traveled to other countries on a number of occasions (to meetings in Togo, Ethiopia, and Senegal). Yet Mr. Crane did not unseal his indictment on those occasions—instead he waited until Taylor left his country solely to attend negotiations designed to bring peace to Liberia. Christo Johnson of Reuters reported that Crane announced, "it is imperative that the attendees know that they are dealing with an indicted war criminal. These negotiations can still move forward but they must do so without the involvement of this indictee."[14] One cannot achieve a peace agreement if one of the parties to the dispute is eliminated from the process.

The reaction to the indictment was both negative and positive, from the involved parties and observers in the region, and throughout the world. The most consistent criticism was on two issues—the court's timing of the release, and the court's jurisdiction to authorize the arrest of Charles Taylor. In its June 9, 2003 edition, Newsweek magazine wrote that

> even backers of an international criminal-justice system questioned the timing: Taylor was in Ghana opening peace talks with two Liberian rebel groups that control most of the country…The court's legal move…may have reduced chances for a negotiated end to the conflict.[15]

Based on the court's legal authority, enforcement of the arrest warrant was at issue; Mr. Crane unsealed, then sought to enforce the indictment of Mr. Taylor before he obtained from the United Nations Chapter VII authority, which would oblige U.N. member states to cooperate with the war crimes tribunal. Not until six days after the indictment did

> the President of Sierra Leone's Special Court, Justice Geoffrey Robertson, write a letter to the United Nations Secretary-General Kofi Annan…asking for a Security Council resolution which would give the court Chapter VII authority under the United Nations charter. A spokesman for Mr. Annan told reporters in New York that since the court did not have Chapter VII authority, there was no enforceable obligation on member states to cooperate.[16]

Cesaré Romano, assistant director of the Project on International Courts and Tribunals at the Center on International Cooperation at New York University and adjunct professor of international law at Fordham University, and André Nollkaemper, professor of public international law and director of the American Center for International Law, Faculty of Law, University of Amsterdam discussed the indictment in an article that was published in the June 2003 issue of *ASIL Insights*, a publication of The American Society of International Law. Romano and Nollkaemper stated: "The timing and methods of unsealing the indictment and issuing of the arrest warrant is questionable." They also revealed:

> The Special Court for Sierra Leone is not a creature of the Security Council. Its powers derive from a treaty that binds only the United Nations and the

Government of Sierra Leone. All other states, including Ghana and Liberia, are third parties to the treaty, and as such are not bound by it.[17]

An observer at the peace conference stated that the presidents in attendance, including President Obasanjo of Nigeria and President Mbeki of South Africa, were astounded and angered by the disruptive move by Mr. Crane, especially since they had neither been consulted nor informed in advance of Mr. Crane's plans to indict Charles Taylor in the midst of their peace conference.[18] Mr. Crane's unilateral action was interpreted as an insult to the leadership in all of Africa.

In Freetown, Sierra Leone, a noted legal expert Sulaiman Banja Tejan-Sie stated that "it was a diplomatic blunder for Taylor to be indicted just as he was on the verge of dialoguing with rebels in his country." Mr. Tejan Sie stated:

> As Head of State, Taylor should not be arrested…Taylor's indictment does not augur well for peace in the subregion…It is fool-hardy for Taylor to be removed out of the current Liberian peace process. If you want Taylor to face justice, let it be done within international law.[19]

On June 6, 2003 National Public Radio's program, *All Things Considered,* presented a segment on the special war crimes court broadcast from Freetown, Sierra Leone. The commentator, Michael Montgomery, reported:

> Prosecutors concede that Charles Taylor's indictment will most likely be challenged. Historically, heads of state have had immunity from foreign courts. The United Nations Tribunal in the Hague was able to indict Serbian leader Slobodan Milosevic, but that court had special authority from the UN Security Council. David Crane does not have that same authority, so in going after a state leader, he's breaking new ground in international law. It's a bold move other governments could find troubling.[20]

A guest on the same program was Madeline Morris, professor of international law at Duke University and senior legal counsel to the prosecutor's office of the Sierra Leone Special Court. She said:

> States see this as potentially becoming a quagmire in which states are grabbing each other's leaders…If it's okay to indict, arrest and potentially convict and incarcerate the head of state or other high official of another country, if one country can do that to another country, then we're in a very different arena than we've been in the past in international relations.[21]

Professor Morris's remarks appear to contradict the action taken by her own chief prosecutor, David Crane.

In Nigeria, Bola A. Akinterinwa, writing in *This Day* on June 10, 2003, raised the questions:

> (T)o what extent can the warrant of arrest restore peace in Liberia and in West Africa? Why should the warrant of arrest be issued at a time Charles Taylor is proposing a government of national unity in which he is not to participate?…President Charles Taylor was in Ghana for peace negotiations with the rebels. He has offered to constitute a national government without his own participation in it. As reported in the press, the timing of the issuance of the warrant was deliberate…The problem is precisely with the objective of

preventing Charles Taylor from attending the peace talks. Can peace be achieved without Charles Taylor?...It is important to allow Charles Taylor to voluntarily ask his followers to surrender their arms and accept peace rather than compelling them to do so...Arresting Taylor will create a vacuum that is likely again to create new tensions of succession in Liberia.[22]

The chief prosecutor's actions were supported by the government of Guinea, a country which the United Nations Sanctions Committee has condemned for arming and supporting the rebels that are causing havoc in Liberia. Guinea's President Lansana Conté's

open support for Taylor's extradition to face war crimes in another country is likely to raise eyebrows in Africa...Diplomats noted that Conté's own government has given strong backing to the Liberians United for Reconciliation and Democracy (LURD) rebel movement...[23]

David Crane, chief prosecutor of the Court, is an American citizen. For over 30 years he served in the government of the United States, most recently as senior inspector general at the U.S. Department of Defense. He previously was assistant general counsel to the U.S. Defense Intelligence Agency (DIA) and was a professor of international law at the U.S. Army Judge Advocate General's School. On April 17, 2002 the Secretary-General of the United Nations appointed Mr. Crane as chief prosecutor of the Special Court for Sierra Leone for a three year term.[24] According to Jess Bravin, writing in the Wall Street Journal, February 12, 2003, "Mr. Crane was named as the chief prosecutor 'after intense lobbying by U.S. diplomats...The U.S. was deeply involved in creating the Sierra Leone court and plans to provide one-third of its $54 million budget...'"[25] These facts lead one to question whether the United States was a party to the decision to indict Taylor at the Ghana peace conference, a notion that the State Department privately denies.

The American imprint on the Special Sierra Leone Court was strengthened on June 13, 2003, when the Committee on International Relations of the U.S. House of Representatives wrote to Secretary of State Colin Powell, urging the Administration to obligate and release to the Special Court, without delay, $10 million in Fiscal Year 2003 Economic Support Funds, bringing the total U.S. contribution to the Special Court to $20 million..."[26]

A dispute arose between those who insisted that the indictment of Charles Taylor be implemented immediately, and those who believed that it was more important to first restore peace to Liberia and make paramount the plight of the Liberian populace, then deal with the status of Mr. Taylor.

The unintended consequence of David Crane's action was that Liberian citizens were imperiled. This was demonstrated by the fact that on the day after Mr. Crane announced the indictment, LURD rebels increased their attacks upon Monrovia, even as their representatives were in Akosombo pledging that they would cease their attacks. The LURD and MODEL factions asserted they would not negotiate with an indicted war criminal, then stated they would only agree to total disarmament and commit themselves to the peace process, if President Taylor resigned immediately without any preconditions.

If the Special Court had waited until after the conclusion of the peace conference and all the provisions were in place (an interim government and an international stabilization force), they could have had both peace and justice. Instead they sacrificed the welfare of the Liberian people in the obsessive pursuit of one man. It is hard to imagine a more counter-productive move than the one taken by Mr. Crane, whether on his sole initiative as he says, or on the instructions of those who financed the Special Court and placed him in his position as chief prosecutor.

Liberia's access to United Nations humanitarian aid was cut off on June 9, because of fighting between government troops and rebels in the capital of Liberia. "French special forces swooped into Monrovia by helicopter…to airlift hundreds of foreigners to safety as rebels crept closer to the centre of the Liberian capital."[27] Secretary-General Kofi Annan called an emergency Security Council meeting that afternoon; at its conclusion the Council "demanded an immediate end to the fighting and appealed to Liberia's government and rebel groups to give peace a chance."

The UN Integrated Regional Information Networks reported that: "Monrovia city centre remained shuttered up, with no water or electricity and all gas stations closed. With no water running in the taps, people were forced to rely on wells, many of which were contaminated…IRIN's correspondent in Monrovia warned of an impending food crisis in the city of one million people…"People will soon die of starvation'," he said.[28]

As of June 10, the rebel attacks continued unabated in Monrovia as ECOWAS sought the assistance of Charles Taylor and the rebel leaders to call a cease-fire. The U.S. announced it was sending in a military force of 35 men to Liberia, but the understanding was their sole purpose was to protect the United States Embassy in Monrovia where U.S. Ambassador Blaney remained at his post. No US. forces were sent to help the people of Liberia. The day before, President Bush had notified the Speaker of the House and the President of the Senate that

> …these movements were undertaken solely for the purpose of protecting American citizens and property. United States forces will redeploy as soon as it is determined that the threats to the Embassy Compound have ended or an evacuation, if necessary, is completed.[29]

There was a sense of déjà vu asthe Liberian people recalled that America sent troops to Monrovia in 1990 to evacuate U.S. citizens, but did nothing to help the embattled citizens of Liberia.[30]

The pessimism of the previous day turned to optimism when, on June 11th,

> Liberia's President Charles Taylor agreed…to halt hostilities against rebels, paving the. way for peace talks to start in earnest and possibly prevent a bloody showdown in the capital…The rebels have also promised West African mediators they will halt their advance so talks can start properly.[31]

Reuters's David Clarke reported that the Special Court "has said it will not drop its indictment and has asked the United Nations to strengthen measures to bring Taylor to trial, but UN Security Council diplomats said the request would have to take a back seat to peacemaking."[32] Anne Boher of Reuters reported Taylor saying: "I am prepared to be the fall guy, to be the whipping post to bring peace to this nation. I will be the sacrifice for the sake of Liberia."[33] At the same time Mr. Taylor lashed out at the Special Court's chief prosecutor, when he said: "No white boy from Washington can walk into Africa and indict a sitting African president."[34]

On Saturday, June 14 (Reuters), the optimism turned to gloom once again, when

> Liberia's main rebel faction backed away from an earlier commitment to forge a truce and said…it would sign no cease-fire until President Charles Taylor stepped down. 'These are our conditions. Mr. Taylor must leave office before

we sign any formal cease-fire agreement. I want to make that emphatically clear,' rebel spokesman Kabineh Ja'neh told reporters...One mediator said the rebels wanted a reference to Taylor's departure to be included in the cease-fire agreement, but that mediators wanted the accord to be unconditional.[35]

Later the same day, however, "mediators said they had ironed out the differences..." and

said that as soon as a cease-fire was signed, full-blown political discussions on a transitional government and the possible deployment of peacekeepers would start...But a key question will be what happens to Taylor. A UN-backed court that indicted him insists he must face justice. But many West African diplomats and officials say this is unimaginable. His aides say he will never leave Liberia, while rebels insist he will have to quit the country.[36]

Taylor himself told journalists at his home town of Arthington on Saturday (6/14): "I think what the international community needs and what Liberians want...is peace and stability. Charles Taylor sees himself as a valuable part of the process."[37]

After herculean round-the-clock efforts by the mediators, on June 17 "Liberia's government and rebels signed a cease-fire...and agreed President Taylor would...step down for a new administration." [38] Kwasi Kpodo, correspondent for the Associated Press wrote on June 17:

Taylor's defense minister, Daniel Chea, who signed the cease-fire in Ghana's capital, appeared to commit the leader personally to the deal. 'President Taylor fully supports this peace accord, and the government will do anything to ensure its success,' Chea said. 'We have done the greatest thing this afternoon by signing this cease-fire. By this, we're letting the world know that the government of Liberia wishes in no way to be part of further bloodshed. Mediators and observers in Accra burst into applause and raucous cheers as Chea shook hands with Kabineh Ja'neh and Tia Sanger, delegates of the two rebel movements...In Liberia, news of the cease-fire sparked celebrations in the streets of Monrovia. Cars with white rags tied to their antennas in symbols of peace, drove through rutted roads, honking. Shoppers burst into dance at one roadside market.[39]

The cease-fire agreement, stated that "the signing of this agreement shall be followed immediately by the engagement of the GOL (Government of Liberia), LURD and MODEL with all other political parties and stakeholders in dialogue, to seek, within a period of thirty days, a comprehensive peace agreement." Among the issues to be included in the peace agreement will be the "formation of a transitional government which will not include the current President..."[40] Although not specifically included in the cease-fire agreement, the parties agreed that, at some point, Charles Taylor will step down as president to be succeeded by an interim government. Discussions are ongoing in Accra concerning political reconciliation, a West African verification mission that would be sent to Liberia to oversee the cease-fire agreement, followed by a West African-led "stabilization force" that might include some form of American assistance. [41]

In yet another twist in the search for peace, however, Reuters reported on June 20: "Liberian President Charles Taylor said Friday he had no intention of stepping down before his term ends in January and reserved the right to run for re-election, despite a ceasefire deal calling for his departure." Reuters quotes Taylor as saying in a radio broadcast on that date: "I intend to complete my tenure as president and turn over to the vice president. I reserve the right, my constitutional right, following the transition, to run for general elections if I decided to do so." [42] This statement of President Taylor drew consternation in many quarters, both within and without Liberia. There was much speculation on his motive. Did Taylor renege on his agreement not to run for re-election because the United States (State Department) earlier had discussed with him possible full or partial amnesty, but withdrew the offer after the Sierra Leone war crimes court's chief prosecutor, an American, indicted him? Taylor knew that if he stepped down as president of Liberia, his immunity from prosecution as a head of state would end, and there was no indication that the court would drop the indictment. (See "The Arrest Warrant against the Liberian President, Charles Taylor" by Cesare P. R Romano and Andre Nollkaemper, ASIL Insights, American Society of International Law June 2003.)

Accusations of violations of the ceasefire agreement soon came from all sides, and, on June 24, 2003, Reuters reported that

> fighting roared toward Liberia's capital…in a serious blow to last week's cease-fire and hopes of a negotiated end to West Africa's deadliest conflict. Aid workers and military sources said rebels Liberians United for Reconciliation and Democracy attacked President Charles Taylor's forces near Plumkor village, barely 13 miles from the fringes of the coastal city of Monrovia.[43]

Later AP reported that the rebels were attacking Monrovia's port on the west side of the city.[44]

On June 25, however, there were new and highly disturbing developments. Early in the day

> U.S. authorities admitted tens of thousands of refugees into the residential complex, as rebels attacked the city with rocket-propelled grenades, mortars and small arms, among other weapons. It marked the first time since 1996, during the height of Liberia's civil war (1989-1996) that authorities opened the compound as a refuge for Monrovia's people[45]

Later the same day

> explosives landed in (the) U.S. diplomatic complex …causing injuries among thousands of people seeking refuge…a U.S. official said…Just before Wednesday's explosions, the U.S. Embassy issued a statement condemning rebels' serious violation of the cease-fire, which has caused unwarranted terror and misery for tens of thousands of innocent Liberians. Rebel groups must realize that if they are to have any international credibility or recognition they must abide by international agreements and respect basic human rights.' the unsigned statement said. UN Secretary-General Kofi Annan also condemned the fighting and urged both sides to resume negotiations.[46]

The next day (June 26)

> angry crowds laid the bloody, twisted bodies of children in front of Liberia's heavily guarded U.S. Embassy…shouting blame at U.S. Marines and America for failing to protect Monrovia's people from fighting overruning the capital…Health Minister Peter Coleman said fighting Tuesday and Wednesday

had killed 200 to 300 civilians and wounded 1000...Large crowds assembled, pushing, shoving and screaming at Marines to intervene to stop the war.[47]

That same day, President Bush addressed the Corporate Council on Africa's U.S.–Africa Business Summit in Washington, D.C. and said:

> In Liberia, the United States strongly supports the cease-fire signed earlier this month. President Taylor needs to step down so that his country can be spared further bloodshed. All the parties in Liberia must pursue a comprehensive peace agreement. And the United States is working with regional Governments to support those negotiations and to map out a secure transition to elections. We are determined to help the People of Liberia find the road to peace.[48]

In response, the Taylor government "urged the United States to remain 'proactive in the peace process' and made no direct mention of Bush's key request." [49] Reuters's Alphonso Toweh (June 27. 2003) reported that "the Liberia government warned of anarchy if anyone tried to put in place a 'quick solution' to violence that has lasted on and off for 14 years." On June 28, however, Charles Taylor, in an interview with CNN, "expressed gratitude" to President Bush and said: "Finally the United States is paying attention to Liberia." Taylor's position, however, remained that "he is willing to step down but not immediately. Doing so would simply plunge the nation into more violence, he said."[50]

The battle between the government forces and the LURD continued as the LURD captured the port of Monrovia, and then was driven out by the government forces. Both sides then declared yet another cease-fire on June 27.[51]

It should be noted that the Liberian political parties, many of which were gathered in Ghana for the peace conference, were furious that the rebel groups were attempting to seize power and seek diplomatic gains through military force, when the political parties had consistently limited themselves to negotiation and peaceful diplomacy in their attempt to forge a peace resolution. They were appalled at the notion that the rebel groups would even be considered for participation in an interim government, by shooting their way to governmental participation. Questions raised by the various Liberian factions regarding U.S. policy include:

> If the U.S. does not intervene and continues to sit on the sideline, what will happen if the LURD wins control of the country? (Joe Wylie of the LURD to AP in Senegal on June 26: "Our plan is to take the whole country.")

> Does the U.S. want to show the world that the only way to succeed in Liberia is through military force and thus reject the political parties' reliance upon diplomatic negotiations and free elections?

> Is not the U.S. risking the possibility of a military take-over of Liberia by the LURD which is predominantly led by fundamentalist Muslims?

> Must parties which support a negotiated peace be forced to mount a military campaign against the LURD and MODEL, thus prolonging the suffering of the Liberian people? [52]

Taylor, in his interview with CNN International on June 28, "clarified" his position by stating that he plans to serve out his term which he asserts ends in January, then step down in favor of a transition government.[53] When eventually new elections are called, although he has the constitutional right to run in such an election, he said he will not do so. The rebel groups, as well as some of the political parties in Liberia, stated they want Mr. Taylor to step down in August, a date which they assert marks the end of his tenure in office. They threatened to boycott the peace conference if he does not comply.

Pressure mounted on the White House to send an American contingent as part of an international peacekeeping force to Liberia. The Washington Post, on July 1, editorialized:

> UN Secretary-General Kofi Annan has called for an international peacekeeping force to prevent further bloodshed, and he has implored the United States to lead it. Britain and France have publicly backed the idea, and several West African nations have offered to contribute 3,000 troops if they are matched with 2,000 Americans. Both sides in Liberia say they would welcome a U.S. led force. Faced with such unanimity, the Bush administration should strongly consider acting…Without foreign intervention, renewed warfare and a humanitarian catastrophe appear likely—and any intervention will be far less likely to succeed without American troops. At a time when many people around the world are questioning U.S. foreign policy, Liberia offers an opportunity for the United States to show that it is still prepared to use its power for more than narrow self-defense.[54]

On July 2, President Bush, in anticipation of his July 7 African trip, met with his top national security advisors at the White House to consider Kofi Annan's request. "The participants did not agree on whether to send U.S. troops into Liberia, said an administration official familiar with the discussions."[55] The report continued:

> At the White House meeting, Defense Secretary Donald H. Rumsfeld resisted an appeal from [Secretary of State] Powell to consider Annan's request, U.S. officials said…The Pentagon believes that the U.S. military…is too stretched to undertake a new peacekeeping mission in a country that is not central to U.S. national security interests. The State Department has contended that announcing a limited U.S. role in a Liberian force would shore up Bush's standing on the evening of a major tour of Africa, the officials said.[56]

This tension between the State Department and the Defense Department permeates many of the United States' policy decisions toward Liberia, in particular, and Africa in general.

As America celebrated the Fourth of July, the Administration apparently made its decision: the U.S. will send troops to Liberia.[57] As for Charles Taylor, he agreed to step down and seek temporary exile in Nigeria. (While welcoming President Taylor's decision, President Bush wanted him to leave the country *before* sending in American troops; Taylor insisted that, in order to avoid a power vacuum, he should remain in office *until* the American troops arrived.) If indeed the Americans come to Liberia, it is hoped that the fighting between the government and rebel forces will stop—that Liberians will form an interim transition government—that no individuals or groups who seek power by military force will be granted a role, either in a transitional government or in Liberia's future leadership—and that eventually a democratic national election is held so that the people of Liberia can freely choose their own leadership. A U.S. presence should begin a new chapter in American-Liberian relations, that focuses on the needs of the citizens and the rebuilding of the war-torn country.

NOTES

[1] Personal communication with U.S. and Liberian government officials.

[2] United Nations, "Security Council Extends Sanctions Against Liberia until May 7 2004, Unanimously Adopting Resolution 1478 (2003): Also Places 10-Month Ban on Import of Liberian Timber," UN Security Council, 6 May 2003.

[3] Ibid.

[4] "Accra Peace Talks on Liberia Set for June 2," *The Inquirer* (Monrovia) posted to The Perspective (Smyrna, GA) <http://www.theperspective.org/inquirer/accrapeacetalks.html>.

[5] Colum Lynch, "U.N.'s focus diminishes efforts on Africa's troubles," *Washington Post*, May 25, 2003.

[6] Personal communication with delegates of the June 4, 2003 peace conference in Akosombo and Accra, Ghana.

[7] Clar Ni Chonghaile, "Liberia's Taylor Indicted for War Crimes," Accra: *Reuters*, June 6, 2003, 5:15 p.m.

[8] Christo Johnson, "Liberia's Taylor Indicted for War Crimes," Freetown: *Reuters*, June 6, 2003, 9:35 a.m.

[9] World-Reuters (Accra), *Indicted Liberian president leaves Ghana for home*, June 4, 2003.

[10] Jibril Abubakar, *Daily Trust* (Abuja), June 6, 2003. On AllAfrica.com. <www.allafrica.com.>.

[13] Irwin Arieff, "UN backs S. Leone court after Taylor indictment," *Reuters,* June 4, 2003.

[14] World-Reuters, "Liberia's Taylor Indicted for War Crimes," June 4, 2003.

[15] "Liberia: Court of Opinion: Is the United Nations doing more harm than good?" *Newsweek*, June 9, 2003.

[16] "June 11 …The president of Sierra Leone's Special Court, Justice Geoffrey Robertson…", Sierra Leone News Archives-June 2003, <www.sierra-leone.org/slnews0603.html>.

[17] "The Arrest Warrant against the Liberian President, Charles Taylor" by Cesare P. R Romano and Andre Nollkaemper, ASIL Insights, American Society of International Law June 2003.

[18] "How Kuffour, Obasanjo, Mbeki Saved Taylor in Ghana," *allAfrica.com*, June 6, 2003, <allafrica.com/stories/200306060456.html>; "Liberia: Vice President quits as Taylor claims coup attempt," *UN OCHA IRIN*, 5 Jun 2003, <http://www.reliefweb.int/w/rwb.nsf/0/59170942aa8a086249256d3d0012ce0d?OpenDocument>.

[19] "How Special Court Bungled President Taylor's Arrest," *Concord Times* (Freetown), June 6, 2003, allAfrica.com.

[20] Michael Montgomery and Deborah George, "War Crimes Trials in Sierra Leone: American Radioworks Documentary Probes Atrocities," *All Things Considered*, National Public Radio, <http://discover.npr.org/features/feature.jhtml?wfld=1289885>.

[21] Ibid.

[22] Bola A. Akinterinwa, Editorial Headline: "Charles Taylor and Warrant of Arrest, *This Day,* Financial Times Information Ltd-Asia Africa Intelligence Wire, June 10, 2003. Available at <http://www.fol.org/late_breaking/june10_worldpress.html>.

[23] *IRIN* UN Integrated Regional Information Network, June 6, 2003, as posted to AllAfrica.com.

[24] Special Court for Sierra Leone, Biography of David Crane, <www.sc-sl.org/bottom2.htm. >.

[25] Jess Bravin, editorial, *Wall Street Journal*, February 12, 2003.

[26] Congressmen Henry J. Hyde, Edward R. Royce, Christopher Smith, and Tom Lantos, letter to Hon. Colin Powell, dated June 13, 2003.

[27] David Clarke, "French pluck foreigners from Liberian fighting," *Reuters*, June 9, 2003.

[28] "Rebels Open Second Front in battle for Monrovia," *IRIN* (UN Integrated Regional Information Networks), June 9, 2003. See archive at <www.irinnews.org \> *or allAfrica.com*.

[29] Hon George W. Bush, "Text of a Letter from the President to the Speaker of the House of Representatives and the President Pro Tempore of the Senate," White House, Office of the Press Secretary, June 9, 2003, <http://www.whitehouse.gov/news/releases/2003/06/20030609-10.html>.

[30] See p. 30.

[31] David Clarke, "Liberian talks set to start after cease-fire," *Reuters*, June 12, 2003.)

[32] Ibid.

[33] "Troops to leave Liberia's streets," *CNN* (Monrovia, Liberia), June 12, 2003, <http://edition.cnn.com/2003/WORLD/africa/06/12/liberia.taylor/>.

[34] Ibid.

[35] Anne Boher, "Liberia's rebels back down from ceasefire," *Reuters* (Akosombo), June 14, 2003.

[36] Ibid.

[37] Anne Boher, "Liberia ceasefire possible on Monday—mediators," *Reuters* (Akosombo), June 14, 2003.

[38] Anne Boher, "Liberia signs ceasefire with rebels," *Reuters* (Accra), June 17, 2003.

[39] Kwasi Kpodo, "Taylor to step down as president under cease-fire deal with Liberian rebels," *Associated Press*, June 17, 2003.

[40] Agreement on Ceasefire and Cessation of Hostilities between the GOL, and LURD and MODEL, June 17, 2003, available at United States Institute of Peace, <http://www.usip.org/library/pa/liberia/liberia_ceasefire_06172003.html>.

[41] Sony Ugoh, an official with the West African regional bloc that oversaw the peace talks, as reported by Kwasi Kpodo, "Taylor to step down as president under cease-fire deal with Liberian rebels," *Associated Press*, June 17, 2003.

[42] *Reuters,* June 20, 2003.

[43] Alphonso Toweh, "Fighting rages again toward Liberia's capital," *Reuters*, June 24.2003.

[44] Jonathan Paye-Layleh, "Shelling Hits Civilian Areas in Liberia," *Associated Press,* June 25, 2003.

[45] Jonathan Paye-Layleh, "Shells Explode in US Embassy in Liberia," *Associated Press*, June 25, 2003.

[46] Ibid.

[47] The U.S. Embassy is across the street from its high-walled U.S. diplomatic residential complex.

[48] Hon. George W. Bush, "President Bush Outlines his Agenda for U.S.–African Relations, Remarks by the President to the Corporate Council on Africa's U.S.–Africa Business Summit, Washington Hilton Hotel, Washington, D.C.," White House, Office of the Press Secretary, June 26, 2003, <http://www.whitehouse.gov/news/releases/2003/06/20030626-2.html>.

[49] Jonathan Paye-Layleh, "Liberian Bloodshed Continues Unabated," *Associated Press*, June 27, 2003.

[50] "Liberia president 'to step down,'" *CNN.com International/WORLD,* June 28, 2003, <http://edition.cnn.com/virtual/editions/europe/2000/roof/change.pop/frameset.exclude.html>.

[51] Paye-Layleh, June 27, 2003.

[52] Personal communication with delegates attending June peace talks in Ghana.

[53] *CNN.com International/WORLD,* June 28, 2003.

[54] Editorial, *Washington Post*, July 1, 2003, OpEd page.

[55] Colum Lynch, "Annan requests U.S. peacekeepers in Liberia," *Washington Post*, July 2, 2003.

[56] Ibid.

[57] "U.S. military team prepares to leave for Liberia," *CNN.com/World*, July 6, 2003; "U.S. 'discussing' Liberia role," *CNN.com International/World,* July 1, 2003, <http://edition.cnn.com/2003/WORLD/africa/07/01/liberia.us.jvt/index.html>.

APPENDIX A

Chronology

1816	Paul Cuffee, a successful Quaker shipowner of African-American and Native American ancestry, advocates settling freed American slaves in Africa. He gains support from the British government, free black leaders in the United States, and members of Congress for a plan to take emigrants to the British colony of Sierra Leone. At his own expense, Captain Cuffee takes 38 American blacks to Freetown, Sierra Leone, but his death in 1817 ended further ventures.
Dec. 21	The Rev. Robert Finley organizes the American Colonization Society for Colonizing Free People of Color—commonly called the American Colonization Society (ACS), to send free African Americans to Africa as an alternative to emancipation in the United States. Finley was a Presbyterian clergyman from Basking Ridge, New Jersey. Others involved in the formation of the ACS in Congress Hall in Washington, D.C., are: Henry Clay, E.B. Caldwell, Hon. Robert Wright of Maryland, John Randolph, Richard Rush, Walter Jones, Francis S. Key, James H. Blake, John Peter, Bushrod Washington, James Breckinridge, and William G.D. Worthington.
1817 Jan.	ACS meets and elects the following officers: Bushrod Washington, president; Hon. William H. Crawford, of Georgia, vice-president; Hon. Henry Clay, of Kentucky, vice-president; Hon. William Phillips, of Massachusetts, vice-president; Col. Henry Rutgers, of New York, vice-president; Hon. John E. Howard, Hon. Samuel Smith, and Hon. John C. Herbert, of Maryland, vice-presidents; John Taylor, Esq., of Virginia, vice-president; Gen. Andrew Jackson, of Tennessee, vice-president; Robert Ralston and Richard Rush, Esqrs., of Pennsylvania, vice-presidents; Gen. John Mason of District of Columbia, vice-president; Rev. Robert Finley of New Jersey; E.B. Caldwell, secretary; W.G.D. Worthington, recording secretary; and David English, treasurer.
1821 Dec 15.	Agents of the ACS purchase Cape Mesurado, about 225 miles south of Sierra Leone, and surrounding coastal land in West Africa, for the colonization of people of African descent. In exchange for the land, the ACS agents offer a number of items with little value. After considerable negotiation, the five African kings who control the area agree to sell the land to ACS and accept their baubles as payment.
1822 Jan.	The first colony is settled at Cape Mesurado. Internal disputes within the ACS lead to the formation of a number of self-supporting state colonization societies that also organize settlements near Cape Mesurado. As a result of the colonization efforts of the ACS and the independent state colonization societies, Liberia is created.
1847 Jul. 26.	Liberia becomes first black independent republic in Africa after being governed by ACS. The capital, Monrovia, is named in honor of the fifth president of the United States, James Monroe, who along with Congress, give the society close to $100,000 for the removal plan.
1862	The United States government officially recognizes Liberia as an independent state.
1876	Scramble for Africa begins with King Leopold
1917	Liberia declares war on Germany, giving the Allies a base in West Africa.
1926	Firestone Tire and Rubber Company opens rubber plantation on land granted by government. Rubber production becomes backbone of economy.
1936	Forced labor practices abolished.

1943	U.S. President Franklin Delano Roosevelt (FDR) visits Liberia to examine labor and airport facilities.
1944	William V.S. Tubman becomes president of Liberia. His administration lasts until 1971. He institutes the Open Door Policy. Government declares war on the Axis powers.
1945 Jun.	Cold War begins.
1948	Liberia's vote breaks tie at United Nations to make Israel a state.
1951 May.	Women and indigenous Liberian property owners vote in the presidential election for the first time.
1958	Racial discrimination outlawed.
1971	Tubman dies and is succeeded by William R. Tolbert, Jr. Tolbert administration lasts until 1980.
1972	Charles G. Taylor enters U.S. to study at Bentley College.
1974	Government accepts aid from the Soviet Union for the first time.
1978	Liberia signs trade agreement with the European Economic Community.
1979 Apr. 14.	More than 40 people are killed in riots following a proposed increase in the price of rice.
1980 Apr. 12.	Master Sergeant Samuel Doe, Thomas Quiwonkpa and other enlisted army personnel stage military coup. Tolbert and more than 12 of his government officials are killed. A People's Redemption Council (PRC) headed by Doe suspends constitution and assumes full powers. Quiwonkpa becomes commanding general of the Armed Forces of Liberia and symbol of the military coup that brought PRC to state power. Doe's administration lasts until 1990; he serves as head of state (1980–85) and then as president (1985–1990).
1983 Oct.	Chairman Doe forces General Quiwonkpa into involuntary retirement from the Armed Forces of Liberia with the forfeiture of all benefits. General Quiwonkpa's dismissal stems from concerns he had with Doe regarding the returning of state power to an elected democratic government.
	General Quiwonkpa and 12 prominent Liberians are implicated in a plot to overthrow the government. Quiwonkpa escapes Liberia and resurfaces in the United States.
1984.	May. Taylor accuses of embezzlement; goes to U.S. jail for 15 months.
	Doe's regime allows return of political parties following pressure from the United States and other creditors.
1985 Sep 15.	Taylor escapes jail; returns to Africa.
Oct.	Jackson F. Doe (no relations to Samuel Doe) wins the presidential election; U.S. still supports Samuel Doe.
Nov.	General Quiwonkpa initiates coup attempt and fails to capture state power; Doe kills him.
1988	President Joseph Momoh refuses Taylor permission to operate out of Sierra. Momoh supports President Doe.
1989	Taylor makes alliance with Sierra Leone guerrilla faction, which is known as the Revolutionary United Front or "RUF") of Foday Sankoh.
Nov. 11.	Berlin wall comes down.
Dec. 24.	Taylor and his guerrilla faction, the National Patriotic Front of Liberia or "NPFL", launch an attack to depose Doe and his government from state power.
1990–1997.	Civil war in Liberia. ECOWAS becomes involved. Momoh provides base for ECOMOG in Sierra Leone.
1990 Jun.	Four U.S. warships with 2,000 marines anchor off Monrovia and evacuate U.S. nationals; no move to restore order.
Jul.	Doe massacres 600 Gio and Mano people sheltered in a church (including

	Taylor's father).
Aug. 24.	ECOMOG moves into Monrovia (mostly Nigerians).
Aug. 27.	Banjul Agreement goes into effect. Amos Sawyer becomes head of the Interim Government of National Unity (IGNU).
Sep. 9.	Prince Y. Johnson kills President Doe at ECOMOG headquarters.
Sep.	First battle of Monrovia takes place.
1991 Mar. 6.	LSH[a] and HPG[b] meet Taylor for first time in Dakar, Senegal.
May 29.	United Liberation Movement for Democracy (ULIMO) is formed in Freetown by former AFL personnel runaways from Doe government, with U.S. and Israeli training—supported by Sierra Leone government (Momoh).
Aug. 5–11.	LSH and HPG meet with Taylor in Harbel.
Sep. 14.	LSH and HPG meet with Taylor in Gbarnga.
Sep. 16.	Yamassoukro III meeting, LSH attends.
Oct. 26.	Yamassoukro IV meeting, LSH attends.
Oct. 30.	ECOWAS rejects former U.S. President Jimmy Carter solution.
Nov. 2–10.	LSH to Liberia
Dec. 11.	Cold War ends.
1992	United Nations (UN) imposes arms embargo on Liberia (never removed)
Oct. 15.	Operation Octopus–2nd battle for Monrovia.
Jun. 6, 1993.	600 people are massacred at Firestone Plantation; UN concludes that AFL (Doe) responsible.
Jul 15.	Cotonou Agreement-cease-fire-signed by NPFL, AFL and ULIMO (supported by ECOMOG–dissolution of Sawyer (IGNU) government-establish Liberian National Transitional Government (including NPFL and ULIMO).
Sep. 1994	Coalition (AFL, LPC, and ULIMO–J) attack Gbarnga.
1995 Aug.	Taylor makes peace with Nigeria; Abuja Agreement to disarm, hold elections.
Aug. 31.	Taylor enters Monrovia (first time since 1983) –looks to ECOMOG for security.
1996 Apr.	Factional fighting resumes and spreads to Monrovia.
Aug. 6.	3rd battle for Monrovia–ECOMOG forces are deployed throughout country; clear land mines and reopen roads, allowing refugees to return. Election in Sierra Leone; Tejan Kabbah elected president.
1997 May 27.	Junta overthrows Kabbah in Sierra Leone.
Jul. 19.	Presidential and legislative elections in Liberia; Taylor wins a landslide and his National Patriotic Party wins a majority of seats in the National Assembly. International observers declare the elections free and fair.
1998 Feb.	Kabbah returns to office as president of Sierra Leone.
Jul. 2.	LSH to Liberia.
Oct. 13.	Massachusetts drops all charges against Taylor.
Nov. 29.	LSH to Liberia.
1999 May 5.	LSH to Liberia
Jul.	Lome Accord brokered by U.S. and Britain; puts RUF in charge of diamonds.
1999.	Last of ECOMOG peacekeepers leave Liberia; LURD begins attacks.
2000 May.	RUF kidnaps 500 UN peacekeepers.
Jul. 14.	LSH to Liberia.
Sep.	Liberian government launch massive offensive against rebels in Lofa County. Liberia accuses Guinea of supporting the rebels.
2001 Feb.	Liberian government says Sierra Leonean rebel leader Sam Bockarie, also known as Mosquito, has left the country.
May.	UN reimposes sanctions on Liberia to punish the Taylor government for trading weapons for diamonds from rebels in Sierra Leone.
2002 Jan.18.	War in Sierra Leone officially ends.

Feb. 27.	Mano River Union summit meeting in Morocco.
Mar.	ECOWAS peace talks in Abuja (LURD) boycotts.
May 6.	UN extends sanctions on Liberia for another 12 months.
May 14.	Election in Sierra Leone; Kabbah reelected.
Sep.	President Taylor lifts an eight–month state of emergency and a ban on political rallies, citing a reduced threat from rebels.
Nov. 26.	UN extends arms embargo to LURD; six months review of sanctions, left in place.
Nov. 27.	Taylor agrees to peace talks with LURD; LURD refuses.
Dec. 5.	President Bush greets Daniel Arap Moi at White House.
2003 Jan. 18.	President George Bush issues Executive Order (Liberia threat to U.S. foreign policy).
Feb. 3.	African Union meets.
Feb. 5.	Taylor urges LURD to join peace talks in Bamako, Mali.
Feb. 23.	International Contact Group (ICG) meets in New York.
Mar.	Security situation deteriorates as rebels open several battlefronts and advance to within 10km of Monrovia. Tens of thousands of people displaced by fighting.
Apr.	New rebel group, Movement for Democracy in Liberia (MODEL), makes gains in southeast.
May.	Annual review of sanctions scheduled.
Jun.	President Taylor attends talks in Ghana aimed at ending ongoing rebellion. Talks overshadowed by indictment accusing Mr. Taylor of war crimes over his alleged backing of rebels in Sierra Leone. An arrest order is not heeded and Mr. Taylor returns to Liberia. Fighters from main rebel group (LURD) sweep south in an attempt to capture the capital.
Jun. 17.	A cease-fire agreement reached at talks in Ghana is signed.
Jun.	President Bush calls for the resignation of Liberian president Charles Taylor; he also calls for unconditional cease-fire in the Liberian civil war. Liberian people call for U.S. to intervene and send troops to Liberia to stop fighting by the government and rebel forces..
Jun. 23.	Sir Jeremy Greenstock, Britain's UN ambassador, calls on the Security Council to form a multinational force to bolster cease-fire between the rebels and government in Liberia.
Jul.	U.S. considers sending troops to Liberia. President Taylor clarifies his posotion, announces he will leave the presidency before the end of his term.
Jul. 6	President Taylor accepts offer of asylum from President Obasanjo of Nigeria, but gives no date for departure. Talks in Ghana continue on planned nterim government.
Oct.	National presidential and legislative elections scheduled. Postponed.

Note: Prepared with assistance from Edward Lama Wonkeryor, Ph.D. See bibliography.

[a] LSH is the author.

[b] HPG is the author's law partner.

APPENDIX B

PRESIDENTS (HEAD OF STATE) AND INTERIM PRESIDENTS OF LIBERIA 1847 to 2003

PRESIDENTS

1. Joseph Jenkins Roberts (1847–1856)
2. Stephen Allen Benson (1856–1864)
3. Daniel Bashiel Warner (1864–1868)
4. James Spriggs Payne (1870–1871)
5. Edward James Roye (1870–1871)
6. James Skivring Smith (1871)
7. Joseph Jenkins Roberts (1872–1876) 2nd time
8. James Spriggs Payne (1876–1878) 2nd time
9. Anthony William Gardiner (1878–1883)
10. Alfred Frances Russell (1883–1884)
11. Hilary RichardWright Johnson (1884–1892)
12. Joseph James Cheeseman ((1892–1896)
13. William David Coleman (1896–1900)
14. Garretson Wilmot Gibson (1900–1904
15. Arthur Barclay (1904–1912)
16. Daniel Edward Howard (1912–1920)
17. Charles Dunbar Burgess King (1920–1930)
18. Edwin James Barclay (1930–1944)
19. William Vacanarat Shadrach Tubman (1944–1970)
20. William Richard Tolbert, Jr. (1971–1980)
21. Samuel Kanyon Doe (Head of State 1980–1986; President 1986–1990)

    INTERIM PRESIDENTS

    1. Amos Claudius Sawyer (November 23, 1990–August 08, 1993)
    2. Bismarck Kuyon (August 18, 1993–November 13, 1993)
    3. Philip Banks (November 13, 1993–February 28, 1994)
    4. David Kpormakor (February 28, 1994–September 02, 1995)
    5. Wilton Sankawulo (September 2.1995–September 03, 1996)
    6. Ruth Perry (September 3rd 1996–August 2nd, 1997)

22. Charles Ghankay Taylor (1997–2003).

APPENDIX C

UNITED STATES DEPARTMENT OF STATE DIPLOMATIC APPOINTEES TO LIBERIA, 1863–2002: AMBASSADOR, ENVOY, MINISTER, CONSUL GENERAL, COMMISSIONER, AND CHARGÉ D'AFFAIRES.

Although not all U.S. State Department diplomatic appointees were black Americans, the posts in Liberia (as were those in Haiti) were commonly referred to as the "Negro" post in the 19th century and the first half of the 20th century.

Name: John J. Henry
State of Residency: Delaware
Title: Commissioner/Consul General
Appointment: Mar 11, 1863
Note: Declined appointment.

Name: Abraham Hanson
State of Residency: Wisconsin
Title: Comm/Consul General
Appointment: Jun 8, 1863
Presentation of Credentials: Feb 23, 1864
Termination of Mission: Died at post on or before Jul 20, 1866
Note: Commissioned during a recess of the Senate; recommissioned after confirmation on Jan 12, 1864.

Name: John Seys
State of Residency: Ohio
Title: Minister Resident/Consul General
Appointment: Oct 8, 1866
Presentation of Credentials: Jan 2, 1867
Termination of Mission: Left post, Jun 11, 1870
Note: Commissioned during a recess of the Senate; recommissioned after confirmation on Feb 21, 1867.

Name: J.R. Clay
State of Residency: Louisiana
Title: Minister Resident/Consul General
Note: Not commissioned; nomination not confirmed by the Senate.

Name: F.E. Dumas
State of Residency: Louisiana
Title: Minister Resident/Consul General
Appointment: Apr 21, 1869
Note: Declined appointment.

Name: James W. Mason
State of Residency: Arkansas
Title: Minister Resident/Consul General
Appointment: Mar 29, 1870
Note: Did not proceed to post.

Name: J. Milton Turner
State of Residency: Missouri
Title: Minister Resident/Consul General
Appointment: Mar 1, 1871

Presentation of Credentials: Jul 19, 1871
Termination of Mission: Left post, May 7, 1878

Name: John H. Smyth
State of Residency: North Carolina
Title: Minister Resident/Consul General
Appointment: May 23, 1878
Presentation of Credentials: Aug 19, 1878
Termination of Mission: Relinquished charge, Dec 22, 1881

Name: Henry Highland Garnet
State of Residency: New York
Title: Minister Resident/Consul General
Appointment: Jun 30, 1881
Presentation of Credentials: Dec 22, 1881
Termination of Mission: Died at post, Feb 13, 1882
Note: Commission (issued during recess of the Senate) not of record; enclosed with an instruction of Jul 19, 1881. Recommissioned after confirmation on Oct 26, 1881.

Name: John H. Smyth
State of Residency: North Carolina
Title: Minister Resident/Consul General
Appointment: Apr 12, 1882
Presentation of Credentials: Aug 4, 1882
Termination of Mission: Presented recall, Dec 14, 1885

Name: Moses A. Hopkins
State of Residency: North Carolina
Title: Minister Resident/Consul General
Appointment: Sep 11, 1885
Presentation of Credentials: Dec 14, 1885
Termination of Mission: Died at post, Aug 3, 1886
Note: Commissioned during a recess of the Senate; recommissioned after confirmation on Jan 13, 1886.

Name: C.H.J. Taylor
State of Residency: Kansas
Title: Minister Resident/Consul General
Appointment: Mar 11, 1887
Presentation of Credentials: Jun 4, 1887
Termination of Mission: Left post soon after Sep 22, 1887
Note: Commissioned during a recess of the Senate.

Name: Ezekiel E. Smith
State of Residency: North Carolina
Title: Minister Resident/Consul General
Appointment: Apr 24, 1888
Presentation of Credentials: Jul 21, 1888
Termination of Mission: Left post, May 20, 1890

Name: Alexander Clark
State of Residency: Iowa
Title: Minister Resident/Consul General
Appointment: Aug 16, 1890
Presentation of Credentials: Nov 25, 1890
Termination of Mission: Died at post, May 31, 1891

Name: William D. McCoy
State of Residency: Indiana
Title: Minister Resident/Consul General
Appointment: Jan 11, 1892
Presentation of Credentials: Mar 28, 1892
Termination of Mission: Died at post, May 15, 1893

Name: William H. Heard
State of Residency: Pennsylvania
Title: Minister Resident/Consul General
Appointment: Feb 23, 1895
Presentation of Credentials: May 6, 1895
Termination of Mission: Presented recall, Apr 28, 1898

Name: Owen L.W. Smith
State of Residency: North Carolina
Title: Minister Resident/Consul General
Appointment: Feb 11, 1898
Presentation of Credentials: On or shortly before May 11, 1898
Termination of Mission: Presented recall, May 13, 1902

Name: John R.A. Crossland
State of Residency: Missouri
Title: Minister Resident/Consul General
Appointment: Jan 16, 1902
Presentation of Credentials: May 13, 1902
Termination of Mission: Left post, Jan 30, 1903

Name: Ernest Lyon
State of Residency: Maryland
Title: Minister Resident/Consul General
Appointment: Mar 16, 1903
Presentation of Credentials: Jul 27, 1903
Termination of Mission: Probably presented recall on or shortly before Aug 25, 1910

Name: William D. Crum
State of Residency: South Carolina
Title: Minister Resident/Consul General
Appointment: Jun 13, 1910
Presentation of Credentials: Aug 25, 1910
Termination of Mission: Left post, Sep 17, 1912

Name: Fred R. Moore
State of Residency: New York
Title: Minister Resident/Consul General
Appointment: Mar 1, 1913
Note: Took oath of office, but did not proceed to post.

Name: George W. Buckner
State of Residency: Indiana
Non-career appointee
Title: Minister Resident/Consul General
Appointment: Sep 10, 1913
Presentation of Credentials: Dec 8, 1913
Termination of Mission: Left post, Apr 15, 1915

Name: James L. Curtis
State of Residency: New York
Non-career appointee
Title: Minister Resident/Consul General
Appointment: Oct 25, 1915
Presentation of Credentials: Dec 29, 1915
Termination of Mission: Left post, Oct 20, 1917
Note: Commissioned during a recess of the Senate; recommissioned after confirmation on Dec 17, 1915.

Name: Joseph J. Johnson
State of Residency: Ohio
Non-career appointee
Title: Minister Resident/Consul General
Appointment: Aug 27, 1918
Presentation of Credentials: Oct 8, 1919
Termination of Mission: Presented recall, Feb 13, 1922

Name: Solomon Porter Hood
State of Residency: New Jersey
Non-career appointee
Title: Minister Resident/Consul General
Appointment: Oct 26, 1921
Presentation of Credentials: Feb 13, 1922
Termination of Mission: Left post, Jan 9, 1926

Name: James G. Carter
State of Residency: Georgia
Foreign Service officer
Title: Minister Resident/Consul General
Appointment: Mar 1, 1927
Note: Declined appointment.

Name: William T. Francis
State of Residency: Minnesota
Non-career appointee
Title: Minister Resident/Consul General
Appointment: Jul 9, 1927
Presentation of Credentials: Nov 30, 1927
Termination of Mission: Died at post, Jul 15, 1929
Note: Commissioned during a recess of the Senate; recommissioned after confirmation on Dec 17, 1927.

Name: Charles E. Mitchell
State of Residency: W.Virginia
Non-career appointee
Title: Minister Resident/Consul General
Appointment: Sep 10, 1930
Note: Commissioned during a recess of the Senate; recommissioned after confirmation on Dec 16, 1930. Did not proceed to post in the capacity of Minister Resident/Consul General; took oath of office as Envoy Extraordinary and Minister Plenipotentiary and proceeded to post, but did not present credentials; left post, Mar 22, 1933, the Government of Liberia having requested his recall, Feb 11, 1933.

Name: Charles E. Mitchell
State of Residency: W.Virginia
Non-career appointee

Title: Envoy Extraordinary and Minister Plenipotentiary
Appointment: Jan 20, 1931

Name: Lester A. Walton
State of Residency: New York
Non-career appointee
Title: Envoy Extraordinary and Minister Plenipotentiary
Appointment: Jul 22, 1935
Presentation of Credentials: Oct 2, 1935
Termination of Mission: Left post, Feb 28, 1946

Name: Raphael O'Hara Lanier
State of Residency: Texas
Non-career appointee
Title: Envoy Extraordinary and Minister Plenipotentiary
Appointment: Feb 13, 1946
Presentation of Credentials: Jul 1, 1946
Termination of Mission: Left post, Jun 8, 1948

Name: Edward R. Dudley
State of Residency: New York
Non-career appointee
Title: Envoy Extraordinary and Minister Plenipotentiary
Appointment: Aug 11, 1948
Presentation of Credentials: Oct 18, 1948
Termination of Mission: Promoted to Ambassador Extraordinary and Plenipotentiary
Note: Commissioned during a recess of the Senate; recommissioned after confirmation on Mar 2, 1949.

Name: Edward R. Dudley
State of Residency: New York
Non-career appointee
Title: Ambassador Extraordinary and Plenipotentiary
Appointment: Mar 18, 1949
Presentation of Credentials: May 6, 1949
Termination of Mission: Left post, Jun 15, 1953

Name: Jesse D. Locker
State of Residency: Ohio
Non-career appointee
Title: Ambassador Extraordinary and Plenipotentiary
Appointment: Jul 22, 1953
Presentation of Credentials: Oct 16, 1953
Termination of Mission: Died at post, Apr 10, 1955

Name: Richard Lee Jones
State of Residency: Illinois
Non-career appointee
Title: Ambassador Extraordinary and Plenipotentiary
Appointment: May 31, 1955
Presentation of Credentials: Jun 24, 1955
Termination of Mission: Left post, Jul 24, 1959

Name: Elbert G. Mathews
State of Residency: California
Foreign Service officer
Title: Ambassador Extraordinary and Plenipotentiary

Appointment: Aug 12, 1959
Presentation of Credentials: Sep 30, 1959
Termination of Mission: Left post, May 4, 1962

Name: Charles Edward Rhetts
State of Residency: Indiana
Non-career appointee
Title: Ambassador Extraordinary and Plenipotentiary
Appointment: Jul 5, 1962
Presentation of Credentials: Aug 7, 1962
Termination of Mission: Left Liberia, Sep 30, 1964

Name: Ben H. Brown, Jr.
State of Residency: South Carolina
Foreign Service officer
Title: Ambassador Extraordinary and Plenipotentiary
Appointment: Nov 25, 1964
Presentation of Credentials: Jan 6, 1965
Termination of Mission: Left post, Jul 17, 1969
Note: Commissioned during a recess of the Senate; recommissioned after confirmation on Jan 18, 1965.

Name: Samuel Z. Westerfield, Jr.
State of Residency: District of Columbia
Foreign Service officer
Title: Ambassador Extraordinary and Plenipotentiary
Appointment: Jul 8, 1969
Presentation of Credentials: Dec 9, 1969
Termination of Mission: Died at post, Jul 19, 1972

Name: Melvin L. Manfull
State of Residency: Utah
Foreign Service officer
Title: Ambassador Extraordinary and Plenipotentiary
Appointment: Dec 2, 1972
Presentation of Credentials: Dec 22, 1972
Termination of Mission: Left post, Dec 15, 1975
Note: Commissioned during a recess of the Senate; recommissioned after confirmation on Feb 8, 1973.

Name: W. Beverly Carter, Jr.
State of Residency: Pennsylvania
Foreign Service officer
Title: Ambassador Extraordinary and Plenipotentiary
Appointment: Apr 6, 1976
Presentation of Credentials: Apr 23, 1976
Termination of Mission: Left post, Jan 1, 1979

Name: Robert P. Smith
State of Residency: Virginia
Foreign Service officer
Title: Ambassador Extraordinary and Plenipotentiary
Appointment: Jul 2, 1979
Presentation of Credentials: Aug 6, 1979
Termination of Mission: Left post, Jan 15, 1981

Name: William Lacy Swing
State of Residency: North Carolina

Foreign Service officer
Title: Ambassador Extraordinary and Plenipotentiary
Appointment: Jul 18, 1981
Presentation of Credentials: Aug 11, 1981
Termination of Mission: Left post, Jun 10, 1985

Name: Edward Joseph Perkins
State of Residency: Oregon
Foreign Service officer
Title: Ambassador Extraordinary and Plenipotentiary
Appointment: Jul 12, 1985
Presentation of Credentials: Aug 28, 1985
Termination of Mission: Left post, Oct 22, 1986

Name: James Keough Bishop
State of Residency: New York
Foreign Service officer
Title: Ambassador Extraordinary and Plenipotentiary
Appointment: Mar 27, 1987
Presentation of Credentials: May 4, 1987
Termination of Mission: Left post Mar 31, 1990

Name: Peter Jon de Vos
State of Residency: Florida
Foreign Service officer
Title: Ambassador Extraordinary and Plenipotentiary
Appointment: Jun 22, 1990
Presentation of Credentials:
Termination of Mission: Left post, July 27, 1992
Note: Arrived at post, Jun 28, 1990. Had not presented credentials before the overthrow of the Government of Liberia on Sep 11, 1990.

Between 1992 and 1999 the following officers served as Chargé d'Affaires ad interim:
William H. Twaddell (Sep 1992–Jul 1995),
William B. Milam (Nov. 1995–Jan 1999), and
Donald K. Petterson (Feb 1999–Aug 1999).

Name: Bismark Myrick
State of Residency: Virginia
Foreign Service officer
Title: Ambassador Extraordinary and Plenipotentiary
Appointment: Jul 7, 1999
Presentation of Credentials: Aug 20, 1999
Termination of Mission: Left post Jul 23, 2002

Name: John William Blaney
State of Residency: Virginia
Foreign Service officer
Title: Ambassador Extraordinary and Plenipotentiary
Appointment: Aug 8, 2002
Presentation of Credentials: Oct 3, 2002
Termination of Mission:

Source: Research by the Department of Protocol, U.S. Department of State. Courtesy of Andrew L. Silski, Country Officer for Liberia and Cape Verde, U.S. Department of State.

APPENDIX D

REPUBLIC OF LIBERIA DIPLOMATIC REPRESENTATION TO THE UNITED STATES

Legation opened July 24, 1947

Charles D. B. King
Appointment: July 24, 1947
Presentation of Credentials: July 25, 1947.
Title: Ambassador Extraordinary and Minister Plenipotentiary.
Legation raised to Embassy May 12, 1949.

Charles D. B. King
Appointment: May 10, 1949.
Presentation of Credentials: May 12, 1949.
Title: Ambassador Extraordinary and Plenipotentiary.

Clarence Lorenzo Simpson
Appointment: April 25, 1952.
Presentation of Credentials: May 5, 1952.
Title: Ambassador Extraordinary and Plenipotentiary.

George Arthur Padmore
Appointment: April 2, 1956.
Presentation of Credentials: April 27 1956.
Title: Ambassador Extraordinary and Plenipotentiary.

Samuel Edward Peal
Appointment: October 13, 1961.
Presentation of Credentials: October 19, 1961.
Title: Ambassador Extraordinary and Plenipotentiary.

J. Urias Nelson
Appointment: June 22, 1976.
Title: First Secretary, Chargé d'Affaires ad interim.

Francis Nelson William Dennis
Appointment: July 15, 1976.
Presentation of Credentials: July 19, 1976.
Title: Ambassador Extraordinary and Plenipotentiary.

Wlliam V. S. Bull, Counselor
Appointment: November 18, 1979.
Presentation of Credentials:
Title: Chargé d'Affaires ad interim.

Herbert Richard Wright Brewer
Appointment: December 12, 1979.
Presentation of Credentials: January 31, 1980.
Title: Ambassador Extraordinary and Plenipotentiary.

William Bull, Counselor
Appointment: October 27, 1980
Presentation of Credentials:
Title: Chargé d'Affaires ad interim.

APPENDIX [CONT.] REPUBLIC OF LIBERIA DIPLOMATIC REPRESENTATION TO THE UNITED STATES

Dr Joseph Saye Guannu
Appointment: April 14, 1981.

Presentation of Credentials: June 4, 1981.
Title: Ambassador Extraordinary and Plenipotentiary.

W. Elwood Greaves, Minister-Counselor
Appointment: September 30, 1983.
Presentation of Credentials: .
Title: Chargé d'Affaires ad interim.

Major General George Toe Washington
Appointment: December 12, 1983.
Presentation of Credentials: January 9, 1984.
Title: Ambassador Extraordinary and Plenipotentiary.

Eugenia A. Wordsworth-Stevenson
Appointment: October 20, 1986.
Presentation of Credentials: November 24, 1986.
Title: Ambassador Extraordinary and Plenipotentiary.

Rachel Gbenyon Diggs
Appointment: January 1998.
Presentation of Credentials: March 16, 1998.
Title: Ambassador Extraordinary and Plenipotentiary.
Departed: November 1999.

William Bull
Appointment: May 19, 2000.
Presentation of Credentials: June 14, 2000.
Departed: August 2000.
Title: Ambassador Extraordinary and Plenipotentiary.

Source: Research by the Department of Protocol, U.S. Department of State. Courtesy of Andrew L. Silski, Country Officer for Liberia and Cape Verde, U.S. Department of State.

APPENDIX E

LESTER S HYMAN INTERVIEW WITH HIS EXCELLENCY CHARLES GHANKAY TAYLOR, PRESIDENT OF LIBERIA

Friday, March 7, 2003 from 8:30 to 9:30am via telephone*

LSH: Mr. President, one of the criticisms most often made against your government is that much of the revenue, for example from timber sales, has gone into your pocket, while nothing is being done to help the people. Recognizing that the costs of defending Liberia against the LURD attacks are extremely high, nevertheless can you tell me what specifically the government is doing to help the people? For example, why is there no electricity or potable water?

CGT: Let me just say this. There are now two timber companies in Liberia, but they are not yet operating at full capacity. 100% of the annual revenues from timber exploration, which amounts to about $5 to $7 million a year, goes directly into the regions where the timber is extracted. These revenues are being used in those counties to build roads, to build schools, to build hospitals and to take care of essential services. The claim that this money goes into the President's pockets is pure nonsense. We cannot do as much as we wish to do for the people of Liberia because, since the civil war, the international community has not engaged in any major program for the reconstruction of Liberia. So everything that is being done in this nation right now is being done with the meager resources that are being generated by the Republic's timber and maritime programs.

As to the issue of light, during the civil war, the major infrastructure for light, which was the hydro system, was destroyed. In the city of Monrovia, we had the production of some 40 megawatts of electrical power which was damaged during the war. In the case of light, light was financed on a grant or loan from the U.S. Government assisted by the World Bank and other financial institutions. The generators were damaged along with the hydro. Because of the capital intensive nature of light and water in third world countries, all Presidents of Liberia have always received international grants and assistance for the construction of electrical power. No government of Liberia has been able to do it, and we've been unable to do it because the cost of electricity in Liberia, the rebuilding of the hydro, and putting lights in Liberia is a minimum cost of $125 million United States dollars. The budget of Liberia is $70 million a year because our economy has not been able to regenerate itself. So all this about the President supposedly pocketing money—that's completely false. I have no foreign bank accounts. I have talked to the United Nations and I have said to the opposition leaders in the country if any of them are aware of any bank or international institution anywhere on the planet earth that has any account for Charles Taylor, to make it known and I will resign and turn the money over to the Liberian people. There is no such thing as money going into the President's pocket.

LSH: The UN Sanctions Committee apparently believes that the RUF is still alive and well; that 1,500 of them have joined your forces in the battle against the LURD; and that sanctions are necessary to prevent you from continuing to help the RUF. Is the RUF still a cohesive group, and, if so, with what agenda?

CGT: The RUF does not exist so far as I know at all. There is no such thing as 1500 RUF being here. The United States and Great Britain have continued to perpetuate these blatant lies …lies designed to interfere with the political process in Liberia. The United States Government is directly involved in equipping the LURD rebels by training them in Guinea under the guise of helping the Guinean government and we are arresting and killing their trainees in Liberia. There are no RUF here. We have *very* good cooperation with the government in Sierra Leone. As a matter of fact, I have just received their Ambassador. President Kabbah and I are working very closely together. We in the Mano River Union are working very, very well together.

LSH: You have indicated a willingness to sit down with the LURD and initially they refused. Now they say that they are willing to meet. The ICG (International Contact Group) apparently will make recommendations to the ECOWAS–sponsored meeting scheduled in Mali. What do you see coming out of that meeting?

CGT: Well, there are many things. One, we believe that war is not going to be the solution. There was a National Reconciliation Commission set up in Liberia on a multi-partisan basis including political leaders, eminent persons, opposition leaders and all. We see that as the proper forum for these discussions. It must be discouraged in Africa and all around the world when, any time a rebel group takes up arms and attacks a legitimate government, you bring them to the table and include them in the government. The answer is for them to lay down their arms and participate in the political process. There are eighteen political parties registered in this country. If the LURD has a political agenda, they should come forward, lay down their arms, and join the political process.

LSH: Would you agree to an immediate mutual ceasefire?

CGT: Well, there are several things that we have to do regarding that. The Government of Liberia is under international sanctions, including an arms embargo. Despite the fact that the LURD has been supported by Guinea and the United States, they weren't able to gain certain territories. If LURD is prepared to confine herself in certain sections of the country, while we bring in a capacity-building force to disarm them, I think this would be reasonable. The issue of a ceasefire with men hunkering down near the capitol of Monrovia is something that needs to be discussed.

LSH: The international community says they will not send funds into Liberia because there is no transparency. Why won't you open up the books? What is there to hide?

CGT: They must understand that Liberia is a democratic country. The legislature of Liberia is responsible for making sure that revenues of this country are properly utilized for the purpose of the Liberian people. Now it is one thing to ask for transparency and it is another thing to ask to come to preside over a country. The United States, to go to the United Nations and say that we want you to audit the Liberian government as if somebody has hidden money here, I think it's a violation of our sovereignty. The issue of transparency I think is fine. The national legislature of Liberia can conduct itself properly. If government is supposed to report to the national legislature of our country, I think it's absurd for anybody to come from the outside and say, well, we want to come in and audit the government of Liberia. That's the function of the national legislature of this Republic. And that process is ongoing. We have submitted to a process by the legislature. We have nothing to hide. But one must protect the government of a sovereign state from the zealous functions of powerful countries that want to rule other countries by subterfuge.

LSH: The international community also condemns Liberia's human rights record. There seems to be little doubt that the ATU and the security forces have committed some egregious violations of human rights. Did you order those violations? If not, did you know about them after the fact? What can be done to stop them?

CGT: The whole issue of human rights and how it is interpreted in some third world countries is all subjective. In the case of Liberia you have opposition groups that are anti-government. These are the people who are paid by certain non-governmental groups to report on alleged human rights violations. So their so-called facts are not always accurate. We do admit that there are some things that are done wrong by certain groups, and people are trying to paint the ATU, but in the case where we have proof of any action or excesses that the police or any security forces have committed, we punish therm. But in dealing with Liberia and some of the information that is flowing out of here regarding so-called human rights abuse, one must be very careful, We have a situation where there is a war as launched by LURD and backed by powerful countries. These LURD people have been videotaped by western journalists laying people down, cutting them open, eating their hearts, eating human flesh, raping women, tearing down the countryside and those people are *not* accused of human rights violations. So one must wonder as to whether this is a genuine attempt to really look at human rights problems which I agree most third world countries have, and we must do something about it, versus whether those individuals intend to keep using lies and deception that human rights is a problem in order to prevent the government from getting international assistance. I think that we have a responsibility as a government to respect human rights. We take that very seriously. But we must separate out lies, deceptions and made-up stories. Everything is being done to arrest those people who truly have violated human rights and put them in jail to serve prison sentences for any excesses that have been carried out by them.

LSH: Can you stop the use of child soldiers? There are claims that some of them, as young as 10 years old, are being conscripted from the displaced person camps?

CGT: Lies. These are all lies. The government of Liberia is not a rebel force. These are all lies and I will challenge anyone—you know, this is where it gets to the point—we challenge any nongovernmental organization in this Republic to identify any child soldier who they claim has been recruited by government. We are aware of international conventions. We are signatories to these conventions, and we will not permit the recruiting of any child soldiers for any purpose to fight on behalf of this legitimate government. That we find terrible and we would not do it.

LSH: What about freedom of the press? Doesn't even the temporary closure of a newspaper have a chilling effect on free speech in Liberia?

CGT: Let me be clear about the issue of free speech. I'd like to know how major countries, including the United States—we are at war—there are certain things that cannot be permitted for reasons of national security during war. Even in the United

States, the good thing about it is that during the Vietnam war journalists were constrained—they were controlled in certain ways and, in fact, those that were not controlled demonstrated respect as patriotic Americans to make sure that certain issues of national security were not compromised. We have a very small population of 5 million [sic] people. You have a situation here where there are some LURD fighters in the bush that have brothers and sisters who are officials in the government. Some of them are press people. Liberia and most third world countries have not reached the mature level toward government as have the press in the United States or most western democracies. But even at that, for those of us who attended school in the west—I was in the United States doing undergraduate and graduate work there—we have a good appreciation for the free press. Right now in Liberia there are about one dozen newspapers operating and about a half dozen radio stations and two television stations. Now, this has never happened before under any president of this country. So we value free speech. We value a free press. But we must understand that we are at war. Look at Kosovo. The United States had forces, NATO had forces in Kosovo. When they got to Kosovo, they shut down certain radio stations. They shut down certain television stations in the interest of peace and national security. This was done by United States forces. So there are circumstances in countries, especially in Liberia where we just came from war, where certain utterances on the radio or in the press could spark up a new war, so we have a duty and a responsibility to making sure that everything is done to preserve national security. Even at that, we have one dozen newspapers operating. There is no censoring of the press. We just urge them to be as responsible as they should be.

LSH: What about campaigning? Some of your critics are complaining that you will not allow people to meet or demonstrate or make political speeches—that they have to wait until June to campaign and they claim that that is in the midst of the rainy season when therefore opposition parties don't really have an opportunity to get around the country and campaign before the election in October. Would you react to that, please?

CGT: Well, I'll tell you something. It's foolish. I've heard Ambassador Blaney say that. Look, the election commission here is independent—the independent election commission. I did not set the date. I would love to start campaigning myself right now because if one were to assume that during the dry season the opposition will be able to campaign effectively because of road conditions, and if that assumption were true, then we must assume that I and my party would be able to amass more logistics than they so it would be better for us if we were to campaign now. There are laws in this country that I did not make. The election rules—when elections are held—are set out in the statutes and laws of this Republic. I didn't make those rules. This has been the modus vivendi—the mode of operation—here for over a century. The Constitution is there, so people must understand that no government, this President especially, would encourage any process that would subvert the constitution, statutes and laws of this Republic. I am not about to try to keep the opposition out of these elections. What we are going to do is we're going to uphold the law and defend the Constitution of this Republic. If the Election Commission moves up the date for campaigning, we will all go by it. But it is not because of the rainy season. In fact it already has started raining in Liberia. For someone to say that the month of June is the height of the rainy season is wrong. The height of the rainy season in Liberia really starts in October. In October,

November, December it's really raining in Liberia. So this whole argument about the rainy season is false.

LSH: You mentioned the Election Commission. I noticed that just the other day you put two vociferous critics of your Administration on the Election Commission. But the opposition parties are claiming that, even with those two people, you still control both the Election Commission and the Liberian Supreme Court. What is your response to that?

CGT: Well, I'll tell you what I think. It could have been said in the United States of the last election that the Republicans controlled the Supreme Court of the United States and that's why George Bush won the presidency. Is there an end to the accusations? The political parties—eighteen of them—got together and said, look, we want the Commission expanded. Mr. President, we want it expanded. So we expanded the Commission. We increased it by two. We asked all political parties in Liberia to nominate a sub-list of seven persons from which we will take two for the Commission. They did. Sixteen—to be exact, 14—excuse me—of those political parties signed on to that list. From that list were chosen two our of our worst critics who now are members of the Election Commission. We want to show transparency. We want to show that we we're going to do this thing above board. The original five members of the present Election Commission, all of them were Commissioners during the last general election, and they were all picked by the international community because of their neutrality. Every member of that Commission served in the last election here. What we did was to say well, fine, if the international community trusted these individuals and felt comfortable with them during the last elections in Liberia, we will continue with them. We did it with the advice and consent of the Liberian Senate. Now for someone to say that we control the Election Commission, that's going too far.

We have credible justices of the Supreme Court across all boundaries in Liberia. The five members of the Supreme Court were selected on a regional basis with the participation of eminent Liberians. The national bar association of this Republic participated in recommending names for justices when I became President of this country. We had political leaders. Everyone took part in a slow but very credible process of nominating and selecting members of the Supreme Court. I believe that it would be, not just unpatriotic, it would be wicked for anyone to try to smear the character of these justices that have their own backing across the length and breadth of this country. Okay? Every member of this court—the original five—were in Liberia, in Monrovia during the war. They were not behind the lines. These were people who have a reputation in this country for being fair and being knowledgeable of the law, and I take great exception to anyone who would make any assertion that these justices are not credible. I mean, I find it appalling that anyone would think this way. We must respect our own people and stop trying to destroy them.

LSH: Why are you opposed to have an international group oversee the October election? And how can an election be held if LURD fighting is still going on? And what do you think about delaying the election to next year as some suggest?

CGT: There are so many complications. My opposition to an international group quote, unquote, "overseeing" our election is a violation of our Constitution and it is also a violation of our sovereign right as a people and a nation. For someone to say that someone should come and "oversee" an election in Liberia when there is a legitimate government is a violation of our Constitution and our sovereignty as a people. However, we have written the United Nations, the European Union, the African Union, ECOWAS to have as many observers as possible and to provide technical assistance. The whole question of " presiding over" diminishes our credibility as a government and it's a mockery of our sovereignty as a sovereign people. We find that unacceptable, we find it insulting that anyone would suggest that someone should come and "preside" over an election, especially when there is a legitimate government. Now about the issue of fighting. The LURD's only ambition is to disrupt elections. But elections are going to be held. And let me just say this. There is precedence in West Africa. In Sierra Leone— we had elections in Sierra Leone. We have other cases where there have been wars in countries that have held elections because elections and the date for elections are not issues that are decided by presidents or governments. The election date is a decision of the Constitution of the Republic of Liberia that I did not write or have amended since I became President. So I don't have the power to subvert the Constitution. So if someone suggests that we push the election into next year, that person is suggesting that we ignore the Constitution of Liberia and I am not prepared to do that. That date is locked in concrete in the Constitution and my own position is that unless the Constitution is amended, no one, the President, no one has the right to change it. Now, if there are exogenous factors that could lead to a delay or what not, those factors have to be taken to the court. Under our Constitution it is only the Supreme Court of Liberia with an issue before it that can rule on the matters of the Constitution, the interpretation of the law or as to whether there are factors that could force the court to rule that such a measure be taken. I do not hold that power, and do not wish to possess such a power. So I have said that we must submit to the courts. All issues regarding the Constitution or issues thereof must be a matter for the courts. We must respect that process and be a country of laws.   .

LSH: Both the New Republic Magazine and the Washington Post here have accused you of having connections with Al Qaeda (apparently through Ibrahim Bah), and specifically that you were given $1 million to provide sanctuary for two of Al Qaeda's operatives. Could you give me a response to that, please?

CGT: I tell you. I couldn't have heard anything further from the fact. But what has happened interestingly is that after we saw that propagandist piece written in the Washington Post, I proceeded immediately to officially inquire of the United States government, and we have been assured by the United States government that there is no such thing from their side and they do not know where that came from because it never existed. Now this is crucial. For close to 200 years we have been in very close, close contact with the United States government. We would never, ever, tolerate, encourage, or any other thing, anyone who would act in violation of international law. For us, there is no room for terrorism. There is no room for terrorists. Because we here have our own terrorists. In fact, we have defined—we have our own meaning of terrorism that would be even a little tougher than the United States on any people who use weapons to destroy innocent civilian lives—men, women and children. In fact we will act even harsher against terrorists than you do in the United States because, you know, you guys, you respect the law a lot—we do too, but there's no room here for that. And so never would we permit that, or encourage it, and we are working very closely with the United States government and the international community to make it absolutely sure that this place will never be a haven for any terrorists. We have condemned all acts of terrorism. We have made our airport, all of our facilities available to the United States government in this global war against terrorism. It is inconceivable that we would ever encourage any action of terrorists. Now, having said that, we know that terrorism and Al Qaeda have cells all around the world, including the United States. Some of them are hard to find, but we all are going to be looking for them, and this is why we are working with your governmental agencies, we are working with the FBI, because there may be some of them that we do not know. We are in touch with the United States Embassy near this Capitol and work very closely with them. Let me tell any terrorist or would-be terrorist: Liberia would be the worst place to come to because you will be caught. Not only are we going to arrest you but we won't even investigate— we immediately will turn you over to the United States. So we want to make this very clear. Liberia and America are one. We have long, historic ties. We want to be your ally, and no one, no one acting against the United States in any shape or form should believe that Liberia will be sympathetic to whatever terrorist cause no matter how minor If you adversely affect the United States, you have adversely affected Liberia.

LSH: How do you account for the fact that so many Liberians living in the United States are adamantly opposed to your government and talk against it constantly?

CGT: Many Liberians are in the United States under a resettlement program. A large majority of those people have to speak evil of the government or they are not given permanent residency. You cannot get political asylum unless you lie. So I want to hold the United States responsible for some of this and let me give you the theory why I say that. I understand that Immigration is just now catching on to this whole phenomenon of people lying just to get into the United States. I'll tell you something and this may be strange. I have relatives of mine that have gone to the United States and have had to lie and I'm helping some of those relatives but they've had to lie. The only the way they can get the documents is to say that President Taylor just killed my aunt. And the aunt is also my aunt. I think it's a policy matter. The second issue you have is that during the civil war, even before the change of policy that I'm talking about, many Liberians went over to America and heard lies and disinformation about what's going on in Liberia. Sometimes people call me from America to tell me there's fighting on a street in Monrovia and I haven't even heard about it. But it appears to be fashionable that unless you say something evil about the government, you cannot stay in the United States, and I think that quality is contributing to what you hear right now.

LSH: Why do you believe that the United States has opposed you from the day you appeared on the national scene in Liberia, going back, way back?

CGT: Oh boy. I wish I knew because it started out with your government supporting me with very good cooperation between the United States government and the then NPFL. We worked very, very closely. I think there's been a very good job done on us by some opposition figures that were originally part of us. For example, such well-known personalities in the diaspora community as Ellen Johnson-Sirleaf have contributed a lot to the bad feelings in the United States. And this is someone who helped me organize the NPFL. We were together in the war. She wanted the leadership. I refused. She got bitter and spread a lot of disinformation

The second problem that we had is that, during the civil war, I had a bump-in with former Secretary of State Madeleine Albright when she was U.S. Ambassador to the United Nations. She came to Liberia and really talked in a rough way to the then Council of State. I took strong exception. She issued a press release after she left and I did, too, and I think she's had it in for me ever since. And when she became Secretary of State she never came to Liberia, and Susan Rice, the Assistant Secretary of State for Africa, never came here. I really regret this very much because we've always wanted to engage the United States—we still want to. We always look at the U.S. as a Big Brother. But I think that the United States government is like a aircraft carrier—it moves very slowly, hard to turn. And some of those old policies and assertions made by certain individuals are still being used as a yardstick for Liberia. We came to this government with 80% victory. We have many non-governmental organizations that are working here. We work along with them. We have a government of national unity here. We have opened up the press. We've done more in terms of free speech, the respect for the tenets of democracy , than any other government before me. But I just have to wait on God's time because I'm a Christian and I *believe* that God is my guide. No matter what happens the truth is finally going to come out that Taylor is doing his best in Liberia and for those that hate me, we invite them to constructively engage us and see where the faults are. We have done everything that the United States government has asked of us. We have no political prisoners in our jails. We have no journalists jailed. We just don't understand. And I hope someone would be able to come out and tell us why they have this anti-Taylor situation going on. In Liberia we still are popular amongst our people. We have the full support of the Liberian people in spite of the international sanctions, embargoes and everything that they have put upon us to disrupt our government. The Liberian people still give us their support. So we hope that the Bush Administration will engage us. You guys may say that Taylor is this, Taylor is that. Whatever the story, let's go in there—let's sit down with Mr. Taylor. Let's see if we can engage that government and the Liberian people for the betterment of the Liberian people instead of this constant destruction of our country.

LSH: I think you just answered my last question which was: what should U.S. policy toward be in your judgment?

CGT: Let's sit down and talk. What are the issues? What are we doing that you don't like? We asked the United States to come back in here. We've asked you to bring back the Peace Corps to Liberia. We asked the United States to help retrain our army. Retrain our police. Retrain our security forces. They have refused. So if we agree that there are, and there are, some human rights problems in Liberia, to change this problem will mean we have to train people. We are not permitted under the Security Council resolution to train anybody. We can't. So it's as if someone wants to bring the government down. And I would think the way out of this is to engage this government. We are very reasonable people and we want to see our country move forward. We cannot stay in a state of war. We cannot have these policies against Liberia continue. They are hurting the ordinary people, and it's wrong.

Note: One caveat. The telephone connection during this interview was of poor quality. At times there was severe static and sometimes words were garbled. Therefore it is possible that, in certain instances, I was unable to hear and transcribe accurately every single word uttered by President Taylor.

APPENDIX F

YAMMASOUKRO IV TALKS, PRELIMINARY SESSION NOTES, OCTOBER 26-27, 1991

At the Yamoussoukro IV (October 29-30, 1991) conference, the author sat in on the private meetings Charles Taylor held with his advisors.* Provided here are some of the notes that he took at the time, useful for analysis of these events:

> The most significant concern involved the October 26-27 visit to Liberia of former President Jimmy Carter whose International Negotiating Network (INN) formally has been invited by the Yamoussoukro leaders to monitor the forthcoming Liberia election and the electoral process leading up to it.

> President Carter held substantive meetings with Dr. Amos Sawyer in Monrovia and with Charles Taylor in Gbarnga. He also toured parts of the country. Thereafter, he sat up most of the night to set forth in his own handwriting a list of suggestions regarding border security, encampment and disarmament, which was delivered to each participating nation's representative at the start of the Yamoussoukro IV conference.

> Charles Taylor immediately made it clear that he would accept totally the Carter proposal and urged his colleagues to do the same. Amos Sawyer told colleagues that he could accept the Carter plan "with minor reservations," although it is my understanding that he made no effort to enlist support for it. Yet the so-called "hard line" countries participating in the Yamoussoukro conference rejected the Carter suggestions. This was very troubling to President Taylor who believed strongly that if the leadership of Liberia (Sawyer and Taylor) was prepared to accept the Carter solution, it was inappropriate for the non-Liberian participants to veto it and impose their own will on Liberia. Especially since the U.S. provides substantial economic assistance to the countries represented at the Yamoussoukro Summit, one might properly ask why we were not more active in trying to convince these nations to accept the Carter initiative.

> On the second day of the conference, matters became even more difficult when an entirely different resolution was presented to Mr. Taylor as a <u>fait accomplis</u>. This document basically would have turned over the entire nation of Liberia to the ECOMOG forces until the election was held. In stark contrast with Yamoussoukro III, this proposal was not one which evolved from the discussions of the leaders; nor was it prepared by them jointly.

> President Taylor called a break in the proceedings in order to meet privately with his Ministers to review this proposal (which, for example, would have allowed ECOMOG forces to enter any home in Liberia without a warrant and would not require them to consult with local administrative officials in any way).

> The reaction of the Taylor advisors ranged from bitter disappointment to anger. Not one person in the room— including those who had been the most accommodating in the past—were willing to have their President sign a document which they considered to be an outrageous surrender of their basic rights and sovereignty.

Taylor then rejoined the meeting of West African leaders and announced that, after meeting with his people, he had concluded that there was no way he could sign the document which had been presented to him.

In response, it was suggested that a working subcommittee headed by President Blaise Compaore of Burkina-Faso be constituted to work with President Taylor to respond constructively to his concerns. This was done.

After several hours of deliberation, a new document was prepared which, while nowhere as realistic as the Carter suggestions, did provide for ECOMOG supervision of border security and the disarmament process in a manner that recognized the appropriate role of local authorities and allowed for cooperation between ECOMOG and the Sawyer and Taylor Liberian governing bodies.

Again President Taylor called together his advisors and Ministers to review the new document. Reactions varied. Some continued to feel that Taylor should hold firm for the Carter proposal. Others believed that the new formulation relied too heavily on trusting ECOMOG to do the right thing. And still others believed that Taylor should accept the plan as the best that could be achieved. Taylor listened carefully to the debate (which was of extremely high quality, with each person effectively articulating his or her position) and then indicated that his best judgment was to agree.

---

* The author also attended the Yamassoukro meeting on September 16-17, 1991.
Source: Hyman, Lester S., Yamoussoukro IV Report, October 29-30, 1991.

BIBLIOGRAPHY

BOOKS

Adebajo, Adekeye. 2002. *Building Peace in West Africa,* Lynn Rienner Publishers.

Armon, Jeremy and Andy Carl, eds. 1996. *Accord: An International Review of Peace Initiatives, the Liberian Peace Process, 1990-1996.* London: Conciliation Resources.

Berkley, Bill. 1986. *Liberia: A Promise Betrayed,* A Report on Human Rights, New York: Lawyers Committee for Human Rights.

Cohen, Herman J. 2000. *Intervening in Africa: Superpower Peacemaking in a Troubled Continent* (Studies in Diplomacy), St. Martin's Press.

Davis, Ossie and Ruby Dee. 1998. *With Ossie and Ruby—In this Life Together,* William Morrow.

Ellis, Stephen. 1999. *The Mask of Anarchy: The Destruction of Liberia and the Religious Dimension of an African Civil War,* London: Hurst & Company.

Enoanyi, Bill Frank. 1991. *Behold Uncle Sam's Step-Child,* SanMar Publications.

Epstein, Edward Jay. 1982. *The Rise and Fall of Diamonds,* Simon and Schuster.

Friedman, Thomas R. 1999. *The Lexus and the Olive Tree,* Farrar Straus Giroux.

Halberstam, David. 2001. *War in a Time of Peace: Bush, Clinton and the Generals,* Scribner.

Horton, S. Augustu P. 1994. *Liberia's Underdevelopment—In Spite of the Struggle,* University Press of America.

Huband, Mark. 1998. *The Liberian Civil War,* Frank Cass.

Hull, Cordell. 1948. *The Memoirs of Cordell Hull, Volume II,* The Macmillan Company.

Kalb, Marvin. 2001. *One Scandalous Story: Clinton, Lewinsky, and thirteen days that tarnished American journalism,* New York: Free Press.

Kaplan, Robert D. 1996. *The Ends of the Earth: A Journey at the Dawn of the 21st Century,* Random House.

Kissinger, Henry. 2001. *Does America Need a Foreign Policy?: Toward a Diplomacy for the 21st Century,* Simon and Schuster.

Kulah, Arthur F. 1999. *Liberia Will Rise Again: Reflections on the Liberian Civil Crisis,* Abingdon Press.

Lyons, Terrence. 1999. *Voting for Peace: Postconflict Elections in Liberia,* Brookings.

Moses, Wilson Jeremiah (ed.). 1998. *Liberian Dreams: Back-to-Africa Narratives from the 1850s,* Pennsylvnia State University Press.

Naess, Erling D. 1972. *The Great PanLibHon Controversy,* Epping, Gower Press.

Newsom, David D. 2001. *The Imperial Mantle: The United States, Colonization and the Third World,* Indiana University Press.

Njoh, Joseph. 1996. *Through the Liberian Storm,* London: Minerva Press.

Pakenham, Thomas. 1991. *The Scramble for Africa: 1876-1912,* Johannesburg: Jonathan Ball Publishers.

Reader, John. 1998. *Africa: A Biography of a Continent,* Alfred A. Knopf.

Stearns, Monteagle. 1996. *Talking to Strangers: Improving American Diplomacy at Home and Abroad,* Twentieth Century Fund.

Timmerman, Kenneth R. 2002. *Shakedown: Exposing the Real Jesse Jackson,* Regnery Publishing.

Ungar, Sanford J. 1985. *Africa: The People and Politics of an Emerging Continent,* Simon and Schuster.

Unoke, Ewa. 1993. *The Untold Story of the Liberian War,* ABIC Publishers.

Wonkeryor, Edward L. 1985. *Liberia Military Dictatorship: A Fiasco Revolution.* Chicago: Struggler's Community Press.

Wonkeryor, Edward L, Ella Forbes, James S. Guseh, George K, Kieh Jr. 2000. *American Democracy in Africa in the Twenty-First Century?*, Cherry Hill: Africana Homestead Legacy Publishers.

Young, James C. 1934. *Liberia Rediscovered.* Doubleday, Doran & Company.

PERIODICALS

Anderson, Jon Lee. "The Devil They Know," *New Yorker,* July 27, 1998. Profile of Charles Taylor.

Coleman, Sarah. "African Union," *World Press Review*, October 2001, Vol. 48, p. 28–29.

Commonwealth of Liberia. *The Constitution of the Commonwealth of Liberia,* January 5, 1839. Adopted by American Colonization Society.

Cockburn, Andrew, Cary Wolinsky (photographs). "Diamonds: The Real Story," *National Geographic,* March 2002.

DeMars, William. "War and Mercy in Africa," *World Policy Journal,* Summer 2000.

Friends of Liberia Newsletter. Interview with Sarah Morrison, former Peace Corps Volunteer in Liberia, regarding Charles Taylor, September 24, 2001.

Gbenyon Diggs, Rachel, "Rumors About Liberia." *Washington Post,* January 23, 1999, Section A, p. 20. Letter by Liberian Ambassador to U.S. to the editor re: Liberia's role in Sierra Leone.

Gregg, Judd (U.S. Senator). "A Graveyard Peace," *Washington Post,* May 9, 2000, OpEd article.

Harden, Blaine. "Who Killed Liberia? We Did, The Ugly American Policy: Create the Mess, Then Stand Back and Watch the Slaughter," *Washington Post,* May 26, 1996, Outlook Section C, p. 1.

Hirsch, John L. "War in Sierra Leone," *The International Institute for Strategic Studies,* Autumn 2001. Article by the Vice-President of International Peace Academy.

Kramer, Reed. "Liberia: A Casualty of the Cold War's End," *CSIS Africa Notes.* July, 1995. Article.

Lizza, Ryan. "Double Take," *The New Republic,* November 9, 2001. Regarding al Qaeda and Charles Taylor.

Loeb, Vernon. "Rumsfeld's Flying Circus: When it Comes to Going Fast, Far and Frequently, The Defense Secretary is Way Out Front," *Washington Post,* May 3, 2003, Style section, p. C1.

Masland, Tom. "The Gems of War: How Illicit Diamonds Finance Africa's Bloodiest Conflicts," *Newsweek,* July 10, 2000.

Wax, Emily. "At the Heart of Rwanda's Horror General's History Offers Clues to the Roots of Genocide," *Washington Post,* September 21, 2002; Page A1.

Wallechinsky, David. "The 10 Worst Living Dictators," *Parade Magazine,* February 16, 2003. Article.

Wonkeryor, Edward Lama. "America's African Colonization Movement: Implications for New Jersey and Liberia," *Liberian Studies Journal,* 2002: Volume XXVII, number 1, pp. 28–42.

Woodward, Bob. "Covert Aid Programs Put Casey's Teams in the Palace to Recruit," *Washington Post,* September 30, 1987. Article re: CIA enlistment of Samuel Doe's personal guard.

Ziamo, Maxwell. "To Kill a Dog: A rejoinder to Jefftey Bartholet's 'An African Strongman,'" *Newsweek*, May 14, 2001.

GOVERNMENT PUBLICATIONS

Economic Community of West African States (ECOWAS), *Final Communique of Yamoussoukro III meeting*, September, 1991.

Office of the Secretary of Defense, International Security Affairs, Office of African Affairs, *Critical Factors in Demobilization, Demilitarization and Reintegration: An Analysis of Ethiopia, Liberia, Mozambique and Zimbabwe*, 2002.

Republic of Liberia, Liberian Department of Public Affairs, *Presidential Papers. Vol. I*, 1998.

———, Ministry of Education, *Fact Sheet on schools in Liberia 1997-2002*, August 24,2002

———, Ministry of Education. *Liberia Education Sector Master Plan 2000-2010*, March 2000.

———, Ministry of Education, *Technical Working Paper on status of education in Liberia*, n.d. Prepared for National Conference on Peace and Reconciliation, August 24, 2002.

———, Ministry of Foreign Affairs. *Official Statement of Government of Liberia on the Sierra Leonean Crisis*, February 19, 1999.

———. *The Constitution of the Republic of Liberia*, January 6, 1986.

U.S. Central Intelligence Agency (CIA), World Factbook: Liberia, 2002.

United States Government Printing Office, Foreign Relations of the United States Diplomatic Papers 1943 re President Franklin D. Roosevelt visit to Liberia, 1964.

U.S. Department of State, Bureau of Democracy, Human Rights and Labor. *Liberia: Country Report on Human Rights Practices: 1997*, January 30, 1998.

———, Bureau of Democracy, Human Rights and Labor. *Liberia: Country Report on Human Rights Practices: 2000*, February 23, 2001 <http://www.state.gov/g/drl/rls/hrrpt/2000/af/845.htm>.

———, Bureau of Democracy, Human Rights and Labor. *Liberia: Country Report on Human Rights Practices: 2001*, March 4, 2002 <http://www.state.gov/g/drl/rls/hrrpt/2001/af/8388.htm>.

———, U.S. Agency for International Development (USAID), *Liberia Overview*, July, 2002.

VIDEOTAPES

Cry Freetown, Insight News Television.

Liberia A Journey Without Maps. James Brabazon, SABC TV, Johannesburg, South Africa.

Bright, Nancy Oku, Jean-Phillipe Boucicaut, *Liberia: America's Stepchild: The Untold Story of America's African Progeny*, Grain Coast Production, © 2002, for PBS Home Video.

PERSONAL COMMUNICATION

INTERVIEWS

Anonymous. International Monetary Fund, April 1, 1999.

Anonymous. U.S. Department of State.

Cohen, Herman J. Former U.S. Assistant Secretary of State for African Affairs, March 1,

2002.

Cooper Gerald. Former Liberian Ambassador to International Maritime Organization (IMO), Washington, D.C., February 27, 2002.

Dalley, George, Chief of Staff to Congressman Charles B. Rangel. Washington, D.C.

Gbenyon, Diggs, Rachel. Former Liberian Ambassador to the U.S., Nashville, Tennessee, February 8, 2002

Kawah, Lami. Liberian Ambassador to the United Nations, New York, October 21, 2002.

Kromah, Alhaji G. V. Leader of ULIMO-K, Washington, D.C., May 3, 2002.

Taylor, Charles G., his Excellency, the President of Liberia, Monrovia, Liberia. March 7, 2003. Via telephone.

Woolsey, James. Former Director of U.S. Central Intelligence Agency (CIA), Washington, D.C., March 7, 2002.

Yerks, Robert. Retired U.S. Army General, Washington, D.C., February 28, 2002.

CORRESPONDENCE

Albright, Madeline K., U.S. Secretary of State. Letter to President Charles G. Taylor re: role in Sierra Leone peace process, October 20, 1999.

Bridgewater, Pamela E., Deputy Assistant Secretary of State. Letter to LSH re: Liberian elections, March 17, 2003.

Carter, Honorable Jimmy. Letter to LSH re restructuring of Liberian security forces, September 10, 1998.

———. Letter to his Excellency President Charles G. Taylor re: Human Rights Commission, August 24, 1998.

U.S. Congressional Black Caucus. Letter to President Clinton re: Sierra Leone, February 3, 1999.

Dalley, George, Chief of Staff to Congressman Charles Rangel. Letter to LSH re: first Congressional Black Caucus visit to Liberia in 1974.

Flynn, Heather, U.S. Senate Foreign Relations Committee. Letter to LSH re: Brooke Amendment, October 29, 2002.

Hyman, Lester S. Letter to U.S. Secretary of Agriculture Daniel R. Glickman, request for food aid for Liberia, September 29, 2000.

———. Letter to the editor of the *New Yorker* re: Jon Lee Anderson article, August 4, 1998.

———. Notes on Liberian Fact-finding Visit, August, 1991, memorandum.

———. Letter to Secretary of State Madeline Albright re: Plymouth charges against Charles Taylor, September 24, 1997.

———. Letter to William Cohen, U.S. Secretary of Defense, requesting appointment to discuss U.S. training of Liberian armed forces, April 22, 1998.

———. Yamoussoukro IV Report, October, 1991, memorandum.

Kern, Vincent D., U.S. Defense Department Deputy Assistant Secretary for African Affairs. Letter to LSH re: training Liberian armed forces, June 10, 1998.

List, Kathleen, U.S. State Department Liberian Desk Officer. Letter to LSH re U.S. aid to Liberia FY 1998, March 25, 1998.

Rice Susan E., U.S. Assistant Secretary of State for Africa Affairs. Letter to General Robert Yerks re International Monetary Fund recommendations, September 8, 1999.

————, U.S. Assistant Secretary of State, Letter to LSH re: Albright visit to Africa, January 13, 2000.

Spencer, Dayle. Letter to LSH re: Yamoussoukro Conference, July 13, 2001.

Taylor, His Excellency Charles G. Letter to H.E. Gunter Pleuger, President of the UN Security Council re sanctions, February 18, 2003.

————. Letter to UN Secretary-General Annan re the election process, February 17, 2003.

REPORTS, STATEMENTS, TESTIMONY, SPEECHES, AND PRESENTATIONS

Blaney, John, U.S. Ambassador to Liberia. Press Conference transcript re: humanitarian situation in Liberia, November 21, 2002.

Captan, Monie R., Foreign Minister of Liberia. Mission of the Republic of Liberia to the United Nations, statement at open hearing of UN Security Council, July 31, 2000.

Cato Institute. "Bush, Ashcroft Run Roughshod over Bill of Rights," June 26, 2002. Report.

Dorley, A. Richard, Liberia Central Bank. Chart of projected and actual development expenditures for 2001–2003, March 12, 2003.

Fahnbulleh, Gayah. Speech to MDCL Conference re: relevance of the Abuja Accord, January 19, 2002.

Gbenyon Diggs, Rachel. Presentation on Liberia to Vanderbilt University faculty and staff, October 25, 2001.

Gongloe, Tiawon S. *Testimony on the State of Emergency, Sanctions and Arms Embargo*, Statement to the Senate of Liberia, February 27, 2002.

Gore, Al, Vice President of the United States. Letter to LSH re: "Rule of Law" speech at National Conference on the Future of Liberia, August 31, 1998.

Grossman, Marc, Under Secretary for Political Affairs, U.S. Department of State. "American Foreign Policy for the 21st Century, Remarks to the Kansas City International Relations Council, Kansas City, Missouri," October 29, 2002. As prepared, <http://www.state.gov/p/14810.htm>.

Human Rights Watch. Report on war crimes by Liberian government and rebels. May, 2002.

Hyman, Lester S. "Rule of Law," Speech to All-Liberia National Conference, Monrovia, 1998.

International Monetary Fund (IMF). Concluding statement of staff visit to Liberia, September 15, 2000.

————. Pamphlet Series No. 51 "Debt Relief for Low-Income Countries, 1999.

Jeter, Howard, U.S. Ambassador to Nigeria. Speech delivered at the Shell Muson Center, Lagos, Nigeria, April 1, 2003 as released by the Public Affairs Office of the U.S. Embassy, Nigeria.

Kennedy, Edward M, U.S. Senator. Remarks at Presentation of Robert F. Kennedy Human Rights Award to Liberia Archbishop Michael Francis, November 22, 1999.

Kollie, Aaron, Liberian Embassy, Washington D.C. "The Perspective," Statement at the Congressional Black Caucus Forum, September 12, 2002.

Multi-Donor Assessment Mission (Paris Donors). Communique of Mission to Liberia, November, 15-19, 1999.

National Conference on the Future of Liberia. Conference Resolutions, August 10 and 19, 1998.

Perry, Robert, U.S., Deputy Assistant Secretary of State for Africa. Speech to National Convention of the Movement for Democratic Change in Liberia (MDCL) re LURD and elections, January 19, 2002.

Powell, Colin L., U.S. Secretary of State. Remarks at swearing-in of John W. Blaney as U.S. Ambassador to Liberia, September 9, 2002.

————. Press Remarks with Foreign Minister Sidibe, Bamako, Mali, May 23, 2001 <http://www.state.gov/secretary/rm/2001/3013.htm>.

Republic of Liberia. Response to Panel of Experts Report re United Nations Resolution 1306. January 26, 1999.

Rice, Susan. U.S. Assistant Secretary of State for Africa. Testimony before U.S. Senate Subcommittee on Africa Affairs re: U.S. policy on Sierra Leone, October 11, 2000.

Special Court for Sierra Leone, "The Prosecutor Against Charles Ghankay Taylor also known as Charles Ghankay MacArthur Dapkpana Taylor Indictment." case No. SCSL-03-1, 7 March 2003.

Taylor, his Excellency Charles G., State of the Union Address, January 30, 2001.

————. State of the Union Address, January 28, 2002.

Taylor, her Excellency Jewel Howard. Activities of the Office of the First Lady, December 19, 2001.

The Carter Center. Preliminary Statement on Liberian Special Election, July 21, 1997.

United Nations. Panel of Experts Report pursuant to Security Council Resolution 1306 (2000).

————. Panel of Experts Report pursuant to Security Council Resolution 1343 (2001).

INDEX

ABOUT THE AUTHOR

Lester S. Hyman is a prominent Washington, D.C. attorney with 48 years of experience in law, government, and politics. A graduate of Brown University and Columbia University School of Law, he specializes in creating and implementing legislative strategies and resolving international disputes for clients, including Fortune 500 corporations, as well as countries and major companies abroad.

In 1990 Mr. Hyman was a member of the International Observer Team headed by former President Jimmy Carter, which monitored the first democratic election in the history of Haiti. He was deeply involved in peace resolution efforts during Liberia's civil war and took part in the work of the International Negotiating Network (INN) at the Carter Center with specific reference to Liberia. He also dealt with legal and governmental issues in Japan, France, Germany, England, Lebanon, Russia, and the Caribbean. In 1996, President Clinton appointed Mr. Hyman to the 8-person Presidential Delegation that represented the United States at the historic Peace Accord signing in Guatemala, ending a 36-year civil war. From 1997 to 1999, Mr. Hyman acted as United States legal counsel for the Republic of Liberia.

Because of his considerable expertise, Lester Hyman has taught "Decision-Making in Politics" at the John F. Kennedy School of Government at Harvard University. He is a member of the Board of Directors of the Center for National Policy, one of the country's leading public policy "think tanks."

Active in state and national politics, Mr. Hyman has served in Massachusetts as Chief Assistant to the Governor, Secretary of Commerce and Chairman of the Democratic Party. His political work at the national-level has been as an advisor to eight U.S. presidential candidates.